Foucault's Challenge

DISCOURSE, KNOWLEDGE, AND
POWER IN EDUCATION

Foucault's Challenge

DISCOURSE, KNOWLEDGE, AND POWER IN EDUCATION

EDITED BY

Thomas S. Popkewitz and Marie Brennan

Teachers College, Columbia University
New York and London

LB880
.F682
F685
1998

Published by Teachers College Press, 1234 Amsterdam Avenue, New York, NY 10027

Poem by Tom Stonier and Cathy Conlin reprinted from *The Three Cs: Children, Computers, and Communication,* by Tom Stonier and Cathy Conlin (Chichester, England: Wiley, 1985). Copyright John Wiley & Sons Limited. Reproduced with permission.

Chapter 1, "Restructuring of Social and Political Theory in Education: Foucault and a Social Epistemology of School Practices," by Thomas S. Popkewitz and Marie Brennan, was originally published in *Educational Theory.* Reprinted with permission.

An earlier version of Chapter 9, "Disciplining Bodies: On the Continuity of Power Relations in Pedagogy," by Jennifer M. Gore, appeared in *International Studies in Sociology of Education, 5* (2) (1995), under the title "On the Continuity of Power Relations in Pedagogy." Adapted with permission.

Chapter 14, "Intellectuals at Work and in Power: Toward a Foucaultian Research Ethic," by David Blacker, was originally published in *O Sujeito da Educação: Estudos Foucaultianos,* edited by Tomaz Tadeu da Silva (Petrópolis, Brazil: Editora Vozes, 1994), under the title "Foucault e a Responsabilidade Intelectual." Reprinted with permission.

Library of Congress Cataloging-in-Publication Data

Foucault's challenge : discourse, knowledge, and power in education /
    edited by Thomas S. Popkewitz and Marie Brennan.
        p.   cm.
    Includes bibliographical references and index.
    ISBN 0-8077-3677-5 (cloth : alk. paper).—ISBN 0-8077-3676-7
(pbk.)
        1. Foucault, Michel—Contributions in education.   2. Education—
Philosophy.   3. Discourse analysis.   4. Power (Philosophy)
5. Postmodernism and education.   I. Popkewitz, Thomas S.
II. Brennan, Marie.
    LB880.F682F685   1998
    370'.1—dc21   97-34270

ISBN 0-8077-3676-7 (paper)
ISBN 0-8077-3677-5 (cloth)

Printed on acid-free paper
Manufactured in the United States of America

05 04 03 02 01 00 99 98   8 7 6 5 4 3 2 1

To our fathers, who died in this past year but whose
life and inspiration will always be with us

Contents

Acknowledgments

There are a number of people whom we would like to acknowledge for their help during the process of putting this book together.

We need to thank Joann Foss. She had the patience to put up with one of the editor's speaking about multiple things at once, often not mentioning the subject in the conversation. She took care of communications that moved across three continents and one island, and through multiple drafts, during the manuscript preparation. She coordinated the process of putting the manuscript together and retyping material when distance and difficulties in e-mail imposed themselves. She also exhibited patience for the multiple personalities among the contributors. In an important sense, she is the alter ego of the book and is responsible for its completion. We would also like to thank Lynn Fendler for all of her help in the preparation of the manuscript for publication. We would also like to thank Brian Ellerbeck of Teachers College Press for his careful and insightful readings during the development phase of this book, and Myra Cleary for the strong copy editing.

As editors of a book concerned with modernism/postmodernism, we both thank and bemoan e-mail. It is a wonderful system when it works. It helps provide quick communications and lends new weight to the need to think about the globalization of the intellectual, the reconstructions of identity and simulacra. At the same time, e-mail colonizes as it erases all vestiges of language that are not Anglo. For someone whose university is off the beaten path and without the proper technical lines to "receive" and "send," as with one of us, it creates hidden mailboxes that are visible only to the machine and that appear only when the machine decides on the need for visibility.

Introduction

The number of studies on Foucault or engaging Foucault's ideas in a conversation with other social theorists has grown considerably in the past few years, reflecting the significance of his challenge to disciplinary production of knowledge and his contribution to intellectual work across the human sciences in the last quarter of the twentieth century. With one exception, there has been a notable absence of work on Foucault in the field of education—perhaps because his challenge asks for an enormous shift in the largely modernist progressive or emancipatory discourses of education that have dominated pedagogical thought. Through Foucault's work, educators are asked about the conditions of construction of their field, and the power/knowledge nexus represented by that construction, including that of political projects, such as reform movements in education.

Educational institutions—including schooling and the tertiary education sector—have been a major focus for government policing/reform in the past few decades. The seeming ruptures of the economic, political, and social boundaries associated with the second half of the twentieth century have been accompanied by a resurgence of new forms of conservatism in education, with discourses re-forming older versions of individualism and producing new forms by which to normalize power relations. As Foucault (1971) himself noted, "Every education system is a political means of maintaining or modifying the appropriateness of discourses with the knowledge and power they bring with them" (p. 46).

Both Left and Right find it difficult in the current period to marshal adequate explanations for the multiple changes occurring in the field of educational practice. Traditionally, both have relied on modernist notions of progress to justify their theoretical, empirical, and political strategies, and tend to use broader-scale interests in the state, society, or politics to illuminate or apply to the field of education. Where Foucault has been used within these concerns, he is largely arraigned as part of the internecine paradigm warfare rather than explored for the challenges he offers—methodological, epistemological, and in terms of the politics of intellectual work. In these cases, he is invoked often, but the modernist discourse continues without the reflexive examination of the almost missionary zeal with which proposals are put forward for the "salvation" of the masses through education. The normative discourses of different political groupings in educational reform, research, and teaching have been little disturbed until now by Foucault's skepticism of the will to truth in those interests.

This volume explores how Foucault's methodologies for the study of power enable us to reexamine and re-vision the "foundations" of critical traditions inherited from nineteeth-century European forebears. We see Foucault's work as both generative and illustrative of movements within social and educational theory to break with certain principles of critical traditions dominating Western leftist thinking since the turn of the century. His concern with how the subject is constituted in power relations forms an important contribution to recent social theory concerned with the politics of identity, as witnessed by the theoretical and historical work within the feminist movement. His consideration of change as ruptures and breaks, related to French philosophical and historical schools, has thrown into sharp relief our conceptions of history and of the conventions of progress that underlie social and educational sciences. The pragmatism of Foucault's scholarship raises important questions about the relation of intellectual production to social practices, questions that are taken up as well within the work of Pierre Bourdieu, among others.

Critics have suggested that Foucault's own work privileged the productive mechanisms, the techniques of power, without allowing adequate room for resistances—competing discourses and mechanisms—to develop. This volume is structured to pay attention to the relationship between the regularities of the will to truth and the multiple spaces for other discourses and politics to emerge. Feminist work, in particular, shows the different spaces that can be made in educational research by working with and against a Foucaultian starting point. Foucault's own work is not to be celebrated uncritically, but rather to be viewed as work in a conversation that draws European continental traditions of sociology, philosophy, and history into American and Australian educational studies.

For our purposes, Foucault offers the possibility of a different kind of theoretical and political project, which does not automatically privilege its own position. This volume provides not only concrete studies of power/knowledge relations in specific educational sites but also a wider focus on the field as a whole and its construction both as an academic field of production and as the work of the teacher and the school.

The volume is the convergence of a number of conversations that have occurred within the past decade. The Wednesday seminar group in the Department of Curriculum and Instruction at the University of Wisconsin–Madison has been reading across literatures to understand the assumptions and implications of certain European continental theories as they relate to the study of educational phenomena, with Foucault's contribution prominent in these discussions. We have explored a range of postmodern, modern, feminist, and poststructural readings to consider the problematics and problems of educational phenomena. Continually in these readings, Foucault introduced a reflexivity to the methodological stances that were constructed for empirical studies of health education, civics education, disability studies, information technology, policy, educational reform, and educational research. The conversations also have continued across the department as issues of pedagogy and feminism were debated. We have continued these discussions across countries and continents, and these transnational perspectives are included in this volume.

The organization of the book revolves around four major strands of contemporary debates about educational scholarship. Part I provides a theoretical overview, and Part II consists of educational studies of what are called "histories of the present." The chapters explore a scholarship produced through engaging Foucault's social historical methods. They are concerned with the power/knowledge relations produced through the systems of reasoning deployed in educational practices. This interest is discussed historically to explain how current forms of educational knowledge are shifts in principles that order action and participation in schools.

Part III points to the possibilities for curriculum practices. These chapters explore how pedagogical practices can be re-visioned by pulling together a number of different intellectual movements that draw Foucault into a conversation with feminism, media studies, literary studies, and poststructuralism.

Part IV provides examples of empirical and textual studies that draw on Foucaultian ideas. The studies entail a rethinking of the methods and interpretive frames for empirical and policy-oriented critical educational sciences.

Part V provides systematic discussions of the relation of intellectual work to the practices of change in schools. This part rounds out the general issues raised in this scholarship. It challenges traditional thinking about the role of intellectuals in the process of education and social change.

We point to these different intellectual strands because they also embody different intellectual styles of writing. The different styles are important for two reasons. First, they embody different scholarly forms of interpretation, as found in history, media and literary studies, and philosophy, among other fields. The range of readings, narrative styles, and content in the book indicate the general theoretical terms and provide a broad orientation to the work of Foucault, which has been misunderstood or poorly presented in education. Second, the different narrative styles make it possible to engage the ideas of the volume on multiple levels.

By organizing the book through weaving together different narrative styles and disciplinary foci, we seek to place educational discourses into a dialogue with a number of important intellectual currents in fields outside of education that previously have been excluded. At the same time, we believe that collectively the chapters indicate the changing terrains in which critical studies are being struggled over.

This book, therefore, is written for multiple audiences. It is for the teacher who has a curiosity about the assumptions and implications of education "reasoning" and pedagogical practices. The chapters of the book also provide ways to challenge the taken-for-granted thinking that organizes the activities of teaching. At the graduate level, the book engages in central problems of educational theory and methodology. Finally, the chapters explore current debates about educational change and its theories of progress.

REFERENCE

Foucault, M. (1971). Orders of discourse (R. Swyer, Trans.). *Social Science Information, 10 (2)*, 7–30.

Foucault's Challenge

DISCOURSE, KNOWLEDGE, AND
POWER IN EDUCATION

PART I

Foucault in a Conversation with Education

1

Restructuring of Social and Political Theory in Education: Foucault and a Social Epistemology of School Practices

THOMAS S. POPKEWITZ & MARIE BRENNAN

Our concern in this chapter is with how Foucault's methodologies for the study of power are related to a more general reexamination and re-visioning of the "foundations" of critical traditions inherited from nineteenth-century European forebears. Through his wide-ranging studies of knowledge, madness, prisons, sexuality, and governmentality, Foucault's historical philosophy interrogates the conditions under which modern societies operate. His concern with how the subject is constituted in power relations has been taken up in various projects across multiple settings, with particular implications for interdisciplinary work. The politics of identity, as witnessed in the theoretical and historical work within the feminist movement, is one such example, crossing nation-state barriers of European and Anglo-American intellectual work.

This chapter moves between the particular contribution of Foucault and the more general intellectual movements to which he has contributed. The attention given to Foucault in the English-speaking world is part of a larger sea-migration of critical traditions of social science since World War II. By

sea-migration, we mean the post–World War II mixing of European continental social theories that integrate historical and philosophical discourses
with the more pragmatic (and philosophical analytic) traditions in the United
States, Britain, and Australia.[1] The translations and incorporation of European Marxist social philosophy (such as that of the Frankfurt School of critical theory from Germany), the Italian Marxist Antonio Gramsci, and, more
recently, French "postmodern" and French and Italian feminist theories are
important to the production of a "critical" space within the education arena.

Our reason for raising the issue of sea-migrations early in this chapter
is to provide a reading of Foucault within intellectual traditions. Translations
of Foucault have provided entree for English speakers to an intellectual tradition that has emerged forcefully in the past two decades to challenge the
hegemony of Marxist theories about issues of power and the politics of social
change. Until then, explicitly Marxist projects had been the main—at times
even the only—means for considering power and politics within and across
social settings at a time when individual and functionalist theories held dominance. This challenge to Marxist theories, we argue, is not to displace them
with another hegemony, but to recognize that there are certain changing conditions in the construction of power that are not adequately articulated
through Marxist theories and that are obscured in some instances in previous
critical traditions. Our interest is with a view of power that is both different
from and, at certain points, complementary to that of the structuralism of
Marxist theories.

We use the term "critical" in this chapter to place the work of Foucault
in a field concerned with issues of power and the political in schooling (for
general discussions of Foucault's contributions, see Burchell, Gordon, &
Miller, 1991; Dreyfus & Rabinow, 1983; Noiriel, 1994). *Critical* refers to a
broad band of disciplined questioning of the ways in which power works
through the discursive practices and performances of schooling. The various
modes of critical inquiry endeavor to understand, for example, how the mar-
ginalization of people is constructed and the various forms in which power
operates. The studies in this book seek ways of interrogating anew "the evidence and the postulates, of shaking up habits, ways of acting and thinking,
of dispelling commonplace beliefs, of taking a new measure of rules and
institutions" (Foucault, 1991b, pp. 11–12).

We see Foucault's work as both generative and illustrative of a critical
intellectual tradition that provides certain breaks with the principles that
have dominated Western leftist thinking since the turn of the century.[2]
Whereas previous critical scholarship has treated knowledge as part of the
epi-phenomena through which social material practices are formed, Foucault's work is illustrative of a move within critical traditions to focus on
knowledge as a material element in social life.

The chapter proceeds through a scaffolding of ideas whose resultant "logic" relates a number of cross-currents in social theory and history. We first discuss Foucault's "decentering of the subject" as part of a broader consideration of the intellectual and political project of intellectuals that we call a "social epistemology." Our interest is to consider knowledge as social practice that generates action and participation. Knowledge, for our purposes, is a material practice that constitutes the "self" in the world rather than part of what Marxist analyses refer to as an epi-phenomenon.

We explore two concepts of power: that of sovereignty/repression and that of the deployment/production of power, arguing, with Foucault, certain feminist theories, and a political sociology of knowledge, that issues of power require making connections between self and self, self and other, and institutional discourses. Central in the linkages is Foucault's concept of governmentality. In the final part of the book, the politics of intellectual work are given attention. We follow Foucault's (1984) argument that the commitments of the Enlightenment are not bound to a particular doctrine or a particular body of knowledge, but that the Enlightenment is "an attitude, an ethos, a philosophical life in which the critique of what we are is at one time the historical analysis of the limits that are imposed on us and an experiment with the possibility of going beyond them" (p. 50).

CHANGING PATTERNS OF POWER AND THE CONSTRUCTION OF SOCIAL THEORY

If we think of critical educational research as a social room of different groups of people, we find that during the later part of the 1980s "new kids" arrived to articulate and explore questions and ideas about the politics of knowledge untouched or undeveloped in other critical traditions; these ideas later were called "postmodernism" and "poststructuralism," as well as, in some cases, a re-visioned Marxism that emphasized what Stuart Hall (1986) called, "a Marxism without guarantees." The new sea-migration of social theories from France and Germany were positioned as central in these debates by their various proponents (see, e.g., Giroux, 1992; Mahon, 1992; Popkewitz, 1992).

The questions raised are not merely about intellectual struggles, but embody changes in the construction of power in modernity, of which intellectual work is an important part. Wagner (1994), for example, argues that since the nineteenth century there has been a re-construction of control in social practices as older boundaries of social trust and security were eroded through processes of modernization. The modernization, however, was not only in the physical landscape in which one worked and lived as a social being. It also included forms of individualization that segmented the person into discrete attributes and behaviors that could be supervised and observed to ensure progress. The social sciences, Wagner continues, were inscribed in the process of modernization to make objectivist knowledge the classificatory criteria through which individuals were disciplined and self-regulated.

This issue of power, taken up by Foucault and certain postmodern social theorists, is different from those of the turn of the twentieth century. Rose (1996), for example, has persuasively argued that neoliberal policies of market, choice, and privatization are themselves embedded in longer-term changes (he calls them "mutations" in "advanced liberal societies") in the ways of understanding, classifying, and acting on the subjects of government, and in new relations between the ways in which individuals are governed by others and the ways in which they govern themselves. These relations are not in the anthropological universe of functional sociology but in the outcome of specific social practices through which subjectivities are constructed (also see Donald, 1992; Hunter, 1994; Rose & Miller, 1992; Shapiro, 1992; Walkerdine, 1990).

Exploring the changing foci and strategies of power, which Wagner and others trace and Foucault's empirical studies underscore, we believe, requires different intellectual practices than those found in previous critical traditions in the social sciences. We initially explore these distinctions and differences by comparing the assumptions of the philosophy of consciousness that has dominated liberal and critical social science with "a social epistemology" through which the work of Foucault can be located.

The Philosophy of Consciousness and the Privileging of the Subject

By the philosophy of consciousness, we mean two ideological legacies of nineteenth-century social thought in contemporary social and educational theory. One is the inscription of progress as a foundational assumption of intellectual knowledge. That strand of social thought brings into clear relief the relation of the past, present, and future. That relation gives direction to new, universal solutions for human emancipation. Second is an assumption that disciplinary knowledge has a subject. For liberal and critical theorists, change was premised on identifying the subjects who gave direction to change, either by locating the origins of repressive elements that prevented progress or by identifying the groups that were to bring about a redemptive world. In one strand of social theory, structural "actors" were identified, and in another strand of theory, individuals were identified in order to be "helped" through organizational and "community" strategies.

The foundational assumptions of progress and actor/agent converge in the liberal and Marxist–Hegelian traditions. Both were constructed within a particular doctrine related to nineteenth-century views of the Enlightenment. It was believed that systematic knowledge was the motor by which "reason" could direct social action and guarantee future betterment in society. That reason was applied by specific sets of actors that were identified through the knowledge of social science. Whereas liberal thought sought progress through managing social change, critical Hegelian thought sought progress through identifying social contradictions. While liberalism tends to place greater emphasis on individuals and the phenomenology of the subject in social change, critical traditions focus on the objectively constituted and constituting subject (see, e.g., Benhabib, 1986).

In contemporary school reforms, these foundational assumptions are deeply embedded as doxa. Dominant and liberal educational reform discourses tend to instrumentally organize change as logical and sequential, although there has been some recognition of the pragmatic qualities of social life (see, e.g., Fullan with Stiegelbauer, 1991). Although the specific focus may change, the agents of redemption are the State and educational researchers, and the agents of change are teachers as "self"-motivated professionals.

Critical traditions, particularly those related to Marxism, also maintain commitments to progress through philosophical assumptions about agents. With some hesitations and some dissent, contemporary critical traditions continue a nineteenth-century view of social redemption through schooling. Intellectual work is to provide universal norms and direction for social change. It is assumed that critical interrogations of social conditions will produce a new synthesis from the identified contradictions. The agents of redemption in critical traditions are universalized notions of the actor who is defined as being marginalized—workers, racially discriminated groups, and, more recently, women. The norms and direction to progress typically appear as an outcome of the research itself (Popkewitz, 1991).

The historical significance of the philosophy of consciousness, it is important to note here, recast and constituted a particular doctrine of the Enlightenment. It was a radical nineteenth-century philosophical strategy that placed people directly into the knowledge about social change, challenging the reigning notions of theology and the chances of birth as the arbiters of progress. Further, it gave continuing attention to the groups (actors) included and excluded through social practices, an important element of contemporary politics in which certain groups have been categorically excluded.

But while recognizing the importance of this nineteenth-century doctrine, we also question whether the epistemological foundations of actors and progress are adequate for the politics of governing and power that circulate in contemporary societies. Two issues appear throughout this chapter and the book:

1. Paradoxically, with different ideological positions, similar images of

the subject as an active and responsible agent within a developmental process of change are utilized. Young (1990) argues historically that the Marxist version of social change is but a negative revision of the history that was imposed by Europeans in their nineteenth-century imperialism. Colonial systems and their dialectics embody rules of knowledge that presuppose a universal governing structure of self-realization in all historical processes. Marxism's reversal of the idealism of Hegel, Young (1990) argues, "remains explicit with, and even extends the system to which it is opposed" (p. 3) because the same universalizing narrative of an unfolding rational system of the world continues to appear. The construction of knowledge, Young argues, expropriates and incorporates the "Other" into a system that is totalizing and thus does not allow the "Other" legitimacy. To place this convergence into contemporary American educational reforms, the very systems of reasoning that are to produce equality, justice, and diversity may inscribe systems of representation that construct "otherness" through concrete pedagogical practices that differentiate, compare, and normalize children along a continuum of value.

2. The second point we want to make here is related to the a priori principle of progress. We will argue later that it is possible philosophically (and theoretically) to accept a view of progress and of human agency without the prior positing of the agent as a principle of disciplinary study. The significance of analytic posture about progress and agents in the philosophy of consciousness is found, paradoxically, in making the intellectual the authority over the subject. The authority occurs as the intellectual is invested with defining the relation of the subject to the developmental process from the past and present to the future. We say "paradoxically" because the often repeated phrase in critical traditions that the politics of knowledge is in "making" the world not in describing it, leaves its own presuppositions of progress and actors unquestioned and unscrutinized.[3]

A Social Epistemology, Decentering the Subject, and Knowledge/Power

The premises about progress and agents in the philosophy of consciousness is one of the major challenges posed in current debates about social and educational theory. In a wide band of intellectual work called "the linguistic turn," there has emerged a focus in research on the constitutive role of knowledge in the construction of social life. Our interest here in the linguistic turn is to explore a specific scholarship that both focuses on the relation of power, knowledge, and change, and historicizes the problems of "knowledge." We call this twofold interest "social epistemology."

We use the phrase "social epistemology" rather than "linguistic turn" as a strategy to place the objects constituted as the knowledge of schooling in historically formed patterns and power relations (see Popkewitz, 1991, 1992). Epistemology provides a context in which to consider the rules and standards that organize perceptions, ways of responding to the world, and the conceptions of "self." Concurrently, social epistemology locates the objects constituted as the knowledge of schooling as historical practices through which power relations can be understood. We argue that the statements and words of schooling are not signs or signifiers that refer to and fix things, but social practices through generating principles that order action and participation. The conception of epistemology, then, is not, as in U.S. philosophy, a meta-discourse to find the ultimate rules of truth, but an effort to understand the conditions in which knowledge is produced.

Our speech is ordered through principles of classification that are socially formed through a myriad of past practices. When teachers talk about school as management, teaching as producing learning, or children who are at risk, these terms are not merely words of the teacher, but are part of historically constructed ways of reasoning that are the effects of power. A social epistemology studies speech as effects of power.

"Learning" as a discourse of schooling is another example. It is an invention derived from behavioral psychology of the 1920s and related to, among other events, concerns with the administration and assessment of the teacher and the child. But the knowledge of the world as "learning" is not only about interpretation. The psychological visioning of the world is also a revisioning of the "self." The "reasoning" inscribed technologies about how the teacher supervise classroom practices as well as a way in which teachers and children become self-governing actors in the spaces of schooling. A social epistemology enables us to consider the word *learning* not as standing alone, but as embodying a range of historically constructed values, priorities, and dispositions toward how one should see and act toward the world.

The governing of reason is a central theme in Fendler's genealogical study of the "educated subject" in this book. Fendler argues that "to be subjected to education has meant to become disciplined according to a regimen of remembering and forgetting, of assuming identities normalized through discursive practices, and of a history of unpredictable diversions." She examines over time the shifting assumptions of "true" and good in the notion of the "educated subject," the practical technologies to educate, the systems of recognition and things "examined," and the ways people are "invited" to recognize themselves as "educated." The epistemological shifts in the organizations of the educated subject enables Fendler to consider the significance of current pedagogical reforms as practices of governing the "self."

The focus on the historical construction of "reason" and the "reasonable person" provides a strategy to make problematic what the philosophy of consciousness assumes. Certain postmodern writers suggest that specific strategies of the nineteenth and twentieth centuries that define progress and the agent as an a priori philosophical assumption of theory need to be rethought. If we look at Foucault (1984) and a feminist philosopher, Butler (1992, 1993), for example, we find that they raise questions about whether the maintaining of the historical subject who brings about change is, in fact, an effect of power. The argument is that the a priori philosophical placement of actors in the narratives of social science obscures more than it reveals. The strategies of naming actors in social practices is construed as hiding the power relations within the rules of classification applied.

Knowledge of the constituted subject, then, is a central concern of a social theory of power. Inquiry is to understand how the rules of reason that structure our practices for change and the classifications and distinctions among groups of people have been constructed. Sawicki (1988), drawing on Foucault in reviewing feminist research, argues that feminine forms of embodiment in dietary and fitness regimes; expert advice on how to walk, talk, and dress; the ways in which hair is styled; and the wearing of makeup are "technologies that subjugate by developing competencies" and aesthetic tastes (pp. 174–175). Sawicki continues that power is deployed through the systems of ideas about the self that are intertwined with performances and "skills" through which an individuality is constructed as natural and desirable for a woman.[4]

In certain ways, this focus on knowledge is not "new" to the scholarship of education. Kuhn's (1970) studies of knowledge to understand scientific change is one example of such an approach, although we use Kuhn advisedly here because of his idealistic conception of change. Kuhn studied an epistemological tradition of history/social science that is tied to European continental scholarship (see, e.g., Richter, 1986; Tiles, 1984) and brought into the study of power in the social sciences through the work of Michel Foucault. Kuhn, the continental historians and philosophers of science, and Foucault shifted the focus of inquiry from the intentions of people to the changing principles through which knowledge itself is structured. Scientific change is then located in the manner in which concepts change and the conditions in which concepts change.

We also can identify the focus on epistemology in Marx and in the Marxist theorist, Louis Althusser, a colleague of Foucault. Althusser worked from the tradition of the history of science prominent in France, although, ironically, Althusser's epistemological approach was criticized as not being Marxist (Young, 1990).

The study of knowledge as a social practice, discussed earlier, is called a "decentering of the subject." The objective of the decentering of the subject is to understand how the subject is constituted within a field that relates knowledge and power. It is not to eliminate subjects seeking to change their worlds but to give historical specificity to the systems of ideas that enclose and intern the "reason" and the "reasonable person" as alternatives are sought.

The decentering of the subject also enables us to problematize our relation to present modes of reasoning through historically examining how an autonomous "self" is constituted. A subject-decentered approach would place the difference as that of studying blackness instead of blacks, femininity instead of women, homosexuality instead of homosexuals, and childhood instead of children. The decentering of the subject, then, is to focus on systems of ideas as historical practices through which the objects of the world are constructed and become systems of action (see Foucault, 1988; also see Dreyfus & Rabinow, 1983; Noujain, 1987; Rajchman, 1985; in feminist theory, see Barrett & Phillips, 1992; Fraser, 1989; Nicholson, 1986; Weedon, 1987).

Foucault, in his later work, calls this historicizing the subject a genealogy, arguing:

> One has to dispense with the constituent subject, to get rid of the subject itself . . . to arrive at an analysis which can account for the constitution of the subject within a historical framework. . . . And this is what I would call genealogy . . . a form of history which can account for the constitution of knowledges, discourses, domains of objects etc., without having to make reference to a subject which is either transcendental in relation to the field of events or runs its empty sameness throughout the course of history. (Foucault, 1980, p. 117)

Social epistemological theory is thus understood as situated within a broad multidisciplinary conversation about the project of social science and history. This intellectual project is, first, a strategy to focus on theory as an epistemological problem; that is, it provides a way of orienting and of problematizing the social conditions in which contemporary social life is constructed (see, e.g., Popkewitz, 1991). It is to treat theory, as does Bourdieu, who is educated within the same intellectual milieu as Foucault, as a "thinking tool"—"a modus operandi which practically guides and structures scientific practices" (Bourdieu & Wacquant, 1992, p. 161; also see Bourdieu, 1984, 1990). Second, the decentering of the subject is a strategy not to reject humanism but to resituate that humanism by historicizing the conceptions of actors and reason through which practice and purpose are constructed. As Hacking (1986) has argued, "Foucault said that the Concept of Man is a fraud, not that you and I are nothing" (p. 39).

The strategy of a social epistemology reverses the interests of the philosophy of consciousness by making the problem of study that of the knowledge that inscribes agents. The terrain of social and educational theory is with a "critical," problematizing theory that focuses on the construction of knowledge itself and "reason" as the problems of inquiry. It makes problematic how the "objects" of the world are historically constructed and change over time. Such a strategy, as will be argued later, is a political theory as well as theory of knowledge, as the two are inseparable. The effect is to disturb narratives of progress and reconciliation, finding questions where others had located answers (Dean, 1994). This can be contrasted to liberal theories that are built on a model of social progress and a theory that proposes a dialectic in which present forms of reason and society are both negated and retained in a higher form.

Regional Study Instead of Context: Individuality in Discursive Spaces

A concomitant interest within social and educational theory is a radical re-conception of space and time. This re-conception shifts attention from notions of geographically bound contexts that develop in chronological sequences to notions of regions bound by a discursive "field" and uneven time dimensions. The latter give focus to how the subject is to be known and knowing in a terrain not bound to geographical landscapes and physical points of reference but to discursively constructed practices.

We can understand this notion of space/time by thinking of the child in schooling. At one level, there is no child in school until we have theories that enable us to talk of a childhood. Childhood normalizes the way in which children are to be seen, talked about, and acted upon as "learners" or as having a "developmental process." Further, the distinctions of adolescence or a learner embody principles for ordering identity that transcend the particular institution of schooling by means of the categories applied. The conceptions of childhood place a child in normalized social spaces that "travel" across different social institutions.

One of the major contributions of Foucault is his directing our attention to how social spaces or regions have been discursively constructed in modern life. The histories that Foucault wrote about, for example, are histories of how the person is made into a subject through particular rules and standards in particular institutional patterns but that are not reducible to the particular institutions. His studies of the prison and the criminal, the asylum and the insane, the clinical medical gaze, and bodily desires in the history of sexuality are examples of the constructions of discursive fields. Each field is an assemblage that spans multiple institutions.

Individuality seems to transcend particular events and the social moorings of place, such as the child as a learner who has no specific geographical location. Thus, for example, the person-as-learner is defined through abstract sets of categories about cognition, affect, and motivation. These sets of categories and distinctions constitute and divide individuals.

We can think of educational studies, then, as a social mapping of the region and its inscribed boundaries. The regional focus enables an understanding of how particular rules and standards of truth cross institutional patterns and are not reducible to those patterns. The notion of region embodies a varied notion of time to account for different patterns of ideas and social practices that come together to produce the subject—the child in childhood, the animal, the medical patient, and so on. This notion of time has no universal sequence or single "origin" that is different from chronological time and different from the philosophy of consciousness that posits as a priori the conditions of the subject for considering social change.

Curriculum becomes, from this point of view, part of a discursive field through which the subjects of schooling are constructed as individuals to self-regulate, discipline, and reflect upon themselves as members of a community/ society (see, e.g., Englund, 1991; Hamilton, 1989; Lundgren, 1991).[5] For example, if we focus on the systems of ideas that merge into the modern curriculum at the turn of the century, we find that the curriculum changes were a part of a visioning/re-visioning of social commitment and of individual service and faith (Popkewitz, 1987, 1991). The ideas re-visioned a pastoral image of the person in relation to a modern, scientific notion of the "rational" citizen. The discourses of the child placed faith in the rational individual as the locus of change (see, e.g., Meyer, 1986).

We can consider the significance of the discursive fields to be explored through returning to the earlier discussion of Wagner (1994). He argued that issues of power have become significantly different from those of the nineteenth-century theories that posited a view of power as sovereignty. The construction of expert systems of knowledge that construct and normalize individuality has increased in important ways. Thinking of our "selves" through such systems seems natural—our individuality involves our personality characteristics and conceptions of the body and desires inscribed through gendered knowledges.

The strategy to locate individuals in discursive spaces is a way to understand and make problematic the classificatory criteria through which individuals are to be disciplined and self-regulated.

The mapping of a discursive field can be found in the historical studies in this book. Earlier, we discussed Fendler's genealogy of the "educated subject." Simola, Heikkinen, and Silvonen's study of the changing regimes of truth in the historical construction of the teacher in Finland, Rabak Wagener's study of "health" education, and Hultqvist's and Baker's chapters on the concept of childhood focus on how power is effected in discursive spaces that traverse multiple institutions. Rabak Wagener, for example, moves among different educational, medical, and social welfare institutions to consider the emergence of the category of health education. In particular, she considers how moral/political categories are deployed as scientific categories in constructing the "students" of objects of sexuality and "desire." Her analysis provides a way to consider how health, sex, and morality intersect contemporary policy discussions about AIDS and sex education.

DECENTERING PROGRESS: FROM EVOLUTION TO A HISTORY OF BREAKS

With progress no longer guaranteed by the reasoned application of scientific principles, another conception for change must be identified. That conception is of ruptures or breaks in the systems of reasoning (knowledge) that generate the principles of action and participation.

The notion of change as breaks or ruptures is found in the history of science developed in France and conceptual history found in German historiography. The distinctions between important periods of scientific ways of reasoning are studied not as cumulative; rather they involve ruptures in belief and cognition that occur within particular historical conjunctures. For example, Bachelard's studies of physics in the 10 years from 1920 to 1930 formed, he suggests from a scientific point of view, as long an era as the previous 500 years (Young, 1990). There occurred, in this period, a remaking of science's own history of itself, as relativity theory and microphysics produced a reaction to the science of the past. Science becomes a series of "nons"—non-Cartesian, non-Euclidean, non-Newtonian, non-Baconian. In Kuhn's (1970) argument about revolutionary and normal sciences as well, historical change did not involve the intent and purpose of actors, even though individuals and particular practices were part of the narrative about science. "Scientific revolutions" gave focus to different sets of rules and standards about truth—what is to be studied, why, and how—from those of normal science. We can turn, as well, to Wittgenstein (1966), who later provided a way of understanding historical change as multiple rates developing across different institutions at different times. Wittgenstein likened historical change to a thread made up of many fibers. The strength of the thread does not reside in the fact that some fibers run its entire length, but in the fact that many fibers overlap.

From this perspective on change, the set of relations that becomes schooling—in its forms of expression and performances—exists across different dimensions of time and space rather than through the development of a continuous history. Mass schooling, for example, was a nineteenth-century invention that emerged from different movements within society that, at a certain level, worked autonomously from each other. Overlapping with changes in classroom teaching were the creations of institutions for teacher education, the rise of the modern university, the formation of social sciences, and the emergence of a discipline of psychology. The multiple arenas of practice occurred at the conjuncture of the emergence of the modern welfare state that governed the new institution of mass schooling. At the same time, systems of ideas appeared about the "educativeness" of the person: ideas of childhood, classrooms, and school administration aligned social/political rationalities to the personal progress of the child.

The focus on change as breaks in discursive fields can be explored in studies of educational reform. Baker and Hultqvist in this volume study how reasoning about the child is a political technology that changes in different historical relations. Baker argues that schooling presupposes a concept of childhood and then she explores historically the multiple and complex interweaving of discourses through which childhood as constructed has produced systems of inclusions/exclusions. The processes of differentiation, for example, in "child study" research at the turn of the century worked to advantage certain categories of white children. Its norms privileged certain white, especially male and middle-class, children, and thereby excluded African-American children from the dominant versions of the child to be cared for in the schooling system. Hultqvist maps the construction and re-constructions of the welfare "child" as a pedagogical principle in Swedish state policies. His analysis points to the development of a "decentralized child" as a historically constituted subject well before that subject became visible in current policy discussions related to "markets" and privatization. His analysis directs attention to the historical limitations of accepting the constituted subject as historical "fact," such as found in much of the critical literature that speaks of "conservative restorations" with labels of "the New Right."

We can think of these studies as mapping the construction of the subject through a genealogical historical mode of analysis. Genealogies, as we discussed earlier, are histories that work to construct historical analyses about how the particular forms of reasoning and "telling the truth" of the present involved shifts in the power relations and kinds of knowledge central to establishing a particular discourse. The studies within this volume work to explore how reason is produced within a set of historical relations that does not emphasize causality. This form of argumentation removes the linearity of much prevalent historical work; more important, it also makes spaces for multiple interrelationships in the construction of a discourse and hence more spaces for multiple openings for contestation and redefinition.

A different dimension of the "linguistic turn" is found in the work of Habermas (1971, 1981, 1987; Bernstein, 1985), a member of the Frankfurt School of Critical Theory. Habermas's writing on cognitive interests in knowledge and his later theory of communicative action embody a theory of language in a social theory of change. Habermas's theory, however, is dualistic in his separation of life-worlds and system, producing an ahistorical view of power as he focuses on a universal pragmatics of reason (see, e.g., Sintomer, 1992).[6]

If we place the work of the Frankfurt School and the French Marxist, Althusser, in historical proximity, we realize that there are important points of continuity as well as breaks with the epistemological assumptions that we are discussing in relation to Foucault. It is the epistemological continuities that those who write about limitations of the "linguistic turn" in social theory and the "structural" needs of inquiry do not recognize in their critiques, as the critics, especially in education, do not understand their own history. (We will discuss these critiques later.) At the same time, the focus of this book is the radical breaks in social epistemology embodied in Foucault's discussion of change and power.

CHANGE AND POWER

Sovereignty and Power

We can pursue further the implications of the social epistemology as social theory by focusing more directly on the concept of power.[7] Foucault reverses the traditional belief that knowledge is power and looks for power in how people effect knowledge to intervene in social affairs. Foucault's concept of power gives attention to its productive dimensions, such as how power works through individual actions to vision and re-vision our "selves" as acting, thinking, and feeling persons. This occurs as we consider the social and conceptual conditions through which we have come to reason about sexuality, criminality, medicine, and sanity/madness as the effects of power (Foucault, 1965, 1973, 1975, 1979).

To explore Foucault's notion of power, it is worth considering the philosophy of consciousness articulated in school studies of power. To be schematic here, the purpose of studying power within the philosophy of consciousness is to identify the origin of power; that is, the objective of the study is to identify the actors who control, and in whose benefit existing arrangements work—for example, asking in whose interest the curriculum is selected or achievement assessed.

The centering of actors as the wielders of power introduces a view of power as sovereignty. For Foucault, this is best illustrated by the symbolic use of the power of the sovereign, the king with power of life and death over his subjects. Taking this notion of sovereign power into research is to give attention to what groups are favored in decision making and how the decisions distribute values to produce a context of domination and subordination—the rulers and the ruled. Power in this landscape is "something" that people own, and that ownership can be re-distributed among groups to challenge inequities—hence the use of the term "sovereignty."

The concept of power as sovereignty is found in much of the sociology of school knowledge, where it is used to explain the origins of domination and subjugation in society. For example, a sovereignty notion of power is embodied in current educational literature that sees social interests inscribed in reform reports and government policies that argue for a "back to basics" curriculum. The consequence of the reforms, it is argued, is to re-produce gender, racial, and class distinctions in society (Carlson, 1992).

Structural concepts of agency, resistance, and contestation have been used to posit ways in which the hegemony of the rulers is challenged and change can be sought. Structural uniformity is assumed, for example, in inquiries to understand how gifted education, school testing, and teacher hiring practices privilege certain groups, or is resisted through students' reading of "romance fictions," teaching practices, and rejecting dominant values of adolescents (see, e.g., Weis & Fine, 1993). Here, sovereign power is attached to actors who have the legitimacy to make decisions and allocate values within communities—a description that continues to inscribe the commitments of the philosophy of consciousness. A central premise is that society includes groups, social interests, and "forces" that historically have formed and whose practices dominate and repress other groups.

The sovereignty notion of power is limited on a number of counts. Whereas the sovereignty notion of power posits unified historical processes and structures, change entails "an amalgamation of institutional and discursive practices that function as a collective assemble of disparate parts on a single surface" (Crary, 1990, p. 6). If one re-examines the "conservative restoration" thesis, for example, the changes reported in economy, culture, and politics are found to begin well before the election of Reagan in the United States or Thatcher in the United Kingdom, and entail a re-organization of knowledge and practices that occurred in an uneven pattern, within multiple institutions, and over a period that is longer than the "Reagan–Bush" era (see Kuttner, 1991; Lekachman, 1982; also see Popkewitz, 1991, 1996). What is reported as structural historical change in the "conservative restoration" is nonhistorical and nonrelational. Power is treated as immanent to the specific setting rather than questioned about how it is possible to exist in this form or what the conditions of its production are.

Another limitation of the sovereignty notion of power is in the tendency to homogenize and essentialize categories of analysis. The historical contingencies and multiple boundaries in which race, class, and gender are constructed, for example, have no single origin or universal characteristics but are constructed in relational fields that are fluid and multidimensional. While one can posit a generalized condition of capitalism as a background to the organization of power, for example, this positing does not provide an adequate theoretical grounding for understanding how the capillaries of power work in modern societies. There is no one "model" of capitalism, and its history is not one of unified development.

Thus, while research and researchers can be sensitive to issues of race, class, and gender, the rules and standards of reasoning by which the subjects are "defined" are not essential categories of logic but need to be treated as historically constructed categories that embody and weave together social, technological, and institutional patterns. Power as sovereignty often creates a dichotomous world in which there is the oppressor and oppressed, thus producing a dualism whose effect is to define particular social groups as monolithic entities. The researcher's story is of one group who dominates while the other carries social righteousness but does not possess power. The dualism of oppressor/oppressed loses sight of the subtleties in which power operates in multiple arenas and social practices (see Popkewitz, 1993). The critical traditions that build on this approach to sovereign power have used ideological critique to uncover the "real" or underlying power relations, which are identified and thereby "fixed."

Power as Deployment and Productive Effects

Foucault suggests that there is a different but not necessarily incommensurate interpretation of power from that of sovereignty. That view concerns the productive quality of power. This productive notion of power concerns its effects as it circulates through institutional practices and the discourses of daily life. Foucault argues that power is embedded in the governing systems of order, appropriation, and exclusion by which subjectivities are constructed and social life is formed. Here, Foucault revises the Nietzschean notion of a "will to know" to consider how available systems of ideas discipline individuals as they act, see, think, and see themselves in the world.

Historically, we can focus on the new deployments of power occurring as the state and the social sciences develop new technologies. The welfare state insurance for unemployment, and classification systems that define people by age, occupation, marital status, and health status serve to re-vision individuality through "civilizing processes," to borrow from Norbert Elias (1978), that produce boundaries and permissible paths for the new citizen. The idea of the deployment of power gives focus to how the subject is disciplined through the rules of knowledge per se.

The changing foci and strategies of power, which Foucault's empirical studies underscore, we believe, require different intellectual practices to explore issues of power than those embodied in the philosophy of consciousness and its critical traditions in the social sciences. Strategically, the study of the effects of power enables us to focus on the ways that individuals construct boundaries and possibilities. In some ways, we can consider the work of Foucault as expanding on and providing a historical specificity to the observations of the early Frankfurt School. The early theorists focused on the expanding rationalization and instrumental reasoning that underlie modernity. Foucault enables us to understand that such reasoning has multiple trajectories and to explore the various strategies through which individuality is constructed as both disciplining and productive of power.

The productive elements of power move from focusing on the controlling actors to the systems of ideas that normalize and construct the rules through which intent and purpose in the world are organized. The effects of power are to be found in the production of desire and in dispositions and sensitivities of individuals. The concern of Marx with the productive characteristics of labor thus is inverted into the productive characteristics of knowledge itself (Dumm, 1987).

It is the effects of power that postmodern and feminist literatures have focused on, with Foucault's work an important generative element of these explorations. For example, Spivak (1992) discusses the problem of translation as a political practice that entails multiple deployments of power. Focusing on the translations of women's texts from the Third World into English, Spivak argues that the specific actor who writes these texts cannot be designated by her subject position of gender or class. She explores how the discursive practices normalize and produce identities through a pervasive orientalism that obliterates Third World specificity and denies cultural citizenship. For Spivak, the concern is not to find the origin of repressive mechanisms of class or gender; her concern is how "sense" is produced through the complex inscriptions of power relations.

We can explore the productive notion of power to re-conceptualize the problem of socialization in teaching and teacher education. Most research on teaching and teacher education assumes the "subject" of children and teacher as stable categories—research questions are asked about how teachers and students learn about the social relations and at points resist those arrangements. The notion of socialization also can be used to ask about the discursive practices that construct what it means to be a teacher who administers children. For example, a recent study of socialization in teacher education was interested in understanding the particular images and visions in schooling that classified children of color and of poverty (Popkewitz, in press). The study described how the discursive practices of classroom teaching and management and conceptions of children's intelligence, behavior, and achievement are constructed and the effects of power. The different systems of pedagogical ideas formed a scaffolding of ideas that normalized children of color in opposition to some general but unspoken norms about personal competence in schools. What was significant (and paradoxical) was that the rules of "reasoning" in the teacher education practices were also the rules of current school reforms concerned with issues of equity.

To summarize, we explored two interpretations of power—as sovereignty and as deployment. Each maintains general political commitments for social change, but with different assumptions in the loci of study and the politics of intervention. We recognize that neither interpretive stance is totalizing but both are complementary; the former considers larger historical structures through which daily life is constructed; the latter focuses on the concrete practices through which power circulates and is productive in daily life. The latter is a political as well as an intellectual strategy for disrupting that knowledge/power relation through making visible and open to resistance the systems of ideas that construct the subject.

GOVERNMENTALITY IN EDUCATION

Foucault's concept of governmentality has received only scant attention from within the field of education as yet (see, e.g., Ball, 1990; Foucault, 1991a). The notion of governmentality provides a way to consider the concept of power as deployment (discussed earlier) and to consider the conceptual scaffolding built through the discussions on decentering the subject and the problematics of power when considering issues of change. We first outline Foucault's own approach to governmentality and then move to discuss education as centrally implicated in the process of modernization within which projects such as the philosophy of consciousness have been constructed. These are also related to discussions of the other chapters in this volume.

The Significance of Emphasis on Governmentality

In current educational debates there has been much discussion about the problem of school governance, usually cast in terms of specific organizational features of the school or school system in relation to state intervention. Building on our discussion above, however, we suggest that it is more fruitful to discuss the issues of governance less in terms of pros and cons about specific policies and more in terms of the conditions by which practices such as site-based management, "the reflective teacher," or "action research" are constructed as plausible.

In his lecture on governmentality, Foucault (1991a) argues that rather than the "Étatisation of society," modernity actually may be characterized by "the 'governmentalization' of the state" (p. 103). The shift from the art of governance of the prince in relation to a principality—exemplified by Machiavelli's treatise—toward governance of a different kind was able to occur during the sixteenth century in large part, he argues, because of the specific development of the phenomenon of "population." Population as an entity can be cared for by government by moving into a more grand arena the practices of the patriarch in caring for the family and managing its "economy." Foucault (1991a) suggests that "the family becomes the instrument rather than the model: a privileged instrument for the government of the population. . . . Population comes to appear above all else to be the ultimate end of government" (p. 100). Population, once it exists as a concept, can be measured, organized, statistically developed into categories, and dealt with in institutions, each with its own techniques of power/knowledge. It is the pre-eminent form of power/knowledge relations of the modern world. In developing the technologies appropriate to population, governmentality then must include a focus on the techniques of the self as well as the institutional technologies that perpetrate the art of government in ways that make it acceptable to the populace.

Gordon (1991) argues that the "focus of Foucault's interest in modern governmental rationalities consists, precisely, in the realization of what he called "the 'daemonic' coupling of 'city game' and 'shepherd-game': the invention of a form of secular political pastorate which couples 'individualization' and 'totalization'" (p. 8). What is of particular importance to this volume is that educational institutions combine in particular ways the pastoral, caring work of the state and the work that makes population categories work (see, e.g., Hacking, 1991; Rose, 1989).

Governmentality and Education

While Foucault himself gave little direct attention to the institution of schooling and its microtechnologies of power/knowledge, much of his work has major implications for understanding the nature of educational work, including education research, and he often refers in passing to such implications. In his lecture on governmentality in 1978, for example, Foucault (1991a) suggests that the explosion of concerns central to his thesis included the "government of children and the great problematic of pedagogy which emerges and develops during the sixteenth century" (p. 87). His work on prisons also has been used as an important corollary to the institution of schooling. Yet while a number of scholars have taken up the challenge of Foucault's governmentality in relation to diverse fields, rarely has this concern with governmentality as a coalescence of different foci for power/knowledge been analyzed within education.

Foucault argued in *Discipline and Punish* (1979) that the invention of the "examination" allowed the "calculable person" to be developed and thus the particular form of the power/knowledge relations characteristic of the modern period. Hoskin (1993), however, working from Foucault's framework, suggests a need to move further than Foucault in understanding the significance of the examination. Foucault (1991a) argues:

> The pastoral, the new diplomatic-military techniques and, lastly, police, these are the three elements that I believe made possible the production of this fundamental phenomenon in Western history, the governmentalization of the state. (p. 104)

Hoskin (1993) suggests that "examination lies at the heart of the transformation" (p. 277). For Hoskin, the new "'calculable person' is the result of the invention of marking: The new panoptical gaze of surveillance-plus-judgment is the result of the new powers of writing-plus-examination. The transformation into the disciplinary world (never directly specified by Foucault) is a direct outcome of a new way of learning to learn, beginning at the top in these elite settings" (Hoskin, 1993, p. 277).

The new pedagogy, discussed in *The Order of Things* (Foucault, 1973) in relation to philology, biology, and political economy, gave rise to new ways of "constructing the self: respectively as critical-interpretive, as technical-scientific, and as rational-economic" (Hoskin, 1993, p. 280). By the early nineteenth century, Hoskin argues, the regulation through the introduction of practices of writing, grading, and examination was firmly entrenched. Thereafter students quickly came to take it for granted that writing, grading, and examination were practices dating back to time immemorial (Hoskin, 1993). The grammocentric world suggested by Hoskin, organized around the discipline of writing, and oriented to a new principle of producing power/knowledge, has been central to the development of the modern world.

This may suggest some reasons why education, both schooling and university sectors, has become so central in the development of new forms of governmentality, exemplifying new strategies, tactics, and techniques of power to furnish what had become the major form of power relations defining institutions and individuals in Western societies. The institutions of formal education, schools and universities, have become central to the "disciplining" in most if not all other fields.

Reforms in education do not occur in a vacuum, but are intricately connected to activity in other fields, particularly the media. Green's explorations of the reform of English as a subject provides an exemplary case of state intervention in education with remarkable parallels across England, the United States, and Australia. As Green shows in this volume and elsewhere (Green, 1995), even a single subject area such as English can be a means of mobilizing particular discourses that alter the content, focus, and relations of teaching. He is also concerned with the way discourses around English are mobilized in the professional and public arenas to construct the "teacher." Exploration of these reform themes, particularly through a genealogical approach, provides detailed evidence of the ways in which the connection of knowledge to power operates to constitute the subject of schooling. "Subject" here is used with at least three referents: the teacher who is subjected to particular reforms, the child who is constructed through marshaling particular discourses, and also the more common usage of the subject as the formal content of schooling.

Shutkin, in this volume, makes clear some of the dimensions of the refocusing of curriculum control through new information technologies, the changes that "technological identity" can make to the teacher–student relationship. Shutkin's concern is with the deployment of power, drawing on Foucault to explore how discursive spaces are constructed through practices in different sites. His concern is how various sites of deployment of new information technologies are related in constructing the teacher and the student in schooling.

Both the pastoral and economic aspects of population, another dimension of governmentality, work at the microlevel of the individual, in the body, in individualizing the particular dimensions of normality, as well as across populations. Thus it is "normal" for young people to be gathered together in age-grouped cohorts, organized around the transmission and production of certain kinds of knowledge, in institutions that we know as schools. Different students in schools are, however, differentiated according to different scales and categories, often through the medium of assessment, but also through the privileging of certain kinds of content and approaches to teaching and learning. Students will be cared for in a range of ways, and different kinds of statistics will be collected and collated in relation to their positioning and achievements. The move to further consolidate the calibration of "outcomes" in testing on standardized content, best represented in moves to "national curriculum" across the Anglo world, can be seen as a further development of the links between individualization and populational overview.

"Caring" or pastoral power is, however, not only connected to the formulation of the preschool and school-age child. It is also constructed as central to educational work, including in universities. Gore, in this volume, takes seriously Foucault's challenge to undertake studies of the microphysics of power by "operationalizing" his genealogical work to consider empirical questions. Gore considers a number of institutional settings across which it often is presumed that the normalizing practices of education will vary. She considers how and whether practices are differentiated in terms of power relations created in both formal and informal settings, ostensibly feminist and not. While the focus of her chapter is methodological in the sense that she explores the extent to which Foucault's categories, developed in his broader studies of power, can be used to conduct more microphysical examination of specific sites, her interest is in the practices of power within and across sites.

Simola, Heikkinen, and Silvolen re-marshal Foucaultian resources to construct a "catalog of possibilities" across what they see as a coherent body of Foucault's work. They argue against working separately on issues of knowledge, subjectivity, and truth in favor of a more relational approach. They textually analyze the production of "truths" of the modern Finnish teacher, to explore how "pastoral professionalism" works as a structuring principle of the discourses constructing the teacher. Such links between the constitution of the subject and the broad themes of educational discourses are central to the project of exploring governmentality.

INTELLECTUAL WORK AS POLITICAL: A RECONSIDERATION

Why focus on a social epistemology rather than maintain the assumptions of the philosophy of consciousness? One could argue that focusing on the intent and purposes of social actors provides an important social as well as scientific commitment; it places people and their social worlds as central in producing social change. To remove people from history, it is argued, is to make the world seem deterministic and outside the possibility of intervention. In fact, efforts to remove the actor have been viewed as reactionary within the dogma of the philosophy of consciousness.[8] Not to have a visible actor—groupings of people and individuals—in narratives of social affairs is asserted as anti-humanistic (and even anti-democratic). It is not uncommon to hear people react to stories about schools by asking, "Where are the people in the story?" The assumption is of a world in which salvation can be found through positing prior universal actors who will carry out good works and whose potential is not prevented through the schemata of theorists who "decenter" the subject (see, e.g., Beyer & Liston, 1992).

Further, since there is no rhetoric of emancipation, it is assumed that power as an issue is not present as well. This argument is a reading that ignores the terrain that is being struggled about. It is a reading that continually brings the ideas in the linguistic turn into an Hegelian set of assumptions about contradictions, resistance, and a humanism based on a universalized notion of progress. The argument becomes solipsistic and intellectually narcissistic.[9]

But as important, the sociological consequence of the philosophy of consciousness has not always been empowering. The practical consequences of an unquestioned centering of a subject entail multiple issues of power that are hidden in the rhetorical constructions. Butler (1992) argues, drawing on feminist and postcolonial literature, that the centering of the subject is a particular invention of Western philosophy. When the subject is taken uncritically as the locus of struggle for knowledge about enfranchisement and democracy, scholarship draws from the very models that have oppressed through the regulation and production of subjects (also see Young, 1990). Such a strategy, Butler argues, is both a consolidation and concealment of those power relations. Where the agency of individuals or groups are made to seem natural, there is a tendency to lose sight of how the agendas and categories that define oppositions are historically formed. The systems of relevancies are taken for granted.

Further, the objective of the decentering of the subject, we have argued, is not to prevent the subject from acting, or to give up the Enlightenment project. The strategy of decentering the subject is itself a product of the very self-reflectivity produced through an Enlightenment ethos. The decentering of the subject has its own sense of irony: There is an acceptance of the need to construct knowledge that can enable people to act intentionally. The subject is made into a dimension of the questionable and of "insistent contest and resignification" (Butler, 1992, p. 7), not as a foundation of research that is taken as the unquestionable. By continually exploring what it meant to remove the self-reflective subject from center stage, Foucault made different approaches to rationality and activity possible. Thus the process of subjectification—central to political projects of varying persuasions and commitments—becomes open to critical scrutiny in ways not previously understood.

Constructing histories about how our subjectivities are formed (making the agendas and categories of the subject problematic) can provide a potential space for alternative acts and alternative intentions that are not articulated through the available commonsenses. The chapters in this volume clearly relate the development of subjects to the power relations in and through which they are formed, and the kinds of knowledges necessary for power to be exercised, and a number demonstrate some of the possibilities. Fendler, for example, in counterposing the regulatory ideals of a number of different moments in educational history, not only shows that change is possible for the individual to be educated, but also makes spaces for considering strategic intervention in the constitution of the educative substance of the subject.

This insertion of the subject, therefore, occurs in a different location than that argued in the philosophy of consciousness; but it is no less an acceptance of the need of and the challenge for more viable and just possibilities. The humanism is reinserted into social analysis by questioning the givenness of the subject as historically constructed and thus re-asserting an individuality that can challenge the rules of reason that subjugate.

The political project of many feminists inscribes this shift in intellectual work. An important strategy in constructing different social relations and social spaces for women is to challenge the hegemonies of "reason" that are inscribed in gendered identities. The "politics of identity" and the "politics of difference" in feminist scholarship are an integral dimension of the political project of feminism itself. Such moves historicize gender constructions in order to dislocate the inscribed identities of women and thereby open up other possibilities.

The life and work of Foucault is another example of the insertion of the agency and the politics of the intellectual (see, e.g., Eribon, 1991; Miller, 1993). Michel Foucault was in his lifetime a major figure in French intellectual life, playing the role of activist intellectual, which has no real counterpart in the English-speaking world, particularly the United States and Australia. Thus, although English speakers may read his work as not directly engaged with the major political debates of his—or the current—era, it is necessary to remind such readers of the significant and close connections that his work had at a metalevel with the issues of lived politics. In addition to his own political connection with the student uprisings in Tunis and France and their aftermath—for example, in the development of a radical faculty at Vincennes—and his work with prisoners, Foucault's focus in his own research lay in the problematics of disruption to order, the ways in which order itself was a fragile but forcible and tangible achievement. Such themes recur from *Madness and Civilization* (1965) through *The Order of Things* (1973), *Discipline and Punish* (1979), and *The History of Sexuality* (Foucault, 1988). Foucault's work, we think, entails a radical politics in intellectual work as it was related to social movements, but without the hortatory claims that privilege the position of the intellectual as an oracle.

At this point we can introduce the notion of resistance into our discussion of the relation of politics and intellectual project. In the philosophy of consciousness, resistance was posed as outside of power. It privileged specific acts of will as if individuals were sovereign agents responding to universal categories and universal claims about emancipation. The discussion here has suggested that resistance is imbricated within power, not outside of it (Young, 1990). The focus on sovereignty neglects a conception of resistance that relates to the disciplinary forms and technologies through which power operates.

It is this sense of resistance imbricated within power that we can read in/through two chapters that focus directly on pedagogical moments. For Orner, resistance is not about replacing a new set of universal truths with an alternative, feminist or otherwise, but about a methodological—in both classroom and research terms—approach to continually making problematic the stories we are given and those we tell. "Poaching" Foucault, like many feminists, Orner is particularly concerned with the gendering effects of the disciplinary technologies of schooling, absent from Foucault's own discussions of the body, bio-power, and sexuality.

Schaafsma, like Orner, moves Foucault's insights into the practical tasks of curriculum and writing among students in inner-city high schools. He moves Foucault's concept of an author into a conversation to consider how classroom talk and writing are performative. He rejects much of the romanticizing of pedagogical thought that naturalized the "voice" of students and teachers. Schaafsma discusses writing as a doublet in which an historical "I" of past constructions of the "subject" intersects with an autobiographical "I" that interrupts the effects of power. Through Schaafsma's writing we can understand that curriculum is continually a practice of inclusion/exclusion, of constructing reason and nonreason that have critical moments in the construction of "self" and the world.

But the politics that Foucault's work engenders, however, is not without controversy. The last chapters, in dealing quite differently with the problematic of political work, attest to the significance of the political impact of Foucault's work in Anglo-American academic work and the debates that continue to be engaged in connection to this oeuvre. Here we re-enter the question of the role of intellectuals in the politics of change that has been so central to the philosophy of consciousness. Jóhannesson points out some of the problems that arise in relation to the politics of educational intellectual work. Jóhannesson's connection of Bourdieu's concept of social strategy with Foucault's technologies of the self offers, he argues, a way to develop epistemic reflexivity in research that goes beyond a universal ethic to the development of ethics related to specific sites (see, e.g., Bourdieu, Chamboredon, & Passeron, 1991). In an extended discussion of "usefulness" and "relevance" of educational research, Jóhannesson draws on both Foucault and Bourdieu to establish an agenda for a progressive politics that neither privileges the conditions of its own scientific production nor refrains from questioning its own investments in certain forms of reasoning. Zipin, like Jóhannesson, also finds reason to connect Bourdieu and Foucault through examining the tensions of anti-foundationism in recent postmodern educational anthropology. Blacker, more aligned with Jóhannesson, suggests that Foucault's work does offer necessary and important dimensions to a research ethic for institutionally situated intellectuals. Rather than seeing Foucault's project as one of refuting humanism, Foucault, he suggests, can be interpreted as, first, offering an immanent critique of humanism, and second, offering specific conceptual apparatus for developing a more political and effective specific intellectual. Blacker focuses on the problem of the intellectual whose role is not to criticize the ideological contents supposedly linked to science, or to ensure that his own scientific practice is accompanied by correct ideology, but to ascertain the possibility of constituting a new politics of truth.

To return briefly to the argument of the philosophy of consciousness: In that argument the actor makes history; and, it is believed, the absence of a visible agent introduces a determinist world that has no possibility of change. The argument of these chapters and of the general foci of this book is to problematize that argument, to focus not on actors but on our forms of reasoning and principles of ordering. Such a strategy destabilizes the reigning forms of "reasoning." A seeming paradox is thus introduced as we re-vision the philosophical issues of agency and actors as a priori conditions of analysis and social action. In the social theory discussed here, the agent is present, not as the actor in the narrative of inquiry, but by destabilizing the conditions that confine and intern consciousness and its principles of order. Making the forms of reasoning and rules for "telling the truth" potentially contingent, historical, and susceptible to critique, is a practice to dislodge the ordering principles, thereby creating a greater range of possibility for the subject to act.

At this point, we can approach a theoretical discussion of social theory and research through focusing on a debate about the relation of a social epistemology to the actual engagements of practices. Often, the lack of signifying differences in practices among groups is cited as a limitation of Foucault's genealogy. It is argued that such engagements are sites for developing shared ethics. From our perspective, such argument erroneously conflates three important distinctions. First, "shared ethics" always involve the predominance of norms within a specific paradigm of rule. The intellectual strategies discussed in this chapter and the rest of the book, while not monolithic, provide methods by which to scrutinize that paradigm historically, rather than assume it within empirical studies. Second, the distinction conflates interpretive and strategic discourses in social change. The latter, the very social contingencies in which the politics of social life is enacted, are always more complex than any interpretive discourse can provide. Not to distinguish between different discourses privileges the intellectual's constructions of the subject in processes of change, which is always dangerous when placed in relation to commitments to a democracy.

Third, the concern for engagement and action involves a different paradigmatic stance and intellectual interest than discussed here. If we can be schematic here, we have focused on a social epistemology as a problematizing theory to discern the salient characteristics of the social formation that predominate within a specific paradigm of rule. This strategy embodies a different problematic from the theory of action that has dominated the human sciences since the early twentieth century. At the same time, we recognize epistemological approaches that can help to understand action and practice and, in certain circumstances, can be woven together with a social epistemology (see, e.g., Popkewitz, 1996). Bourdieu's (1990) sociological theory is an exemplar of a strategy that focuses on action through considering how specific power/knowledge relations differ according to their articulation with other practices. Our focus here, in contrast, is with the social historical mechanisms that generate the principles of action, participation, and the "other" with the sociological sites of engagement in action, although Gore's study attempts to bridge these two theoretical positions from a Foucaultian perspective.

We draw attention to these different paradigmatic approaches to direct attention to how issues of change, ethical dimensions of power/knowledge relations, and contestation are raised. But at the same time, and important from our point of view, is the need to be sensitive to how different intellectual traditions raise epistemological and political foci and different sets of relevances in research projects. The intellectual and political danger is to universalize and colonialize thought by saying, for example, that all research needs to inscribe action as an a priori epistemological principle.

SOME CONCLUDING THOUGHTS

We have argued that the linguistic turn and a social epistemology embody political commitments to question injustice and domination, but the current strategies of intellectual work are different from the leftist scholarship of the 1970s and 1980s. Some authors have argued that the utopian energies that gave birth to modern politics have been either realized or exhausted, such as the successes and failures of the union movements and role of the media in modern societies (Rasmussen, 1992). Whether or not we agree with these assessments, it is important to recognize the changing terrain of political struggles that are exemplified in the politics of identity of postmodern social theory found in, for example, feminist and postcolonial literatures. The disruption of how we "tell the truth" about ourselves and others is viewed as a practical strategy for constructing options as the rules through which power is deployed are themselves made visible.[10]

If we are to make the rules for telling the truth visible and open to critique, this requires a careful use and problematization of the work of Foucault himself. While the epistemic figure of Foucault looms large on the intellectual landscape of the late twentieth century, what is important for research is not a slavish cult of Foucaultian implementation studies but a continual problematization of the categorizations, foci, and methodological considerations to which he has given emphasis. This is not to invite methodological pluralism or unbridled eclecticism. Rather, it is to emphasize the need for rigorous questioning of the will to truth embodied in educational work and education research in particular. In an arena that is centrally concerned with training in truth production, such an invitation may be difficult to accept.

In moving to closure of a pragmatic kind, we turn to an historical argument about science. Toulmin (1990), in examining the history of science, argues that we have been living under the specter of certainty since the late seventeenth century, even though the first work in science involved norms of skepticism. He suggests that possibly it is time that we give skepticism a try since certainty has not worked. To put this in a different way, there is a continual rhetorical stance in U.S. critiques of the linguistic turn that if one does not make explicit the normative commitments and the subject in the knowledge of social science, no one will act and the people of the world will be incapacitated. This argument is an act of tremendous hubris as well as an odd historical argument. We can point to no instance of people being incapacitated to act because of intellectual knowledge; in fact, people typically act in ways that intellectuals do not approve of. Nor have social movements been disbanded when the identification of actors is intellectually blurred. The dualism of a problematizing knowledge versus social reconstruction has no historical validity. People continually act; they have no option but to act in their daily and collective lives. Perhaps, to return to Foucault and Toulmin, a problematizing theory may be one way to consider the politics of knowledge, the politics of intellectual work, and the politics of change.

NOTES

We wish to thank James Marshall, Lynda Stone, Nick Buburles, Geoff Whitty, and members of the University of Umeå Peagogiska Institutionen for comments as we wrote this draft. But most important are the conversations of the Wednesday Group during the past decade, which enabled us to consider the different terrains in which critical intellectual work was occurring. Without these readings across fields, this chapter would not have been possible.

1. We borrow the phrase "sea-migration" from the social-intellectual historian, Hughes (1975). Our intent, however, is not to suggest a single movement of ideas from Europe, but to recognize a certain globalization of ideas.

2. One of the first books in education to explore this was Ball, 1990.

3. This self-reflectivity, which Bourdieu, Chamboredon, and Passeron, 1991, call an "epistemological vigilance," applies in this study as well. While such self-

reflectivity is always different, as resistances operate within power relations and not outside of them. Our focus is on historicizing the present.

4. These practices are not totalizing, but include ambiguities and resistances, as Sawiki (1988) acknowledges.

5. We use the words *community* and *society* as distinctions that are of historical significance. The former involves space/time relations that were local; the latter involves more abstract conceptions of self as a citizen of a nation, as a worker, or as an ethnic group within some larger sets of relations. As these abstract notions of society are made part of one's definition of self, the meaning and relationships of "self" in communities are constructed. For discussion of these concepts in relation to changing terrains of politics, see Rose, 1996.

6. One also can understand the Frankfurt School as a reaction to fascism, while French social thought was a more general critique but at the same time responsive to its colonial wars in the post-World War II period (Young, 1990).

7. Also see Marshall (1990) on different conceptualizations of power.

8. One needs to read current literature theory, feminist scholarship, as well as critiques of postmodernism in education to realize that privileging the subject is deeply political.

9. See, for example, Pignatelli (1993), who turns from a problematized theory to dialectical theory of change without any notice of the shift in epistemology.

10. It is an interesting side note to our discussion that Foucault's work has been influential in institutional reforms in multiple countries. This occurred without posturing an epistemology of progress in his scholarship. He rejected privileging the intellectual through arguments about some universal notion of the intellectual bringing progress through the a priori positioning of the "subject."

REFERENCES

Ball, S. (1990). *Foucault and education: Disciplines and knowledge.* London: Routledge.

Barrett, M., & Phillips, A. (1992). *Destabilizing theory: Contemporary feminist debates.* Stanford: Stanford University Press.

Benhabib, S. (1986). *Critique, norm, and utopia: A study of the foundations of critical theory.* New York: Columbia University Press.

Bernstein, R. (Ed.). (1985). *Habermas and modernity.* Cambridge, MA: MIT Press.

Beyer, L., & Liston, D. (1992). Discourse or moral action? A critique of postmodernism. *Educational Theory, 42,* 371–393.

Bourdieu, P. (1984). *Distinction: A social critique of the judgment of taste* (R. Nice, Trans.). Cambridge, MA: Harvard University Press.

Bourdieu, P. (1990). *The logic of practice.* Stanford: Stanford University Press.

Bourdieu, P., Chamboredon, J., & Passeron, J. (1991). *The craft of sociology: Epistemological preliminaries* (R. Nice, Trans.). New York: Walter de Gruyter.

Bourdieu, P., & Wacquant, L. J. D. (1992). *An invitation to reflexive sociology.* Chicago: University of Chicago Press.

Burchell, G., Gordon, C., & Miller, P. (Eds.). (1991). *The Foucault effect: Studies in governmentality.* Chicago: University of Chicago Press.

Butler, J. (1992). Contingent foundations: Feminism and the question of "postmodernism." In J. Butler & J. Scott (Eds.), *Feminists theorize the political* (pp. 3–21). New York: Routledge.

Butler, J. (1993). *Bodies that matter: On the discourse limits of "sex."* New York: Routledge.

Carlson, D. (1992). *Teachers and crisis: Urban school reform and teachers' work culture.* New York: Routledge.

Crary, J. (1990). *Techniques of the observer: On vision and modernity in the nineteenth century.* Cambridge, MA: MIT Press.

Dean, M. (1994). *Critical and effective histories: Foucault's methods and historical sociology.* New York: Routledge.

Donald, J. (1992). *Sentimental education: Schooling, popular culture and the regulation of liberty.* London: Verso.

Dreyfus, H. L., & Rabinow, P. (Eds.). (1983). *Michel Foucault: Beyond structuralism and hermeneutics* (2nd ed.). Chicago: University of Chicago Press.

Dumm, T. (1987). *Democracy and punishment: Disciplinary origins of the United States.* Madison: University of Wisconsin Press.

Elias, N. (1978). *The history of manners: The civilizing process* (Vol. 1; E. Jephcott, Trans.). New York: Pantheon.

Englund, T. (1991, April). *Rethinking curriculum history—Towards a theoretical reorientation.* Paper presented at the annual meeting of the American Educational Research Association, Chicago.

Eribon, D. (1991). *Michel Foucault* (B. Wing, Trans.). Cambridge, MA: Harvard University Press.

Foucault, M. (1965). *Madness and civilization: A history of insanity in the age of reason* (R. Howard, Trans.). New York: Pantheon.

Foucault, M. (1973). *The order of things: An archaeology of the human sciences.* New York: Vintage.

Foucault, M. (1975). *The birth of the clinic: An archaeology of medical perception* (A. M. Sheridan Smith, Trans.). New York: Vintage.

Foucault, M. (1979). *Discipline and punish: The birth of the prison* (A. Sheridan, Trans.). New York: Vintage.

Foucault, M. (1980). *Power/Knowledge: Selected interviews and other writings by Michel Foucault, 1972–1977* (C. Gordon, Ed. and Trans.). New York: Pantheon.

Foucault, M. (1984). What is enlightenment? In P. Rabinow (Ed.), *The Foucault reader* (pp. 32–50). New York: Pantheon.

Foucault, M. (1988). *The history of sexuality: Vol. 3. The care of the self* (R. Hurley, Trans.). New York: Random House.

Foucault, M. (1991a). Governmentality. In G. Burchell, C. Gordon, & P. Miller (Eds.), *The Foucault effect: Studies in governmentality* (pp. 87–104). Chicago: University of Chicago Press.

Foucault, M. (1991b). *Remarks on Marx: Conversations with Duccio Trombadori* (R. Goldstein & J. Cascaito, Trans.). New York: Semiotext(e), Columbia University.

Fraser, N. (1989). *Unruly practices: Power, discourse and gender in contemporary social theory.* Minneapolis: University of Minnesota Press.

Fullan, M., with Stiegelbauer, S. (1991). *The new meaning of educational change* (2nd ed.). New York: Teachers College Press.

Giroux, H. (1992). *Border crossings: Cultural workers and the politics of education.* New York: Routledge.

Gordon, C. (1991). Governmental rationality: An introduction. In G. Burchell, C. Gordon, & P. Miller (Eds.), *The Foucault effect: Studies in governmentality* (pp. 1–52). Chicago: University of Chicago Press.

Green, B. (1995). Post-curriculum possibilities: English teaching, cultural politics, and the postmodern turn. *The Journal of Curriculum Studies, 27* (4), 391–409.

Habermas, J. (1971). *Knowledge and human interest* (J. Shapiro, Trans.). Boston: Beacon Press.

Habermas, J. (1981). *The theory of communicative action: Reason and the rationalization of society* (Vol. 1; T. McCarthy, Trans.). Boston: Beacon Press.

Habermas, J. (1987). *The theory of communicative action. Lifeworld and system: A critique of functionalist reason* (Vol. 2; T. McCarthy, Trans.). Boston: Beacon Press.

Hacking, I. (1986). The archeology of Foucault. In D. C. Hoy (Ed.), *Foucault: A critical reader* (pp. 27–40). Oxford: Basil Blackwell.

Hacking, I. (1991). How should we do the history of statistics? In G. Burchell, C. Gordon, & P. Miller (Eds.), *The Foucault effect: Studies in governmentality* (pp. 181–196). Chicago: University of Chicago Press.

Hall, S. (1986). The problem of ideology—Marxism without guarantees. *Journal of Communication Inquiry, 10*, 28–43.

Hamilton, D. (1989). *Towards a theory of schooling.* London: Falmer Press.

Hoskin, K. (1993). Education and the genesis of disciplinarity: The unexpected reversal. In E. Messer-Davidoff, D. R. Shumway, & D. J. Sylvan (Eds.), *Knowledges: Historical and critical studies in disciplinarity* (pp. 271–304). Charlottesville, VA: University Press of Virginia.

Hughes, H. (1975). *The sea change: The migration of social thought, 1930–1965.* New York: Harper & Row.

Hunter, I. (1994). *Rethinking the school: Subjectivity, bureaucracy, criticism.* New York: St. Martin's Press.

Kuhn, T. (1970). *The structure of scientific revolutions* (2nd ed.). Chicago: University of Chicago Press.

Kuttner, R. (1991). *The end of laissez-faire: National purpose and the global economy after the cold war.* New York: Knopf.

Lekachman, R. (1982). *Greed is not enough: Reaganomics.* New York: Pantheon.

Lundgren, U. P. (1991). *Between education and schooling: Outlines of a diachronic curriculum theory.* Geelong, Australia: Deakin University.

Mahon, M. (1992). *Foucault's Nietzschean genealogy: Truth, power, and the subject.* Albany: State University of New York Press.

Marshall, J. (1990). Foucault and educational research. In S. Ball (Ed.), *Foucault and education: Disciplines and knowledge* (pp. 11–29). London: Routledge.

Meyer, J. (1986). The politics of educational crisis in the United States. In W. Cummings (Ed.), *Educational politics in crisis.* (pp. 44–58). New York: Praeger.

Miller, J. (1993). *The passion of Michel Foucault.* New York: Simon & Schuster.

Nicholson, S. (1986). *Gender and history: The limits of social theory in the age of the family.* New York: Columbia University Press.

Noiriel, G. (1994). Foucault and history: The lessons of a disillusion. *Journal of Modern History, 66,* 547–568.

Noujain, E. (1987). History as genealogy: An exploration of Foucault's approach. In A. Griffiths (Ed.), *Contemporary French philosophy* (pp. 157–174). New York: Cambridge University Press.

Pignatelli, F. (1993). What can I do? Foucault on freedom and the question of teacher agency. *Educational Theory, 43,* 411–432.

Popkewitz, T. (1987). *The formation of school subjects: The struggle for creating an American institution.* London: Falmer Press.

Popkewitz, T. (1991). *A political sociology of educational reform: Power/knowledge in teaching, teacher education, and research.* New York: Teachers College Press.

Popkewitz, T. (1992). Social science and social movements in the U.S.A.: State policy, the university and schooling. In D. Broady (Ed.), *Education in the late 20th century: Essays presented to Ulf P. Lundgren on the occasion of his fiftieth birthday* (pp. 45–79). Stockholm: Stockholm Institute of Education Press.

Popkewitz, T. (Ed.). (1993). *Changing patterns of power: Social regulation and teacher education reform.* Albany: State University of New York Press.

Popkewitz, T. (1995). Critical traditions and its linguistic turns. In P. Higgs (Ed.), *Metatheories in the philosophy of education* (pp. 139–174). Durban, S. A.: Heinemann.

Popkewitz, T. S. (1996). Rethinking decentralization and the state/civil society distinctions: The state as a problematic of governing. *Journal of Educational Policy, 11*(1), 27–51.

Popkewitz, T. (in press). *The spatial politics of urban & rural education: Discourses of School Reforms as Systems of Exclusion.* New York: Teachers College Press.

Rajchman, J. (1985). *Michel Foucault: The freedom of philosophy.* New York: Columbia University Press.

Rasmussen, D. (1992). Reflections on the "end of history": Politics, identity and civil society. *Philosophy and social criticism, 18,* 234–250.

Richter, M. (1986). Conceptual history (Begriffsgeschichete) and political theory. *Political Theory, 14,* 1219–1230.

Rose, N. (1989). *Governing the soul: The shaping of the private self.* New York: Routledge.

Rose, N. (1996). The death of the social: Re-figuring the territory of government. *Economy and Society, 25,* 327–356.

Rose, N., & Miller, P. (1992). Political power beyond the state: Problematics of government. *British Journal of Sociology, 43,* 173–205.

Sawicki, J. (1988). Feminism and the power of Foucauldian discourse. In J. Arac (Ed.), *After Foucault: Humanistic knowledge, postmodern challenges* (pp. 161–178). New Brunswick, NJ: Rutgers University Press.

Shapiro, M. (1992). *Reading the postmodern polity: Political theory as textual practice.* Minneapolis: University of Minnesota Press.

Sintomer, Y. (1992). Power and civil society: Foucault vs. Habermas. *Philosophy and Social Criticism, 8,* 357–379.

Spivak, G. (1992). The politics of translation. In M. Barrett & A. Phillips (Eds.), *Destabilizing theory: Contemporary feminist debates* (pp. 177–200). Stanford: Stanford University Press.

Tiles, M. (1984). *Bachelard: Science and objectivity.* Cambridge: Cambridge University Press.

Toulmin, S. (1990). *Cosmopolis: The hidden agenda of modernity.* New York: Free Press.

Wagner, P. (1994). *The sociology of modernity.* New York: Routledge.

Walkerdine, V. (1990). *School girl fictions.* London: Verso.

Weedon, C. (1987). *Feminist practice and poststructural theory.* London: Basil Blackwell.

Weis, L., & Fine, M. (Eds.). (1993). *Beyond silenced voices: Class, race, and gender in United States schools.* Albany: State University of New York.

Wittgenstein, L. (1966). *The philosophical investigations: A collection of critical essays* (2nd ed.; G. Pitcher, Ed.). Notre Dame: University of Notre Dame Press.

Young, R. J. C. (1990). *White mythologies: Writing, history and the West.* New York: Routledge.

PART II

Historical Constructions of the Reasoning of Schooling

2

What Is It Impossible to Think? A Genealogy of the Educated Subject

LYNN FENDLER

Αχορευτοζ απαιδευτοζ
Anyone who cannot sing in a choir is not educated.
—Laws II 654b

A typical objective of genealogy is to problematize commonplace assumptions. A typical objective of critical educational discourse is to interrupt existing power relations. Foucault's genealogies do not take the subject[1] for granted, but rather analyze the constitution of subjectivity as an effect of power relations. Therefore, Foucaultian genealogy is a fruitful approach for critiquing the effects of power in the commonplace meanings of "educated" today.

In this chapter, I examine social constructions of "educated" through history. I try to understand what sorts of relations and techniques could account for the values normalized in the various meanings of educated. In other words, what is assumed to be educated today embodies particular values by defining what is normal and what is not normal. Therefore, those values can be said to have inscribed power; normative values are pieces of evidence that give clues to how power has been exercised.

This genealogy examines six assumptions that exemplify the construction of the educated subject of the present. The first assumption that characterizes current educational discourse is teachability. The second assumption is that the knowledge constituting the educated subject is scientific, in the sense of worldly or secular. The third assumption in current discourse is that there is a generalizable procedure for becoming educated. This assumption forms the basis of assertions about "learning styles" and "learning disabilities." The fourth assumption is that the educated subject has the capacity to reflect objectively. In a Foucaultian genealogy (see, e.g., Foucault, 1988, 1990a, 1990b), this knowledgeable means of self-control is known as "technologies of the self." The fifth assumption is that the educated subject has become individualized and identified according to populational referents. This assumption is evident in the commonplace ways of labeling individuals as "woman," "intelligent," "learning disabled," "at risk," "developmentally normal," and so on. Lastly—and this is a relatively recent development—the educated subject is one who takes pleasure in becoming educated and desires to be self-disciplined.

This genealogy seeks to examine some early formulations of these characteristics, which are now assumptions, about the educated subject. That is, features of the educated subject that are now taken for granted were at one time or another controversial. For example, today it is generally assumed that "educated" is an effect of teachable knowledge, not an effect of divine dispensation or natural evolution. This didactic tradition was debated by Plato, but is now largely taken for granted. For each of the six assumptions, I explore an historical instance in which a characteristic was debated, not assumed, in order to suggest alternatives to current assumptions and to "make the familiar strange."

Throughout the genealogy, radically other images of what it has meant to be educated emerge, and by analyzing these I hope to problematize what it has meant to be educated. In doing so, it becomes possible to gain some purchase on a few of the assumptions that bind and constrain current definitions of educated. In this sense, my project is a political one in which I assume that the meanings of educated were effected by power and are subjects of power—what is called a "socially constructed," "regulated," or "normalized" subject.

WHAT IS TEACHABLE? PAIDEIA AND DIDACTICS

In current educational discourse, it is generally taken for granted that teaching is part of education. "What knowledge is of most worth?" is perhaps the most famous framework for the debate about what should be taught, and that debate is characteristic of current educational discourse. However, the characteristics of the educated subject emerge through an analysis of current assumptions about what can be taught. Assumptions about what can be taught are vastly different today than they were even a century ago.

In this section, I examine Plato's *Protagoras* (1956) in order to analyze some early formulations of the debate about what can be taught. The central question of the dialogue is, "Can virtue be taught?" In the debate between Socrates and Protagoras, it is possible to read some of the initial formulations of the principle of didactics (i.e., teachability of virtue) versus paideia (i.e., natural accrual of virtue).

In *Protagoras*, the educated subject consisted of what appears now as an amalgamation of mind/body/soul (see, e.g., Jäger, 1939; Marrou, 1948/1956; Despland, 1985). The substance to be worked over by education was, by today's standards, relatively undifferentiated, a holism that has contributed to the common designation of Greek education as being "humanistic." Historians and commentators have used various translations of the Greek *physis*, including "nature," "soul," and "spirit"; it is generally accepted that the conception of "nature" replaced previous conceptions of "divine descent" through developments in the field of medicine (see, e.g., Jäger, 1939). In any case, it is possible to read the Greek philosophical position as allowing for an overall commensurability within a "nature" whose goodness consisted of a harmonious mind/body/soul.

Plato's educated subject had a holistic nature; and the criteria by which educated could be determined was also relatively undifferentiated. That is, Plato's dialogues indicate the foundation of a natural and necessary commensurability among "divine law," "natural law," and "reason." The mode of such a holistic conception is commonly referred to as "universal law" or "universal principle" in which all entities and events can be attributed ultimately to a single homogeneous causal Idea. In this sense the Platonic notion of power can be described as sovereign, insofar as power was conceived as having a clearly delineated and identifiable form. Platonic sovereign power was manifest as an Idea or standard against which all particulars could be judged.

Sovereign power for Plato, however, was unlike sovereign power in later medieval times, in that Plato's educated subject did not strive to reconcile reason with God or to articulate the relationship between God and human nature. Rather, for Plato, the task was to cultivate one's true nature, which was necessarily virtuous, which meant in harmony with reason, divine dispensation, beauty, and pleasure.

Protagoras (speaking for the Sophists) and Socrates agreed that the regimen constructing the educated subject consisted of knowledge and care for the self. However, the Sophists and the Socratics deployed radically different technologies to mean "care and knowledge." The Sophistic regimen called for didactic techniques in which virtue was teachable by an expert. Protagoras, himself, was the model Sophist teacher whose rhetorically structured arguments provided the knowledge that could impart virtue. For the Sophists, knowledge and care for the self could be taught—in the didactic sense—to the educated subject.

In contrast, the Socratic regimen of paideia assumed that knowledge—and virtue—were part of a person's nature. This assumption supports the Socratic technology of dialogue and the assumption of the undifferentiated "whole" of human nature. That is, Socratic virtue was actively cultivated by the educated subject, but not taught to—in the Sophist didactic sense—the educated subject. The tension was between, on the one hand, paideia, in which virtue was cultivated when the educated subject engaged in dialogue, musical performance, and athletic feats; and, on the other hand, the technology of didactics in which virtue could be taught to a "student" by a "teacher."

The different technologies of paideia and didactics embed different assumptions about the constitution of the subject. On the one hand, paideia embeds the assumption of a holistic and complete nature; there is no need to intervene in the "natural" growth of the person toward virtue. By the same token, the possibility of becoming educated was determined by birth, and not available to most people. On the other hand, didactics embeds the assumption of an incomplete or imperfect nature that requires the intervention of a teacher in order to cultivate virtue. Simultaneously, the technology of didactics embeds the assumption that the possibility of being "educated" was not limited by birthright.

In classical Greece, the intimate family tradition of education as paideia was gradually replaced by the more public technologies of didactics. Even Plato, in his last writings, *The Republic* and *The Laws*, constructed the educated subject less in terms of paideia and more in terms of didactics.[2] However, the terms of the debate between Socrates and Protagoras are helpful in understanding that didactics—or teachability—was not always taken for granted as constituting the educated subject.

The educated subject of Plato's discourse is virtually unrecognizable by current standards. The educated subject of the 1990s is not only assumed to be teachable, but has individual characteristics such as "learning style" and "developmental stage" that specify the nature of teachability. This way of thinking would have been utterly alien to both Socrates and Protagoras.

"EDUCATED" BECOMES SECULARIZED

The source of knowledge in Greek and Roman times was godly, and therefore more or less mysterious. What was "true" could change according to the dictates of a God or gods. An educated person today, however, is assumed to have access to knowledge through scientific or rationalizable means. What circumstances could account for the revolution in what it was possible to know? How did the source of knowledge shift from the realm of the sacred and mysterious to the realm of the secular and worldly? One instance of a break from sacred to secular knowledge can be explored through the writings of Thomas Aquinas (ca. 1225–1274).

For Plato, the mind/body/soul had been inseparable and inevitably virtuous; however, in medieval times, Christian thinkers were obligated to fulfill the theological imperative of a soul that was godly and eternally good and still explain the existence of "sin." In order to do so, Christian thinkers eventually supposed that there must be something definitively human but separable from the soul. This something, which could be declared the ungodly source of sin, came to be understood as the body—as in carnal knowledge (see, e.g., Riley, 1988). By positing a physical entity of "body" as differentiable from the earlier integrity of "self," and by declaring the body sinful, medieval Christian thinkers could maintain a coherent doctrine in which God could be omnipotent and good, and a person could be sinful while still being endowed with a divine soul. The medieval educated subject, then, according to Thomas Aquinas, practiced the devotional nurture of a disembodied soul.

A Christian soul differed from a Platonic soul in two salient ways: First, the Christian soul was godly, but subject to the Fall. Goodness and virtue were no longer natural and inevitable; in fact, sinful was now the human condition. Second, the Christian soul could be educated separately from the body. The early Christian educated subject was constructed through technologies that resulted in separate entities of soul and body: prayerful devotion and obedience in order to nurture the spirit, and abstinence, suffering, pain, and celibacy in order to diminish and weaken the flesh. The technologies of Christian education constructed bifurcated possibilities for subjectivity through technologies that privileged the mystical and degraded the visible.[3]

A thirteenth-century "educated" subject was inscribed at the nexus of science and theology. On the one hand, educated meant subject to cathedral-based theology, prayerful devotion, contempt for bodily sensation, study of Platonic grammar and rhetoric, reconciliation of prophecy and revelation, deduction from scriptural principles, loyalty to authority, and faithful acceptance of sacred design.

On the other hand, cultural contacts with Middle Eastern philosophers facilitated the development of non-Christian, scientific technologies. So, educated also implied university-based science, including induction from empirical observation (i.e., bodily sensation), experimentation, analysis through Aristotelian logic, interrogation of assumed principles, and reasonable hypothesis testing.[4]

Some scientific knowledge was incommensurable with Christian doctrine. So it became incumbent upon educated subjects to clarify the "truth" either by reconciling apparent contradictions or by labeling irreconcilable knowledge as "heresy" and therefore false.

Thomas Aquinas systematically attempted to discriminate the sacred from the secular. He employed rational argumentative strategies, and at the same time believed ultimately in a "First Cause" or an "Unmoved Mover" beyond reason as the ground of truth. For a Christian, to be educated meant to be subject to revelation and to practice piety. At the same time, educated Christians had begun to understand astronomical and physiological mechanisms about how the world worked. The discursive technology that came to be used in order to explain the relation between the sacred and the secular was allegory. Educated subjects generated imaginative and elaborate allegories in efforts to reconcile discoveries in astronomy and medicine with scriptural referents. Furthermore, the educated subject assumed a place in the allegory of heaven and earth. Technologies of allegory constructed subjectivity that was simultaneously sacred and secular.

To contemporary readers, the theological-scientific regimen of education may seem incoherent or contradictory; but both the cathedral and the university regimens assumed that "educated" meant more God-like. Medieval scientists could hardly be considered atheists or even spiritual agnostics; in fact, the absence of a theological dimension in intellectual work would have been considered impious and therefore uneducated. A "conflict" between theology and science is produced only when one assumes that subjectivity is rationally coherent, a position that was not generally assumable until much later. Thomas Aquinas's purpose was to distinguish knowledge that was susceptive to reason from knowledge that could only be miraculously revealed; an educated person knew the difference.[5]

In summary, the educated self of medieval times was subject to divine dispensation, mystical revelation, Aristotelian logic, empirical phenomena, and perils of the flesh. Both Thomas Aquinas, whose works were canonized, and William of Ockham, whose works were excommunicated, exemplify the characteristic assumptions about the educated subject in which sacred knowledge became distinguishable from secular knowledge. The educated subject tended to ask ontological questions in attempts to reconcile Church doctrine with empirical observation, such as the paradigmatic How many angels can dance on the head of a pin?

Not until later times, when the subjective self became an object of scientific study, was it possible to question epistemology in such a form as, "What are the mechanisms by which an individual subject can 'know'?" In this sense, the medieval educated subject can be characterized as "transcendent" insofar as the pious, sensible, knowing self was sacred and therefore unexaminable; subjectivity was not yet differentiated (or mediated) on the bases of individualized perception, experience, or language.

The medieval Christians' attempts to separate the sacred from the secular had an ironic effect. The effect was not as intended: to establish an orthodox canon and obliterate heretical notions. Rather, the effect was to create two viable realms of knowledge: the sacred and the secular. The domain of knowledge with which the educated subject was identified had been irretrievably fractured into those two realms. Thereafter, it became possible to think of the educated subject as having a secular identity.

THE ABSTRACTION OF COGNITION

Another assumption in today's educational discourses is that the educated subject possesses a faculty of "cognition." This cognitive faculty generally is understood as abstractable from other faculties of the self such as "affect" or "behavior." However, the faculty of cognition was not always taken for granted. In fact, Descartes, who is widely assumed to have "discovered" cognition, did not assume a separability of cognition from the self. However, Descartes's *Discourse on Method* serves as an instance in which the abstraction of cognition was debatable.

Descartes assumed a transcendent subjective self; in fact, he assumed a generalized human nature: "Good sense is the most evenly distributed commodity in the world . . . [and] is equal in all men" (Descartes, 1637/1980). Significantly, Descartes grounded his philosophy in the evidence he obtained from his dreams. In this sense, Descartes trusted his subjective (i.e., "dreaming") self to provide the basis for truth; the basic premises for truth required no "objective" referent for justification.

How did cognition come to be understood in abstract terms as constitutive of the educated subject? Descartes's contribution is the assertion that the thinking process is abstractable from the body. The Cartesian abstraction of thought process as the self often is described as a mind–body dualism, but this description can be somewhat misleading. Descartes did not posit a complement of dual substances of mind and body; rather, he maintained that the person—as body and soul—was whole and divinely determined. "Real" substances were repudiated in favor of "laws" or "principles." Descartes's contribution was to bestow the status of "reality" to a set of rational principles. After all, Descartes did not become famous for saying, "I have a mind, therefore I am."

Descartes's break with tradition was the assertion that thinking as a process or method could be abstracted and perfected—educated, as it were. Hence, the Cartesian subject to be educated no longer corresponded to a human soul, but rather to a set of generalizable principles that were abstractable. It is this abstraction of principles that provided the groundwork for the development of a "scientific method."

Moreover, Descartes's formulation constructed an educated subject of an entirely new sort because that set of abstract principles was posited as the self. That is, to be educated referred not to the care and cultivation of a virtuous human nature, and not to the ascetic regimen of piety separating the soul from the body, but rather to the personal identification with rational principles. Descartes did not construct rationality as an object of education; Descartes constructed rationality as constitutive of the educated subject: "I am rationality, and rationality is me." The educated subject assumed a rational identity.

The technologies of the educated subject shifted from devotional practices that emphasized the distinction between the body and the soul to methodological practices that emphasized the distinction between the True and the False. As the educated subject became more and more identified with rationality, the previous entities of nature, soul, and body drifted out of focus.

As it turns out, Descartes's method was a crucial step in making the educated subject rationalizable and objectifiable. Just as Thomas Aquinas's work had the effect of formulating a secular realm of knowledge by its systematic distinction of the sacred from the secular, Descartes's work had the effect of formulating the rational self by its systematic distinction of the irrational from the rational. However, the particularly modern ways in which the self would become rationalizable could not have been predicted from the initial formulation of *cogito ergo sum*.

The educated subject of an Enlightenment ethos was not yet rationally coherent. To be educated meant to encounter various forces—godly, satanic, natural, logical, and appetitive—that were all construed as "real," sovereign entities. One could never predict what sort of power might be immanent in strange or foreign ideas or emissaries. Power, then, could be ascribed to various conflicting sovereignties of the universe. The educated subject of the time was identified as "rational" by an attitude of critique (Foucault, 1984).

Technologies of abstraction and rationality began to be formalized at institutional as well as subjective levels. Hamilton (1989) traced the incipient groundwork for formal schooling to the beginning of the seventeenth century. Hamilton historicized the progressive differentiation of "education," which was tutorial and individual-based, from "schooling," which was class or "batch"-based. Regarding the establishment of seminaries between 1620 and 1692, Hamilton observed, "Theology began to be opened up to the influence of logic, rationality and systematization" (p. 65).

The educated subject of the Enlightenment began to be constructed in accordance with rational principles. Rationality formed the basis for self-identification, methodological technologies of investigation, and institutionalized regimens. Batch-based schooling constructed subjectivity as having rationalizable capacities that were shared by a batch and therefore could be classified. However, for Descartes, knowledge was still accessible to and produced by individual educated subjects; and knowledge could be generated, evaluated, and validated by subjective experience, including dreams.

The educated subject of the early seventeenth century could debate in good faith between rationalism and empiricism. Descartes struggled to make sense of the complex relations among Aristotelian logic, subjectively revealed truths, and empirically observable phenomena. The educated subject was one whose subjective rationality formed the basis for critique. In this sense, since method was still a subjective function, the subject was transcendent and incontrovertible.

The epistemological consequences distinguishing Descartes's methodology are indicative of the eventual shifts in the constitution of the subject: from the transcendent godly self to the principled rational self. The educated subject eventually came to be understood as a subjective un-mediated knower—an individual immediately related to truth—whether truth was construed rationally or experientially.

THE OBJECTIFICATION OF THE SUBJECT

Current educational discourse generally assumes that the subjective knowing self is itself an object of study and that knowledge of the self is the basis for an educated identity. However, this was not always the case. In fact, the notion that the subjective self could have an objective identity is particularly characteristic of modernity. An early formulation of the self-as-object can be examined in the work of Immanuel Kant (1949/1785, 1950/1783).

Modernity is characterized as a break or rupture from the Enlightenment on three grounds. First, Kant's compelling synthesis of rationalism and empiricism effectively ruined both analytic systems as discrete plausible foundations, and so the central debate that constituted Enlightenment philosophy was rendered moot. Kant's questions were not about the objects that were seen, but about how seeing itself occurred. Second, the categorical imperative posited a subject-as-point-of-view. This means that the subject of modernity was no longer given as transcendent; the subject-as-point-of-view became the object of investigation. The educated subject began to question the faculties of perception, such as seeing and knowing. The taken-for-granted subject could no longer be taken for granted. The Enlightenment subject as tabula rasa or naivete was replaced by a modern a priori objective consciousness. Modern subjective experience would be examined using the same technologies that had been developed for examining objects of science. The third dimension was that the meaning of educated shifted from the transcendent subject of the Enlightenment to the institutionally identified subject of modernity. The process of becoming educated shifted from a predominantly philosophical enterprise to an institutionally framed enterprise, namely, schooling.

In Kant's work, the Enlightenment debates between rationalism and empiricism reached their culmination. In Kantian epistemology, insofar as rationalism and empiricism finally were "synthesized," neither rationalism nor empiricism could be deployed in its previously discrete form. Kant investigated not objects, but our knowledge of objects. That is, when Kantian epistemology called the knowing subject into question, there was no longer an assumable relation between the object and the subject. A new form of subjectivity emerged wherein the educated self became both the investigator and the investigated. The educated subject assumed an identity as one who selfconsciously examined the subject-as-knower.

In place of earlier debates that moved back and forth between rationalism and empiricism, there emerged the "categorical imperative": "Not being but consciousness is the starting point." This shift is important because it provides an early formulation that made possible the study of the subject as object. Moreover, this shift provides the mechanism for a shift from sovereign (objective) power to a dispersed (subjective) exercise of power. The investigation of the subject as an object in its historical context eventually would lead to the disappearance of the subject-as-subject and the subsumption of the subject into objectivity.

It was no longer possible for the educated subject to cite dreams as evidence because the perceptual capacities of the subject had been called into question. This is the shift that defined "subjective knowledge" to mean "invalidated opinion," and "objective knowledge" to mean "validated truth."

The way the objectification of the subject was taken up historically in British modernity is exemplified in the writings of John Stuart Mill (1961/ 1865). Mill's philosophical discourse, like Locke's before him, focused precisely on the relationship of the individual to society. It is important to note, however, that "society" is a modern object of investigation that did not pertain to previous historical contexts. The constitutional monarchy created by the democratic bourgeois revolution of 1688 in England provided the historical forum in which society became an object (or subject) of rational inquiry, of sociological classification, and of political administration. The rise of social and political institutions compelled administrators to define and resolve issues of difference among people in order to manage society.

When the upshot of Kant's epistemological revolution is analyzed in relation to Mill's utilitarianism and the development of social institutions, another node in the genealogical legacy of the educated subject is situated. Kant's educated subject was constituted in terms of a priori "categories." The Enlightenment aspect of educated subjectivity was the liberation of human reason from the determinations of law or authority. For Kant, to make the self an object of conscious inquiry was to free the self from determinism imposed by laws of nature: "Actually freedom is only the spontaneous activity of which we ourselves are conscious. The words 'I think' already indicate that even in my representations, I am not passive, but a free agent" (Kant, quoted in Jaspers, 1962, p. 78).

The revolutionary aspect of this shift was to extricate possibilities for human knowledge from the uncontrollable determinations of natural or divine law. By placing the perceiving subject under the microscope of science, the educated subject created a vastly greater potential for scientific study. Moreover, if the educated subject was no longer determined by natural law, then the educated subject could be changed—that is, controlled—through scientific intervention. Furthermore, knowledge of the self would serve as the means by which the educated subject could become a member of modern society. Power, then, is no longer conceived as strictly sovereign. Modern exercise of power began to take the form of the control of the subjective self by the subjective self.

The constitution of the modern educated subject, then, can be described as a complicated and reflexive objectification. That is, scientific methodologies previously had been applied to the investigation of objects in the outside world; the reality of a perceiving subject was taken for granted, so the subject "self" was sacrosanct and unquestionable. But modern science regarded the perceiving subject as also susceptive to investigation by scientific methods. Moreover, the historical context of modernity identified the educated subject as a member of society (see, e.g., Lasch, 1979; Wagner, 1994).

"Reflexivity" describes the situation in which the subject perceives the subject. Without the objectification of the subject, Freudian psychoanalysis would have been unthinkable. Modern reflexivity is an inversion of Cartesian subjectivity in which the subject/self was transcendent, and the objective of science was the development of methodology. In contrast, technologies of reflexive objectification construct the educated subject/self as the object of an assumed scientific method and in relation to a social whole. This, in effect, rendered the society transcendent and the individual subject objectified.

Modern science was not a hypothetical endeavor. To be educated meant to be concerned with a whole new realm of problems, namely, those of a society and the relationship of the individual to institutions of administration and regulation. Unity and truth were understood in terms of social science, and the scientific "discovery" of difference entailed political consequences of a new sort. Questions of rights and justice emerged in contexts of institutional administration, economic management, and legality. The educated subject was constructed in relation to society, with "educated," "subject," and "society" all being contested categories.

For example, in educational discourse, the construction of the educated subject allowed for two very different kinds of arguments about social identities (see, e.g., Gatens, 1991). One possible argument was that genders and races were "really" different, wherein the assumption of difference was based on objectively perceivable phenomena; this meant that perceptible differences justified correspondingly differentiated pedagogies, laws, rights, and identities. A different argument was that races and genders were "really" similar, wherein similarity was based on the assumption of subjectively endowed natural rights; differences were merely perceptual variations, which meant that pedagogies, laws, rights, and identities were universally ascribed. Then the problem would be how to administer a society with apparent diversity.

In either case, the mode of subjectification was no longer a personal issue, but a trans-personal one. The epistemological borders of the self were no longer individual (personal) but grounded in a social (trans-personal) context with such terms as nation and class. In those circumstances, the social context of modernity made it possible to justify a proposition—produce knowledge—by appeals to rationally apprehended "realities" beyond personal (subjective) experience and specifically grounded in social (objective) terms. Concomitantly, the self was understood as subject to and object of regulation in terms of rationalized social identities.

In systems other than modernity, the epistemological model of subject and object did not pertain. "Traditional" versions of idealism, metaphysics, formalism, deism, and humanism had all assumed an unmediated or transcendent subject—at least to some degree. The impact of the Kantian epistemological break was so profound in philosophical discourse that all previous constructions of subjectivity—in which a "knower" was assumed—thereafter were classified as "naive realism." Outside of modernity, the point of view was not questioned, not examined, not "seen," ergo "naive." Modern revolutionary objectivity constructed an apprehensible point of view. In the construction of the modern educated subject, what traditionally had been held sacred—the soul/self—was recast as occult and in need of examination. Thenceforth, to be educated meant to examine not only objects of the world, but also one's own point of view.

The educated self of modernity was epistemologically complex. Not only did the educated subject have a greatly extended capacity for scientific observation, but the educated subject was itself also identified as the object of scientific investigation, part of society, and simultaneously the negotiator between the positions of the knower and the known, the manager and the managed. Politically speaking, modern subjectivity is in some sense paradoxical. That is, the subject was endowed with unlimited perceptive and regulatory capacities; at the same time, the subject lost its transcendent sovereignty insofar as it was subsumed or objectified into a regimented abstraction and regulated in terms of social-scientific categories.

INDIVIDUAL ACCOUNTABILITY AND SELF-DISCIPLINE

The relationship of the individual to society was a controversy of modernity, but controversy over the social role of the individual eventually became commonplace. The notion of "education for citizenship" became widely embedded in institutions and discourses. The discursive controversy about the individual's relationship to society shifted to become a controversy about the individual's identity and personal well-being. In what circumstances did it become possible to see the individual as the site of disciplinary accountability?

The Progressive Era (ca. 1880–1920) in the United States provides an example of historical shifts in technologies of verification, namely, statistics, and in technologies of governance, namely, psychological self-discipline. Sociological categories, which were the objects of vigorous debate throughout modernity, eventually became taken for granted as statistical "realities." That is, many aspects of the political and scientific debates of modernity (e.g., Are races "really" different?) became administrative debates and eventually were "resolved" and formalized through various processes of legislation, institutionalization, and discursive practices (see, e.g., Baker, this volume). Furthermore, progressive movements amplified the role of psychology in education. The institutional and discursive upheaval of that time has been well documented and analyzed (see, e.g., Kliebard, 1986).

The substance of earlier Greek, medieval, and Enlightenment subjectivity corresponded in some sense to an individual human being. Modern epistemological upheavals constituted a subjectivity that was trans-personal in the context of the formation of social institutions and (neo) Kantian metaphysics. By the turn of the twentieth century, social and political institutions were being established, and new sets of social and political issues were being raised. Academically, psychology's split from moral philosophy inscribed a new relation of the educated subject to society and to knowledge; and statistical methods became increasingly influential in the social sciences.

This generated a new configuration of what could be known and how anything could be known. The knowledge of social science became expressible in terms of statistics, and the educated subject became recognizable in terms of psychology. That is, social phenomena became testable and verifiable on the basis of statistical measurement, correlation, and prediction. At the same time, education became increasingly a psychological endeavor, and the sociological categories of modernity were appropriated by emergent psychology. In educational discourse, statistically established categories—such as intelligence quotients—were appropriated as psychological norms constituting the educated subject (see, e.g., O'Donnell, 1985; Popkewitz, 1991).

In this pattern of knowledge production, the subject to be educated was identified as a conglomeration of statistically defined attributes, such as race and gender, that were appropriated as attributes of the individual in the forms of personality, affect, perceptual sensibilities, and cognition. At the same time, however, knowledge was not seated in an individual mind, body, or soul; and knowledge could no longer be based on personal (subjective) experience as it could have in earlier times.

In education, the language and descriptors of psychology are among the technologies of individualization, an outgrowth of the objectification of the subject. This epistemological shift eventually would have a double effect: It would construct knowledge in terms of statistical categories, and it would construct the knower as an individual instantiation of those categories.

One significant aspect of the changes in the constitution of the subject from modern times is the conflation of the site of power and the subject of power. In previous eras, power had been conceived as sovereign and outside the self; and the subject of power had been the natural/social self. That is, subjectivity previously had stood in an agonistic relation to sovereign power. However, the effects of formal modernization were to shift power from external or sovereign structures onto self-disciplinary practices. The educated subject, then, became endowed with a new sort of power, namely, the power to govern itself. The rationalizing capacities of the discipline of psychology made self-governance an aspect of the educated subject. Thenceforth, the educated subject was identified according to psychological capacities, mediated by expert knowledge, and regulated in terms of social institutions. In these circumstances, the power to be self-governing was simultaneously the discipline to be psychologically normal.

The mode/regimen of governance in its disciplinary capacity as "biopower" has been analyzed by Foucault as governmentality (Foucault, 1991). In this pattern of governance, when subjectivity is constituted through practices that identify the self, the mode of subjectification and its regimen become indistinguishable. That is, in Foucault's analysis, traditional (other than modern) governance was a pattern in which power was exerted by an "other"—something outside the "self." The site of this traditional sovereign power was discrete and identifiable; therefore, it was possible to conceive of a subject constituted in a positively agonistic relation to the site of power.

In contrast, modern governance is a pattern in which the educated subject as psychologically regulated citizen is expected to exercise the power that governs the self. The power relations of governing include not only behavior but also "mentality" or the "soul." A pattern of governmentality had been evidenced in modernity, but then the degree to which politics entailed government of the self was arguable. In educational discourse by the turn of the twentieth century, this concept of politics-as-governmentality had crossed an epistemological threshold from a disputable issue to become a tacit assumption. There was no question that the educated subject would be self-disciplined.

Just as modern knowledge was a kind of reflexive objectification—the subject perceives the subject—governmentality is a kind of reflexive governance—the subject disciplines the subject. The subject is recognized as "educated" and "civilized" precisely because of its "self-discipline." Conversely, the subject, insofar as it is constituted as not self-disciplined, is regarded as "uncivilized" and "uneducated."

In order to think about the educated subject, it is helpful to use the metaphor of the actuarial table; the term *actuarial* combines the concept of statistical methods with an allusion to the psychological concept of "self-actualization." The educated subject can be described as actualized in psychological terms that were derived from statistical norms. Statistics were developed as a solution to the theoretical/practical/political problems of difference; since society consisted of differentiated roles, education would have to serve differentiated purposes. The educated subject, then, would be expected to assume differentiated identities in accordance with various statistical—that is, actuarial—ascriptions, which would be ordered and regulated by means of psychological diagnosis and intervention.

THE EDUCATION OF DESIRE

In the last years of the twentieth century, what discourses are authorized to speak about education in the United States? What amalgamation of discourses constitutes the educated subject? In classical Greek times, an aristocratic elite addressed issues of education; in medieval times, certain theological scholars were authorized by the church; during the Enlightenment, scientific philosophers exemplified the educated subject; throughout modernity, the site of educational discourse became institutionalized and shaped by social science; and at the beginning of the twentieth century, the responsibility for institutionalized education was assumed by the state and influenced greatly by national political projects.

Going into the twenty-first century, the rhetoric of education in the United States has become one that proposes "partnerships" among schools, researchers, governments, and businesses. Partnership negotiations typically are complicated by disparate foci, fluctuating political commitments, competing self-interests, intractable institutional structures, and incompatible perceptions of how the world works. Educational reform, as arbitrated by state agencies, increasingly has required official legitimation by a caucus of academic, governmental, business, and institutional representatives.

Epistemological shifts are multiple and far-reaching. However, this analysis of current educated subjectivity does not presuppose a complete overhaul of the educated subject; rather it focuses on emerging trends of curriculum and pedagogy in the United States and what those trends assume about becoming educated.[6] This characterization of the educated subject is based on an analysis of a particular wave of recent reform in education. This wave of reform is signaled by such pedagogical reform practices as outcome-based curriculum, site-based management, professional development schools, metacognitive guidance, the reflective teacher, cognitively guided instruction, critical pedagogy, feminist care pedagogy, culturally relevant pedagogy, constructivism, and character education. What assumptions about the educated subject are being constructed through these educational discourses?

Teaching Desire

Plato's *Protagoras* debated the relative merits of paideia and didactics. Today, a didactic approach to education is generally assumed; however, what precisely is assumed to be teachable has changed significantly in the past decades.

Nineteeth-century educational reform was concerned primarily with intellect, behavior, and citizenship, so pedagogies and assessment techniques were designed to cultivate the intellect, discipline behavior, and encourage social responsibility. Today, classroom management techniques generally maintain intellectual, behavioral, and civilizing disciplines, but more recent reforms have tended to assert that intellectual mastery and behavioral compliance are not enough. In fact, educational goals now require that students be "motivated" and have a "positive attitude." Therefore, it has become the task of educationists to teach children the "desire" for education. The aspects of the self most recently made teachable include love, pleasure, feelings, wishes, fears, and anxieties—constituents of "the private self" that Rose (1989) calls "the soul."

A child's soul has become the focus of considerable research and attention especially since the 1950s when "non-intellectual behaviour was . . . rendered into thought, disciplined, normalized, and made legible, inscribable, calculable" (Rose, 1989, p. 147) through technologies of psychological observation, measurement, and intervention. Hence, constructions of desire, fear, and pleasure have become teachable disciplinary strategies of the self.

Evidence of the teachability of desire can be found in various pedagogical techniques. For example, in "metacognitive monitoring," a student is required not only to solve a math (or writing, or science) problem, but also to reflect on and attest to the motivational steps involved in that computation: "Why do you want to do that?" Some forms of reflective and autobiographical learning, such as writing journals, require allocutions of a student's attitudinal or affective state as a part of the learning process. Similarly, in teacher education, reflective and autobiographical research methodologies teach desire in the process of becoming a teacher. In "constructivist" approaches, a teacher or student participates actively in the construction of an identity that is compatible with the desire to be educated. Character education, which regulates affect and disposition, is replacing behavioral modification, which regulates actions, as a disciplinary pedagogical technique. Finally, complex batteries of standardized tests and assessment portfolios, no longer limited to assessing an informational knowledge base, have been developed to measure students' and teachers' attitudes, self-discipline, personality, disposition, type and level of motivation, and willingness to adapt.

Critical pedagogies acknowledge the social aspects of educated subjectivity, and the critical response often has been to insert a (semi)autonomous or resisting subject. The educated subject of most critical pedagogies is identified on the basis of a desire for social justice and a moral commitment to democracy; it is a subject position that implies the mutual identification of social goals and subjective desires.

Recent reports from the employment sector specify that businesses prefer to hire people less on the basis of technical skills or knowledge, and more on the basis of a "good attitude," communication skills, and a flexible personality. The implication is that education should adapt accordingly by teaching the motivation and desire to work in order to prepare students for successful employment. "Parents and teachers were now to take responsibility for regulating not just their habits and morals, but their feelings, wishes, and anxieties, if they were not to produce troubled and troublesome children" (Rose, 1989, p. 156). Becoming educated, in the current sense, consists of teaching the soul—including fears, attitudes, will, and desire.

Rationalizing Pleasure

For Plato, pleasure was aesthetic, sensuous, and erotic; and education worked to enhance those pleasures. For Thomas Aquinas, pleasure was also sensuous and erotic, but sinful; therefore, education imposed an ascetic regimen to diminish those pleasures and redefine pleasure to mean piety. Descartes assumed the dangers of sensuous pleasure and tacitly shifted pleasure—even identity—from feeling to thinking. Cartesian rational methods have since been extended into realms such as politics, government, economics, and psychology. Recently, educational pedagogies have tended to show evidence of the rationalization of pleasure as an individual's commitment to society.

Recent trends in pedagogy rhetorically invoke pleasure in the service of discipline and classroom management. Sensuality, aesthetics, and erotics have been recast as self-indulgence, and pleasure is now constructed according to criteria of social and psychological impact; pleasure has been discursively positioned as indistinguishable from social service.

The second volume of *The History of Sexuality* (1990) is entitled *The Use of Pleasure*, and in it Foucault explores historically how "pleasure" was defined and redefined in discourses that eventually constructed sexuality (and not eating) as a moral issue. Further, Donzelot (1991) analyzes how "pleasure in work" constructs a new moral relationship between a person and work:

> Pleasure in work diverts people from individual egoism as much as from nationalistic hysteria, putting before them instead a model of happiness in an updated, corrected social domain, where attention to the social costs of techniques and to techniques for reducing the cost of the social create the possibility and necessity for a new social concert, in which the effacement of the juridical status of the subject removes inhibitions about his participation. (p. 280)

For the educated subject, the construction of a kind of pleasure is used as a technique to "remove inhibitions about participation." The techniques of the confessional, in the forms of autobiography, reflection, and metacognitive monitoring, are deployed to educate the innermost desires of the subject:

> The obligation to confess is now relayed through so many different points, is so deeply ingrained in us, that we no longer perceive it as the effect of a power that constrains us; on the contrary, it seems to us that truth, lodged in our most secret nature, "demands" only to surface. (Foucault, 1990, p. 60)

· This deployment of power serves to erase the distinctions between the subject and the socially stipulated goals of education. Furthermore, in the context of recent pedagogical practices, it becomes impossible to think of becoming educated as enhancing the enjoyment of aesthetic, sensuous, and erotic pleasure.

Objectifying the Subject

Since modernity, the methods and procedures of schooling had been stipulated by policy, and the outcome was expected to follow. In that model, there was always the theoretical possibility of "unexpected" results. Now, however, there is a reversal; the goals and outcomes are being stipulated at the outset, and the procedures are being developed post hoc. The "nature" of the educated subject is stipulated in advance, based on objective criteria, usually statistical analysis. Because the outcome drives the procedure (rather than vice versa), there is no longer the theoretical possibility of unexpected results; there is no longer the theoretical possibility of becoming unique in the process of becoming educated. There is only the possibility that discipline will have been effective or ineffective in reaching the stipulated goals. The objective now functions less as a result and more as a target.

The objectification of subjectivity is being constructed through various pedagogical technologies. One is in the writing of educational policy. For example, state curriculum in the past was written in terms of procedures and methods, but state curriculum standards now are increasingly being written in terms of objectives or goals. A system of site-based management then is made accountable for developing procedures to meet those goals. In this new system, evaluation of educational policy reform is limited to an evaluation of the degree to which any given procedure yields the predetermined results.

The same pattern of governance operates at the pedagogical level through the implementation of outcome-based curricula in which the educational goals are specified in advance—"the student will be able to. . . . " Technical procedures then are developed for effective realization of those results and are evaluated only on their degree of effectiveness. The same pattern is evidenced at the classroom level in which a lesson plan is written by specifying the objectives first and the methodology afterwards. The way these policies are written gives evidence that the educated subject now is being constructed by means of articulating the results of an educational regime first, and then evaluating the procedures accordingly.

Governing Individuals

Recent pedagogical trends have emphasized an ethos of ministry, or caring—pastoral power—in an effort to counter perceived dehumanizing and militarizing effects of regimentation and technology. In such approaches, designed to be personalizing and humanizing, education as self-discipline takes on a familiar welfare dimension: "Disease or poverty could no longer be considered to be at the heart of the problem families, for the welfare state had ensured that these problems did not have the disastrous consequences they had had in a previous era" (Rose, 1989, p. 173). In the context of a ministerial and caring regimen, the educated subject is positioned as a member—as in body part—of the social matrix. In this model, the self is no longer in any kind of agonistic relation to the educational system or to society as a whole. The educated subject is adopted and nurtured by the educational system; in fact, the subject is dependent on the system for its welfare and identity, and therefore desires what is best in terms of social well-being.

The significant effect in the present constitution of the educated subject is the dissolution of moral barriers between the subject and the institution, and the concomitant shift of their relation from autonomy to mutual identification. At the same time, the individual is held responsible for disciplining the "self." One consequence of this political positioning is that "desirable" is now defined by what is institutionally demanded, and deviance is rendered literally "undesire-able." As a result, to the extent that the subject is subsumed in the social context, it is impossible to think of normal subjective desire as antisocial.

These pedagogies of disciplining desire are remarkably widespread, and they carry across different political positions. For example, in fundamentalist character education, to be educated means to embody certain stipulated character traits and to hold particular moral commitments. Similarly, in constructivist pedagogies, which are advocated for their nonimpositional pedagogies, to be educated means to be motivated to engage in problem solving; the educated subject of constructivism is a "constructed" learner who does not rely on authority for motivation to engage in scientific inquiry. The constructed learner—that is, the educated subject of much of educational psychology—embodies the desire to identify with the educational curriculum. Furthermore, for political projects of emancipation and empowerment, which promote inclusive representation of marginalized groups, to be educated means to be committed to social justice. No longer is the educated subject one who has learned, or one who learns; now the educated subject is one who desires to learn. In the current sense, educated subjectivity must be understood in the context of pastoral modes of disciplinary power.

In current times it is impossible to think of a normal self without constitutive relation to the social. Social identification was a debatable discursive practice of modernity, became increasingly formalized through the nineteenth and twentieth centuries, and is a virtual assumption in current discourses. As evidence, a subjective identity without relation to the social now is generally regarded as pathological or autistic. Other diagnostic terms in current use connote the normalcy of the self/social identity: sociable, anti-social, sociopath, socially adjusted, dissociated, civilized.

The mutual identification of the subject and the social is a new subjective relation. This relation did not come about as any sort of necessary result, causal principle, or teleological inevitability; history is not predictable. The situation in which the subject and society become reflexively constituted can be called (oxymoronically) a priori representation.

INFERENCES BY WAY OF CONCLUSION

> O body swayed to music,
> O brightening glance,
> How can we know the dancer from the dance?
> —W. B. Yeats, "Among School Children"

Pastoral pedagogies as ministry of desire can be understood as technologies of normalization through Foucault's notion of governmentality. The concept of governmentality facilitates a recognition of the productive effects of power in which social relations repeatedly constitute and reconstitute power through subject positions in history. It is useful to remember that no forms of differences—personal, psychological, ethnic, cultural, political, aesthetic—exist in neutral contexts, free of power relations. Therefore, categorization and deviance have always occurred as effects of power.

In this genealogy, subjectivity has not been conceived as a homogeneous, normative, or rationally consistent state. When it is analyzed discursively, subjectivity is impossible to define on the basis of objective criteria. In the context of genealogy, the educated subject is offered as descriptive of and productive of history. Accordingly, the educated subject of current educational discourse was characterized here as an assumed composite of socially constructed desires and shifting patterns of governance through effects of power.

Seen from another perspective, formerly objective categories have colonized the space of subjective existence through pedagogical practices and technologies of educational psychology. The language and assumptions inscribed in current discourses are conducive to the development and improvement of ever more efficient techniques of meeting objectives, and at the same time inhibit thinking outside the parameters of the stipulated objectives. The "subject" is then identified with the context, and the possibility of being outside the system becomes unthinkable. Moreover, power is exercised "through the unceasing reflexive gaze of our own psychologically educated self-scrutiny" (Rose, 1989, p. 208). This subject, because it is assumed, identified with, and theoretically indistinguishable from its social matrix, is then effectively lost or dead. In some sense, however, the "loss of the subject" may not be as suitable a description as "appropriation and assimilation of the subject into a socially defined objective."

Therefore, in an analysis of the educated subject that recognizes governmentality and pastoral power as disciplinary technologies, it becomes meaningless to distinguish among formerly bounded political positions—such as oppression, agency, liberation, and empowerment—in old ways. That is, in previous patterns of governance, wherein power relations constituted a transcendent subject, it was plausible to define a sovereign site of resistance—as in liberation from domination. However, in a pattern of power wherein the subject disciplines the subject and the soul/self is reflexively identified with the social, the identification of an "agent" or an "oppressor" is problematic. Moreover, ironically, when an analysis assumes a transcendent subject or interpolates an autonomous subject—that is, when the "loss" of the subject is implicitly or explicitly denied—then the resulting subject is tacitly determined by its power relations. Conversely, if the subject is problematized—if I consider the possibilities of having a lost soul—then the self can be understood as constitutive of power relations, and it becomes possible to critique effects of power that otherwise would be obscured.

One inference that can be drawn from this historical analysis is that if current political projects in education continue to assume a traditional modern (i.e., autonomous) subject, then it becomes impossible to recognize or critique the subtle ways in which power currently is being exercised in the construction of educated subjectivity. It is only when research makes the constitution of the subject theoretically problematic that power, in its current forms of governmentality, can be critically analyzed. In other words, if a transcendent or autonomous subject had been assumed in this analysis of current practices, then the degree to which the subject has become colonized by the social context, and the ways in which disciplinary power can be exercised by the self, would have been invisible. In that case, the effects of power in its current forms would have gone undetected. Perhaps the educated subject is now one who questions the subject.

Another inference is that the conceptual tools appropriate for analyzing one set of historical conditions are not necessarily transferable for analyzing a different set of historical conditions. For example, terms developed for analyses of modernity—such as "decentralization," "class," "the state," "the Left," "women"—have been useful in the critique of certain patterns of discrimination and domination. However, when such terms are assumed to be comprehensive and universally applicable, they can serve to obscure other forms of power relations. Political projects that seek to be critical of the power relations being constituted in current social configurations require analytic tools and concepts that take into account innovations, changes, shifts, and adaptations of those (re)configurations.

Certain discourses of postcoloniality, postmodernity, and feminism have begun to develop tools of analysis more adequate to the task at hand (see, e.g., Young, 1990; Riley, 1988). In the process, these discourses have issued challenges, uncertainties, and complexities into critical traditions in education, thereby recasting the theoretical debate, revitalizing the political engagement, and posing new dangers by engendering new configurations of discipline.

Just as in Plato's time Socrates and Protagoras contested educational issues within a framework of common assumptions about the world, so too in the United States at the end of the twentieth century, conflicting reform efforts share certain underlying presuppositions. Plato's epistemological assumptions consisted largely of cultivating memory for one's "true" self and remembering the inherent Ideal of the soul, an Ideal created in the image of free adult males of the Athenian ruling caste. Twenty-three centuries later, Nietzsche's polemic focused on the governmentality of forgetting:

> Man himself must first of all have become *calculable, regular, necessary* even in his own image of himself. . . . The task of breeding an animal with the right to make promises evidently embraces and presupposes as a preparatory task that one first *makes* men to a certain degree necessary, uniform, like among like, regular, and consequently calculable . . . with the morality of mores and the social straitjacket, man was actually *made* calculable. (Nietzsche, 1887/1969, pp. 58–59; emphasis in original)

Nietzsche argued in effect that first we make up our claims to truth, then we forget that we made them up, then we forget that we forgot (see, e.g., Ferguson, 1993). To be subjected to education has meant to become disciplined according to a regimen of remembering and forgetting, of assuming identities normalized through discursive practices, and of a history of unpredictable diversions.

NOTES

My thanks to the Wednesday group at the University of Wisconsin–Madison, and especially to Thomas Popkewitz for patient and critical readings of many drafts.

1. I use the term "subject" instead of "person" in order to signal that I do not assume an essentialist, authentic, humanistic individuality—what is called an "a priori," "transcendent," or later "autonomous" subject.

2. It could be argued that a tradition of paideia was maintained to some degree in monastic and religious orders through the practices of devotion and subjective receptivity to mystical visitation, revelation, and miracle; but didactics is more recognizable today as a technology associated with "educated."

3. There was not yet, however, any abstract entity of "mind" either individually or collectively.

4. However, the regimen of education was still primarily an individual, and not a social, endeavor.

5. In subtle contrast, William of Ockham professed the belief that scientific investigation itself was a divine practice and therefore not heretical—a belief that eventually led to his excommunication. See Tachau (1988) for a thorough discussion of Ockham's position.

6. Many, perhaps most, current schooling practices are legacies from Progressivistic times and can be analyzed according to more traditional assumptions and categories. The focus of this chapter is on more incipient technologies.

REFERENCES

Descartes, R. (1980). *Discourse on the method of rightly conducting one's reason and of seeking truth in the sciences* (D.A. Cross, Trans.). Indianapolis: Hackett. (Original work published 1637)

Despland, M. (1985). *The education of desire: Plato and the philosophy of religion.* Toronto: University of Toronto Press.

Donzelot, J. (1991). Pleasure in work. In G. Burchell, C. Gordon, & P. Miller (Eds.), *The Foucault effect: Studies in governmentality* (pp. 251–280). Chicago: University of Chicago Press.

Ferguson, K. E. (1993). *The man question: Visions of subjectivity in feminist theory.* Berkeley: University of California Press.

Foucault, M. (1984). *The Foucault reader* (P. Rabinow, Ed.). New York: Pantheon.

Foucault, M. (1988). *The history of sexuality: Vol. 3. The care of the self* (R. Hurley, Trans.). New York: Random House.

Foucault, M. (1990a). *The history of sexuality: An introduction* (R. Hurley, Trans.). New York: Random House.

Foucault, M. (1990b). *The history of sexuality: Vol. 2. The use of pleasure* (R. Hurley, Trans.). New York: Random House.

Foucault, M. (1991). Governmentality. In G. Burchell, C. Gordon, & P. Miller (Eds.), *The Foucault effect: Studies in governmentality* (pp. 87–104). Chicago: University of Chicago Press.

Gatens, M. (1991). *Feminism and philosophy: Perspectives on difference and equality.* Bloomington: Indiana University Press.

Hamilton, D. (1989). *Towards a theory of schooling.* London: Falmer Press.

Jäger, W. (1939). *Paideia: The ideals of Greek culture* (G. Highet, Trans.). Oxford: Basil Blackwell.

Jaspers, K. (1962). *Kant* (H. Arendt, Ed.; R. Manheim, Trans.). New York: Harcourt Brace.

Kant, I. (1949). *Fundamental principles of the metaphysic of morals* (T. K. Abbott, Trans.). Indianapolis: Bobbs-Merrill. (Original work published 1785)

Kant, I. (1950). *Prolegomena to any future metaphysics.* Indianapolis: Bobbs-Merrill. (Original work published 1783)

Kliebard, H. M. (1986). *The struggle for the American curriculum, 1893–1958.* London: Routledge & Kegan Paul.

Lasch, C. (1979). *The culture of narcissism: American life in an age of diminishing expectations.* New York: Norton.

Marrou, H. I. (1956). *A history of education in antiquity* (G. Lamb, Trans.). Madison: University of Wisconsin Press. (Original work published 1948)

Mill, J. S. (1961). *Auguste Compte and positivism.* Ann Arbor: University of Michigan Press. (Original work published 1865)

Nietzsche, F. (1969). *On the genealogy of morals* (W. Kaufmann, Trans.). New York: Vintage Books. (Original work published 1887)

O'Donnell, J. M. (1985). *The origins of behaviorism: American psychology, 1870–1920.* New York: New York University Press.

Plato. (trans. 1956). *Protagoras* (G. Vlastos, Ed.; B. Jowett, Trans.; M. Ostwald, Rev.). New York: Liberal Arts Press.

Popkewitz, T. S. (1991). *A political sociology of educational reform: Power/Knowledge in teaching, teacher education, and research.* New York: Teachers College Press.

Riley, D. (1988). *"Am I that name?" Feminism and the category of "women" in history.* Minneapolis: University of Minnesota Press.

Rose, N. (1989). *Governing the soul: The shaping of the private self.* New York: Routledge.

Tachau, K. (1988). *Vision and certitude in the age of Ockham: Optics, epistemology and the foundations of semantics, 1250–1345.* New York: Brill.

Wagner, P. (1994). *A sociology of modernity: Liberty and discipline.* New York: Routledge.

Young, R. J. C. (1990). *White mythologies: Writing, history and the West.* New York: Routledge.

3

A Catalog of Possibilities: Foucaultian History of Truth and Education Research

HANNU SIMOLA, SAKARI HEIKKINEN, & JUSSI SILVONEN

Education is a phenomenon with very obvious links to three main themes of Michel Foucault's work, themes of knowledge, subjectivity, and power. Foucault has been characterized, and with reason, as a philosophical nomad, always on the move. This unceasing movement might make his work appear as series of provocative desertions of promising themes and standpoints. However, we should not let this prevent us from seeing that, like a nomad, he was always practicing the same trade. The name of the trade, we want to argue in this chapter, was a history of truth. Therefore, we emphasize the continuity and coherence of Foucault's work rather than its ruptures. We also believe that treating knowledge, subjectivity, and power as interrelated, which in our opinion is the essence of a Foucaultian history of truth, can open new insights to research on education.

In this chapter we first will formulate our interpretation of a Foucaultian history of truth that connects knowledge, subject, and power to each other as technologies of truth, as an intertwining of techniques of discourse, self, and government. Then we will demonstrate the use of this "catalog of possibilities" in studying the "truths" of modern teacherhood.[1] This will be done in the sections on the truths of the modern Finnish teacher and tacit principles of discourse that are based on findings of a recent historical study. Finally, we will discuss further possibilities for a Foucaultian history of truth in the field of education research.

TECHNOLOGIES OF TRUTH

By reading Foucault (1985) as an historian of truth we mean that truth as "something that can and must be thought" (p. 7) is for him a phenomenon to be studied. The question Foucault asks is not "What is true?" but "How is truth created?" The "games of truth" that he is interested in might be seen played in the three-dimensional space of knowledge, subjectivity, and power. Foucault examines practices and techniques for the production of truth, the constitution of truth-willing subject, and the separation of true and false; that is, techniques of discourse, self, and government. We call the ensemble of these techniques technologies of truth.[2]

Knowledge: The Techniques of Discourse

A field of knowledge is to Foucault a twilight zone between or beyond several dichotomies conventional in the history of ideas or sciences: those of science versus ideology, internal to science versus external to science, true versus false, logic versus linguistics, words versus things. From the point of view of truth-production, however, the central question is not whether the truth is true or false, scientific or ideological, but how it is produced, circulated, transformed, and used. Foucault's (1991b) analysis of discourses attempts to illuminate that twilight zone of knowledge, "to reveal a positive unconscious of knowledge" (p. xi). Discourses, in the Foucaultian sense of the word, are first and foremost techniques, practices, and rules, which can be divided into three sets: those concerning the speaking subject, those connected with power relations, and those internal to discourse itself. In this section we try to clarify the key points in Foucault's arguments on knowledge, discourses, and truth.

First of all, Foucault rejects the notions defining knowledge purely as a linguistic or logical phenomenon. There is a domain where discourse "exercises its own control," but that is not the domain of pure ideas but of internal rules of discourse. These rules Foucault (1971) classifies into three forms of identity controlling and regulating discourse: (1) the identity of "repetition and sameness" effected by the rule of "commentary," the play between primary texts and secondary texts; (2) the identity of "individuality and the I" achieved by the principle of "author"; and (3) the identity "taking the form of a permanent reactivation of the rules" of discourse, produced by the rule of "disciplines" (pp. 12–17).

Second, Foucault (1971) rejects "the philosophy of a founding subject" (p. 21), that is, the absolute priority of the knowing subject, and defines the subject in discourse as "a particular, vacant place that may in fact be filled by different individuals" (1972, p. 95). But that place cannot be filled by anyone. There are certain discursive rules that regulate access to the place of a speaking subject. Foucault (1971) divides these rules of rarefaction among speaking subjects into four categories: (1) "verbal rituals," which determine "individual properties and agreed roles of the speakers" required; (2) "fellowships of discourse," whose function is "to preserve and to reproduce discourse within a closed community"; (3) "doctrinal groups," the effect of which is "a dual subjection, that of speaking subjects to discourse, and that of discourse" to the doctrinal groups; and (4) mechanisms of "social appropriation" regulating the access to subject status (pp. 17–19).

Finally, Foucault rejects the presumption that the relationship between knowing subject and knowledge could be immediate. It is always mediated by power relations, says Foucault (1977), who thus abandons the assumption that "knowledge can exist only where power relations are suspended" and claims that there is no "knowledge that does not presuppose" power relations (p. 27). Power relations are seen not as external to the field of knowledge but immanent to it: "Indeed, it is in discourse that power and knowledge are joined together" (Foucault, 1980, p. 100). The functioning of power relations in a field of knowledge takes most distinct shape in those discursive techniques that Foucault calls procedures of exclusion. These procedures he divides into three categories: (1) "prohibited words," which make it obvious "that we cannot simply speak of anything, when we like or where we like"; (2) the principle of "division and rejection," "the division of madness," which defines the border between reason and folly; and (3) "will to truth," a historical form of "will to knowledge" (Foucault, 1971, pp. 8–10).

Subject: The Techniques of Self

Foucault stated in 1983 that the aim of his work during the previous 20 years had been "to create a history of the different modes by which, in our culture, human beings are made subjects" (1983b, p. 208). He rejected an a priori theory of the subject: The subject is not a substance but a form. The basic question is thus "how the subject constitutes him/herself through practices that are basically related to power and knowledge" (1988a, p. 10). These practices and techniques of subjectivation might be divided into three dimensions: modes of subjectivation, will to knowledge, and art of governmentality.

In subjectivation there is first an ethical axis referring to self–self relations. Foucault writes about four modes of subjectivation. (1) Ethical substance refers to "the way in which the individual has to constitute this or that part of himself as a prime material of moral conduct" (1985, pp. 26–27), the material that is going to be worked over by ethics (1983a). (2) The mode of subjection determines "the way in which people are invited or incited to recognize their moral obligations" (p. 239). This way might be formulated, for example, by a divine law, natural law, cosmological order, or rational rule. (3) The practices of the self are "the means by which we can change ourselves in order to become the ethical subjects" (p. 239). (4) The goal of the ethical life or telos determines "the kind of being to which we aspire when we behave in a moral way" (1983a, p. 239). It is the moral teleology (1985), a mode of ethical fulfillment (1986).

The second dimension of subject creation is its power axis, because subjectivation also involves being "subject to someone else by control and dependence" (1986, p. 212). While will to knowledge constitutes techniques that relate the subject to knowledge, through the art of governmentality the subject is related to the others. It is the capacity simultaneously to govern and to be governed. It concerns those practices that "are frequently linked to the techniques for the direction of others as, e.g., in educational institutions" (1983a, p. 250). The question is one of (moral) behaviors that always will be realized in relation between forces or in power relations (1985). We can find at least three modes here: (1) stylistics of existence, which are a mode of being as one's response to certain relationships with others in an extensive and complex field of power (1985, 1986); (2) mastery of norms, which means both subjection to rules of social games and the ability to capitalize on them; and (3) the link between the technologies of domination of others with those of the self, which Foucault calls governmentality (1988b). It refers to "the totality of practices, by which one can constitute, define, organize, instrumentalize the strategies which individuals in their liberty can have in regard to each other. It is free individuals who try to control, to determine, to delimit the liberty of others and, in order to do that, they dispose certain instruments to govern others" (1988a, pp. 19–20).

The third dimension of subjectivation, its truth axis, consists of techniques for constituting the self both as a subject of knowledge and as a knowing subject (1988a). It is not possible to construct oneself as a knowing subject without having a certain (practical and material) stance to knowledge. This stance is called here will to knowledge (e.g., 1983a). We can find at least three elements constituting this will: (1) The subject is to be willing and able to undertake self-examination, ready to produce knowledge from the self for him/herself (1988b; see also 1983a). (2) The subject has to be willing to be codified and classified (see, e.g., 1985); one cannot become a subject without a certain number of rules of conduct or of principles that are at the same time truths and regulations. It is to fit oneself out with these truths (1988a). Finally, (3) the subject has to be willing to confess, ready to produce individual knowledge for institutions of knowledge. Examples of forms of confession might be the Christian confessional or psychotherapeutic session (1983b).

Power: The Techniques of Government

Foucault tried to outline an "analytics" of power rather than to create a general theory of it. Power is not only negative, ruling, prohibiting, censoring, and uniform domination, but also positive, productive, and creative (Foucault, 1980). It is exercised over free subjects, and only insofar as they are free (1983b). Power is a total structure of actions brought to bear upon possible actions, a set of actions upon other actions. To govern in this sense is to structure the possible field of action of others (1983b). A "regime of truth" (1980, p. 133) is linked with systems of power that produce and sustain it. In this relational sense, Foucault uses the term *gouvernmentalité,* which, besides its meanings of control and guide, might be seen referring to a certain mentality that is willing and able to be governed. In the following, we summarize the Foucaultian analytics of power in three techniques: ordering of forces, disciplining practices, and individualizing practices.

First, there is a specific domain of power and its techniques that we call ordering of forces, which focus on how power is exercised as a tactical and strategical game, exercised from innumerable points, from below, immanently on other relationships, both intentionally and nonsubjectively. It is a question of the multiplicity of relations and positions immanent to power relations in their own organization (Foucault, 1990). The techniques of this specific domain of power include concepts like microphysics of power, bio-power, political economy of body, and political technology of the individual.

Second, there are techniques of government connecting knowledge and power (1983b). They might be called disciplining practices that constitute a strategic dimension of power realized as maneuvers of normativity, strategical integration, and tactical productivity. Discipline here means being subjugated both under a certain specialized domain of knowledge and under a certain regime and order. Disciplining refers not so much to an increase of obedience and allegiance as to the ordering and organizing of the mutual relation between the basic relationships so that they become more sophisticated, rational, and economical as they are surveyed more and more. Perhaps one of the best examples of disciplining practices is the examination, where the exercise of power and the production of knowledge are linked together.

The third dimension of techniques of government is the level connecting self and power. These techniques here are called individualizing practices, while at the same time they produce facts, subject domains, and rituals of truth. Foucault (1983b) speaks also of dividing practices in which the mad and the sane, the sick and the healthy, the criminal and the "good boy" are divided both inside themselves and from the others. In the modern regime of power, it works inside local communities rather than from the outside or from the top down. The pastoral techniques of power might be seen as the most typical individualizing practices (1983a).

A Catalog of Possibilities

We have tried to demonstrate above that it is reasonable to describe Foucault as a historian of truth. The domain of a Foucaultian history of truth, according to our interpretation, might be summarized in the form of a knowledge–subject–power (K–S–P) triangle, which illustrates the elements of the processes of truth production that we have called technologies of truth. This triangle of technologies of truth consists of three K–S–P subtriangles, each of which then is further divided into three dimensions (see Figure 3.1). Foucaultian "totality" thus has three dimensions and at the same time each of these dimensions has a totality in it. Thus, for example, techniques of self is an element of technologies of truth, but at the same time it contains the three dimensions of knowledge (will to knowledge), power (art of governmentality), and subject (modes of subjectivation). Foucault's work, in our interpretation, resembles an onion revealing layer after layer when peeled.

A Foucaultian historian of truth, in our sketch, is a person asking "How?" in the middle of the "What–Who–Why" triangle. She or he is trying to answer the following questions: What is the truth that "can and must be thought"? What is the field of knowledge in which the truth is produced? Who can take the place of the truth-speaking subject? Why is that truth produced? How is the truth produced? What are its technologies? In what way are techniques of discourse, of subjectivation, and of government connected to each other to produce simultaneously certain "fields of knowledge, types of normativity and forms of subjectivity" (Foucault, 1985, p. 4)?

We started this chapter claiming that education as a social phenomenon is tightly linked with Michel Foucault's basic themes: knowledge, subjectivity, and power. For us it is now evident that the Foucaultian problematic of knowledge is relevant in studying systems of education, whose main purpose is precisely to transmit knowledge. It is also quite clear that education is one of the "modes by which, in our culture, human beings are made subjects" (1983b, p. 208), which again turns to Foucaultian techniques of self. Further, it would require a huge amount of naivete to dispute the claim that education as a social apparatus is itself a game of power and is dependent on other relations of power. One might, thus, apply Foucault's ideas to education re-

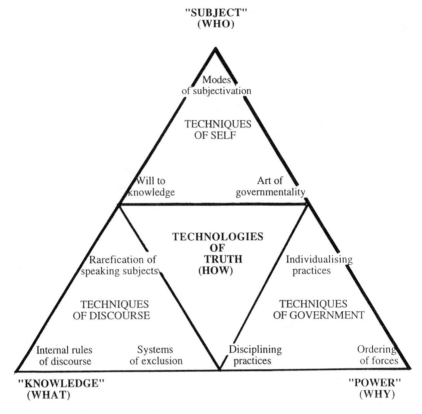

FIGURE 3.1   Technologies of Truth

search using some of these three aspects, for example, by examining educational systems as promoters of knowledge subordinated to games of power, or scrutinizing how schooling produces the modern individual, or analyzing school as a disciplining and punishing institution, a crypto-prison. Without denying the possibilities of these kinds of approaches, however, we would like to emphasize another kind of usage of Foucault's work, namely, the interaction of themes of knowledge, subjectivity, and power, which in our interpretation is the central and most fruitful angle of his work.

Although we emphasize the coherence and systematicity of Foucault's thinking, we do not regard the triangle presented in Figure 3.1 as an omnipotent theory. Actually, we find it futile to look for a grand theory in Foucault's work, which consists of empirical studies characterized by the author himself as "philosophical fragments put to work in a historical field of problems"

(1991c, p. 74). Therefore, the contribution of Foucault's work, besides his empirical results, is not a theory to be used as an explanation when studying historical problematics of knowledge, subjectivity, and power, but rather a "catalog of possibilities," a "meta-methodological device," or a "heuristic tool" to be used in various kinds of empirical studies. This is what our triangle is supposed to be. As a "catalog of possibilities" it can be used also in education research, which we will try to prove with the help of an example that deals with the birth of the modern Finnish teacher.

TRUTHS OF THE MODERN FINNISH TEACHER

The modern Finnish teacher came into being in the 1970s—sometimes described as the "Golden Era of Educational Reforms." First, in the Comprehensive School Reform (1972–1977), the dual-track school system of an 8-year compulsory school and the parallel grammar school was replaced by the single comprehensive school in which the whole cohort of pupils were schooled together for 9 years. Second, the Teacher Education Reform (1973–1979) was carried out, radically changing training particularly of primary school teachers—those who now teach at the lower level, grades 1–6, of the comprehensive school. Their training was removed from teacher training colleges and small-town "teacher preparation seminaries" to the brand-new university faculties of education established as part of the reform. In 1979 the training of primary school teachers was raised to the master's degree level. This dramatically upgraded the role of educational studies in teacher training, and education as an academic discipline expanded rapidly. All this was due, at least in part, to the third reform, the General Syllabus and Degree Reform in Higher Education (1977–1980), which abolished the bachelor's degree, which was brought back only recently (see Simola, 1993a, 1993b).

Discursive changes accompanying these reforms, both as their product and as their producer, were no less dramatic. The comprehensive school presented itself as the New School and did its best to distinguish itself from the old elementary school, and in the same manner new teachers and educational scientists distanced themselves from their predecessors. It is not an exaggeration to say that a new "truth" about both school and teacher was created. The following discussion is based on a study (Simola, 1995) analyzing the state educational discourse in Finland from the 1860s to the 1990s. We will present four truths of the modern teacher and two discursive principles for serious and authoritative use of language about the modern Finnish teacher. While the study is based on official text material, it is limited to an archaeological analysis. Thus, it will tell more about the field of knowledge than of self and of power. We will show, however, that the immanent existence of all three dimensions is of essential importance.

Where are the truths of the modern teacher to be found? In the case of Finland, the institution of governmental committees is a central instrument in planning and justifying reform policy—and in producing and articulating truth. This is especially true in the case of education.[3] In some cases committee proposals have become the official curriculum, both in the strict and in the broader meaning of the term. Committee reports also are scientifically legitimated because of the important role that educational scientists have attained in the committees since the late 1960s. Besides the committee texts on schooling and teacher education, the material of the study consists of the national curriculum documents for elementary and comprehensive schools from 1925, 1952, 1970, 1985, and 1994. These were written to be models for more precise curricular documents that were to be formulated at the local level—in 1925 and 1952 by the school, in 1970 and 1985 by the municipal authorities, and in 1994 again by the school.[4]

Committee and curricular texts are serious and authoritative verbal acts of experts who speak as experts and who with their speech form the official truth on teaching. They are—to quote Foucault (1972)—discursive "practices that systematically form the objects of which they speak" (p. 49). Although they are products of individuals, they have (especially when circulating as law texts or as administrative orders but also as state documents) the appearance of anonymity, of an official truth. We may assume that in these texts there are to be found traces and marks of what is the "true" knowledge about teaching, what the "good" teacher is like, and what kind of power is "right" in the field of schooling.

As the first step in Simola's (1995) study, the Foucaultian K–S–P triangle was used as a "catalog of possibilities" to formulate the following questions and subquestions, with the help of which the text material was "interviewed" (see Figure 3.2). These questions formed a springboard for the research process, to start a hermeneutic circle between the empirical data and the theoretical framework, where the questions were reformulated again and again and where four truths of modern Finnish teacherhood finally were distilled. In the following we try to show how "new" truths of teacherhood (*T*1–*T*4) have replaced the "old" ones in educational state discourse.

The "True" Knowledge About Teaching

Since ethics and psychology separated from religion at the beginning of this century, the knowledge base of teaching, that is, educational studies, has consisted of pedagogical, psychological, philosophical, societal, and practical knowledge. Until World War II—and in certain aspects even until the

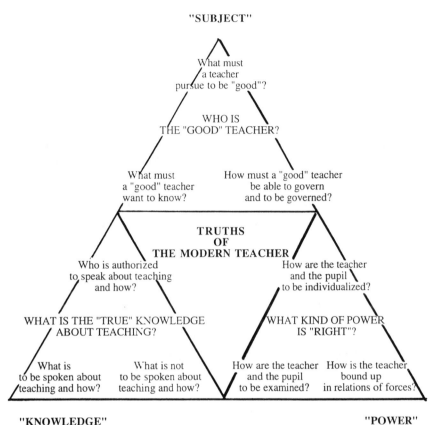

FIGURE 3.2   Truths of the Modern Teacher: An Initial Questionnaire

1960s—the educational aims came from ethics, and the prerequisites from psychology. The task of pedagogy was to combine these two premises into practical teaching methods. The character of educational studies was on the one hand ideological because they were to develop the devotion to and consciousness of the mission of the teacher. On the other hand, educational knowledge was to be practical and provide a repertoire of teaching methods to apply in the various circumstances of the teacher's work. The stance toward the empirical academic educational science that had been changing since the 1950s was rather lukewarm. One may conclude that, until the mid-1960s, educational studies in teacher training were multiple, pragmatic, and ideological, based on psychology and ethics, and related to the needs of teaching practices as interpreted by the National Board of Education (NBE).[5]

The 1967 teacher training committee report (CR) was the turning point. The teacher as a well-educated handyman was replaced by the teacher as a science-legitimated expert. In the 1969 report, responsibility for teacher education was to be wholly assigned to the universities and, in the 1975 report, the training was to be raised to the master's degree level. Through scientification of teacher education, it was hoped that teaching would be transformed from "a haphazard activity into a rational one" (CR, 1975, p. 40). The new teacher was to become a "didactic thinker"[6] and "researcher into his/her work" (CR, 1967, 1975). The student teacher of the 1990s would grind his or her way through educational studies five times longer than his or her fellow student in the 1960s.

Practical and philosophical knowledge as well as societal knowledge was almost completely deleted from the knowledge foundation of the teacher's work beginning in the late 1970s. This "disciplination" of the teacher's knowledge base culminated in the 1989 committee's view of didactically oriented educational science as virtually the only source of true knowledge for teaching. While the report discussed the multiplicity of teachers' work, there was only one reference to educational psychology and none to the sociology or history of education, for example. We can conclude that the "old" truth—that the knowledge base of teaching is a multiple, pragmatic, and ideological combination of ethical, psychological, pedagogical, historical, and content knowledge determined by the NBE—was replaced beginning in the late 1960s by the "new" truth (*T*1), whereby a didactically oriented educational science forms the knowledge base for teachers' work.

The "Good" Teacher

The concept of the teacher as a "model citizen" has been very vital in official discourse. Since the duty of primary school teachers was to guarantee that every citizen would achieve the proper level of decent manners and behavior, they themselves were carefully recruited according to the same premises. Traditionally, the teacher was to be an exemplary citizen both externally and internally (see also Rinne, 1986, 1988a). The claims of external exemplariness vanished from the official texts only during the 1980s, and finally from the legislation in the 1990s. Teachers' inner exemplariness has been even more persistent, although its content has changed. Democratic values gradually replaced the Christian ethos between the 1940s and 1970s. The "pedagogical love" for children shifted to the more cognitive "correct educational attitude." As a curricular committee report for teacher training put it in the late 1960s, the student teacher should have a "positive attitude towards the school and the career of teacher, and an interest in pupils and their development" (CR,

1968, p. 9). Emotions thus were directed toward the institution and the profession rather than toward the pupils.

In the 1970 curriculum, goal consciousness emerged as a central quality of the teacher for the new comprehensive school. In 1984 teachers' obligations "to pursue the attainment of goals stated for the comprehensive school" were written into the legislation (Curriculum, 1985, p. 59). The commitment to the goals then formed the point at which the institutional belief in mass schooling intersected with conviction about the power of the official curriculum as the main tool for the development of school practices. Further, it was believed that these goals were, in some reasonable sense, attainable and realistic. We thus may conclude that the old truth—that the model citizenship and consciousness of the mission are the most central occupational qualities for a teacher—has little by little given way to the new truth focusing on the internal rather than the external exemplariness of the teacher. The good intention, the right attitude, and the deep belief in schooling form the core of the model citizenship of the modern teacher. The consciousness of the goals has replaced both the traditional consciousness of the mission and the external exemplariness. Thus, the second truth ($T2$) of the modern Finnish teacher may be formulated as follows: Goal consciousness is the most central professional quality of the teacher.

The third truth deals with the object of teachers' work: Is it a group of pupils or the individual pupil? Before World War II, Finnish curricular and committee texts rarely spoke about pupils as individuals. Although the benefits of mass schooling for the people were mentioned, it was legitimated principally by the needs of society, of the nation, of the Fatherland. When a child or a pupil was spoken of in the singular, it was in the sense of the generalized individual, that is, as a member of the group of country children who were to be educated.[7] Only after World War II did the modern individual emerge at the side of society as the legitimate basis for compulsory schooling. However, the individual clearly was still subordinated to the interests of society: The clear mission of the compulsory school was to train citizens for society.

In Finland the modern individual has surpassed society as the primordial source of legitimation for schooling only since the late 1960s. The curriculum code[8] broke into an individualist one in which the main ethos was found in the new promise to respond to the individual learning needs and qualities of each pupil. The 1970 curriculum proposed the core of new individualist discourse while stating that pedagogical expediency and flexibility are more important than the number of pupils. At the same time, the basic problem of teaching as stated in official texts shifted from the number of pupils to the diversity of pupil personalities. The work of teachers changed from molding the school life of a group of pupils to an individual-centered task.

Corresponding with this break, the skills that were officially seen as necessary for a teacher changed dramatically. Talking about discipline and order in the classroom was replaced first by concepts of "peace for work" (Curriculum, 1970). Later the whole issue of maintaining "a socially positive order" in the classroom—including such topics as classroom management and social psychology—was removed completely from theoretical studies in teacher education texts and was shifted to practice teaching (CR, 1975). The courses were filled with educational science instead. The new pedagogical idea of "differentiation in teaching" was proposed as a basic tool for taking the diversity of pupils into account in classroom teaching. While the teacher in the "old school" was supposed to consider as individuals only those with problems in adapting to the disciplined life in the classroom, the "new teacher" promised to treat everybody as an individual. A teacher should know every pupil and "be aware of the learning-related factors of the individual pupils' home environment." The teacher ought "to be aware of the previous learning results, abilities, attitudes, expectations and the health condition of the pupil" (CR, 1975, pp. 32–33)—no matter whether she or he was a class teacher with 20 pupils or a subject teacher with 200 pupils.

The promise to respond to the diversity of pupils culminated in the most recent texts, wherein the individual-centered task of the teacher is strengthened by emphasis on the ethical character of the teacher's work (CR, 1989). In the 1994 curriculum, the teacher is seen as a "counsellor of learning" or a "designer of the learning environments" of individual "learners." The school now undertakes to offer "individual study plans" or even "personal curriculums" in accordance with learning needs and qualities of pupils (Curriculum, 1994, pp. 10, 20). While the omnipotence of the school in the 1970s and 1980s was based on didactics, it seemed in the 1990s to lean on flexible organization and school-based curriculum. Therefore, we may say that in the late 1960s the old truth—that teachers' work is to mold the school life of a group of pupils—changed to the new one (*T*3): Teachers' work is an individual-centered task.

The "Right" Power in Schooling

Grading and assessing pupils were not problematized before the 1960s in official school discourse. The theme was not even mentioned in curricular or committee texts, although in all the decrees that determined the tasks of teachers it was clearly prescribed that the teacher should check and supervise the exercises, carry out the grading and prepare the report cards of pupils. This state of affairs is explained by the existence of the parallel school system, which made the selective function of the elementary school very limited. It was only in 1960 that "the assessment of learning results and grading the pupils" (CR, 1960, p. 77) was mentioned for the first time as one aspect of pedagogy in teacher training.

A dramatic change occurred in comprehensive school texts. Since the 1966 report (CR, 1966), the examination had been a constant and central element of the official school discourse. The 1966 report noted the problem that the traditional grading and assessing of pupils gave both quantitatively and qualitatively limited knowledge about the progress of pupils in their studies. Pupils, parents, and teachers, following educational institutes and employers, were seen as in need of comprehensive and individual evaluations during the school years and of objective and comparable assessments in the leaving certificate. Verbal reports for the former and standardized tests for the latter purpose were proposed. These two main techniques of examination—grading by marks and assessment by words—have appeared ever since as the basis for two central functions of schooling: grading for selection of pupils and assessment for the inscription of self-selection into them. Educational science thus was seen both as legitimating the profound intervention into the personality of the pupil and also as offering the tools for it.

The 1985 curriculum was a rupture in the tradition according to which "the assessment carried out by the teacher would be focused on the performance and certain concrete behavior of the pupil but not on his/her personality as a whole" (Curriculum, 1970, 52). Since 1985, in addition to the criteria of knowledge and skills, "the achievement of general educational goals that are notable for the whole development of the pupil" (Curriculum, 1985, p. 30) also would be taken into account in grading of school subjects. Examples of such criteria were mentioned, including, for example, "active participation," "ability and willingness to cooperate," and "the positive attitude and willingness of the pupil to act according to the educational goals" (Curriculum, 1985, p. 31). The examination was presented in 1985 above all as a service to the pupil him/herself while "giving a realistic picture of his/her possibilities, for example, in continuing studies" (pp. 29–30). This emphasis on the examination as an objective and comparable, comprehensive, and individual source for self-selection of the pupil culminated in the 1994 curriculum. The examination "supports most effectively the progress of the individual learning process of the pupil, strengthening the self-confidence and identification of his/her own abilities and skills" (Curriculum, 1994, p. 25).

Thus, one may see here the move from the old truth of the limited and partial, external, and formal elementary school examination that guaranteed citizenship to the individual to the profound, exact, and multifaceted comprehensive school examination system that works for objective selection but, more and more, also for the inscription of the self-selection into the pupil.

Therefore, the fourth truth (*T*4) may be formulated as follows: Comprehensive assessment and objective grading of pupils is one of the basic tasks of the teacher.[9]

TACIT PRINCIPLES OF DISCOURSE

The four truths we have reconstructed above have emerged from an "archaeological" analysis of the official texts undertaken in order to trace various veins of the concept of modern teacherhood, veins originating in different decades and emanating from different sources. These truths are the cornerstones of modern teacherhood in Finnish state educational discourse. They constitute the positive unconscious of knowledge in the field of schooling, the unconscious that determines what knowledge is accepted as "true" for the teacher, what is the essence of the "good" teacher, and what is the "right" way to use power in schooling. These "truths" in summary are the following:

T1. A didactically oriented educational science forms the knowledge base for teachers' work.

T2. Goal consciousness is the most central professional quality of the teacher.

T3. Teachers' work is an individual-centered task.

T4. Comprehensive assessment and objective grading of pupils is one of the basic tasks of the teacher.

In this section we try to put these truths into a larger context. On the one hand, this leads us to widen the "archaeological" perspective and analyze the official Finnish school discourse as part of a broader "epistemological space" (Foucault, 1991b, p. xi) specific to the period, say, from the 1960s onwards. On the other hand, we come to the threshold of a "genealogy" of institutions and practices of education. However, we remain standing on the threshold, because the official texts we are using as source material do not tell us about actual nondiscursive practices in schooling. While the truths *T*1–*T*4 describe what must be said in order for one to be taken as a serious expert speaker in this specific discursive field, in the following we try to outline answers to other questions: How is the truth to be spoken? Who can speak it? Why is it spoken? We will summarize our tentative, and in no way exhaustive, answers as two tacit principles of discourse. They are sort of "metatruths" defining rules or codes of the truth-game in this and obviously also in other discursive fields. These principles are characterized as tacit because they have never been articulated explicitly. We call them tacit principles of rationalism of hopes and pastoral professionalism.

Rationalism of Hopes

By rationalism of hopes we mean a composition of two elements: goal rationalism and decontextualism. First, and as its rational dimension, the school is spoken about as if it were a goal-rational organization. Although heavily criticized over the years in academic discussion, the well-known "Tyler Rationale" (Tyler, 1950) has maintained its position as a paradigmatic basis for planning both the general curriculum and the individual work of the teacher.[10] The belief that the starting point for virtually any educational activity is a clearly stated goal or set of goals was formulated in the Tyler Rationale, and it has become a basic truth in the world of curriculum studies (Kliebard, 1995). Once determined, the goals will guide the other curricular decisions on learning experiences, organization, and evaluation. What is important here is the relation between the goal-rational Tylerian model and the context of educational activity. We cannot claim that the model per se would exclude the context from consideration. However, we may assume that the intellectual focus is very strongly on goals and means. The context of action is seen as secondary to the scrutiny of goals and means. It seems given, taken for granted, and self-evident, as something natural and durable, something out of the range of influence of the actor.

Indeed, with the rise of goal rationalism in Finnish state educational discourse in the late 1960s, the context of school as a historically and culturally formed institution became more and more a marginal domain of knowledge. Therefore, the second dimension of rationalism of hopes is called decontextualization of the state educational discourse. This way of speaking might be crystalized as a "family tutor illusion" (Simola, 1993b, p. 179): speaking as if the basic social relation in the school were one teacher–one pupil. In Finnish texts, it was realized mainly through a curious "naturalization" of the school, a universalization of school learning, and a concealment of certain peculiarities of schooling.

First, before the Comprehensive School Reform, the arbitrary character of the school often was referred to, even in official texts. In the 1950s, schooling was seen as a necessity for civilization, but also as "unnatural because it is so comprehensive and begins already at the age of seven." It was claimed that "schooling, even at its best, intrudes onto the children a lot of strange things that will be resisted by the nature of the child" (Curriculum, 1952, p. 27). This confrontation between the "natural" child and "unnatural" schooling disappeared during the 1970s, while the problem of unnaturalness changed into one of "pedagogical expediency."[11] Second, there was also an essential break in the way of speaking about learning. Before the 1970s, references to learning nearly always dealt with learning the elementary skills and values. "School learning" as a special type of learning often was spoken about explicitly, an expression that completely disappeared during the 1970s. Since the 1970 curriculum, learning in school has become a synonym for general learning. The third mode of decontextualization was the concealment of certain peculiarities of schooling, especially its compulsory and mass character. The compulsory character of the school was still an issue of moral reasoning in 1970, but no trace of it can be found in the official texts after 1975. The mass character of the school also was explicitly articulated before the late 1960s, but in the 1970s became paradoxically irrelevant—in spite of the evident contradiction between the mass character and individualist promises of the school.

To summarize, in Finnish state educational discourse, there is a curious combination of utopian promises and pursuit of their rationalistic realization. Seeing the school as a rational institution makes it seem omnipotent: advanced, fulfilling its tasks, and thus deserving continuous public faith (e.g., Weick, 1976; cf. Popkewitz, 1991). One could say that the expansion of comprehensive schooling is to a large extent justified by the benevolent goals and rationalism of the school discourse. They are both constitutive elements of "education as a religious foundation of modern society," to quote John W. Meyer (1986, p. 358). This also explains those "functionalist blinders" that unite both liberal and critical educationists in their faith in schooling: the former optimistically developing school toward the ideal, the latter blaming it for fulfilling the ideal only partly (Meyer, 1986; cf. Hunter, 1994).

Knowledge, subjectivation, and power come beautifully together, while the millennial dream (Popkewitz, 1991) of completely developed personalities is paradoxically to come true through the bureaucratic machinery of schooling (cf. Hunter, 1994). To see learning in school as a model of universal human learning rather than as a very specific type of learning framed by institutional constraints of mass schooling also has made innovations and reforms rather easy and fluent on paper. Educational problems are reduced to psychological ones, and obstacles to school improvement seem to be found in teachers and pupils rather than, say, in the structural constraints of compulsory schooling, educational policy, or curricular ideology (cf. Lundgren, 1991). It is also possible to see that rationalism of hopes, boosted by the rhetoric of accountability, brings at least two curious elements to the teacher's subjectivity: first, a constant self-reflectivity and self-evaluation as a new technique of the self, and second, a market-oriented "new entrepreneur" (Mac an Ghaill, 1992) as the telos of teacherhood.[12]

The emergence of rationalism of hopes, however, cannot be explained simply by factors internal to the field of education, but should be seen as part of a more general development, starting in the 1960s, in which a new "epistemological space" of planning and regulation was established in Finland. Developments similar to those described above might be found in the fields of, for example, economic and social policy in the process of creating the Finnish welfare state (cf., e.g., Alestalo, 1986).

Pastoral Professionalism

If rationalism of hopes constitutes mainly an institutional discourse of schooling, the second discursive principle constructs directly the modern teacher. It is called pastoral professionalism. Pastoral professionalism in teaching consists first of individualism. It generally is known that a basic argument for accepting teaching as a full profession is that it must be seen as comparable to the archetypal professions such as medicine and law. However, we have not seen much attention paid to the difference under consideration here. While a doctor or a lawyer meets his or her client individually, a teacher meets a group of clients.[13] One might say that this individualism makes it possible to create an individual-centered professional ethos for teaching. This is an essential issue because individualism is related to changes in the way the teacher uses power.

In the case of obligatory mass schooling, it is the question of justifying more and more systematic, comprehensive, and sophisticated examination. These changes can be revealed by comparing the power relations between teacher and pupil in the "old" elementary and the modern comprehensive school. While the teacher in the old school was supposed to consider as individuals only those with problems in adapting to the disciplined life in the classroom, the modern teacher promises to treat everybody as an individual and, by offering individual study programs and personal curricula, to respond to the learning interests and qualities of every pupil. The truth about the individual pupil, which the teacher of the old school was supposed to know and tell, was partial and limited to a pass–fail scale for general conduct and a numerical scale for school subjects. The modern teacher needs to be convinced of his or her ability and justification for penetrating into the most secret nooks of the personality of the pupil and to promise to tell the whole truth about the pupil. While for a teacher in the old school it was clear that school success was not available to all pupils, the new teacher, believing in the egalitarian omnipotence of the school as an institution and in the science-legitimated humanism of academic pedagogy, promises salvation for every child. Finally, while in the old school there was a clear and open, coercive, and sanctioned obligation to follow the commands of compulsory schooling, the modern school invites and induces, declaring and underscoring a right to learning. Power in the modern school seems to work inductively and invitingly rather than through coercion and command, positively and productively rather than negatively and preventatively.

One may see here a certain "pastoralization" of power, in the sense in which Foucault (1983b) used the word.[14] The new forms of pastoral power create first of all the new pupil who is willing and able to engage in self-evaluation and self-selection. This means that pupils undergo constant assessment and grading, and invest in and incline themselves toward the faith of schooling. While the old school demanded allegiance and obedience for only a few years and for a stated period, the new school presupposes them forever, in the name of lifelong education—or perhaps life-sentenced schooling. Individualized knowledge is now to be based on an ever more penetrating gaze from the teacher, the "observation of constant evidence" (Curriculum, 1985, p. 30). It creates the new field of individual knowledge, accumulated in complete archive of generalized knowledge. The 1952 curriculum proposed creating a certain system of pupil register for continuous and cumulative documentation of notes and observations about "the mental development and particularities of the child." However, it was planned especially for pupils "at risk," for those whose "mental balance and working capacity may easily get disturbed" (Curriculum, 1952, p. 36). Only the 1970 curriculum introduced the full-fledged archive that was supposed to consist of a massive information load of "gifts, character, family background, hobbies, physical development and school performances" that was to be gathered through "testing, questionnaires, interviews, home visits, exams, etc." (Curriculum, 1970, p. 186). This personal "pupil register" was a "confidential document"—and as such was closed to the pupil and his or her parents but open to teachers, school officials, and researchers.

The second element of the principle of pastoral professionalism is disciplining.[15] The disciplining of speaking about teachers' work includes at least three dimensions. First, it means that, instead of different domains of knowledge, one academic discipline—educational science or, finally and more precisely, didactically oriented educational science—was given a monopolistic position in determining the true knowledge for teachers' work. In this sense, one might characterize the disciplining of teachers' knowledge as "didactization," where the practical, multiple, and ideological teachers' knowledge, interpreted by the NBE officials, is displaced by academic "teaching science."

The second dimension of disciplining refers to increasing discipline in the use of language when speaking about teaching. Here it seems that there is a strong continuity in the texts. The contents of the preservice studies of teachers had been determined exactly, course by course, in reports of the 1920s, 1960s, and 1970s. Effective administrative regulation of the reform has guaranteed that the shift from the "shadow" of the NBE to the "light" of the university would not threaten the traditional unity and uniformity of teacher training discourse in Finland. Only in the 1989 report were the possibilities of "profilization" of departments spoken about, although there is still an emphasis on "structural uniformity" (CR, 1989, p. 73).

There seems to be a continuity in the third dimension of disciplining, too. It is the question of who is able to take the place of the speaking subject. Educational scientists (later, didacticians) and officials of the NBE (later, also those of the Ministry of Education) have been able to take the position of authoritative speaker in committees on teacher education. To be a classroom teacher has never been enough for those positions. Although a few professors of subject disciplines have been members of some committees, the subject knowledge has had no voice in outlining true knowledge for teacher education. Nor has any sociologist or historian of education—not to mention the clients of schooling, the parents—participated as a member of any committee on teacher training.

To conclude, pastoral professionalism as a tacit principle of discourse is a combination of individualism and disciplining. One may say that it creates both the new expert teacher and the new pupil, both willing to take part in the continuous and comprehensive examination. If the mission of the teacher of the old school was to be a gatekeeper to fully authorized citizenship, the mission of the modern comprehensive school teacher might be seen, writes Rinne (1988b), as "to inscribe into the pupils the sense of 'self-selection' and 'suitability,' to guide the pupils to the free choices and routes that are fitting and suitable for them" (p. 443). Pastoral professionalism forms a specific type of professionalist discourse that is much more analogous—at least in its relations to knowledge, institution, and clients—to that of the priest than that of archetypal professional such as the physician or lawyer. What is more important, however, is that the teacher using the pastoral power of the modern comprehensive school seems to practice par excellence what Foucault described:

> This form of power is salvation oriented (as opposed to political power). It is oblative (as opposed to a principle of sovereignty); it is individualizing (as opposed to a legal power); it is coextensive and continuous with life; it is linked with a production of truth—the truth of the individual himself. (Foucault, 1983b, p. 214)

It is clear that pastoral professionalism cannot be understood as a phenomenon belonging to the world of discursive practices only, or as a phenomenon characteristic of the world of education only. To understand it fully we would have to analyze not only official texts but also the institutions and practices of education. To understand the *dispositifs* of education, we would have to bring the fields of knowledge, social apparatuses, and subjects together in a manner similar to Foucault's in his analysis of the birth of the clinic (Foucault, 1991a). In this analogy educational science equals clinical medicine, school equals hospital, teacher equals physician, and pupil equals

patient. We then would have to analyze the general processes of individualization and disciplining as developments more general than limited to school
and education. Thus, to explain fully the principle of pastoral professionalism we would have to reach beyond the domain of "archaeological" analysis
for "genealogical" comprehension and for Foucaultian "ethics" of subjectivation. But that is another story.

CONCLUSION

The aim of this chapter has been to show, first, that Foucault's work can be
summarized as a project of "a history of truth," and second, that this approach is fruitful in empirical studies. We have tried to demonstrate this
through the example of a history of the modern Finnish teacherhood. Although our reading of Foucault has been an experimental one and the scope
of application has been limited, we believe it opens some promising perspectives in two directions: in "Foucaultian studies" and in education research.

While a first reading of Foucault often gives a confusing impression of
ideas going in multiple directions, we have, on the contrary, emphasized the
coherence of his work. We tried to read it as a systemic whole consisting of
three basic themes of knowledge, subjectivity, and power. We do not try to
deny the fruitfulness of studying these themes separately, but we simply wonder whether such approaches do justice to the full potency of Foucault's original and divergent thinking. We believe that the analytic power of Foucault's
work comes precisely from bringing together these three dimensions, from
seeing knowledge, subjectivity, and power in their immanent relationality.
The games of truth are played in the intermediate space of these three dimensions, games with specific rules and strategies that stay invisible if one looks
for them from only one corner of the game.

It should be emphasized, however, that we do not see the Foucaultian
triangle constructed earlier as a theory in a strict deductive sense of the word,
but rather as a "catalog of possibilities," as a tool to raise and analyze new
problems. The aim of the device is not to act as a decontextualized, universal
model for answers, but rather to unfold space for new ways to ask questions.
It is not a method for concrete empirical research, but a way to ask questions
about conditions of empirical inquiry, going beyond dichotomies of essen-
tialism and nominalism or deduction and induction. As such it is compatible
with different types of empirical methods and applicable to various kinds of
material, permitting deviating theoretical preferences in fields that include
education research.

What possible use, then, would our Foucaultian triangle have in education research? The example we have presented has dealt mostly with the
"knowledge corner" of the triangle, with the discursive techniques of creating

the "truth" of the modern Finnish teacher. We hope, however, to have showed that this truth is not purely a phenomenon of knowledge. It is not independent of relations of power in the field of education or of processes in which not only teachers but also pupils, administrators, educational scientists, and teacher educators are creating their subjectivities. The birth of the modern Finnish teacher—and that of other actors in the field—could have been studied also from the point of view of the other corners of the triangle: from the points of view of subjectivity and power, giving stronger emphasis to techniques of self and techniques of government. But, and this we would like to stress, it is unfruitful to see the teacher only as a pawn in a game of power or simply as an independent individual agent. Although the point of view and emphasis would be different, we believe that all three elements should be kept in view while analyzing the birth of the modern teacher. We even believe that this applies to education research in general, because education deals exactly with questions of knowledge, subjectivity, and power.

NOTES

1. The word "teacherhood" is used in this chapter to refer to properties and attributes ascribed to the "model teacher" in official texts.

2. The following discussion is based on Heikkinen, Silvonen, and Simola (1996).

3. According to a Finnish study, education "has traditionally been an area in which government committees have played a particularly central role in the planning and preparation of government action and in drafting government policy for the sector as a whole. It is through the institution of the committee that education has been brought under strict governmental control, and the committee has become a vital instrument of educational policy as practiced by the state" (Hovi, Kivinen, & Rinne, 1989, p. 243).

4. In accordance with the Finnish state-centered and centralized administrative tradition, the national curricula have been very comprehensive documents. Their extent generally varied from 300 to 700 pages. The exception was the 1994 curriculum, with only 111 pages. In 1952, the curriculum was ambitiously defined as "a series of those experiences that the pupil meets in his/her school work" (Curriculum, 1952, p. 40). The definition of the 1970 curriculum was even more complete. The curriculum must consist of "the explanations of all the most important measures and procedures by which the school proposes to reach the aims imposed for it. . . . The curriculum includes all those learning experiences that the pupils have under the guidance of the school, including outside the classrooms" (Curriculum, 1970, p. 56).

5. Training and its content were directly and strictly controlled and administered by the NBE, which confirmed the curriculum and the syllabus, and approved the textbooks; if desired, its representative even chaired the examinations.

6. The term *didactics* is a very problematic one in English. It is used here in the meaning that it has in the education literature of Germany and the Nordic countries. Kansanen (1995, p. 351) states that "in UK as well as in US frameworks for educa-

tion, the sub-area of didactics seems to be lacking. . . . [M]uch of its content belongs to educational psychology. In Germany and [the] Nordic countries, didactic problems define an independent sub-discipline of education. The scope of didactics covers that of Anglo-American curriculum theory and educational psychology including also much philosophical and theoretical thinking." In Anglo-American literature, there are just a few texts concerning the relation between didactic and curriculum theory but see, e.g., articles on the German *Didaktik* tradition in the *Journal of Curriculum Studies*, vol. 27, issues 1 and 4.

7. Actually, there was one important exception to this. The "founding father" of the Finnish elementary school, Uno Cygnaeus, noted in 1860 that the task of the elementary school is "to awake and to develop those individual inclinations that nature has implanted in each child" (Cygnaeus, 1910, p. 295). It is remarkable that, during the next 80 years, there were no references of this kind to the solitary and original individuals whom the school would promise to take into account.

8. Here we follow Lundgren (1991) in defining curriculum first, as "a selection of contents and goals for social reproduction, that is a selection of what knowledge and skills are to be transmitted by education"; second, as "an organization of knowledge and skills"; and third, as "an indication of methods concerning how the selected contents are to be taught; to be sequenced and controlled, for example" (p. 5). A "curriculum code" is for Lundgren a "homogeneous set" of "principles according to which the selection, the organization and the methods for transmission are formed" (p. 5; also see Rinne, 1987).

9. For a more detailed discussion on this theme, see Simola 1996.

10. On criticism, see, e.g., Kliebard, 1975, 1995; Wise, 1976; Miettinen, 1990; on the Tyler Rationale as a rule of thumb, see, e.g., Madaus & Stufflebeam, 1989; Goodlad & Su, 1992; Doyle, 1992; Hlebowitsh, 1992.

11. A beautiful example of this "naturalization" was the changed stance toward the predictive power of school marks and reports. While in 1952 the school marks were seen as lacking predictive power because of the one-sided character of school life itself, for the curriculum of 1970 the only problem was the insufficiently developed technical means of evaluation (Curriculum, 1952, 1970).

12. New patterns of teacher regulation have been noted in recent literature emphasizing features like centralized assessment (e.g., Ball, 1994; Lingard, 1990; Lundgren, 1991), school-based management (e.g., Angus, 1994; Hatcher, 1994; Mac an Ghaill, 1992), and new collegiality (e.g., Hartley, 1986; Hatcher, 1994; Lawn & Ozga, 1986; Smyth, 1991).

13. The work of the teacher is still a work with masses, where the possibility of dialogue interaction is very limited. Consider just two hypothetical situations. How would a physician survive in a situation where, say, 25 patients with their individual problems had to be attended to in the same room? Or how would a lawyer cope if she or he had to plead for a group consisting of rapists, pick-pockets, drunken drivers, and tax dodgers all at the same time? (Simola, 1993b)

14. Foucault characterizes pastoral power as being an historically unique, "tricky combination in the same political structures of individualization techniques and of totalization procedures" (1983b, pp. 213–216). Pastoral power was born with Christianity, and its modernized form can be seen as a basic technique of Western nation-states. According to Foucault, Christianity is the only religion that has organized itself as a church in which certain individuals can serve others as pastors, first,

working for the salvation of parishioners; second, sacrificing themselves for these parishioners if necessary; third, treating them as individuals; and finally, possessing a special knowledge of their souls. Foucault sees pastoralization, therefore, as a vital technique of the process of governmentalization, which is the essence of the modern state. There are three characteristics of this new pastoral power that distinguish it from its ecclesiastical precursor. First, the promised salvation concerns this world rather than the next. Second, the officials of the pastoral power have changed. Finally, "the multiplication of the aims and agents of pastoral power focuses the development of knowledge of man around two roles: one, globalizing and quantitative, concerning the population; the other, analytical, concerning the individual" (Foucault, 1983b, p. 215).

15. For a more detailed discussion on the professional interests of teacher educators related to the "true" knowledge of teaching, see Simola, Kivinen, and Rinne, 1996.

REFERENCES

Alestalo, M. (1986). *Structural change, classes and the state. Finland in a historical and comparative perspective.* University of Helsinki, Research Group for Comparative Sociology.

Angus, L. (1994). Sociological analysis and educational management: the social context of self-managing schools. *British Journal of Sociology of Education, 15*(1), 79–91.

Ball, S. J. (1994). *Education reform: A critical and post-structural approach.* London: Open University Press.

Committee Report. (1960). *Seminaarilainsäädännön uudistamiskomitean mietintö.* [Report of the Committee for the Reform of Seminar Legislation] (KM 1960:7). Helsinki: Valtioneuvoston kirjapaino.

Committee Report. (1966). *Koulunuudistustoimikunnan mietintö* [Report of the Committee for School Reform] (KM 1966: A 12). Helsinki: Valtioneuvoston kirjapaino.

Committee Report. (1967). *Opettajanvalmistustoimikunnan mietintö* [Report of the Committee for Teacher Preparation] (KM 1967: A 2). Helsinki: Valtion painatuskeskus.

Committee Report. (1968). *Opettajanvalmistuksen opetussuunnitelmatoimikunnan mietintö* [Report of the Committee for Teacher Training Curriculum] (KM 1968: A 6). Helsinki: Valtion painatuskeskus.

Committee Report. (1975). *Vuoden 1973 opettajankoulutustoimikunnan mietintö* [Report of the 1973 Committee for Teacher Education] (KM 1975: 75). Helsinki: Oy Länsi-Suomi, Rauma.

Committee Report. (1989). *Opettajankoulutuksen kehittämistoimikunnan mietintö* [Report of the Committee for Development of Teacher Education] (KM 1989: 26). Helsinki: Valtion painatuskeskus.

Curriculum. (1952). *Kansakoulun opetussuunnitelmakomitean mietintö II* [Report of the Committee for Elementary School Curriculum II] (KM 1952: 3). Helsinki: Valtioneuvoston kirjapaino.

Curriculum. (1970). *Peruskoulun opetussuunnitelmatoimikunnan mietintö I* [Report of the Committee for Comprehensive School Curriculum I] (KM 1970: A 4). Helsinki: Valtion painatuskeskus.

Curriculum. (1985). *Peruskoulun opetussuunnitelman perusteet* [Framework curriculum for the comprehensive school]. Helsinki: Valtion painatuskeskus.

Curriculum. (1994). *Peruskoulun opetussuunnitelman perusteet.* [Framework curriculum for the comprehensive school]. Helsinki: Painatuskeskus.

Cygnaeus, U. (1910). *Kirjoitukset Suomen kansakoulun perustamisesta ja järjestämisestä* [Writings on the establishment and organization of the Finnish elementary school]. Helsinki: Kansanvalistusseura.

Doyle, W. (1992). Curriculum and pedagogy. In P. W. Jackson (Ed.), *Handbook of research on curriculum* (pp. 486–516). New York: Macmillan.

Foucault, M. (1971). Orders of discourse. *Social Science Information, 10*(2), 7–22.

Foucault, M. (1972). *The archaeology of knowledge and the discourse on language* (A. M. Sheridan Smith, Trans.). New York: Pantheon.

Foucault, M. (1977). *Discipline and punish: The birth of the prison.* New York: Vintage.

Foucault, M. (1980). *Power/Knowledge: Selected interviews and other writings by Michel Foucault 1972–1977* (C. Gordon, Ed. and Trans.). New York: Pantheon.

Foucault, M. (1983a). On the genealogy of ethics: An overview of work in progress. In H. L. Dreyfus & P. Rabinow, *Michel Foucault: Beyond structuralism and hermeneutics* (2nd ed.) (pp. 229–252). Chicago: Chicago University Press.

Foucault, M. (1983b). The subject and power. In H. L. Dreyfus & P. Rabinow, *Michel Foucault: Beyond structuralism and hermeneutics* (2nd ed.) (pp. 208–226). Chicago: University of Chicago Press.

Foucault, M. (1985). *The history of sexuality: Vol. 2. The use of pleasure.* London: Penguin.

Foucault, M. (1986). *The history of sexuality: Vol. 3. The care of the self.* New York: Vintage.

Foucault, M. (1988a). The ethic of care for the self as a practice of freedom. [Interview]. In J. Bernauer & D. Rasmussen (Eds.), *The final Foucault* (pp. 1–20). Cambridge, MA: MIT Press.

Foucault, M. (1988b). Technologies of the self. In L. H. Martin, H. Gutman, & P. H. Hutton (Eds.), *Technologies of the self: A seminar with Michel Foucault* (pp. 16–49). Amherst: University of Massachusetts Press.

Foucault, M. (1990). *The history of sexuality: Vol. 1. An introduction.* New York: Vintage.

Foucault, M. (1991a). *The birth of the clinic: An archaeology of medical perception.* London: Routledge.

Foucault, M. (1991b). *The order of things: An archaeology of the human sciences.* London: Routledge.

Foucault, M. (1991c). Question of method. In G. Burchell, C. Gordon, & P. Miller (Eds.), *The Foucault effect: Studies in governmentality* (pp. 33–86). London, Toronto, Sydney, Tokyo, Singapore: Harvester/Wheatsheaf.

Goodlad, J. I., & Su, Z. (1992). Organization of the curriculum. In P. W. Jackson (Ed.), *Handbook of research on curriculum* (pp. 327–344). New York: Macmillan.

Hartley, D. (1986). Structural isomorphism and the management of consent in education. *Journal of Education Policy, 1*(3), 229–237.

Hatcher, R. (1994). Market relationships and the management of teachers. *British Journal of Sociology of Education, 15*(1), 41–61.

Heikkinen, S., Silvonen, J., & Simola, H. (1996). *Technologies of truth: Peeling Foucault's triangular onion.* Unpublished manuscript.

Hlebowitsh, P. S. (1992). Amid behavioural and behaviouristic objectives: Reappraising appraisals of the Tyler rationale. *Journal of Curriculum Studies, 24*(6), 533–547.

Hovi, R., Kivinen, O., & Rinne, R. (1989). *Komitealaitos, koulutusmietinnöt ja koulutuspolitiikan oikeutus* [Institution of the Government Committee and the Justification of Educational Policy in Committee Reports]. Turku: University of Turku. (Annales Universitatis Turkuensis ser. C, tom. 73.)

Hunter, I. (1994). *Rethinking the school.* New York: St. Martin's Press.

Kansanen, P. (1995). The Deutsche didaktik. *Journal of Curriculum Studies, 27*(4), 347–352.

Kliebard, H. (1975). The Tyler rationale. In W. F. Pinar (Ed.), *Curriculum theorizing: The reconceptualists.* Berkeley: McCutchan.

Kliebard, H. M. (1995). The Tyler rationale revisited. *Journal of Curriculum Studies, 27*(1), 81–88.

Lawn, M., & Ozga, J. (1986). Unequal partner: Teachers under indirect rule. *British Journal of Sociology of Education, 7*(2), 225–238.

Lingard, B. (1990). Accountability and control: A sociological account of secondary school assessment in Queensland. *British Journal of Sociology of Education, 11*(2), 171–188.

Lundgren, U. P. (1991). *Between education and schooling: Outlines of a diachronic curriculum theory.* Geelong, Australia: Deakin University.

Mac an Ghaill, M. (1992). Teachers' work: Curriculum restructuring, culture, power and comprehensive schooling. *British Journal of Sociology of Education, 13*(2), 177–199.

Madaus, G. F., & Stufflebeam, D. (Eds.). (1989). *Educational evaluation: Classic works of Ralph W. Tyler.* Boston: Kluwer Academic.

Meyer, J. W. (1986). Types of explanation in the sociology of education. In J. G. Richardson (Ed.), *Handbook of theory and research for the sociology of education* (pp. 341–359). Westport, CT: Greenwood Press.

Miettinen, R. (1990). *Koulun muuttamisen mahdollisuudesta* [On the possibility for change in schooling]. Helsinki: Gaudeamus.

Popkewitz, T. S. (1991). *A political sociology of educational reform: Power/Knowledge in teaching, teacher education, and research.* New York: Teachers College Press.

Rinne, R. (1986). *Kansanopettaja mallikansalaisena: Opettajuuden laajeneminen ja opettajuuteen rekrytoimismekanismit Suomessa 1851–1986 virallisen kuvausaineiston ilmaisemana* [Teacher of the common people as the model citizen: Expansion of teacherhood and the recruitment to the teacherhood in Finland from 1851 to 1986 as expressed in the official documents] (Research Reports A: 108). Turku: University of Turku, Faculty of Education.

Rinne, R. (1987). Has somebody hidden the curriculum? The curriculum as a point of intersection between the utopia of civic society and the state control. In P. Malinen & P. Kansanen (Eds.), *Research frames of the Finnish curriculum*

(Research Report 53; pp. 95–116). Helsinki: University of Helsinki, Department of Teacher Education.

Rinne, R. (1988a). The formation and professionalization of the popular teachers in Finland in the 20th century. In T. Iisalo & R. Rinne (Eds.), *Läraren i 1900-talets kultur och samhälle* (Report B: 26). University of Turku, Department of Education.

Rinne, R. (1988b). Kansan kasvattajasta opetuksen ammattilaiseksi: Suomalaisen kansanopettajan tie [From the educator of the people to a professional teaching: The path of the Finnish primary school teacher]. *The Finnish Journal of Education Kasvatus, 19*(6), 430–444.

Simola, H. (1993a). Educational science, the state and teachers: Forming the corporate regulation of teacher education in Finland. In T. S. Popkewitz (Ed.), *Changing patterns of power: Social regulation and teacher education reform in eight countries* (pp. 161–210). Albany: State University of New York Press.

Simola, H. (1993b). Professionalism and rationalism of hopes: Outlining a theoretical approach for a study on educational discourse. *International Studies in Sociology of Education, 3* (2), 173–192.

Simola, H. (1995). *Paljon vartijat: Suomalainen kansanopettaja valtiollisessa kouludiskurssissa 1860-luvulta 1990-luvulle* [The Guards of plenty: The Finnish teacher in state educational discourse from the 1860s to the 1990s] (Research Report 137). Helsinki: University of Helsinki, Department of Teacher Education.

Simola, H. (1996). From exclusion to self-selection: Notes on construction the modern citizenship through examination of behavior in Finnish compulsory schooling from 1866 to 1996. Paper presented at the international seminar State Regulation, Citizenship, and Democracy. Research Unit for the Sociology of Education, University of Turku, May 24–25, 1996.

Simola, H., Kivinen, O., & Rinne, R. (1996). Decontextualizing pedagogy: The rise of didactic closure in Finnish teacher education. In T. Sander & J. M. Vez (Eds.), *Life-long Learning in European Teacher Education. European Yearbook of Comparative Studies in Teacher Education* (pp. 188–214). Osnabrück: COMPARE-TE European Network. (Available also in ERIC Resources in Education, document number ED 399 243)

Smyth, J. (1991). International perspective on teacher collegiality: A labour process discussion based on the concept of teachers' work. *British Journal of Sociology of Education, 12*(3), 323–346.

Tyler, R. W. (1950). *Basic principles of curriculum and instruction.* Chicago: University of Chicago Press.

Weick, K. (1976). Educational organizations as loosely coupled systems. *Administrative Science Quarterly, 21*(1), 1–19.

Wise, R. I. (1976). The use of objectives in curriculum planning: A critique of planning by objectives. *Curriculum Theory Network, 5*(4), 280–289.

4

A History of the Present on Children's Welfare in Sweden: From Fröbel to Present-Day Decentralization Projects

KENNETH HULTQVIST

In this chapter my aim is to throw some light on what I believe is a change in the discourse about the child and modern childhood in Sweden, as a result of decentralization of the political rationality—a process that is taking place in the Western world at large but is perhaps more dramatic in Sweden because of its centralistic traditions. By "political rationality" I mean, roughly, the different ways through which political reason tries to insert itself in the world as a practice (see Rose, 1993). My view is a rather narrow segment of the sociopolitical field—the preschool and the child produced by it, the preschool child. I do not believe, however, that this is a disadvantage. At the base of the system of Swedish sociopolitical institutions there is quite broad agreement on the subject of how children and young people should be steered. From that viewpoint, the preschool child is used as a synecdoche, that is, a part that gives a perspective of the "whole."[1]

My inspiration comes mainly from Michel Foucault,[2] especially his elaborations on the theme of governmentality.[3] In this composite word, is contained the idea that power is not just power, but that all wielding of power

Foucault's Challenge: Discourse, Knowledge, and Power in Education. Copyright © 1998 by Teachers College, Columbia University. All rights reserved. ISBN 0-8077-3676-7 (pbk), ISBN 0-8077-3677-5 (cloth). Prior to photocopying items for classroom use, please contact the Copyright Clearance Center, Customer Service, 222 Rosewood Dr., Danvers, MA 01923, USA, tel. (508) 750-8400.

is accompanied by an attitude toward the object of power—a mentality. In Western society this mentality (or, as I call it alternatively, rationality) is mainly of a liberal character. The liberal political rationality is multifaceted, but one of its important characteristics is that it attempts to respect the individuality and nature of its objects, while it also attempts to fulfill its purposes and aim. It is this position on the wielding of power that creates the opportunity for the development of knowledge in modern times (see Hindess, 1993). From the very moment that such a rationality presents itself in history, power must be wielded against a background of knowledge about what is to be controlled—a child, a family, an economy, a society, and so on.

On a fundamental level, liberal rationality is straightforward and uncomplicated—all wielding of power is to be done in relation to "natures"— but in practice things are different. Nature can be understood, on the one hand, as the reality to which knowledge refers, and, on the other hand, as a construction or an ideal worthy of pursuit. As Hindess (1993) points out, there are hardly any clear delineations between these two definitions. The concepts exist in order to manifest a distinction, but the contents of this distinction have been changed continuously during the liberal era. With the aid of the governmental theme, Foucault, as pointed out by Popkewitz and Brennan in Chapter 1, vaults over a long tradition to define human emancipation in education and child raising—the child as a given natural creation just waiting to be liberated. School, education, training, and similar social activities, then, not only are concerned with reality; they contribute, in their capacities as depositories of political rationalities, to producing children and young people as subjects of particular ways of living.[4]

This is the insight I will apply to the preschool child. In the first section I report briefly on the set of problems that lays the foundations for Swedish preschool education, as well as for a new conception of the child—the preschool child. The premise of my historical description includes the idea that the preschool child is a product of a new method of leading children that inscribes a new political rationality. This rationality springs from and presupposes a deeply rooted concept that the child has two affiliations: on the one hand, the world of culture, and on the other, that of nature. This divided world played a central role in legitimizing various control rationalities, both within and outside the preschool. The second section of the chapter ties the preschool child to today's efforts to achieve decentralization—and thereby also a changed view of what children are, can be, and should be.[5] Before turning to history, though, I will introduce the Swedish welfare child, a child that is an integral part of the Swedish welfare model of the 1930s and 1940s. This child is still with us, although he or she is about to change.

To understand the formation of the Swedish welfare child, we need to consider the Swedish welfare model and its conception of social engineering.

The construction of the welfare model involves a shift not only in political institutions, but in the language of its institutions. Language is one of the key instruments when society and individuals change course in their social and political life.[6] Within the social sciences, the active role that language plays in securing and restructuring social practices and social relations has not always been considered. Clarence Karier (1986), for example, has shown in a series of interesting works how the pioneers of the social sciences introduced the necessary terminology for recreating and restructuring social and cultural life in America at the turn of the century. Everyone—George Herbert Mead, William James, John Dewey, Charles Sanders Pierce, and others—contributed to a secularization in culture and to the decentralization of the traditional thinking universe, which continues into our time. They were not necessarily writing about the truth itself in the world, but rather supplying rough drafts for our orientation in a secularized culture.[7]

There was a similar process in Sweden in the 1930s and 1940s when the Swedish welfare model was being created. When the social scientists entered the scene, they came mostly as a team in the construction of a series of welfare programs, such as the gigantic state investigations called the Population Commission and the Population Investigation.[8] This entire administrative apparatus served to hasten industrialization by creating a social infrastructure that corresponded to the direction of movement of the times.

In this process of change, social scientific thinking played a much more active role than is indicated in the internal history of the social sciences. Social scientific thinking involves problematizing and diagnosing current problems, and finding ways to solve them. A rather good example of this is the important role that Alva and Gunnar Myrdal played in creating the Population Commission and the Population Investigation.[9] Their influential book *The Crisis in the Population Question* (1934) created an opening for a wider merger between politics and the social sciences, a merger that had important consequences for viewing adults/children.

The Myrdals were not empty-handed when they entered the Swedish scene. First of all, there were the social reforms and the network of social institutions that had been initiated in the beginning of this century. Elementary schooling was being established; social welfare, as well as child psychiatry and other modern types of institutions, were beginning to take shape. Yet another circumstance should be pointed out. It has to do with the role that the Swedish *folkrörelse* (national movements) played in this development. The temperance movements, labor movements, and the evangelic church organizations produced a great number of practices that, despite wide differences in the goals and social status of their members, have in common a new view on the individual's relationship to society. At the core of this new liberal and free view is an individual who is autonomous in his or her relationship to individual life circumstances—but who simultaneously, on the strength of being an individual, can participate in a larger social and cultural community, home district, nation, or international organization (Ambjörnsson, 1987; also see Larsson, 1994). This is the social matrix from which the welfare model of the 1930s and 1940s was created. Second, as mentioned above, there was a new vocabulary in use for depicting and implementing what had become a more distant relation between the individual and society, the best expression of which is the language of the "people's home" (see Hultqvist, 1990). In the language of the people's home, the individual is depicted both as a universal being (a citizen and a member of the nation) and as a private being, tied to his or her private or personal existence (i.e., his or her own family home). Through the contribution of the Myrdals and others, these elements of the past were remolded and put to use in a new historical context.

The starting point for the Myrdals' book was that Swedish society during the 1930s went through a modernization process, a process that they considered to be natural and inevitable. However, modernization was impeded by antiquated organizational forms and a way of thinking about the individual and society that the Myrdals associated with the liberalism of the 1800s and its strong emphasis on the individual. The weakness in the liberal viewpoint was, according to the authors, its inability to see the connection between the individual's well-being and that of the population on the whole. The effects of the liberal rule were noted on all levels of society—on the population level in the forms of decreasing nativity and an uneven distribution of age groups, and on the individual and family level in the form of a laxity in attitudes and mentality. These factors produced the risk of Sweden falling behind in international competition, which also had consequences for the individual citizen. To prevent this situation—and that is the main point of the Myrdals' book—individuality must be organized into a social form backed by the state. Through a wide network of institutions of social security, public health and sick care, and education (preschool, school, social care), the kind of person able to carry Sweden forward in the new era would be created. Envisioned was a highly qualified individual characterized by the norms that lead to the welfare of the population as a whole and of the individual: *omnium et singulorum* to allude to the proud motto of the Enlightenment tradition.

The population question, as it was framed by the Myrdals, became the prism through which a series of problems of the 1930s and 1940s were seen and acted upon. This new way of seeing made possible new political combinations and a framework within which the welfare policy could operate.

This framework provided the conditions of possibility for the social sciences. The social sciences contributed to and became permeated by the new mentality,

> the purpose of which was to achieve economic growth through the agency of social policy guided by the ideas of prevention, where the whole nation is responsible for the children that are about to become the next generation. It is through the realization of such a society that it will be possible to erode the narrow kind of individualism that has become part of the daily life of the citizens and which now is a threat to its existence. . . . The population question is first of all a sociological problem, a sociopsychological problem, a sociopedagogical problem, and at last a problem of social politics. (Myrdal & Myrdal, 1934, pp. 16–18)

A whole new language took shape. Children's growth, to give an example, was incorporated into a psychological language that provided the set of norms through which it became possible to distinguish human differences. What could be expected of children at different ages? Will they succeed or will they fall below the achievement norms set by the school or other institutions? In a similar manner youths' crises and trials became characterized as adolescent problems and were acted upon as such.[10]

For the Myrdals' generation, questions of values and ethics belonged to the order of politics, while the social sciences became a neutral instrument of change, an art of social engineering to be compared with instrumental reason (see Habermas, 1967). Gunnar Myrdal (1931), one of the most influential advocates of this mentality, has described this particular position in the following way:

> That which was for the most part a common political ideology (social liberalism, that is the kind of updated form of liberalism I referred to earlier) had the effect of making socio-political discussion gain a very peculiar air of objectivity. These questions come to be treated by experts—experts on unemployment, housing issues, prostitution etc. (p. 13)

Equipped with a universal rational knowledge, these social engineers "were to calculate and regulate social, economic and moral affairs" (Popkewitz, 1996a, p. 29).

Clearly the idea of a neutral expertise is an ideology in the Marxist sense of the word. But there is more to it than that. The language of expertise also improves the technical capacity of government. Formal theories, the scale, the tabula, and written reports are not only scientific tools, but also media of communication that simplify the task of transmitting knowledge from one center of calculation to another, that is, from the periphery of a local preschool or school to a distant administrative center, where the knowledge will be put to use in some regulatory scheme (see Latour, 1987, 1988). The introduction and distribution of this language across the social field during the 1930s and 1940s probably was the most significant contribution of the social science expertise. Deployed through the framework of the welfare state, this language opened up a new social space for the rational government of individuals, families, and the population; to reverse the statement, the "objective" social sciences were a condition for this kind of government. In the name of welfare, the private was redefined as part of social space, which made possible new forms of interventions in the lives of individuals and families. The social sciences inserted themselves within this social space, and in doing so they helped to produce the kind of individuality of which they spoke.

The governing schemes of the 1930s and 1940s made a difference with regard to the past, but they were not the first of their kind. Concern for the population and for the individual—in terms of health and longevity—extends further back in time, to the eighteen and nineteenth centuries (Beronius, 1994). Gradually there developed a politics of life, or to use the words of Foucault, a bio-politics, first under the cover of a moral language and later in the shape of the social sciences. For Foucault (1977; see also Bell, 1995) bio-politics is the name for a political strategy, the aim of which is to enhance and control the forces of life. Preschool (like school and other modern institution) is part of that development. In the beginning of this century when the preschool movement in Sweden took off, preschool was not involved in the formal system of government, but even so it played a role with regard to it. Furthermore, the ideas of how to govern the child was developed and put to use in relation to that system, sometimes even in opposition to it.[11] I will argue that this opposition emerged from within a kind of bio-political reasoning. The pre-school child, then, is about social regulation, that is about the regulation and construction of the child as an agent of change in relation to "administrative patterns found in larger society" (see, e.g., Popkewitz, 1996a, 1996b). Consequently, I will argue that the "history" of the preschool child is not about a preexisting object, but about the ever-changing rationalities for government.

I will now turn to my historical case, the preschool child that was constructed at the beginning of this century. This child shares many of the characteristics of the welfare child of the 1930s and 1940s. I would even say that this child is still part of our present. I will refer to the *barnträdgården* (kindergarten). The name alludes partly to a journal having the same name, which in the early 1900s was the "mouthpiece" for the Swedish preschool movement, and partly to the preschool program that was taking shape at this point. The great figure in this context is the German pedagogue and philosopher Friedrich Fröbel, who developed the idea of a kindergarten. Fröbel's romantic conception of children's nature as well as his ideas of a kindergarten gained a foothold in Sweden as well as in many other Western countries at the turn of the century.

KINDERGARTEN AND THE MORAL CRISIS

The preschool child was constructed in a time of dissolution as modernization swept away the old—customs, traditions, the order of authority, indeed everything connected with the small-scale society. There was anxiety about the breaking up of the family, and anxiety for all the children who wandered around in the streets without adult supervision. On society's main stage the battle for equality between the sexes was being fought, and there was "a ferment of hatred and jealously between the social classes" (*Barnträdgården*, 1918, p. 17); nothing, not even the most private, could escape the dissolution of the times.

The kindergarten teachers saw the signs of dissolution and moral decay in all corners of social life. The preschool was a site of battle for the child:

> Do not go with the current, but follow time instead if you want to keep yourself young in the battle. If the current takes you, it will devour you, and if times goes away from you, it can't take you. . . . Oh, mankind, like a fall storm fleeing over the earth, never tied by your heart. You who desire to be curious all your life, but who forget the source of life, seek yourself in God, and be calm. (Wulff, 1922, pp. 4–5)[12]

I believe that these lines capture what is essential about kindergarten. Kindergarten is a program to remedy the disorder in the outer social world (or community) as well as in the inner world of the subject. In fact, it is a program for connecting one with the other. I also will suggest that neither of these entities—the community or the child—pre-exists the discourses or programs from which they emanate. Kindergarten, then, is a positive and creative program, with the aim of reorganizing the souls (or psyches) of children to the demands of a new age. The reorganization of the family was also on the agenda. New principles for the government of the family evolved from this program and were put into practice, partly with the help of the preschool child him/herself—who was supposed to bring some order and reason into the home—and partly through organizing parents' meetings. As I have suggested elsewhere, this twofold commitment—to the child and to the family— is part and parcel of a broader concern with mobilization of the community at large (the people's home idea).

Central to kindergarten is a new idea about wielding power. As suggested above, the struggle for the child concerns the relation between the child—his or her inner life or identity—and the social environment. We must be tied both to our hearts and to this turbulent modern world from which there is no escape. This is the recurrent theme in the journal *Barnträdgården*. The emerging ideas of power are related to this context:

> The power of the law and financial security means a lot, but the spirit among those working with children is more significant than the decisions made by the parliament or the words of the law. (*Barnträdgården*, 1927, pp. 3–4)

Envisioned was an individual both capable and willing to contribute to the building up of modern society—which includes the task of building up the subjects themselves. This task could be accomplished neither through the use of brute force nor through the "words of the laws," but only through a strategy of regulated freedom, the aim of which was to guide and develop the actions of free subjects. The kindergarten is, to associate it with modern terminology, a psychosocial construction, a construction for the managing of "souls" and social relations.

On a comprehensive level, kindergarten (and the childhood project at large) deals with reconciling that which has been divided in modern society—male and female, social and cultural gaps—to find a formula for the set of problems of change and stability. The unity for this is found in the shape of a children's garden or, in German, *Kindergarten*. Through the language of gardening, the social divisions of the twentieth century were arranged in the shape of a simple opposition between nature and culture, or between what is natural to all human beings—their natural freedom[13]—and what is specific to the cultural and social life-form (community) the program is directed at. For lack of better words, I would like to characterize the life-form pertinent to this program as a socioliberal way of living. To fulfill such a program—that is, to make it legitimate on its own terms—knowledge about the child and the child's nature is needed.

Several connections may be found between this variant of socioliberal thinking and the one developed by the Myrdals and others during the 1930s and 1940s, the most salient of which is the very strong attempt to naturalize the existing order. However, there are also differences. The kindergarten was still concerned with a discourse that strongly emphasized so-called ultimate moral values[14] (what is good and bad and what is right and wrong). It was not yet built around scientific norms and experties. Viewed from the standpoint of the 1930s and 1940s, kindergarten still lacked the technical language of expertise, that is, a language for governing at a distance. The kindergartners clearly were able to run a practice; they could even transmit this practical knowledge to their colleagues, but the way they spoke about the child or about other aspects of their pedagogical practice—mostly in metaphors—could not be transmitted easily to administrative centers or other centers of calculation and computation (Latour, 1987, 1988; also see Popkewitz, 1996a;

Rose, 1994). I will pursue this line of thought in a forthcoming study (Hult-qvist, 1997).

A New Way of Thinking

So far I have suggested that kindergarten is partly about the construction of subjectivity and partly about the construction of community. What is sought is the kind of individual that freely conducts him/herself in accordance with the laws and social norms of the community. I also have suggested that "community" for the kindergartners is something akin to the peoples home, a home for each and all. Kindergarten is one of the links in the peoples home; other examples are the family and the school.

From this broader approach a series of considerations emerged regarding pedagogical practice. This is very apparent in the journal *Barnträdgården*. It is crammed with examples about the rethinking of community and the subjective lives of children. Even the position of the adult with regard to the child becomes an object of reflection. The following is one of the more inventive:

> He (Liegthart) tells the students about his own boyish pranks—which are not such tame ones—and allows them to enjoy the excitement of them, magnified by the knowledge that it is their teacher who has done this. Then he allows them to judge him. He greets a new pupil who has been expelled from another school because he played hooky, with these words: "Aha! You've played hooky! I did that when I was your age, so I understand. You can go to my school, but on the condition that you play hooky again if you think it's boring here." (The boy's father thought that the school-inspector had gone mad, but the boy came to school and never played hooky again.) (*Barnträdgården*, 1922, pp. 2.1–2.2)

This draft for a new pedagogical practice is paradigmatic. It contains all the "elements" upon which the kindergarten is built. Authority climbs down from its pedestal and stands beside the pupil. Indeed, the relationship becomes quite comradely. This stepping down is also the condition for power's so-called positivity, that is, for the ability to do positive things like making the pupil feel sympathetic toward the school's order and toward comrades as authorities. The example of the sympathetic teacher also demonstrates another central action in the modern wielding of power—the emphasis on freedom. The pupil should not be forced into the classroom. On the contrary, free will is stressed—the pupil is encouraged to play hooky when he needs to. The thinking behind this power play is, of course, that the pupil should be encouraged to govern him/herself in accordance with the norms and values of the school.

This attitude is radically different from an older type of wielding power.

Instead of prescribing, deciding, and interfering, "training should be generally more positive, supervising and correcting" (Fröbel, n.d.).[15]

I would like to stress once more that this changed view of power is not unique to the preschool area. A new rationality for the wielding of power makes its way throughout the entire social field, a rationality that includes a new mentality or position on the so-called human issues. This position takes shape with the increasing insight that modern social life rests more and more on the individual's own self-regulating capacities and willingness to conform. The following example, which I take from *Söderpojken* (boy from the southern part of Stockholm), a yearly bulletin from the YMCA in Stockholm,[16] can serve as an illustration of how this power mentality expresses itself in the "youth council":

> The undersigned hereby applies for membership in the YMCA Söders boys' section in Stockholm, as I wish to be a member of a Christian organization and to take advantage of those benefits accorded such a member. I wish to volunteer my services in the section, as well as always try to be truthful and clean in thought, word, and deed, and work to develop my body, soul, and spirit, and to use my influence among my comrades to the furtherance of that which is right, good, and true (Contract for Entrance into the YMCA). . . . If, however, the newcomer objects to signing such a contract, he can cross out whatever he wishes to leave out. It is important that he knows right away that the YMCA does not wish to interfere or put any undue pressure on his thinking or desires, but only wishes to expose him to other viewpoints and crossroads. He must make his own choices according to his own beliefs. (KFUM, 1930, p. 63)

As in the former example, the new way of life is built upon the idea that goodness in the world (community) is the result of freedom of choice and the will to truth—in this case enhanced by the act of signing a contract (which is, of course, typical of the liberal tradition).

Searching for the Good Nature

The ideas of Fröbel were a source of inspiration for the pioneers. They even named their organization after the German pedagogue (The Swedish Fröbel Organization). However, the attention and respect that was paid to Fröbel cannot be accounted for only in terms of the quality of his pedagogical system. My suggestion is that Fröbel's success is due to the emergent governmentality at the turn of the century.

It is hard to say to what extent Fröbel's ideas or his pedagogical tools, the so-called Fröbel gifts,[17] influenced practice. Also, many of his ideas were transformed by others before they reached Sweden; in fact, many of the pedagogical inventions that we today associate with the name of Fröbel are only distantly related to him (see Johansson, 1994). Bearing this in mind, I believe that it is rather safe to assume that Fröbel's ideas (transformed by others or not) became a vital resource for the kindergartners as regulatory ideals, that is, concerning how to govern the child from a "natural" point of view.

There are two lines of thought in Fröbel's writings that caught the interest of the pioneers. One of these is the development of the child. Fröbel sees development as a natural process and, as in modern developmental psychology's theory formation, he holds that development takes place in sequences or stages. The second line of thought is the child's inherent goodness. The idea is that "evil" happens to the child from the outside, in the form of unhealthy environments, poverty, bad upbringing, and so on. Evil is therefore not natural; it is a deviation from the natural state. If man is inherently anything, then he is de facto good.

In this formula, Fröbel articulates the view of knowledge that is connected to the change in the wielding of power. It is no longer a case of limiting the spread of evil in the world, but rather of laying the foundation for the victory of good. As Walkerdine (1984) points out, even current developmental psychology's theory formation is based on similar ideas.

It is thus upon these two elements of thinking (the natural and the good) that the preschool child is built. By referring to the developmental thoughts, it can be claimed that training aims at supporting an inherent tendency in development; and with the argument about goodness, it can be claimed that what is natural is good. That is the essence of kindergarten. The preschool should be a blossoming garden for children. The child is compared to a plant, which with the proper care will grow into the beautiful flower it was meant to be. The metaphor structures the educator's job of being a gardener in God's nature. The educator nourishes the plant and pulls out all the weeds that threaten to invade the garden.

The Natural and the Normal

Fröbel's interpretation goes hand in glove with set of problems that were of concern to the pioneers. If the child/human being is good, then half the victory is won. The rest will be won with the help of modern directed pedagogical practice.

However, the problem is that the basis for this enterprise, the set of moral problems, never becomes the object reflected upon. "Grass" and "weeds" are discussed, but there is a fundamental obscurity about the social and cultural bases of these classifications. Who or what decides which is grass and which are weeds? Or, to be very clear about it, who or what decides what is true/false, good/evil, beautiful/ugly, and so forth?

The Fröbel child—the child in general—is, of course, not a solution for the problems facing the pioneers. Nor is this the strategic point of this construction. The preschool child does not denote anything real, but is a drafted plan for a new age, for a reality in the making, for when a more divine condition than that of the present has arrived. Consider this example of the child's missionary role in the building of the society:

> We make a false diagnosis when we assume that the intellect occupies the seat of honor in our times. On the contrary, it is darker, and we must be able to return to common sense. This can be done by going back to the child, that inspiring creature, that renewer of the race and the society. Let us come to the child like the Wise Men, laden with rich gifts and led by the star of hope. (*Barnträdgården*, 1934, p. 68)

The preschool child—the renewer of the race—is something of an historical zero, a dividing line in the so-called human development, when all the old trash is to be thrown overboard and replaced by something new and lasting.

At this stage it may be of interest to note that there are points of intersection between the moral discourse of the pioneers and the discourse of psychology. To illustrate this and to foreshadow the events of the 1930s and 1940s—when Fröbel was replaced by psychology—I will bring in the example of Maria Montessori. Montessori may not be a "mainstreamer" with regard to the Swedish context—she is too much concerned with the intellectual development of the child to fit the social profile of Swedish preschool—but her ideas about the child, especially the child's freedom, met a growing interest in Sweden during the 1930s. I do not believe that this was a coincidence. The freedom theme is what connects the moral language of the pioneers with the more technical language of the psychology of the 1930s and 1940s. In 1912, Montessori sketched the foundations of modern scientific pedagogy in the following way:

> The fundamental principle of scientific pedagogy must be, indeed, the liberty of the pupil—such liberty as shall permit a development of individual spontaneous manifestation of the child's nature. If a new and scientific pedagogy is to arise from the study of the individual such a study must occupy itself with the observation of free children. (p. 69)

Maria Montessori is an almost exemplary case of the modern connection between scientific building of knowledge and political reform programs. One is so interwoven with the other that the two can hardly be separated. On the one hand, she says, freedom is necessary if knowledge of the child is to be possible, and on the other hand, as we have noted, the same freedom is a tool for the political reform programs that will bring about the natural child, "that renewer of the race and the society" (Montessori, 1912, p. 69).

In another of Montessori's books, *The Secrets of Childhood* (1936), this connection is perhaps even more clear. A main theme of the book is "the nature of the child." This nature is, she says, a nearly unexplored landscape. We thus know very little, but what we do know indicates that there is more to find out. How can we know, however, that there is such a thing as the nature of the child, when we are so ignorant of its existence? Here Montessori (1936) not only is honest, but also expresses a new age's insight on the limitations of knowledge: "It is impossible to observe something that is not known, and it is not possible for anyone, by a vague intuition, to imagine that a child may have two natures, and to say: 'Now I will try to prove it by experiment.' Anything new must emerge, so to speak, by its own energies; it must spring forth and strike the mind, evoked by what we will call chance" (p. 124).

What was seen by Maria Montessori and her peers, a vision shaped by cultural and historical contingencies, was an embryonic child, a child still not liberated from an obstinate adult dominance (i.e., patriarchal order). With this, the discovery of the child's nature, on the strength of its moral charge, becomes not just an object of knowledge among others, but also an incitement to a fight for freedom; a fight, in Montessori's own words, to make the child normal. For Montessori and others, the natural child represented the vision of a normal state, while all praxis up to that point represented a deviation from this. Normal and natural, then, are interchangeable terms. To be normal is to be governed by natural tendencies (rules).

Maria Montessori thought that she had transcended the limits of history (by pure chance, to use her own expression), but the actual results of her efforts were in fact quite similar to Fröbel's ideas about good development. "Good" and the divine natural order have been replaced by "normal," and the battle for the good and the right can now and henceforth be waged in terms of normalization.

From the Good Nature to the Psychobiological Nature

Since the latter 1930s, there has been increasing demand for the modernization of preschool discourse. The center of the old discourse has disappeared. Everything has been set in motion, including the human subject itself:

> Life really has become a stage for us, where we enter and play out our parts, and leave when our roles end. The difference between us and the actor is that for us there is no director who can tell us ahead of time what to do. Nor is there a prompter who helps us with our dialogue when we lose our places. Each and every one must be on his guard himself, invent his own dialogue, and leave when his part is finished. (Gästrin, 1948, p. 85)

Thus we should rely on ourselves and our own abilities. A triumph for the Enlightenment project! It is not, of course, quite that easy or "good"; what we witness here is just another example of the "return of the old." In this case it is respect for the old order that is replaced by respect for a new deity, the psychobiological order:

> The most important general principle for all pedagogues, regardless of their other views, should be that they promote the children's sound development in both body and soul. To be able to do this it is necessary to have thorough knowledge of the laws of development, since both the children's physical development and their spiritual development are bound by laws. Respect for the laws of nature is an imperative requirement. (Ulin, 1951, p. 128)

We encounter these sentiments in Alva Myrdal's influential book *Stadsbarn* (1934). In this book, whose title means city children, Myrdal sketches a modern preschool program, liberated from Fröbel's "Metaphysics." The ties to the past remain, however, just as in the case of Carin Ulin, despite Myrdal's energetic appeals for a rational upbringing on a scientific basis. This discursive foundation was adopted later by the first national reports in this area, the so-called Barnkrubbor och Sommarkolonier (day nurseries and summer camps), and several others, before it finally reached, in the 1970s, the so-called Barnstugeutredningen (Day-Care Center Report) (1972).[18]

The differences that exist between the Day-Care Center Report and its predecessors are differences not so much of basic patterns as of "levels of abstraction." Concerning *Stadsbarn*, for example, the historical context is present in the form of constant references to the great changes in society. As time goes on, however, these connections are sketchier, and in the Day-Care Center Report the historical context has nearly disappeared. The child is introduced as a purely psychological creature, without connections to either "society" or history. Perhaps this freely floating existence is an expression of the hope that the twentieth-century child has finally found a home, the home that was lost in the era of great social change!

Finally, I would like to point out that there is discontinuity in this discourse production. The Fröbel child and the welfare children of the 1930s are not identical, even if they are similar. The Fröbel child is set into a moral order in which the goal of human development is perfection, in fact, to reach God under earthly conditions. The "fate" of the welfare child is not quite so divine. It belongs to a finite psychobiological order, subject to the conditions of normality. Beyond this transformation lie new observation techniques, research methods, and so on.[19]

The "outer" incitement for this change in discourse about the child is more closely connected to the construction of the modern welfare state during the 1930s and 1940s. The attempts at modernization, which I described earlier, constituted a break with the past, to the extent that the need for a vital population of energetic and healthy individuals was emphasized more than ever.

It is this bio-politics, as Foucault (1977) calls it, that psychological research uses as a lever when it becomes time to make a scientific object of the child. Psychology, in turn, actively contributes to this bio-politics and promotes it through its theories, research methods, and practical instruments (not the least of these being test psychology).[20] The psychology of the 1930s and 1940s is consistently comparable to a bio-political flood, where the actors on the stage of time compete with each other on referring to and cross-referencing everything said and thought about "the constitution," "sexual energy," "psychic energy," "giftedness," and so on.

This bio-political way of thinking is not, as I suggested earlier, completely new even in the area of the preschool. The idea of setting the subject in motion, of getting the subject to develop all his or her energy resources, was, however, incorporated in quite a different ideological context than that prevalent during the 1930s.[21]

A NEW ASSIGNMENT?

In this chapter I have used the discursive construction of the preschool child to gain a perspective on the welfare child, that is, on those types of discourses on children related to institutions dealing with welfare politics. These constructions of children—the preschool child, the school child, and others—are, of course, not alike in all respects. They do, however, have in common the fact that the discourses are grounded in the same basic terminology—the individual and society.

This way of thinking about the child/human being is perhaps most apparent within social liberalism, which has without doubt been the dominant political rationality in Sweden in this century. In its purest form, social liberalism is a synthesis between liberalism and socialism, between the emphasis on the one hand on the individual and his or her freedom, and on the other hand on community, solidarity, and justice. As a political rationality, social liberalism is foremost a language for the reformers of the order of things, but it also wields quite a decided influence on the pioneers of the social sciences. It should be pointed out, however, that social liberalism is not identical with expertise and the kind of welfare programs developed during the 1930s and 1940s. In the early part of this century, social liberalism was associated with other mentalities and with other ways of organizing practices. Kindergarten is an example of this. During the 1930s and 1940s these programs were coordinated and centralized within the framework of the welfare state. Even though the basic terminology, the individual and society, was preserved in that process, this terminology assumed quite a new meaning when it was incorporated into an area of society that increasingly was becoming the object of scientific knowledge and expertise. As I suggested before, the major difference is about language. To be able to govern at a distance, which is a prerequisite for modern forms of governing, knowledge is needed about the different parameters of the entity (a preschool, a school, or a child) to be governed. Furthermore, knowledge must be put in a language that makes it easy and safe to transport it from the "source" to an administrative center of calculation. The poetic language of kindergarten may have had many qualities, but it lacked the precision that was sought during the 1930s and 1940s. I also believe that this explains why the language of Fröbel was replaced by the language of the social sciences, in particular the language of developmental psychology. The language of psychology provided "the technology for rendering individualism [and sociability—K. H.] operable as a set of specific programmes for the regulation of existence" (see Rose, 1989, p. 31).

Today, this "scientific" formula of social liberalism is about to change. During the 1970s and 1980s some social changes took place that were based on another, more flexible view of the relationship between individuals and public institutions. What we are discussing here is the extensive process of decentralization that started in Sweden during the 1970s. At the heart of it is the relatively far-reaching attempt to mobilize individuals and organizations on all levels of society—the individuals themselves, of course, but also their families, relatives, voluntary organizations, and so forth—in order to better utilize society's resources. Concealed in this production is a new definition of an individual life's limits and responsibilities. It is easy to see the change[22] in linguistic usage by comparing the current national documents about children and young people with those produced in the post–World War II years (Hultqvist, 1990). In the latter documents freedom and personal responsibility are mentioned, but their meaning was guaranteed not by the individuals themselves but rather by a welfare state that was taking over responsibility for social issues. Also, new interpretations were brought out in the social sciences, which with all their dissimilarities have in common the emphasis on difference, variability, and instability. This change is part of a new power/knowledge agenda that I will call decentrism.

Decentrism is not an entirely new concept when compared with the political rationality of the 1930s and 1940s. But while earlier politics aimed at a detailed regulation of the political apparatus, decentrism is more about governing the actions of self-governing and autonomous individuals (Lindensjö & Lundgren, 1986; also see Popkewitz, 1996a). Formulation of goals is, as earlier, confined to the central political apparatus, but what is new is that the interpretation of those goals, as well as their realization, is the responsibility of the local actors. Governing now occurs in the shape of goal-steering practices (Popkewitz, 1996a). Related to this is the professionalization of governing systems of schools, preschools, and the social field at large. As I have suggested elsewhere (Hultqvist & Petersson, 1995b), this reinvention of political rationality is part of a broader concern over mobilizing and making effective use of society's resources.

In the concluding part of the chapter, I will argue that the reinvention of political rationality in the 1990s also has an impact on discourse and practices of childhood. I will suggest that the locale for the inscribing of this rationality is on the one hand the nature of the child, and on the other the child's social environment. Within this discourse, nature provides the raw material for development, while the social environment (the family, the preschool, the school, etc.) stimulates and nurtures the child's development.

DECENTRISM AND THE REINVENTION OF THE CHILD

Fundamentals ought to behave as fundamentals. We expect the sun to rise every morning and we also expect that Newton's apple will continue to fall to earth. However, if we take a closer look at the fundamentals of the preschool child, they do not seem to behave like fundamentals. They are more like mobile constants. There is, as we have seen, a huge gap between the Fröbel child and the psychological child of the 1930s; the former is a moral actor of God's natural order, while the latter belongs to the biological order. Even the psychological child is not entirely consistent. During the 1930s, discourse was about maturation and inborn sequences of development (e.g., Gesell and Ulin). In this discourse, the child's own activities were governed by the "laws of nature." What the child did or did not do, had no significant effect on his or her development. The discourse of maturation prevailed until the 1950s and 1960s, when a slightly different discourse emerged that stressed the importance of the child's own activities. According to Jean Piaget, the activities of the child were important since they fed back into the developmental sequence. This made the child co-responsible for his or her own development. Likewise, the new discourse positioned the adult as an active agent, able to guide and influence the actions of the developing child.

From the 1970s onwards, there has been another move within this "unmovable" discourse about nature. We are now about to construct a discourse (and practices) in which (1) both the environment and the child are becoming more active and (2) the boundaries between "nature" and "environment" tend to overlap and become blurred. I will use the contextual child as an illustration.

Until the 1970s all children were universal children. The Fröbel child was a universal child, as was Piaget's. There were no exceptions to that rule.

During the latter 1970s, this changed! Perhaps the most important sign here is the critique of the stage model in Piaget's theory, a model that assumed that development is universal. The critiques relied on new empirical data that tended to show that development was much more varied and unpredictable than the stage model prescribed (Callewaert & Kallos, 1976; also see Kallos, 1979). Contextual factors (e.g., home environmental conditions, the pedagogics of the local preschool, the local surroundings, etc.) were invoked to explain this variation. Today, the idea of context is everywhere; it has permeated research (Pramling, 1983, 1994), higher education (Hultqvist & Petersson, 1995b), and the preschool sector (Förskola-skola, 1985).

The idea of an active environment is now accompanied by another important idea, namely, the child as capable; another version of the autonomous child. The idea of capacity, which I borrow from Basil Bernstein, replaces the idea of competence[23] (i.e., Piaget). Capacity enables the child to respond flexibly to the demands of a changing external world (i.e., economics or the market). According to Bernstein, the idea of capacity emerges "where life experience cannot be based on stable expectations of the future and one's location in it" (see Bernstein, 1996, p. 72). Of course, we still believe with John Stuart Mill, David Hume, and others, that children must be civilized— brought to a state of culture—before they can enter the world of obligations and rights. That is why we need pedagogy and education. However, during the last two decades or so, this idea about the child as capable has emerged. Children seem to be able to do a lot of things they are not supposed to be able to do—they can read and write at a much earlier age than before; they can go to school at age 6 (not age 7, as we are used to in Sweden); they can be granted more responsibility, both with regard to the adult world and in relation to their peers; and they are supposed to be *increasingly able to respond flexibly to the demands of an unstable and changing world* (see Popkewitz, 1996a). These new ideas are now elaborated within different fields, especially in research based on constructivistic and pragmatic ideas, and preschool practices themselves (see, e.g., Dahlberg & Åsén, 1994; Dencik, 1995; Kristjànsson, 1995; Näsman, 1995).

To conclude my argument in this section, I will make a few suggestions concerning the ways in which this conceptual development inscribes the new political rationality in self-governing practices of individuals.

Basically, decentrism is a rationality for governing through what perhaps may be called the responsivity of the subjects (Rose, 1994; also see Hultqvist & Petersson, 1995a, 1995b; Popkewitz, 1996a). This presupposes a subject who knows not only how to follow universal rules (the welfare subject) but also how to interpret them and apply them with regard to continuously changing circumstances or contexts. Today, the preschool and other parts of the social field are saturated with concepts like context, silent knowledge, and practical knowledge; those are the kinds of concepts that inscribe the new political rationalities in practice. The mechanisms for this are on the one hand reflection—constant reflection about practical knowledge and its conditions—and on the other the will to recover and conceptualize the silent undercurrents of knowledge.[24] Theoretically this is a futile "program." Practical knowledge can never exceed its own limits, as these limits are immanent in the distinction between practical and theoretical knowledge. But this fact has now turned into a productive advantage. The decentered person of today is confronted by the endless task of chasing his or her own shadow (which is always elusive). This may be a (very) successful "method" to deal with scarce resources.

Decentrism may be more about adults and youth, but, as I have suggested, the child seems to be following a similar route. Obviously, there is a close affinity between the ideas of community and the autonomous individual on the one hand, and the corresponding ideas within the psychology of development on the other. This and similar examples suggest that the map of childhood is about to be slightly redrawn. It will be redrawn through research about the child (the contextual child), through the way we instruct our preschool teachers, and through the way we organize and reorganize the pedagogical space of preschools and schools, a space that acts as a relay for concepts like autonomy and self-realization.

CONCLUSIONS

Many working within the field of preschool research (see, e.g., Tallberg-Broman, 1991; also see Johansson, 1994) are of the opinion that today's preschool in Sweden belongs to the Fröbel tradition. Following tradition, they also believe that the child is governed by "laws of nature," first discovered by the great pioneers like Rousseau, Pestalozzi, and Fröbel, and later by the psychologist. I will not deny that there is something to both parts of this argument. I do not think, however, that such arguments can deal with the facts of change that I have considered in this chapter. For example, how do we account for the fact that the nature of the child keeps changing all the time? Reference to the object (the child per se) will not do, and the idea of internal development or evolution of ideas is probably not much better. Instead of retreating into either of these positions, I have argued that the preschool child (and the welfare child) is related to the changing rationalities of government. From this point of view, there are no necessary links—in terms of tradition—between the child of the kindergarten or the child of the 1930s and 1940s, and the preschool child of today. Of course, there are links in the sense that we today use ideas of the past to construct our own actuality. I will conclude this chapter with a few examples.

Today, there is a growing interest in ethical and moral issues. There are debates about these issues at different levels of the school system (Colnerud & Granström, 1994), and there also is a growing interest in ethical questions within the field of research (Hultqvist & Petersson, 1995b) and in Läroplaner (curricula) (Skola för Bildning, 1992), to give a few examples. This points to a link between 1990s and the kindergarten project at the turn of the century. But this should not be overstated. Today's issues are part and parcel of decentrism and the increasing professionalism (and the need for a code of conduct) at all levels of the governing system. There are also links between the metaphorical language of Fröbel and the somewhat hermeneutic style of expression in today's curricula for schools and preschools (Skola för Bildning, 1992). Even so, today's qualitative language is different from Fröbel's. It is used not to recall the order of God but to inscribe the rationalities connected with the goal-steering practices of the 1990s. It is a language that works "in a flexible environment that contains a constant flux" (Popkewitz, 1996a, 1996b p. 10).

What we are witnessing today is not the repetition of the past, but the construction of the present. Elements drawn from the past are utilized as links in the ongoing reconstruction of the welfare state model, a model that was initiated by the Swedish national movements and the pioneers of the modern institutional network at the beginning of this century. No one can make any absolute predictions as to how the new socioliberal life-form (Hindess, 1993) will look, but we can perhaps conjecture that it will be inhabited by free autonomous subjects. We should observe, though, that this freedom and autonomy do not belong to the individual per se, but rather create links for the development of a new political rationality.

NOTES

1. For a discussion on the methodological points of the synecdoche concept, see Richardson (1990).

2. I should point out that I perceive Foucault's works as both a continuation of and a radicalizing of the Enlightenment's great legacy. Perhaps the most concise expression of this may be found in Foucault's article "What Is Enlightenment," published in, among other places, *Power/Knowledge* (Gordon, 1980). There are, of course, other opinions on this issue. See Habermas (1987).

3. The subject of governmentality has been treated thoroughly in Burchell, Gordon, and Miller (1991). Also see Barry, Osborne, and Rose (1993). In Swedish there is Hultqvist and Petersson (1995a).

4. There are, of course, limits to this argument, in the sense that human beings obviously "have a biology." No serious person would deny that, not even Foucault. The point, however, is that we will never know what these limits are in themselves, since our knowledge will always be influenced by, as Gordon (1980) puts it, our place

on an historical gradient of power/knowledge. Consequently, and this is the methodological moral of a history of the present, the study of ourselves must proceed from within our own history, the history that has made us what we are.

5. The material that I use to illustrate my line of reasoning is taken primarily from Hultqvist (1990). I also use a follow-up project (Hultqvist, 1993).

6. One of the most prominent advocates of this sort of view is neo-pragmatism, represented by Richard Rorty (1979, 1989, 1991).

7. From a rather different point of view, Nikolas Rose has drawn a similar picture, in this case of the modern child and developmental psychology's growth in England and the United States. See Rose (1985, 1989).

8. These investigations introduced the so-called Swedish Model, which is assumed to be based on a harmonization of social interest and the economy, of society and the marketplace. During this period several economists played an important role in launching this project. The most significant was, of course, John Maynard Keynes, but Gunnar Myrdal, Bertil Ohlin, and others were also influential. This phase of Sweden's social development has been commented upon and written about by many. In Swedish there is Ulf Cervin (1975). In English there is, for instance, Carlson (1989).

9. In many of the Myrdals' writings, especially *The Crisis in the Population Question*—which can be seen as a forerunner of the welfare programs of the 1930s and 1940s—they claimed that science and social techniques were the solution to the "social question." A series of works have been published in Sweden lately that focus on the Myrdals' role in this context. See, for example, Hirdman (1990), Larsson (1994), and Nilsson (1994).

10. The role of psychology in this connection has been described by Nikolas Rose (e.g., 1985, 1989). According to Rose, child and developmental psychology has been interpreted objectively, i.e., as an objective image of the child's development. It is because of this that the positive and productive role played by psychology in the description of the child, as an idea and as reality, has been underestimated. The nature that we thought was inscribed in the child in the shape of predetermined developmental sequences was inscribed in the child instead as a result of the scientific language and the system of observation techniques that reveal the child as a specific object for psychological science. Attaching these forms of description to pedagogy, child raising, and the administrative apparatus has a direct effect on children, their behavior, their attitudes, and their ideas.

11. One of the main targets for critique was the elementary school. From the point of view of the pioneers, the pedagogical traditions of schools were mainly restrictive and paid no attention to the vital needs of children. See Hultqvist, 1990.

12. Bertha Wulff was one of the pioneers of the Danish preschool movement.

13. In the preschool tradition, the nature of the child was an expression of the child's freedom and autonomy with regard to the adult world.

14. In the 1990s there is a renewed interest in so-called ultimate moral values. See, e.g., Skola för Bildning, 1992.

15. The effects of this transformation are very obvious. Instead of forbidding actions, a generalizing system of supervision is created. It aims at regulating and limiting the spread of "wrong" or immoral actions.

16. See KFUM (1930).

17. The Fröbel gifts are composed of different geometrical forms, like the sphere, the cylinder, and the cube. For Fröbel these forms reflect the basic structures of reality, its unity and transformation. Through play the child becomes aware of the objective structure of the gifts and also "develops an awareness of himself as an active human subject" (Johansson, 1994, p. 35). Fröbel's ideas are drawn mainly from German natural romantic philosophy.

18. The Day-Care Center Report (1972) is the most comprehensive report on preschool activities in Sweden. One of its main characteristics is the emphasis on psychological theory construction. The psychology of child development becomes applied psychology. Among the psychological theory constructions that play a part here, we can mention Jean Piaget's, on the child's cognitive development, and E. H. Eriksson's, on the child's psychosocial development.

19. One of the pioneers in this area was Carin Ulin. The so-called Pedagogiska seminariet (Pedagogical Seminary) at the Södra KFUK (Southern YWCA) in Stockholm was started on her initiative. Here Ulin carried out psychopedagogical research that was quite radical for Sweden. This and similar pioneer projects will be described in "Psychology Makes Its Appearance in the Preschool" (Hultqvist, 1993; see also Hultqvist, 1997). The great pioneer in this context is, of course, Arnold Gesell. Gesell's works, as well as those of Charlotte Bühler in Austria, set a fashion for many countries, and it was mainly these that gave Carin Ulin the impulses for her own pedagogical reform activities.

20. This theme will be developed in "Psychology Makes Its Appearance in the Preschool" (Hultqvist 1997).

21. The bio-political metaphors used by the preschool movement in the beginning of this century came mainly from the mining business. For example, the souls of children should be treated like precious metals. See Moberg and Moberg (1909). But there also are references to the "improvement of the race" (p. 18).

22. Today these themes are almost mandatory in official contexts. Mention can be made here of the Swedish "Youth Policy" bill (*Ungdomspolitik,* 1993), as well as the curriculum report Skola för Bildning (1992). Both give a good introduction to the "new" terminology.

23. Piaget's concept of competence concerns the generalized ability "to creatively create structures, i.e., creativity in the process of accommodation" (Bernstein, 1996, p. 56), while "capacity" is about the "set of general skills underlying specific performance" (Bernstein, 1996, p. 69).

24. A very good example of this idea of governing through the self-governing (and reflective) subject is the government report "Lärarutbildning i förändring" [Teachers' Education in Change], Utbildningsdepartementet, Ds, 1996: 16.

REFERENCES

Ambjörnsson, R. (1987). *Den skötsamme arbetaren* [The conscientious worker]. Stockholm: Carlssons.

Barnträdgården [Kindergarten]. (1918–1955). (Vols. 1–89/9).

Barry, A., Osborne, T., & Rose, N. (Eds.). (1993). Liberalism, neo-liberalism, and governmentality [Special issue]. *Economy and Society, 22* (3).

Bell, V. (1995). Bio-politik och incestens spöke: Sexualitet och/i familjen [Bio-politics and the ghost of incest: Sexuality and/in the family]. In K. Hultqvist & K. Petersson (Eds.), *Michel Foucault, namnet på en modern vetenskaplig och filosofisk problematik: Texter om maktens mentaliteter, psykologi, pedagogik, sociologisk medicin, feminism och politisk filosofi* [Michel Foucault, the name of a modern scientific set of problems: Texts on governmentality, psychology, pedagogics, sociological medicine, feminism, and political philosophy]. Stockholm: HLS Förlag.

Bernstein, B. (1996). *Pedagogy, symbolic control, and identity. Theory, research, and critique.* London: Taylor & Francis.

Beronius, M. (1994). *Bidrag till de sociala undersökningarnas historia: Eller till den vetenskapliggjorda moralens genealogi* [A contribution to the history of social investigations]. Lund/Stehag: Symposion Förlag.

Burchell, G., Gordon, C., & Miller, P. (Eds.). (1991). *The Foucault effect: Studies in governmentality.* Chicago: University of Chicago Press.

Callewaert, S., & Kallos, D. (1976). Den rosa vågen i Svensk pedagogik [The rose-colored wave in Swedish pedagogics]. *Forskning och Utbildning, 3*(1), 31–38.

Carlson, A. (1989). *The Swedish experiment in family politics: The Myrdals and the interwar population crisis.* London: Transaction.

Cervin, U. (1975). *Makarna Myrdal och befolkningsfrågan* [The Myrdals and the population issue] (Reports from the Historical Institute in Lund, No. 10). Lund: Meddelanden frîn Historiska Institutionen i Lund.

Colnerud, G., & Granström, K. (1994). *Respekt för lärare: Om lärares professionella verktyg-yrkesspråk och yrkesetik.* Stockholm: HLS Förlag.

Dahlberg, G., & Åsén, G. (1994). Evaluation and regulation: A question of empowerment. In P. Moss & A. R. Pence (Eds.), *Valuing quality in early childhood services: New approaches to defining quality* (pp. 157–171). New York: Teachers College Press.

Dencik, L. (1995). Modern childhood in the Nordic countries: "Dual socialization" and its implications. In L. Chrisholm, P. Büchner, H-H. Krüger, & M. du Bois-Reymond (Eds.), *Growing up in Europe* (pp. 105–119). Berlin/New York: de Gryuter.

Förskola del I och II, betänkande avgivet av 1968 års [Preschool parts I and II]. (1972). (Barnstugeutredningen, SOU [Reports of the 1968 Day-Care Center Investigation, Swedish Government Official Reports], Nos. 26 and 27). Stockholm: Allmänna Förlaget.

Förskola-skola. (1985). *Betänkande av Förskola-skola-kommitén* [Preschool–School] (Reports of the Preschool–School Committee, Swedish Governmental Official Reports, No. 22). Statens offentliga utredníngar [SOU], Stockholm.

Foucault, M. (1977). *Histoir de la sexualité* (Vol. I). Paris: Editions Gallimard.

Foucault, M. (1979). *Discipline and punish: The birth of the prison.* Harmondsworth: Penguin.

Fröbel, F. W. (n.d.). *Om uppfostran, dess mål och medel i allmänhet* [On upbringing, its aims and methods in general]. Norrköping: Municipal Archive Collection. (Swedish translation)

Gästrin, J. (1948). Självstudium och självuppfattning [Self-studies and self-awareness]. *Barnträdgården* [Kindergarten], 5, 85.

Gordon, C. (1980). *Power/Knowledge.* New York: Pantheon.

Habermas, J. (1967). *Zur logik der socialwissenschaften.* Tübingen: J.C.B. Mohr.

Habermas, J. (1987). *The philosophical discourse of modernity, twelve lectures.* Cambridge, MA: MIT Press.

Hindess, B. (1993). Liberalism, socialism, and democracy: Variations on a governmental theme. In A. Barry, T. Osborne, & N. Rose (Eds.), *Liberalism, neoliberalism, and governmentality, economy and society* (pp. 300–313). London: Routledge.

Hirdman, Y. (1990). *Att lägga livet tillrätta* [The streamlining of life]. Stockholm: Carlsons Bokförlag.

Hultqvist, K. (1990). *Förskolebarnet—En konstruktion för gemenskapen och den individuella frigörelsen, en nutidshistorisk studie om makt och kunskap i bilden av barnet i statliga utredningar om förskolan* [The preschool child—A construction for community and individual freedom]. Stehag/Stockholm: Symposion Förlag.

Hultqvist, K. (1993). *Psykologin gör entré i förskolan* [Psychology make its appearance in the preschool]. Forskningsprogram finansierat av HSFR.

Hultqvist, K. (1997). *Changing rationales for governing the child: A historical perspective on the emergence of the psychological child in the context of pre-school: Notes on a study in progress.* Manuscript submitted for publication.

Hultqvist, K., & Petersson, K. (Eds.) (1995a). *Michel Foucault, namnet på en modern vetenskaplig och filosofisk problematik: Texter om maktens mentaliteter, psykologi, pedagogik, sociologisk medicin, feminism och politisk filosofi* [Michel Foucault, the name of a modern scientific set of problems: Texts on governmentality, psychology, pedagogics, sociological medicine, feminism, and political philosophy]. Stockholm: HLS Förlag.

Hultqvist, K., & Petersson, K. (1995b). *Vad händer med synen på barndom och ungdom—Om postmodernism och polititisk rationalitet* [What is happening to the view of childhood and youth—On postmodernism and political rationality] (Didactica Minima, No. 32). Stockholm: HLS Förlag.

Johansson, J-E. (1994). *Svensk förskolepedagogik under 1900-talet* [The pedagogics of Swedish preschool during the twentieth century]. Lund: Studentlitteratur.

Kallos, D. (1979). *Den nya pedagogiken, en analys av den sk. dialogpedagogiken som svenskt samhällsfenomen* [The new pedagogics, an analysis of the so-called dialogue pedagogics as a Swedish phenomenon]. Stockholm: Wahlstrom & Widstrand.

Karier, C. J. (1986). *Scientists of the mind: Intellectual founders of modern psychology.* Champaign-Urbana: University of Illinois Press.

KFUM [YMCA]. (1930). *Söderpojken. Årskrift från Södra KFUM i Stockholm* [The YMCA South's boy section in Stockholm].

Kristjànsson, B. (1995). Vardandets barndom—(Be) varandets barnforskning. In L. Dahlgren & K. Hultqvist (Eds.), *Seendet och seendets villkor: En bok om barns och ungas välfärd* [Seeing and the conditions of seeing: A book about the welfare of children and youth] (pp. 29–59). Stockholm: HLS Förlag.

Larsson, J. (1994). *Hemmet vi ärvde* [The home we inherited]. Stockholm: Bokförlaget Arena.

Latour, B. (1987). *Science in action*. Cambridge, MA: Harvard University Press.

Latour, B. (1988). *The Pasteurization of France*. Cambridge, MA: Harvard University Press.

Lindensjö, B., & Lundgren, U. P. (1986). *Politisk styrning och utbildningsreformer* [Government and educational reforms]. Stockholm: Skolöverstyrelsen/Liber Förlag.

Moberg, M., & Moberg, E. (1909). *Vår tioåriga verksamhet—Kindergartens* [Our ten-year enterprise—Kindergartens] (I Norrköpings Verksamhetsberättelse [Annual Reports of the Town of Norrköping]).

Montessori, M. (1912). *The Montessori method*. London: Heinemann.

Montessori, M. (1936). *The secrets of childhood*. Bombay: Orient Longmans.

Myrdal, A. (1934). *Stadsbarn, en bok om deras fostran i storbarnkammaren* [City children, a book about their upbringing in collective nurseries]. Stockholm: Kooperativa Förbundets Bokförlag.

Myrdal, A., & Myrdal, G. (1934). *Kris i befolkningsfrågan* [The crisis in the population question]. Stockholm: Bonnier.

Myrdal, G. (1931). Socialpolitikens dilemma I och II. [The dilemma of social politics, I and II]. *Spektrum*, *3*, 13–31.

Näsman, E. (1995). Vuxnas intresse av att se med barns ögon [The interest of adults in using the gaze of the child]. In L. Dahlgren & K. Hultqvist (Eds.) *Seendet och seendets villkor: En bok om barns och ungas välfärd* [Seeing and the conditions of seeing: A book about the welfare of children and youth]. Stockholm: HLS Förlag.

Nilsson, J-O. (1994). *Alva Myrdal—En virvel i strömmen* [Alva Myrdal—A whirl in the stream]. Stehag/Stockholm: Symposion Förlag.

Popkewitz, T. S. (1996a). Rethinking decentralization and the state/civil society distinctions: The state as a problematic of governing. *Journal of Educational Policy*, *11* (1), 27–51.

Popkewitz, T. S. (1996b, May 26–29). Systems of ideas in historical spaces: Educational reform, "constructivism," and the changing patterns of governing the self. Paper presented at Conference on Democracy and Changing Governing Patterns of the State, University of Turku, Finland.

Pramling, I. (1983). *The child's conception of learning*. Göteborg: Acta Universitatis Gothenburgensis.

Pramling, I. (1994). *Kunnandets grunder: Prövning av en fenomenografisk ansats till att utveckla barns sätt att uppfatta sin omvärld*. Göteborg: Acta Universitatis Gothenburgensis.

Richardson, L. (1990). *Writing strategies, reaching diverse audiences*. London: Sage University Press.

Rorty, R. (1979). *Consequences of pragmatism*. New York: Harvester/Wheatsheaf.

Rorty, R. (1989). *Contingency, irony and solidarity*. Cambridge: Cambridge University Press.

Rorty, R. (1991). *Objectivity, relativism and truth* (Vol. 1). Cambridge: Cambridge University Press.

Rose, N. (1985). *The psychological complex.* London: Routledge.

Rose, N. (1989). *Governing the soul: The shaping of the private self.* London: Routledge.

Rose, N. (1989a). *Social psychology as a science of democracy.* Paper presented at Eighth Annual Conference of Cheiron-Europe, Gothenburg, Sweden.

Rose, N. (1993). Government, authority and expertise in advanced liberalism. In A. Barry, T. Osborne, & N. Rose (Eds.), *Liberalism, neo-liberalism, and governmentality, economy and society* (pp. 283–299).

Rose, N. (1994). Expertise and the government of conduct. *Studies in Law, Politics and Society, 14*, 357–359.

Skola för Bildning [School for Cultivation]. (1992). *Läroplanskommittén* [Curriculum report]. Stockholm.

Tallberg-Broman, I. (1991). *När arbetet var lönen: En kvinnohistorisk studie av barnträdgårdsledarinnor som folkupplysare* [When work itself was the salary]. Stockholm: Almqvist & Wiksell International.

Ulin, C. (1951). Lekskola för sex-åringar. *Barnträdgården, 7,* 1–11.

Ungdomspolitik [Youth policy]. (1993). Government bill 135. Stockholm.

Walkerdine, V. (1984). Developmental psychology and the child-centered pedagogy: The insertion of Piaget into early education. In J. Henriques, W. Hollway, C. Urwin, C. Venn, & V. Walkerdine (Eds.), *Changing the subject: Psychology, social regulation and subjectivity* (pp. 153–202). London: Methuen.

Wulff, B. (1922). Börnehavelederens forhold till tiden och dens krav [The kindergarten leader's relation to time and its demands]. *Barnträdgården, 2,* 4–6.

5

"Childhood" in the Emergence and Spread of U.S. Public Schools

BERNADETTE BAKER

A child is not, in itself, anything. Any image, body or being we can hollow out, purify, exalt, abuse, and locate sneakily in a field of desire will do for us as a "child."

—James Kincaid, *Child-Loving*

At the end of the twentieth century, having a childhood and going to school are frequently taken for granted as a "normal" part of life. Child*hood* and public schooling are not phenomena that have existed across time and space, however (see Hultqvist, this volume). While "the young" have always been identifiable by their physical size and age, the meanings these differences have been given are not universal. Present-day Western beliefs that children are dependent, vulnerable, require segregation, and require a delay from responsibility represent a particularly modernist shift in views of the young (see Ariès, 1962).

Even more recent are notions of having a normal childhood (Archard, 1993). Childhood today is often perceived as a universal, stable category bound by norms of development and ways of assessing deviations. When ideas of childhood as a special and romantic period of life emerged during the Enlightenment, however, they were the subject of much debate. Treating the young as though they were vulnerable, required special treatment, and required delay from contributing to the activities of living was thought by some observers to be dangerous. It would create silliness in the young, spoiling them through overindulgence and too much attention. It would not offer an adequate introduction to the demands of life. It was not until the nineteenth century that modernist/romantic childhood gained a wider acceptance in the United States and materialized in institutionalized forms, such as public schooling.

Today, both schooling and childhood are mutually reinforcing classificatory schemes and social practices. The "child" is a taken-for-granted subject central to the structure of the educational field. While much educational work flows around assumptions about children and their development, what is meant by being a "child" is not debated. Further, reform efforts continue to express how children should be cared for, neglecting the impact that discourse that structures the "child" may have on ideas of "care," "reform," and "development" in the first place.

Thus the focus of this chapter is the production of childhood in the public school movement in the United States. I explore the shifting constitution of the child and childhood through a "history of the present" (see Foucault, 1979, p. 31). A history of the present is a form of history that enables a questioning of how questions are currently posed. It accounts for the constitution of knowledges through the use of genealogy, a Foucaultian strategy that locates "the modification of rules of formation of statements which are accepted as scientifically true" (Foucault, 1980, p. 117). Thus histories of the present point to the cultural and historical specificity of categories and concepts used to debate and practice schooling today.

I focus first on the production of public schooling and modernist childhood as practices of rescue. I use the slogan childhood-as-rescue, adapted from the work of Roger Schnell (1977), to signal the new ways of reasoning about the young that romanticism suggested.

Second, I trace the reconfiguration of childhood-as-rescue in Childstudy, the first educational movement directed toward reforming U.S. public schools. I explore the historical convergence of discourses of race and nature that enabled the romantic child/adult division to be redefined as developmental at the turn of the twentieth century. I argue that systems of inclusion/exclusion were reconstituted in the reasoning surrounding a developmentalist rescue in Child-study and that this became manifest in recommendations for the differential provision of public schooling.

Third, I sketch shifts in the meaning of childhood-as-rescue that occurred after Child-study's peak. I examine the appropriation of developmentalist discourse in a state survey published in 1917 on the provision of public schooling for children in the South. I use Foucault's (1991) notion of "populational reasoning" to locate how systems of inclusion/exclusion circulated through efforts aimed at extending and governing rescue via public schooling.

Last, I consider the constitution of the child in present-day educational discourse. I question childhood as natural, as an apolitical site for rescue and reform, and as a unitary space for the administration of care.

CONSTRUCTING CHILDHOOD-AS-RESCUE AND PUBLIC SCHOOLING

A child/adult division was one of the discursive conditions that made public schooling possible. The European Enlightenment was not the first space in which a child/adult division emerged, however. What is unique about the Enlightenment is the new, romantic meaning given the child/adult division, which enabled public schools to come into existence. In particular, the inscription of children as morally vulnerable and dependent posited childhood as a period of life requiring special protection and a delay from adult responsibilities.

In North America, histories of the simultaneous emergence of modernist childhood and common schooling fall primarily within the field of psychohistory (see deMause, 1974; Finkelstein, 1989). A central premise of psychohistorical narratives is that without the idea of (modernist) childhood, there could be no idea of the school, and with the idea of the school came reinforcement of the idea of childhood (deMause, 1974; Finkelstein, 1975, 1976, 1989; Hawes & Hiner, 1991; Schnell, 1977).

Despite this commonality there are more frequently disputed themes related to the philosophy of history. Schnell (1977) identifies evolutionary idealist and social control and/or conflict theories as the major frameworks informing psychohistories. Evolutionary idealist histories posit that childhood and schooling are the results of an evolutionary process—a process that has moved humanity from barbarism and cruelty toward children to a softer, more Rousseauian, and "civilized" stance.[1] For example, Lloyd deMause, probably the best-known psychohistorian of childhood in the United States, invokes a "catastrophe" mentality regarding the past:

> The history of childhood is a nightmare from which we have only recently begun to awaken. The further back in history one goes, the lower the level of child care, and the more likely children are to be killed, abandoned, beaten, terrorized, and sexually abused. (1974, p. 1)

Sociological accounts drawing upon social conflict or control theories have been posited in opposition to evolutionary idealist reasonings. The accounts point to broader, actor-centered changes as the motors of history (see Finkelstein, 1975, 1976, 1989; Kaestle, 1983; Katz, 1968; Sandin, 1988; Sommerville, 1982).

In particular, conflict and control issues related to the effects of a class-based system are emphasized. The rise of industrialism, the emergence of the middle classes, urbanization, a desire to acculturate European immigrants and anxiety on the parts of middle-class parents and religious workers at having the young "on the streets" are often cited as major catalysts for schooling and modernist childhood (see Schnell, 1977).

Different psychohistorical accounts, then, have posited different relationships between the emergence of modernist childhood and schooling in the United States. Schnell (1977) argues that what has been missed in accounts that deal centrally with this conjuncture is an understanding of childhood as an ideology of rescue:

> If the centuries following the Middle Ages were in a sense a pilgrimage to "childhood," the school promoters of the nineteenth century erected society's most ornate shrine to that concept. The common school, the physical expression of popular education, represented the final institutionalization of childhood. Before the nineteenth century, the concept had gained mastery only among the elites of western societies, and then only for sons and on a voluntary basis. The common school advocates preached a gospel of universal childhood. . . . Unlike the asylums for abandoned, dependent, and delinquent children, the common school operated on the principle that children were intrinsically innocent but vulnerable and all needed to be rescued. (1977, pp. 47–48)

Schnell thus argues that the ascription of vulnerability to children was a new concept. It promoted children's segregation, protection, and delay in entering into the risk-taking of the adult world on moral grounds. The social groups whose children were "still largely independent, not segregated, exposed to drink, crime, neglect, and hard labor, and made to assume responsibilities early" became identified as not providing their young with a childhood (Schnell, 1977, p. 47).

Further, Schnell (1977) suggests that it was not just public schooling that embraced a new rescue mentality in the 1800s. The proliferation of new services solely for children, such as orphanages, corrective institutions for "juvenile delinquents," and children's hospitals also produced modernist childhood, sanctioning its institutionalization and the systematic surveillance of its morality (Finkelstein, 1975; Schnell, 1977). Schnell posits that the fundamental meaning of childhood implied "rescue" and that the simultaneous rise of common schooling in the 1800s represented "the most ordered of rescues" (Schnell, 1977, p. 39).

I have dwelt at length on Schnell's analysis because he introduces an idea of rescue in relation to childhood that I both draw upon and critique. "Childhood-as-rescue" is a slogan I have adapted from Schnell's discussion to capture the new redemptive themes in discourse on the young. That is, it suggests the new relations of rescuing and being rescued that romanticism brought to the child/adult division.

In the following section, I describe the major themes of rescue that are posited in psychohistorical narratives. In doing so, I accept the slogan as signaling a rupture in the meaning of being young.

Childhood was not produced simply amidst an unvariegated discourse of redemption, however. The analysis of Child-study that follows suggests that rescue had become reconfigured by the turn of the century and was in fact a more nuanced and specific idea than psychohistorical accounts have posited in the present.

RESCUE IN PSYCHOHISTORICAL NARRATIVES

As I noted above, one point of agreement in psychohistorical narratives is that a modernist concept of childhood was important to the creation of common schools. Middle-class activism in the early 1800s is often cited as the mobilizing force for childhood and schooling:

> The central role of the middle classes in the promotion of common schooling is a commonplace in all the major interpretations of nineteenth century education. Whether their influence is viewed as beneficial or pernicious, all agree that middle class humanitarianism, Christian or secular, provided the campaigning that fired the cry for popular education. That the middle classes first assimilated childhood as part of their ideology gives us a key with which to unlock the meaning of those campaigns. (Schnell, 1977, p. 46)

Thus, a central tenet of psychohistorical accounts is that in economic, moral, and intellectual terms, the emergence of childhood-as-rescue as a global concept was the result of strategies surrounding the local preferences of the middle class.

Economic Rescue

The campaigns for common schooling have been described as middle-class strategies for socioeconomic betterment. While some men of the middle classes had access to older forms of training, such as apprenticeships, other forms of training were needed if more economic mobility was desired. More forms of training would lead to more future choices and social improvement.

The four criteria for defining romantic childhood as identified by Ariès (1962), dependence, protection, segregation, and delayed responsibility, "coincided nicely with their [middle-class] existing preference for extensive instruction" (Schnell, 1977, p. 46). A period of training ("childhood") and a place of training ("school") made sense.

Psychohistorical narratives generally posit, then, that middle-class campaigns articulated romantic views of childhood and schooling in order to increase opportunities for economic betterment. Finkelstein (1975) suggests that such functionality did not simply rest with a desire for economic mobility of men alone, but that it also sprang from the desire of some middle-class and working-class women to be freed (rescued?) from several of their younger children for part of the day.

Moral Rescue

Psychohistorical narratives also posit that rescue was delineated by middle-class moral preferences. It was not just any kind of morality that undergirded childhood as a practice of rescue. Ideas of "the family" as a safe haven for the young were integral to the form of morality desired (see Finkelstein, 1975, 1976; Hunter, 1983; Katz, 1968; Marsden, 1990; Sandin, 1988; Sommerville, 1982). The family as a nuclear entity, as a home or nest, and as a space where the segregation of the young and of the genders was lived out, structured the meaning of childhood and the form of moral protection deemed appropriate for it by the middle classes.

In addition, psychohistorical narratives often note the religious discourse that underpinned the first campaigns for common schooling in Massachusetts. The campaigns frequently spoke in terms of Christian salvation, moral protection, and the moral improvement of the young. Morality was often judged by the degree to which a person moved toward or away from "godliness." To be saved from the "old deluder, Satan" and to demonstrate one's destiny as rescued meant to entertain a belief in falling, in the possibility of hell.[2]

Morality in the form of middle-class Protestantism, then, has been cited as a catalyst for inscribing children as weak in physical and spiritual terms and in need of rescue. Schooling and literacy, in regard to the Bible in particular, were middle-class solutions for guarding against the possibility of "moral depravity" and of demonstrating one's rescued destiny.

Intellectual Rescue

Last, the middle classes have been further cited as the catalyst behind schooling's intellectual focus. Childhood-as-rescue required belief in the need for intellectual salvation (see Summerfield, 1984). Childhood was to be considered a time of inferior intellectual abilities relative to adulthood. To move beyond this, the middle classes organized an intervention. The Boston School Committee, for instance, in the 1860s defined the teachers' role as

> [t]aking children at random from a great city, undisciplined, uninstructed, often with inveterate forwardness and obstinancy, and with the inherited stupidity of centuries of ignorant ancestors, forming them from animals into intellectual beings, and . . . from intellectual beings into spiritual beings, giving to many their first appreciation of what is wise, what is true, what is lovely and what is pure. (quoted in Katz, 1968, p. 120)

Middle-class conceptions of what counted as wise, true, lovely, and so forth have thus been posited in psychohistorical accounts as a universalizing discourse informing the intellectual rescue of the young.

In summary, psychohistorical narratives have linked middle-class conceptions of economic mobility, morality, and intelligence to the production of modernist childhood as a segregated stage of life. "Having" a childhood meant being able to be rescued in all three dimensions. Childhood-as-rescue was a call for "social and individual improvement" in a particularly middle-class direction (Schnell, 1977, p. 46). Common schools were a response in pursuing this direction. Together, having a childhood and attending public school were to protect and save the young.

RE-READING CHILDHOOD-AS-RESCUE—ENCODING RACE AND GOVERNING NATURE

Psychohistorical narratives assume a certain logic about schooling's spread as a form of conscious class-based activism. While there is much in the analyses that is helpful for understanding the relative newness of institutions specifically for children and the "mentality" of rescue emerging in discourse on the young, the narratives often posit a relationship between a priori subjects and action as psychological and causal. The economic is taken as a pivotal structure that spawns notions of morality and intelligence that further determine action and outcome. A teleological view of change results amidst a descending notion of power.

My re-reading of childhood-as-rescue accepts a less telic perspective on history and operates from an ascending view of power (Foucault, 1980). That is, the confinement that schooling enabled, the mechanisms of schooling, and the techniques of organizing children were strategies that cannot be assumed to have emerged from "middle-class interests," spreading downwards, but need to be understood as strategies that emerged in relation to local interests and needs, and could subsequently be appropriated in the constitution of broader interests.

Thus, my reading of the Child-study movement, the first to center in or on the child, posits that rescue was reconfigured under developmentalism through a conjuncture of discourses, not simply through middle-class activism. Further, I suggest that developmentalism enabled both preexisting and new systems of inclusion/exclusion to be taken up in the new ways of judging the young.

I briefly outline, first, the central ideas of Child-study. Second, I explore the ways in which oppositions of "race" and ideas of "nature" circulated through the reasoning.[3] It is at this point of delineating the convergence of discourse on the young that I draw upon Toni Morrison's (1992) idea of encoding. The unity given childhood can be understood as a product of discourse on difference. In particular, I focus on the construction of Blackness/Whiteness as key distinctions giving meaning to childhood.

Third, I explore the construction of rescuability as a complex conjuncture of distinctions that included but went beyond Blackness/Whiteness. And last, I trace shifts in developmentalist childhood-as-rescue that can be discerned by the time of the publication of *Negro Education: A Survey of Private and Higher Schools for Colored People in the United States* (Bureau of Education, 1917).

Child-Study, "Race," "Nature," and Defining Childhood— Central Theories of Child-Study

The Child-study movement was the first curriculum reform movement in U.S. public schools, burgeoning in the 1890s and early 1900s (Kliebard, 1986). It is an appropriate site for exploring childhood and its boundaries because it was the first reform movement to define childhood, prescribe child-centered pedagogies, and posit "stages of development" for the young.

The key idea of the movement was that children needed to be studied closely so that a curriculum could be constructed in relation to their "nature" (Hall, 1888). Which traits were studied closely and what inferences were to be drawn were guided by a theory called culture-epoch theory. It is through culture-epoch theory that discourses of race and of nature met to define the child.

Culture-epoch theory was a response to the new Darwinistic theories of biological evolution as applied to the social realm (Social Darwinism). It posited that children develop in ways that parallel the evolution of the "human race." That is, over the centuries, a higher form of humans was thought to have evolved from "savagery" to "civilization" through the biological imperatives of genetics and "natural selection." The child, in its growth toward adulthood, developed in stages marked by this history of evolution:

> The parallelism was known as the "law of recapitulation." The most general formulation of all the facts of development that we yet possess is contained in the *law of recapitulation*. This law declares that the individual, in his development, passes through stages similar to those through which the race has passed, and in the same order; that the human individual of the higher races, for example, in the brief period from the earliest moment of life to maturity, passes through or represents all the stages of life, through which the race has passed from that of a single-celled animal to that of present adult civilised man. (Partridge, 1912, pp. 27–28)

"Child development" was newly posited as "racial evolution." The four stages of development—kindergarten, transition, juvenile, and adolescence—marked the evolution from the "savage" to the "civilized." A correspondence between childhood and "savagery" thus constituted the beginning of child development:

> That the passing traits of the child resemble the characteristics of the savage in many particulars cannot be denied. In regard to fickleness and lack of power of long-sustained effort, optimism, and freedom from care and work, close relation to nature, the tendency to personify natural objects, and to confuse the animate and inanimate, in readiness to imitate, and to act upon suggestion, the child and primitive man are much alike. Both child and savage confuse the real and ideal, the waking life and the dream life. They are alike in the manner in which they see resemblances, in their use of analogy, in the way in which they construct language forms. The sayings of the child much resemble the folklore of primitive peoples. (Partridge, 1912, pp. 76–77)

Culture-epoch theory guided what teachers were to observe in children. Physical traits, such as complexion, head circumference, and limb length, moral traits, such as obedience or disobedience, and intellectual traits, such as how many objects in the environment could be recognized, were recorded. "The passing traits of the child" were expected to manifest themselves in ways that demonstrated a growth through "savagery." Teachers were encouraged to monitor the child's nature so that curricula could be designed to facilitate evolution to the next stage of development.

Reconstituting Rescue Through "Race" and "Nature"

The Limits of the "Child." Culture-epoch theory embodied in its reasoning a particular narrative about "races." It was a narrative dependent upon oppositional constructions of populational groups—oppositions that Morrison

(1992) suggests historically structure the meaning of many concepts in the United States. Morrison argues that it is the opposition of Blackness/Whiteness that drives the understanding of many nineteenth-century literary texts, such as *The Adventures of Huckleberry Finn*. The idea of "freedom," for example, was historically dependent upon the pervasiveness of slavery. It was the slavery of Africans and the "one step removed" work of Africans after slavery's uneven and drawn-out abolition that was crucial to understanding what freedom meant (Du Bois, 1918). Thus, freedom, encoded a dependence of "Whiteness" on constructions of "Blackness" as unfree.

Morrison's literary criticism has significance for how culture-epoch theory and the notions of rescue it enveloped were reconstituting the child. Defining child development as a linear progression through "cultural epochs" was dependent on oppositions to give meaning to "development." The reasoning in culture-epoch theory posited differences between children and adults as differences of savagery and civility. The differences were attributed to "nature" via the "law of recapitulation." The description of evolution and child development along axes of opposition was not, however, a value-free narrative about "nature." Discourse on difference generated productive and repressive moments for developmentally defined children.

Sylvia Wynter (1995) argues, for instance, that what had been learned in the nineteenth century as genetic facts about the survival of particular species had mapped onto them bourgeois and culture-specific discourses that gave higher value to the evolution of "Whiteness" in the human realm. The development of eugenics in the 1890s (the term was coined by Sir Francis Galton) coincided with the rapid rise of Child-study's popularity. Eugenics gave a moral and intellectual commentary to the nature of races. The moral, the intellectual, and "nature" became grounded in the deployment of scientific techniques, which were used to create "data" about race (Gould, 1981).

The practice of scientific techniques as "evidence gathering" acted to normalize oppositions of race. The techniques employed assumed differential values in what was measured. Measurements of Africans were positioned as evidence of "savagery," low morality, and limited intelligence. Measurements of fair-skinned northern Europeans were positioned oppositionally as signs of civility, high morality, and advanced intelligence. The "data" gave race *what appeared within the discursive context* to be objective, material, and "natural" qualities.

At the turn of the century, for instance, there were a variety of tools through which "data" were collected and used to justify *social* hierarchies between people in terms of "nature." In Western contexts, the construction of races was particularly dependent upon a range of pseudo-scientific theories heavily reliant on physical classification. The practice of craniology, phrenology, and physiognomy posited that measurements of physical attributes, such as head size, brain weight, jaw angle, and limb length, could indicate human character and potential.

Frequently, the techniques of sciences such as anthropology were interwoven with justifications drawn from biblical or literary references (Marsden, 1990). By the turn of the century, the techniques of external measurements had moved "inside" the head and gained popularity in reference to intelligence testing especially (Gould, 1981; Wynter, 1995). "Backwardness" had become a category of schooling (see Franklin, 1994).

Child-study saw as its central task the measurement and observation of qualities of "race" and "heredity" in children. Because the nature of the child could not be divorced from the nature of the race, the techniques used to produce "truths" about race were transplanted to produce "truths" about the child. Both childhood and race were thus given a newly reinforced salience in a biologically determined form.

In the 1890s the salience given race permeated actions both within and beyond education. The violence directed at African Americans, for instance, took on a new intensity. The large rise in lynching of African American men, the reaching of new peaks of abuse of African American women and girls, the disenfranchisement of African American men after gaining the vote (theoretically) through the abolition of slavery, and the lack of provision of public schools for African American children marked the depth to which subjectivity was based on a racialized hierarchy of "worth."[4]

Educational discourse imported this hierarchy through the mechanisms and techniques of power that constituted the new scientific study of the child. The convergence of discourse and techniques in/as Child-study held differential implications for newly differentiated children. Not all children studied could equally occupy the site of the "child." While all children were posited to have a "nature," the subject that could occupy the site of the "child" (and especially *the* child) could not have been African American. Africanism, positioned as the embodiment of both "Blackness" and "savagery," also occupied the base of the evolutionary pyramid in culture-epoch theory. Blackness was thus constructed as synonymous with "savagery" and with childhood at all ages. Being a child and having a temporary childhood encoded "Whiteness" as the epitome of civility and rescuability, while Blackness became the marker of alterity that defined its boundaries.

The limits of the child and of having a childhood come into view. One could have a childhood only if one was eventually able to occupy adulthood. One could not occupy adulthood if one was thought to have inherited "savagery." Nature was thought to have endowed different races and the young with particular limits. In Child-study, Blackness dominated the "space of otherness" in giving meaning to these limits. To move beyond childhood meant in part to move beyond Blackness.

The Limits of Rescue. The intersection of race and nature reconstituted the rescue imaginable for children. For children positioned as permanently "savage," schooling was thought to have no effect because "savagery" was aligned with permanent childhood and irrationality. Hence public schools were not recommended for African American, Native American, or "defective" children:

> [T]here are many who ought not be educated, and who would be better in mind, body and morals if they knew no school. What shall it profit a child to gain the world of knowledge and lose his own health? Cramming and over-schooling have impaired many a feeble mind, for which, as the proverb says, nothing is so dangerous as ideas too large for it. . . . Thus, while I would abate no whit from the praise of learning and education for all who are fit for them, I would bring discrimination down to the very basis of our educational pyramid. (Hall, 1901, p. 25)

The developmentalist rescue of the child thus embodied very specific systems of inclusion/exclusion.

Further, developmentalism encoded not only differential practices of rescue, but also an idea of saving "Whiteness" from "Blackness." Blackness, positioned as the ancestor from which others grew or which they playfully revisited, was integral to the growth or "evolution" of Whiteness. To interfere in the growth of a White child would be to disturb its trajectory toward a destiny of "superiority" (e.g., "the higher race"). Good teaching, then, was the building of a curriculum that facilitated the growth of Whiteness beyond its first "savage" stages (i.e., childhood).

The rescue of Whiteness from Blackness was pivotal in what it meant to learn, to care, and to respect "nature." Going against what was believed to be "educational," "caring," and "natural" meant being a "bad teacher."[5]

Blackness/Whiteness, then, operated as a system of inclusion/exclusion that became inscribed into the new developmentalist child/adult division. Encoded in the meaning of "scientific pedagogy" and circulating in the production of developmentalist childhood itself were new means of making Blackness the property through which Whiteness could again secure itself.

Complexities in Child-Study's Children

Educational movements such as Child-study both enabled and were enabled by a positioning of Blackness as the means to Whiteness. Blackness/Whiteness was not the only kind of populational distinction that made Child-study possible, however. Child-study incorporated into its theories of development and the systems of schooling it recommended, distinctions that in specific and complex ways went beyond and yet included Black/White binaries. That is, it drew upon preexisting "differences" and simultaneously generated further distinctions in positing a new developmentalist conception of childhood. I focus on some of the complex conjunctures that made Child-study possible both as a recognizable reform with recognizable limits and as a reform generating new limits of its own.

Savage/Civilized. "Blackness" and "Whiteness" were undeniably positioned as oppositional in many ways and were drawn into the meaning of savage/civilized in Child-study. However, the savage/civilized binary was conjoined to more than polar conceptions of color. "Savagery" could be occupied by groups constructed as "Indian" or "Oriental" or "Immigrant," and "civilized" required a very particular alignment of qualities that included not just "Whiteness" but Protestant Christianity, English-speaking, law-abidingness, maleness, sedentariness, adulthood, heterosexuality, and economic independence. For example:

> The mixed and roving character of our people makes good schooling hard. New waves of humanity are constantly breaking on our shores. There are something like a million newcomers each year. But for this supply what would become of our increase of population, our industries, etc.? Once immigrants were Celtic, Teutonic, and from the north of Europe; now they are from the south and east, Italians, Armenians, Russians, Finns, and even Orientals, despite the checks put upon the yellow peril. More and more of these fresh arrivals speak a tongue remote from our own, and the most the school can do is to teach them a little English and induct them into our ways of living and thinking. All must be smelted in one crucible. . . . Again, having immigrated here, they continue to wander, and the traditions of their migratory, nomad life are very strong in all classes of our population. . . . Truancy and other laws are easily evaded where humanity swirls, and education on the fly is sure to be superficial with these peek-a-boo pupils. (Hall, 1911, pp. 596–597)

"Savagery," could then, be permanent in several alignments that fell outside of Blackness. To grow away from it required very specific configurations of Whiteness that included more than just "Whiteness" per se. Hence, *The Ideal School as Based on Child-Study* projected a very narrow range of what "ideal" meant (see Hall, 1901). Being ideal meant being "the right race" in addition to an array of other markers of identity that signified one as "rescuable."

Special Child/Normal Child. In *The Ideal School* pedagogical strategies were differentiated for girls and boys at different stages of their "development." The pedagogies embodied a reasoning that naturalized categories of children, their potentials, and their perceived futures. *The Ideal School*, though, did not educate boys or girls of any class or "race" who were deemed "special" and hence without "potential" or future at all.

Rather, physically and mentally impaired children were discussed as "educational problems" (see Hall, 1911). They were new kinds of children, newly posited as different or "special" in relation to developmentalism. In a chapter explaining "the special child" (Hall, 1911), a convergence of discourse on difference implied the special child's race:

> If the rate of increase of the best children diminishes and that of the worst increases, the destiny of our land is sealed and our people are doomed to inevitable decay and ultimate extinction. These three big D's we deal with, the defectives, delinquents, and dependents, the great Biologos or spirit of life would designate or describe by another adjective big D not fit to print or speak, for they are a fearful drag upon our civilization. . . . From the standpoint of eugenic evolution alone considered, these classes are mostly fit only for extermination in the interests of the progress of the race. On the principle of selection and the survival of the best, they should be treated as Burbank treats the huge pile of plants he has cultivated and bred from what would not yield the best products and so burns. These are the tailings of the mine, the wastage and by-product of civilization. (p. 77)

It is here that categories of "race" and categories of physical and mental health subliminally intersected. "Nature" (God, "the great Biologos") had created "defectives, delinquents, and dependents" who interfered with "the progress of the race." The "three big D's" could be occupied by various children of Whiteness and by either gender. The impulse that the reasoning embodied, though, was stacked toward filling the D's with population groups that already were constructed elsewhere as a "drag upon our civilization."

The special child was a new subject encircled by preexisting distinctions, such as Blackness/Whiteness and savage/civilized. In the convergence of new ways of reasoning about reason, the special child became articulated to a deficit view that developmentalism enabled, encoding and constructing Blackness as savage and abnormal.

Child-study, then, like any other movement, was not a simple matter of liberation versus constraint, production versus repression, or desire versus fear. Rather, the convergence of discourse that gave meaning to the child embodied a range of productive and repressive moments that were played out through the uneven provision of schooling and the differential images of rescuing children. While inspiring a protective and romantic stance toward the child, the developmentalist logic that Child-study ushered into education's discursive field simultaneously decentered the protection of many children through its multiple "spaces of otherness."

State Discourse, "Race," and "Nature" in the Provision of Public Schools

By the time of "World" War I the provision of public schooling was at issue in state discourse on education in the South.[6] Populational groups who previously had been excluded from public schooling were now to attend state-funded schools. In 1917, the Bureau of Education (1917) published *Negro Education: A Survey of Private and Higher Schools for Colored People in the United States*. Its (much disputed) central theme was that publicly funded elementary and high schools should now be provided for all African American children.

How, in such a short period of time, could the basic tenets of the immensely popular Child-study be so questioned by the state as to generate new policy? What I trace below, using Foucault's notion of "populational reasoning," are some shifts in childhood-as-rescue and schooling as a site of redemption that the publication of the survey embraced.

The survey was an artifact predicated upon "populational reasoning." Foucault argues that "populational reasoning" emerged in relation to ruptures in the form of social organization in Europe in the mid-eighteenth century. Prior to the emergence of the concept of a "population," the art of government and management of the economy were based on a model of the family with the father as head. The patriarch determined the economy of the household, monitored the morality of its members, and corresponded with other families or the prince of the region.

By the middle of the eighteenth century, an increasing number of people and changes in agricultural production had led to a shift in human affairs. The economy and the art of managing individuals were no longer reducible to the family alone. Thus, the family became an instrument, a point of application, in the monitoring of a larger group (the population), rather than a unit concerned with and monitoring itself. Population groups became constructed, defined, and counted through such techniques as statistics-keeping. Management of the population became an end of government in itself. Interventions based on the records' being kept became a means of demonstrating government in a "rational and conscious manner" (Foucault, 1991, p. 99).

By defining groups in particular ways and maintaining records that gave material qualities to the construction of groups, populational reasoning "normalized" certain characteristics. What were socially constructed criteria appeared in time as "natural attributes" (e.g., "racial characteristics"). The historical and cultural specificity of the reasoning became submerged, and the appearance of the criteria as "natural" became reinforced through scientific techniques that were built around gathering data about the attributes. Populational reasoning thus flowed through the educational reforms of the turn of the twentieth century as much as it did through state policy.

While I have generalized and applied Foucault's analysis here, the main point is that the construction of groups and specific group characteristics (such as those attributed to and cataloged as "race" in the nineteenth century) emerged at a very specific historical moment. The art of governing required a kind of "governmentality" related to the role of the state as a definer, watcher, and manager of difference. Hence, the construction of groups and group differences gave rise to identities that were crystallized in many techniques of government by the turn of the twentieth century (Foucault, 1991).

Shifts in Rescue. Foucault's idea of populational reasoning enables a view of how reasoning African American children could be imagined as a legitimated task by the state only after oppositional identities were taken for granted as something to be "managed." In Child-study, many lessons were offered to teachers, teacher educators, and normal school students as to how and why "differences" between races were to be seen as "natural" and "scientifically" valid. By the time of the *Negro Education* survey, these understandings were so implicit that no explanation was required as to why a document would be constructed around oppositional conceptions of race or why the rescue of African American children via inclusion in public schools had not been a concern of the state before.

The survey represents an art of government demonstrated through the management of groups that appear as givens (i.e., "children" and "races"). As in Child-study, African American children were positioned as objects or property to be decided about and managed by others in relation to inclusion/exclusion. The importance given elementary schooling for children and the existence of the survey itself was explained commonsensically through juxtaposed categories of race:

> In view of the importance of the public-school education of Negro children both to the Negro race and to the economic and moral welfare of the South, effort has been made to obtain an accurate financial measure of the interest in this phase of education. (Bureau of Education, 1917, p. 27)

Similarly, in explaining why better-trained teachers were needed for African American children, oppositions of race were further invoked:

> The future development of the Southern States in industry, in agriculture, in sanitation, and in morality requires the effective education, not only of the white youth but also of the colored youth of the those States. The high death rate of the Negroes, largely due to ignorance and low economic status, is a menace to themselves and the communities in which they live. Since the Negroes now constitute at least a third of the southern labor supply, their lack of industrial skill

will hamper the economic development of the South so long as adequate public-school facilities are not provided. The high percentage of illiteracy among Negroes is not only a measure of ill-health but also an indication of moral limitations and consequent dangers to the welfare of the colored race, as well as to that of its white neighbors. (Bureau of Education, 1917, p. 25)

The populational reasoning embodied in the discourse here "naturalized" "race" into a Black/White binary used to explain the provision of education. While this is no different in some senses from the "order of things" in Child-study, what had shifted by 1917 was the concept of rescue and its relationship to developmentalist childhood. "Whiteness" was still constructed through "Blackness" as in Child-study, but "the Negro race" was newly represented as a discrete entity that could be rescued from itself. Blackness, then, was deployed as requiring urgent rescue from Blackness.

Despite the new extension of a developmentalist childhood to African American children, though, what remained central in state discourse was the role of Blackness in defining the welfare and meaning of Whiteness. Without the rescue of "Black" children through public schooling, Whiteness would be "in danger." Thus, the new meaning of rescue for African American children was not "spiritual reintegration" via exclusion (see Foucault, 1965). Redemption was not to be rendered for "Whites" or "Blacks" through keeping African American children out of public schools, but by their inclusion. Thus the move toward inclusion of African American children in tax-funded systems embodied in its "good intentions" benefits to Whiteness.

This is an important point to note. The survey's structure acknowledged that the rescuing of children had previously taken the form of differential practices. The state's aim was now to extend the rescue of the child via the inclusion of Blackness in "the public." Simultaneously, however, Blackness and Whiteness maintained their antithetical discursive positions. In efforts to overcome exclusions, in efforts to "include" Blackness, exclusions still prevailed.

Through applying a reasoning that assumed inherent differences between groups what appears as an extension of rescue, as a broadening, reinforced the idea of "races" as differently valued. *Which* subjects could now occupy the location of the child had shifted, but the child at the center of educational discourse maintained similar discursive limits.

Shifts in "Nature." The paradoxes that redefined the practice of rescue were enabled by a new orientation to nature. That is, if African American children were positioned in 1917 as educable, the relationship between one's nature and the ability to be governed by the self or others had to have changed. The nature of Blackness could not remain immutable if a child was to qualify for rescue. It had to be able to "develop."

In the *Negro Education* paragraphs quoted in the previous section, the biological dimensions of nature are noticeable in reference to such things as "high death rates," "illiteracy," and "moral limitations," but the limits of reason permeate the document elsewhere:

> It is not the educated Negro that fills our penitentiary and jails, works in our chain gangs, and fills our poorhouses. These places are given over to the ignorant and depraved. It is not the educated Negro that makes up our idle vagrant class, that commits our murders, and despoils our women. Here again it is the illiterate and degraded Negro. The trained Negro lives in a better home, wears better clothes, eats better food, does more efficient work, creates more wealth, rears his children more decently, makes a more decent citizen, and in times of race friction is always to be found on the side [of] law and order. These things seem to be worthy fruits, and whatever system produces them should have our approval. If we are to be fair to the section in which we live, and fair to the Negro race, we must see that a common-school education is given to the majority, and that a more thorough and complete training shall be given to the capable few who are to become the leaders of this race. (Bureau of Education, 1917, p. 26)

Thus, despite the strength of biological imprints of nature, nature was now mutable via an educational rescue. The environment was newly posited as affecting "Black" and "White" children.

African American children were not positioned as *fully* rescuable, though, because race was still being invoked as a "natural" phenomenon with natural limitations. The rescue demonstrated by the "educated Negro" was limited to "the capable few who are to become the leaders of this race." Thus, while the environment could play a part, it was as though it had certain limited raw material to work with.

"Improvement" and "educatedness," then, still encoded a movement toward very specific alignments of Whiteness. The reasoning that aimed to extend rescue and to modify African American children's nature through the environment reinscribed a deficit "logic." Thus, the very scaffolding of the child that had limited schooling's uneven provision in the first place was reinvoked in efforts to implement "inclusive" schooling.

This does not mean that a shifting meaning of "nature" was absolutely reproductive, however. In Child-study, educating Blackness was positioned as an impossibility. By 1917, *Negro Education* was discussing the most efficient means of implementing public schooling for African American children. I am not suggesting that this is a singular, linear, and causal result of a shifting conception of nature free from political expediencies, activism, or conditions in social and global relations at the time. Instead, I am arguing that a shift in how nature was theorized was significant within the logic of educational discourse. What was "reasonable" for the state to pursue had changed.

It is interesting to consider the discursive context that enabled the articulation of this shift. What context enabled a view of nature that embodied "biological determinism" and also saw space for the management of nature through regulating childhood and races?

The Child-study movement came to prominence in a social context that seemed to be changing rapidly. Modernity had brought to the North American continent industrialization, urbanization, massive immigration, internal migration, a meeting of religions, languages, dispositions, values, labor knowledge and styles, family formations and foods. By creating categories of classification that helped define the form that inclusions and exclusions would take in educational realms, Child-study cast certainty into what appeared to be disarray. Limits on the egalitarian principles of liberal modernity were thus set through notions of caring for and centering the child.

The "normalizing processes" that centered the child in Child-study were based upon modes of knowledge production at the time that were developing a high status outside of education or already had significant appeal. In particular, producing knowledge about "race," children, and nature was dependent upon the techniques of science (in a secular and broad sense) and upon a concept of a Christian God (in a particular Protestant sense) who had already established what science would pursue, that is, the "laws of nature."

The converging discourses that set limits on the child did not generate a static conception of childhood and its rescue however. The production of knowledge about children and about races and the normalizing processes that this incorporated was a never-quite-complete task. Hence, by 1917, the provision of public schooling for African American children was a discernible concern in state discourse in the South.

Simply noting the emergence of new ways of thinking about children in educational discourse is simplistic, however. What is more difficult is understanding how the shifts appeared as "truths" at a particular time. That is, what was it that enabled the *Negro Education* survey to construct the arguments that it did?

The publication of the survey during World War I is a notable indication of its context. What had opened up with the coming of war in Europe were debates and fears of internal domestic crisis in the United States. During the latter stages of World War I, the debates were noticeably structured by discourse surrounding race and government. The debates, often on the floor of state legislatures and Congress, frequently conveyed a sense of fear and anticipation of "uprising" or "revolt" similar to that expressed immediately after the Civil War.

Perhaps part of the shift from nature as immutable to nature as able to be contoured and managed by humans to some degree was a response to the uncertainty that was exacerbated by the onset of large-scale warfare in Europe. It would be a more expedient way to regulate groups if African American children's natures were controllable rather than on a predetermined ballistic pathway to "savagery."

This does not suggest that a shift in "nature" arose as a conscious plan, arose as a conspiracy of suppression, or had a singular originary point. There were other aspects of rescuing the child that did not emerge in relation to the war. For instance, the rise of institutionalized and formalized sciences that undertook projects for understanding "Man" was simultaneous with the emergence of a developmentalist notion of childhood and its extension to African American children.

The establishment of social science paradigms in the latter half of the 1800s enabled a more humanist grasp on knowing and regulating humans than previous Judeo-Christian doctrines of nature could. The hotly debated formalization of such disciplines as anthropology, sociology, and psychology in the latter half of the 1800s in the United States is indicative of the fumbling for this grasp during the shift from a religious to a secular view of "Man" (see Popkewitz, 1991; Wittrock, Wagner, & Wollmann, 1991; Wynter, 1995).

The secularization of "Man" enabled belief in the ability to exact some measure of control and predictability over events. Intellectual space was required for being able to develop what was known about humans. In addition, space was required for developing what could be changed about humans on the basis of this knowledge. Nature as immutable did not provide the space needed. Nature as being able to be capitalized upon, contoured, managed by others, and regulated by the self did. The nature of the child was thus a key site for articulating shifts in reasoning about human limits and in controlling the social world through "the management of difference."

Shifts in Populational Reasoning. New discourse on nature and rescue also arose in relation to a new way of thinking about populational reasoning. As I indicated above, the relationship among nature, children, and evolution toward adult reason incorporated very specific ideas about "racial" oppositions. The unreasoned child was, as a concept, set in contrast to the reasoned adult, but the notions of reason were related to images of Blackness as savage, impulsive, emotional, and undeveloped. An array of other limits combined with Blackness to tighten the picture of "normality."

The construction of groups as intellectually vulnerable or inferior acted to define the concept of reason itself. The specific form in which populational reasoning played itself out in the United States was dependent upon concepts of race and nature that set limits on intelligence and rationality. Thus, interventions pursued in relation to the population could not be divorced from what different populational groups were thought to be capable of.

This is an important point. In Child-study, Blackness and Whiteness were based on the assumption that African American children could not reason. African American children were thereby positioned as "ineducable." By 1917, African American children (or more accurately, in the term of *Negro Education*, "the capable few") were positioned as "educable" in official discourse. Educability, though, was defined in terms of the extent to which Blackness could be moved away from. While Blackness was positioned as educable, to be able to think/reason/show educatedness was to demonstrate movement toward the multiple alignments of Whiteness.

There was a shift, then, in the reasoning deployed regarding population groups. Under the premises of Child-study, no intervention would effect the rationality of Blackness. By 1917, the intervention that *Negro Education* represents assumes the reverse. Reasoning about the management of population groups embodied a different sense of the boundaries constructing the child.

It is important not to exaggerate the effects of such a shift, however. Subtle changes in populational reasoning did not dramatically reconstruct groups and the character alignments they had been given. A change in how populational groups were reasoned about incorporated Blackness as educable, but only on terms that already had established a very specific form of Whiteness as the pinnacle of educability. Thus, while a different sense of the child was discernible in state discourse by 1917, there was also a sense of the assimilating and repressive effects that the extension of rescue embodied.

It seems, then, that reasoning about the child and childhood held continuous and discontinuous moments across the public school movement in the United States. The establishment of schooling centered a notion of rescue in reasoning about the young. The centering of child development reconstituted rescue, placing limits on participation, rationality, and ability through new techniques for governing races and natures.

Under developmentalism, the child became the new carrier of the future, but only in terms of a recapitulated past. Childhood-as-rescue now had a set order and a way of determining deviation. State appropriation of a developmentalist logic by 1917 indicated a continued attempt to struggle with time and to manage difference—to bring predictability and certainty to the future while maintaining the order of things from the past. In educational discourse, the shifting meaning of what and who was meant by childhood represented both a marker of rupture and an effort to contain the wounds.

NONCONCLUDING THOUGHTS: CHILDHOOD IN EDUCATIONAL WORK IN THE PRESENT

How might this view of the shifting constitution of the child inform a view of childhood in the present? That is, how can a "history of the present" be made use of tactically today?

First, childhood can no longer be perceived as a natural phenomenon with natural laws guiding its natural unfolding. The child seems to be a product of categories, techniques, and reasonings through which we perceive things as being "natural." The naturalness attributed to childhood can be better viewed, then, as a cultural conjuncture that generated multiple effects.

Second and related, destabilizing the naturalness of childhood opens it up as a political space. Childhood was not and is not an objective concept. While I have argued that its production was not a top-down plan of the middle classes, but eventuated through a convergence of discourses, childhood, from its romantic rescue to its developmentalist order, produced differential effects for children. It remains in the present, like the child's body itself, as a space that certain distinctions made possible and upon which further distinctions can be made.

Currently, the developmentalist order of childhood is being extended, and so, too, are its productive and repressive effects. New kinds of children are being produced through new categories for assessment. Categories such as "ready to learn," "at risk," "attention deficit disorder," "emotionally disturbed," "learning disabled," "cognitively disabled," and so on, suggest the limits of a normal childhood at the end of the twentieth century.

The categories of deficit owe less to nature, though, and more to culturally specific practices. These practices privilege concepts of intelligence, orderliness, rationality, self-control, speed of recall, willingness to submit to authority, a love of reading, writing and coloring, a willingness to sit still, and formal English proficiency. The categories of deficit thus help constitute the current meaning of childhood as preparation for school and school as preparation for work.

The categories of deficit do not have neutral effects, however. They are disproportionately filled with children further labeled as "minority" and "poor." Being "not quite the ideal child" for teachers to teach in "the regular classroom" seems a space of otherness reserved for children already othered through a variety of discourses. Embodied in the very techniques for identifying and helping children "having difficulties," then, are both productive and repressive moments—moments that signify the operation of power in the extremities of its reach, in the very mechanisms of "care" for the child.

Lastly, the above calls into question the administration of childhood as "care" in an unvariegated or unitary form. This is particularly the case in present educational reforms that push for child-centered teaching. Currently, for instance, there are many educational reform efforts dependent upon a notion of "good" teaching as "child-centered" teaching. Strategies that pay some homage to whole language, multicultural education, feminist pedagogies, the analysis of learning styles, or portfolio assessment, for example, rely implicitly or explicitly upon a well-studied knowledge of one's students as central to the strategies' success. Centering the child as a prerequisite for further action seems so embedded as a sign of sensitivity, care, and reform that it is now difficult to imagine a "good" teacher as not being a child-centered teacher.

While acts of great love, self-sacrifice, empathy, or anger at injustice have generated the above reforms it is important to question what the centering of the "child" *decenters.* At the end of the twentieth century, it seems that the centering of the "child" as a form of rescue contained moments of slippage. The normalization of "childhood" as "stages of development" produced "others," whose protection was not guaranteed.

Questions arise in the present then as to how the "child" at the center of educational movements is being constituted in efforts that are thought to mark "civility," "progress," or "justice." Do new projects of rescue require a dependent child who can be rescued economically, morally, and intellectually? Are characteristics ascribed to the child—who is to be both centered and reformed—as though they were "natural" features of "populational groups"?

If child-centeredness historically required margins to give meaning to rescue, then how might reforms presently aimed at rescuing the young deploy systems of inclusion/exclusion? Have the effects of power been left behind in projecting alternative forms of rescue? Which subjects can occupy the space of rescuer and rescued? And what are the boundaries of "care" that our new forms of rescue imply?

These are questions that a history of the present of the "child" brings to mind at the same time that we can note that the educational field has been dependent upon the child and the idea of childhood for existence. The current feel-good coherence given childhood-as-rescue has obscured the cultural inventions, the historical specificities, and the foreclosing that have inhabited its deployment in educational discourse across the public school movement in the United States. One has to wonder, then, despite the administration of "care" and the good intentions of educational reform, whether the place of "childhood" in our memories is as "natural," protective, or innocent as Rousseau would have us believe.

NOTES

1. Debate in childhood history exists over whether Ariès's social history of childhood (translated as *Centuries of Childhood: A Social History of Family Life*) is accurate in asserting that prior to the seventeenth century French cultures had no conception of childhood. The debate, which crosses scholarship primarily in France, England, and the United States, generally divides between those who agree with Ariès's contention on the basis of the evidence of paintings, iconography, literature, games, pastimes, schooling and so forth (see Stone, 1977; deMause, 1974) and those who maintain that previous European societies did have a conception of childhood (see Pollock, 1987, 1983; Hanawalt, 1993). Archard (1993) argues that the debate has occurred primarily because of confusion over distinctions among "concepts," "conceptions," and "sentiments" of childhood. While Ariès's book was translated into English as a discussion of the "concept" of childhood, Archard argues that the original French text speaks of a "sentiment" of childhood. Archard concludes that previous societies did have a concept of childhood, but its particular modern form (as related to the historical shift called modernity) did not become apparent until around the seventeenth century. Thus, the sentiment, or a particularly modern conception, of childhood seems to have emerged at the same time that the changes in the effects and technologies of power that Foucault identifies in relation to systems of sexuality and the family, prisons, sanity, and so forth, emerged in Europe.

2. The "old deluder, Satan" refers to what is called the "old deluder law" of 1647, the first general school law recorded in the thirteen colonies that concerned the compulsory provision of (but not attendance at) common schools in New England. The reason given for the need for a school reads: "It being one chief object of that old deluder, Satan, to keep men from the knowledge of the Scriptures, as in former times by keeping them in an unknown tongue, so in these latter times by persuading from the use of tongues, that so at least the true sense and meaning of the original might be clouded by false glosses of saint-seeming deceivers, that learning may not be buried in the grave of our fathers in the Church and Commonwealth" (quoted in Williams, 1937, pp. 80–81).

3. My focus is narrowed here primarily to the construction of Blackness and Whiteness as essentialized poles in educational discourse at the time. This certainly does not represent the vast array of configurations of ethnicities that were being "cataloged" in social science literature and popular parlance at the turn of the century. References to "Indians," "Orientals," "Southern and Eastern Europeans," "Jewish immigrants," "the Irish," "native whites," and "foreign whites" proliferated in this period of mass immigration to the American continent, mass migration within it, and mass deportation to elsewhere. Conceptions of Blackness and Whiteness in educational literature today occupy such a strong grasp upon identity politics, educational and social explanations, and revisions of explanations that it seems pertinent to pursue the reasoning by which such constructions became accepted as a plausible way of explaining behavior and of organizing and practicing education in the first place.

What I am also not addressing at this point are the complexities surrounding different configurations of gender as they related to the construction of children and adolescents of different races and ethnicities. By the 1890s, the majority of elementary school teachers in all U.S. states were female. Arguments over the creation and expansion of schooling for older children ("adolescents" or "youths") frequently invoked a "commonsensical" assumption of the time that men were more appropriate teachers of boys at these ages. This is certainly the view espoused by Hall (1901, 1902, 1911) in conjunction with his argument for educating some girls for robust procreation as the apex and reflection of their evolutionary status.

4. These constructions generated the formation of many oppositional interest groups in education who aimed to overcome or maintain the disparities associated with these positionings. This chapter is not focused upon the arguments that different groups employed in these debates, but rather upon the discursive context of oppositional categories that made such debates plausible. For examples of the ways in which African American activists in education argued against the disparities in its provision and quality during and after the first crisis of modernity by utilizing what Bell (1980) refers to as the "interest convergence principle," see Du Bois (1918, 1973) and Woodson (1933). These works give some sense of the range of positions articulated within interest groups forming around racial categories in educational discourse.

5. The permeation of these discourses at the time not only positioned the way in which teachers could be perceived but also the way in which they could act or respond to such perceptions. The *Handbook of the Wisconsin Child-study Society* (Wisconsin Child-study Society, 1898), coauthored by teachers and sent to every teacher in the state, is an example of how many teachers attempted to do their jobs well in relation to the ideas of the time. For example, the handbook urges teachers to "[a]scertain the child's physical characteristics by individual observation, consultation with parents, and tests," and states that the "mental and moral characteristics are to be ascertained by observation, consultation and language exercises." Limb length, jaw angle, and moral "virtues and perversions" could then be recorded on the worksheets provided, and demonstrations of care could follow, based upon the inferences made. The many teachers who joined the Child-study movement did not see categories of "race" as "bad" but rather as a commonsensical way of explaining behavior and guiding work. These categories were normalized in a way that was seen to be positive and helpful for the individual child and for society at large. For a fuller account of how educational reform movements in the United States, including Child-study, influenced teacher education, see Herbst (1989).

6. I use the terms "provision," "spread," and "extension" (of public schooling) interchangeably, although I feel comfortable with none of them. They are not meant to imply the presence of an "actor" who deliberately and conspiratorially plans public schooling's uneven presence.

REFERENCES

Archard, D. (1993). *Children: Rights and childhood.* London: Routledge.
Ariès, P. (1962). *Centuries of childhood: A social history of family life.* New York: Vintage.

Bell, D. (1980). *Brown* and the interest-convergence dilemma. In D. Bell (Ed.), *Shades of Brown* (pp. 90–106). Boston: Harvard Law Review Association.

Bureau of Education. (1917). *Negro education: A survey of private and higher schools for colored people in the United States* (Vol. 1). Washington, DC: Department of the Interior.

deMause, L. (Ed.). (1974). *The history of childhood.* New York: Psychohistory Press.

Du Bois, W. E. B. (1918). Negro education. *The Crises, 15* (4), 173–178.

Du Bois, W. E. B. (1973). *The education of Black people: Ten critiques, 1906–1960.* Amherst: University of Massachusetts Press.

Finkelstein, B. (1975). Pedagogy as intrusion: Teaching values in popular primary schools in nineteenth-century America. *History of Childhood Quarterly, 2* (3), 348–378.

Finkelstein, B. (1976). In fear of childhood: Relationships between parents and teachers in popular primary schools in the nineteenth century. *History of Childhood Quarterly, 3* (3), 321–336.

Finkelstein, B. (1989). *Governing the young: Teacher behavior in popular primary schools in 19th century United States.* New York: Falmer Press.

Foucault, M. (1965). *Madness and civilization: A history of insanity in the age of reason.* New York: Vintage.

Foucault, M. (1979). *Discipline and punish: The birth of the prison.* New York: Vintage.

Foucault, M. (1980). *Power/knowledge: Selected interviews and other writings, 1972–1977.* New York: Pantheon.

Foucault, M. (1991). Governmentality. In G. Burchell, C. Gordon, & P. Miller (Eds.), *The Foucault effect* (pp. 87–104). Chicago: University of Chicago Press.

Franklin, B. (1994). *From "backwardness" to "at-risk": Childhood learning difficulties and the contradictions of school reform.* Albany: State University of New York Press.

Gould, S. (1981). *The mismeasure of man.* New York: W. W. Norton.

Hall, G. S. (1888). *The contents of children's minds on entering school.* New York: Kellogg.

Hall, G. S. (1901). The ideal school as based on child study. *The Forum, 32* (1), 24–29.

Hall, G. S. (1902). The high school as the people's college versus the fitting school. *Pedagogical Seminary, 9* (1), 63–73.

Hall, G. S. (1911). *Educational problems* (Vol. 11). New York: Appleton.

Hanawalt, B. (1993). *Growing up in medieval London: The experience of childhood in history.* New York: Oxford University Press.

Hawes, J., & Hiner, R. (Eds.). (1991). *Children in historical and comparative perspective: An international handbook and research guide.* New York: Greenwood Press.

Herbst, J. (1989). *And sadly teach: Teacher education and professionalization in American culture.* Madison: University of Wisconsin Press.

Hunter, E. (1983). This was your life: Studying the history of childhood. *Educational Leadership, 40* (6), 18.

Kaestle, C. (1983). *Pillars of the republic: Common schools and American society, 1780–1860.* New York: Hill and Wang.

Katz, B. (1968). *The irony of early school reform: Educational innovation in mid-nineteenth century Massachusetts.* Cambridge: Harvard University Press.

Kincaid, J. (1992). *Child-loving: The erotic child and Victorian culture.* New York: Routledge.

Kliebard, H. (1986). *The struggle for the American curriculum.* New York: Routledge.

Marsden, W. (1990). Rooting racism into the educational experience of childhood and youth in the nineteenth- and twentieth-centuries. *History of Education, 19* (4), 333–353.

Morrison, T. (1992). *Playing in the dark: Whiteness and the literary imagination.* Cambridge: Harvard University Press.

Partridge, G. (1912). *Genetic philosophy of education: An epitome of the published educational writings of President G. Stanley Hall of Clark University.* New York: Sturgis & Walton.

Pollock, L. A. (1987). *A lasting relationship: Parents and children over three centuries.* Hanover, NH: University Press of New England.

Pollock, L. A. (1983). *Forgotten children: Parent-child relations from 1500 to 1900.* Cambridge: Cambridge University Press.

Popkewitz, T. S. (1991). *A political sociology of educational reform: Power/knowledge in teaching, teacher education, and research.* New York: Teachers College Press.

Sandin, B. (1988). Use and abuse of the historical perspective on the history of children. In *Proceedings of the Conference on Historical Perspectives on Childhood* (pp. 93–113). Trondheim: The Norwegian Centre for Child Research.

Schnell, R. (1977). "The most ordered of rescues": A reinterpretation of childhood history and the common school. Paper presented at the Annual Meeting of the Midwest History of Education Society, Chicago.

Sommerville, J. (1982). *The rise and fall of childhood.* Beverly Hills, CA: Sage.

Stone, L. (1977). *The family, sex, and marriage in England, 1500–1800.* New York: Harper & Row.

Summerfield, G. (1984). *Fantasy and reason: Children's literature in the eighteenth century.* Athens, GA: University of Georgia Press.

Williams, E. (1937). *Horace Mann: Educational statesman.* New York: Macmillan.

Wisconsin Child-study Society. (1898). *Handbook of the Wisconsin Child-study Society.* Milwaukee: Wisconsin Teachers' Association.

Wittrock, B., Wagner, P., & Wollmann, H. (1991). Social science and the modern state: Policy knowledge and political institutions in Western Europe and the United States. In P. Wagner, C. H. Weiss, B. Wittrock, & H. Wollmann (Eds.), *Social sciences and modern states* (pp. 28–85). Cambridge: Cambridge University Press.

Woodson, C. (1933). *The mis-education of the Negro.* Washington, DC: Africa World Press.

Wynter, S. (1995). 1492: A new world view. In V. Lawrence & R. Nettleford (Eds.), *Race, discourse and the origin of the Americas: A new world view* (pp. 5–57). Washington, DC: Smithsonian Institute Press.

6

The Construction of the Body Through Sex Education Discourse Practices

JUDITH RABAK WAGENER

In the past several decades there has been a constant although shifting debate regarding sexuality education in the schools. While in the 1960s, 1970s, and early 1980s there were clear divisions among proponents and those who believed that nearly any form of sexuality education would whet teenagers' sexual appetite, leading to irresponsible and immoral behavior, since the onset of HIV/AIDS proponents have expanded to include the latter group. Now, previous opponents argue that human growth and development courses, with a return to traditional family values and abstinence-only instruction, must supplant instruction in which students are given information regarding contraceptive technologies, discuss multiple forms of family, and have access to school health clinics in which contraceptives, including condoms, are made available.[1]

However, this debate is inextricably connected with certain notions of sexuality, desire, male and female bodies, and social and cultural norms that have become institutionalized and yet remain invisible in their historical specificity. By this, I refer to the roots of what presently is considered normal and appropriate sexual and social behavior. While critics and proponents of sexuality education alike debate the role that schooling in sexuality plays in creating, demanding, or denying sexual experimentation in youths, each side is grounded in the theoretical presupposition that there exist eternal, universal, and natural essences of sexual desire and behavior that must be controlled or shaped in various manners. What the current public discourses veil are the social and historical constructions and reconstructions of "normal" sexuality, and thus the critical role that sexuality education has played, in this century, in social administration.

I will argue that this century of school sexuality education is an important arena for investigation and debate not because of its controversy or because it can be proven that it either caused or prevented irresponsible teenage sexual activity, but because of its role in the larger context of modern pedagogical practices in which the lives, thoughts, actions, and behaviors of schoolchildren have come under increasing scrutiny and management. Underlying the continual debates about sex education, with their moral and religious underpinnings, are curriculum discourses in which normalizations about human behavior were and are institutionalized. It is, as Michel Foucault (1977, 1979, 1980a, 1980b, 1986) has theorized, the continual and changing conceptualizations (but at any given time normalized constructions of male and female and adolescent sexual behavior) that become part of the governance of individuals and social groups in modernity.

A brief discussion of Foucault's theoretical positions and their application to a study of early-twentieth-century school sexuality education would be helpful in an effort to locate power in such pedagogical practices. As Foucault argued, particularly in his later works, *The History of Sexuality* (1980a) and *Discipline and Punish* (1979), modern schooling in health and sexuality has been and is a project tied into the state, but not simply government institutions. Rather, these school subjects contain multiple and interweaving discourses, which, in their modern and technical construction, make possible a continual and micro-management of individual behavior. Particularly since the early decades of the twentieth century, curriculum technologies, such as those that clearly define, categorize, examine, evaluate, distinguish, and standardize appropriate and inappropriate behavior, have enabled pedagogical practices, including those found in sexuality education, to participate in the multiple ways in which lives of school students are governed.

In this chapter, I focus on the public school system in Milwaukee, Wisconsin, and show how the semiautonomous notions of health, social hygiene, human growth and development, and other curriculum topics constitute what can be described as a political economy of male and female bodies. Milwaukee city, county, and state documents, school board reports, news clippings, curriculum files, and other educational materials are investigated between 1910 and 1960.[2] During this time, normalizing techniques are noted revealing the multiple schemata by which human bodies are monitored and disciplined toward socially appropriate conduct. Relational discourses representing the broader social and political debates within which curriculum practices became institutionalized are also recorded.[3]

While the various institutions that form public life and shape the lives of children, such as all social, religious, political, government, and educational institutions, are implicated in power, they are not solely power nor are they easily defined in their power. Rather, argued Foucault, power can be located at the smallest levels of life activities and practices: The public statements, debates, curriculum guides, and district policies that are constitutive of sexuality education in any school district, can be examined for the ways in which individuals or groups of individuals are constructed as capable, limited as inherently defective, and eternalized as biologically given or psychologically hopeless. This, in a Foucaultian sense, is a form of government and power over individuals that cannot be traced to the sovereignty, but, in a more dangerous and insidious fashion, permeates daily life through that which is uncritically seen to be true.[4] In the case of sexuality education, the authority for such truths resides primarily in the human sciences, such as human biology, genetics, and psychology, which since the turn of the twentieth century have provided the overarching legitimation for theories about male and female sexual and gender roles, childhood sexuality, and adolescence.[5]

The project described in this chapter involves an investigation and analysis of the historical continuities and discontinuities in conceptualizations of male and female bodies, sexual desire, gender roles, childhood sexuality, and so on. The analysis is predicated on the assumption that present-day notions of sexuality, as found in school discourses, can be investigated for their roots in past discourses that shaped and framed sexuality education in this century. Rather than focus on sex education as a national movement, which presumes it is monolithic and without relationship to a cultural, social, political, and economic geography, one particular school district, the Milwaukee Public Schools, is investigated and placed within its broader contexts of social, political, and religious frameworks.

In the first section of the chapter, I present an overview of social and political discourses that framed the ways in which Milwaukee's citizens were categorized and disciplined. This is followed by a description of the various and overlapping strategies by which the human body became available to scrutiny through health and pedagogical institutional discourses. In the second section, I describe the formation and reformation of normalizations of the self through the biology of the sexes. Shifts in the normalization of female, male, and adolescent bodies are described within a context of changing epistemologies.

THE BODY SCRUTINIZED

In the early 1900s, as in other industrialized cities of the time, the movement toward technological modes of production was found not only in business and labor but in schooling as well (Kliebard, 1975, 1986). While Milwaukee maintained a unique population base that was noted as more "ethnic" in nature than that of other cities, and while this German- and Polish-based population was politically aligned with the Socialist Party more than in most U.S. cities during this period, the tenets of industriousness, efficiency, and social engineering were as common in Milwaukee as elsewhere (Reese, 1981).

In fact, it is in consideration of Milwaukee's unique citizenry and political history that the study of the embodiment of sexuality becomes even more important. Whereas it is convenient and tempting to position Milwaukee's predominantly German political, religious, and social character as institutionally dominant, archival evidence of strategies of regulation and normalization practiced at multiple sites and in multiple discourses weakens such structural thinking. That is, even in consideration of Milwaukee's unique heritage, Milwaukee civic and school discourse practices made evident the broader twentieth-century shifts in bureaucratic and technological thinking that pervaded all levels of life activities—which simply cannot be traced to an imposition of power from the dominant political leadership to the "masses."[6]

Before proceeding, I would like to draw out a Foucaultian position central to the analysis. As previously mentioned, this study concerns the various and changing political economies of the body. By this, I refer to the importance of placing human behavior, as defined in discourses of sexuality education, within the political and social contexts in which women and men are defined and examined in public life in Milwaukee. Foucault argued that it is in discourse that historical struggle takes place; appropriate knowledge as verified through the human sciences becomes a practice of power when males and females and adolescents and children are viewed and disciplined toward a set of norms and standards that are largely uncontested. Thus, power resides in the hidden ways in which the political and social struggles to define common knowledge become embodied by men and women.

A brief mapping of Milwaukee's social, health, political, and religious foundations in the early decades of the twentieth century will be incorporated at this point as a way in which to show, relationally, the discourse practices of schooling and broader institutional discourses.

Milwaukee: The "Ethnic" City

In the early decades of the century, Milwaukee's population, as mentioned previously, was dominated by Germans, Austrians, and Poles, which contributed to the overall Teutonic flavor of the city. Other ethnic groups settled in Milwaukee as well, including Irish, Italians, Greeks, Eastern European Jews, Russians, and Scandinavians (Olson, 1987). Of the 88,991 foreign-born citizens of Milwaukee in 1900 (31% of the total population), 61% were German and 17% were Polish. In the same year, there were only 892 people of "Negro descent," out of a total city population of 285,315 (U.S. Census, 1900).

Sentiments toward Milwaukee's ethnic population ranged from admiration to disgust. Germans and Poles were described as thrifty and industrious and superior to Italians, Hungarians, and Greeks. Italians often were viewed as intemperate and prone to violence and, along with the "detested Irish," were to compete with African-Americans for unskilled jobs (Korman, 1967).

In religious affiliation the vast majority of immigrants were Lutheran or Catholic, because of the German and Polish domination (Korman, 1967).

The political and social influence of the Turnvereine Society, a German cultural society, was evident in both political and pedagogical practice in the early twentieth century. Many of these society members were anticlerical, supported Socialist policies, and believed in enlarged scientific instruction in the schools (Still, 1948). Other prominent German groups included the Old Lutheran group, noted for its adherence to fundamentalist beliefs and opposition to rationalism and secularism, and the German Catholics (Woehrmann, 1987).

By the early years of the twentieth century, Milwaukee had established itself as a city in which social reforms were notable. Among the victories of the Milwaukee Socialists, who governed City Hall for 38 of the 50 years between 1910 and 1960 (Olson, 1960), were public housing, social security, workmen's compensation, expanded public education, and free medical services in the public schools.

However, the city government was not without its opposition, including, but not limited to, the Milwaukee Catholics, led by Archbishop Messner, who feared that public schooling would supplant the family (Reese, 1981). Messner argued that parents—not the schools—should have the primary responsibility for educating the child in "family values" (Ring, 1968).

While Milwaukee's reforms were designed to benefit particularly low-income residents, including recent immigrants who were largely of Southern and Eastern European descent, Milwaukee was not immune from the national movement toward social efficiency or "race betterment." Interestingly, while Milwaukee's Catholics opposed the Socialist push toward public education, they allied themselves with the Socialists in their strenuous opposition to Wisconsin's sterilization statute, put forth in 1913. Even so, the statute passed, allowing for the sterilization of inmates at the state's penal and mental institutions, a practice advanced under the banner of "negative" eugenics—or prevention of procreation among those deemed "unfit" (Vecoli,

1960). However, other eugenic principles, including "positive eugenics," which was the program designed to educate people regarding the science of selective breeding, were more easily masked by discursive practices that had their basis in the twentieth-century tenets of social control and efficiency.[7]

A primary illustration of eugenical practices was public discourses that made clear the hierarchical positioning of Milwaukee's ethnic groups. Medical professionals, social workers, educators, city officials, and religious leaders alike spoke to the position of minorities and women. Addressing the Sunset Club in 1909, Dr. Sellinger of the University of Chicago stated that the criminal is "usually the immigrant who can't adjust himself to the industrial system."[8] Sellinger's remedy was to provide detention homes for "tramps" and to restrict immigration based on IQ tests.

Milwaukee newspapers were rife with negative descriptions of immigrant communities. For example, in 1906 the mayor, building inspector, and fire chief combined forces to clean up what were described as the "Badlands" (which were part of "Nigger Alley"), and the "Ghetto," inhabited by Russian Jews. Another section was described as a "nest of Slovaks," people "herded together like sheep," where "filth and vermin crawled."[9]

Even the noted Milwaukee settlement worker, Lizzie B. Kander, contributed to these categorical discourses. In a letter on philanthropic policy, she claimed that men were superior to women, even in character, and that sterilization would be the most humane way of eliminating the unfit.[10]

While Milwaukee was noted for its progressive public health reforms, including regulation of the meat packing industry, water quality improvement, and enactment of tenement laws (Leavitt, 1975), its city physicians also participated in the campaign for social order. This was no more evident than in the health programs against the spread of venereal diseases, which were rampant in Milwaukee following World War I, as elsewhere. Moralizing judgments became public health mandates, in the name of hygiene and sanitation. George Ruhland, Commissioner of Health in 1919, claimed:

> One of the most difficult problems confronting the committee in charge of protecting returning soldiers from vice conditions is the large number of apartments occupied by women of loose moral character.[11]

It is interesting to note the message that returning soldiers needed protection and that the enemy, this time, were immoral women. Implicit is the designation of men as incapable (biologically) of controlling their own sexual impulses, while women clearly were deemed capable of and responsible for acting in a moral and careful fashion. It is difficult not to read "biology is destiny," or "boys will be boys," into this passage.

The above excerpt also can be read as the normalization of male sexual

activity and the pathologization of female sexual activity, which would become a consistent discursive practice of the Milwaukee Health Department
through the 1910s, 1920s, and 1930s.

A reference to Foucault's unique postulate on modern power is again
valuable. While in the monarchical periods of the Middle Ages power clearly
was imposed from top to bottom (juristic), in modern centuries power inheres in the multiple strategies by which human life activities are defined,
sorted, examined, and monitored. Through modern scientific methods, monitoring and measuring the productivity and worth of humans and groups became possible and widespread. And yet it is in the ability of individuals to
control and discipline their own thoughts and actions, that power becomes
diffuse and omnipresent at the same time.[12] Thus, normalizing judgments are
those techniques by which the lives, thoughts, and desires of modern humans
have become microscopically examined and strategically rather than juridi-
cally regulated.

In summary, these brief descriptions of Milwaukee's political and religious formations, and health reforms in the early decades of the century, give
focus to the ways in which individuals and groups of individuals would be
classified and categorized. Of importance is the notion that multiple and often conflicting institutional discourses allowed for the viewing, examining,
and subsequent hierarchization of Milwaukee's citizens. Of even more significance, as illustrated by Lizzie Kander's discourse, is the Foucaultian notion that modern techniques of surveillance—those forms of self- and social
observation and judgment made possible through modern measurements—
allowed self-examination and self-limitation to seem normal.

Up to this point the focus for discussion has been on a chronological
history of actors. In the following, I turn to a description of the shifts in how
the body is placed, discursively, within a social, political, and economic
space.

The "Dangerous Teen"

There were many different facets of sex instruction in Milwaukee between
1910 and 1960. There were parallel movements to instruct Milwaukee youths
in several different topics pertaining to sexuality education, including sex
hygiene, particularly in relation to body cleanliness and sanitation; social hygiene as it pertained to grooming, etiquette, and appearance; eugenics; human growth and development; and family living. There was also parallel instruction in sexuality across different organizations: The city and state health
departments provided lectures and classes in the schools, the churches, and
the YMCA; and the Milwaukee Public Schools (MPS) integrated information
about sexuality across several subject areas, including physical education,

health education, biology, home economics, social studies, and ethics. Throughout most of the period under study—at least until approximately 1950—these subjects often were taught at the same time through both the schools and the health departments.

Throughout the first section of this chapter, I noted the theme of social efficiency: This was an overriding assumption for sex education and other curricular practices throughout the period under study. The social conditions to which this assumption refers, however, are varied. In the early decades of the century, the primary focus of sex instruction was on the prevention and control of venereal diseases. Along with instruction in hygiene and sanitation, however, students were instructed in social hygiene—social grooming, human relationships, preparation for marriage, and family life. In the 1940s, with venereal diseases in check in the middle-income population, and divorce on the increase, instruction in human relationships and social living became even more predominant. However, whether it was education about venereal diseases or education in human relationships and family living, the overarching presupposition was that sex instruction could provide an order to social living in an increasingly pluralistic society.

The social context for sex instruction not only influenced the form of instruction, but created new ways in which the self and social body were defined. In later years, there were shifts in the ways in which bodies were constituted, with new bodily constructions again becoming normalized. The documents of sex education—the curriculum guides, reference materials, scientific statements, and public debates regarding sex instruction—tell the story of the changing ways in which the curriculum defined and disciplined individuals toward certain norms. Technical ways of thinking about, sorting, and ranking social life were carried into curriculum practices so that individuals were disciplined to monitor their own thoughts, desires, and behaviors.

These historical constructions can be given more coherence through a discussion of teenage conceptualization and supervision in early-twentieth-century Milwaukee. In the 1920 annual report of the city's Board of School Directors (Milwaukee Public Schools, 1920), an editorial discussed the problems associated with the long hours of "leisure" thrust upon young people. It suggested that idleness created a "dangerous teen." The Milwaukee Health Department records show that these teens were particular teens, however. The April 1921 *Bulletin of the Milwaukee Health Department* (Milwaukee Health Department, 1921) stated that statistics showed that youths, "especially those of the *class* which is ordinarily considered most likely to be infected, leave school long before the age at which sex education in regard to the twin diseases [syphilis and gonorrhea] is given" (p. 7; emphasis added). The earliest incidences of venereal disease in boys are at age 15, and reach a maximum at ages 19 to 23, according to the article. "The ages of sixteen to

twenty-three are those between the most usual ending of school and beginning of married life" (p. 7). For girls, the incidences of venereal disease
ranged approximately 2 years earlier than for boys.

The *Bulletin* suggested that the sex education that was offered through
lectures in the upper grades of the high schools often started too late to "be
of real service in safeguarding young people against venereal disease" (p. 7).
However, the particular leisure activities of the "class" of students described
distinguished these youths from other youths. Through health department
statistical analysis, specific sexual and social bodies are constructed. As the
city monitored incidences of communicable diseases in youths, other life activities were tabulated and available for scrutiny: school attendance, marriage
rates, and so on.

A February 1926 booklet entitled *Our High School Girls* (Milwaukee
Public Schools, 1926) offered similar discourses regarding the "problem" of
teen leisure. In this booklet, girls are warned of their various "impulses."
Although it does not describe these impulses, it concludes that "a busy girl
is a safe girl" (p. 4). It is difficult to ascertain the precise meaning of these
warnings; however, it is likely that they meant that industriousness decreased
the likelihood of time available for sexual "experimentation."

In the early decades of the century, teenage activities were measured and
enumerated; particular youthful behavior was targeted as an object of sexual
concern. Contained within these discourses, however, was an exercise of discipline; young people were to manage their time to behave in a socially approved manner. This meant that youths were to exercise a certain diligence
in thought and action, in both school and "leisure" time.

Although space limitations in this chapter do not allow for a more thorough discussion of the various ways in which the life activities of youths were
monitored and classified according to certain social mores, it is important
to emphasize the shift in authority regarding sexual matters. Although the
Milwaukee Health Department educators were the primary instructors of sex
hygiene in the early decades of the century, by the 1940s the demands for
instruction in sex and social hygiene by city and state health educators became too much to handle, resulting in a shift in responsibility to the public
schools. At the same time, there was a shift in attitudes regarding sex instruction: By the late 1930s, parental authority regarding sex matters was gradually supplanted by the schools. The schools were to provide the categories
and distinctions by which the body was to be thought about, but within the
context of familial and moral guidance.

Colonization of the Home

The deployment of micro-managing practices, made possible through new,
scientific curriculum objectives and standardized expectations for sexual and

social conduct, was integral in the shift toward the institutionalization of the Milwaukee Public Schools as authorities in sexual matters.

The city health department would still play an integral role in sexuality education in the 1930s and 1940s, however. John Koehler, Commissioner of Health, stated in the September 1936 *Bulletin* (Milwaukee Health Department, 1936): "Next to homes and parents, schools and health departments play the most important part in disease prevention and health promotion" (p. 2). As had been argued by other reformers before, Koehler stressed that "as much emphasis should be laid on proper teaching of personal health and hygiene as is laid on other subjects" (p. 2).

The campaign to incorporate social hygiene education into school subjects was conducted largely by medical leaders, school administrators, women's groups, the YMCA, and health educators for the State of Wisconsin and the City of Milwaukee. In the 891 Series of the State Board of Health, there are many references to the work done in social hygiene education by Aimee Zillmer, health educator for the state, and Urania Rauter and later Joyce Reiss, health educators for the City of Milwaukee Health Department. In the many letters exchanged between Ms. Zillmer and Ms. Rauter during the 1940s, one can see the building of a firm partnership in efforts to bring the social hygiene "message" to youths, not only in Milwaukee schools, but throughout the state. Dwight Warner, also a social hygiene educator for the state, lectured in social hygiene to boys from 1929 to 1947. By the 1940s, health educators for the city and state began to feel that they could not meet the increasing demands to speak to students about social hygiene.

In the volumes of materials, mostly correspondence from the State Board of Health, one can locate a subtle, mid-century shift toward the usurpation of the home in matters of sex instruction. An important element in the push for more sex education through the guidance of the schools was an increasing acceptance of the position of the school as authority.

Notions of the moral body as provided through parental guidance were to be given new distinctions and definitions through scientific instruction in the schools. In a Milwaukee reference booklet, *Sex Education for the Adolescent*, Corner and Landis (1941) stated:

> In an ideal education system having a thoroughly sane attitude about the matter, parents would not need to teach the biology of sex, for it would be taken up in due course at the various stages of science teaching in the schools as a part of the general training in biology. This is already being done excellently wherever competent teachers have been given the opportunity. The lucky parents of children so taught have a background against which they can more easily develop socially approved values and attitudes in their children. (p. 3)

Later, the same volume described the new view of the parent's role in teaching her or his children about sex. "The best contribution the parent can make to the sex education of his child is to see that the boys and girls are properly taught the elements of biology and hygiene, preferably in school" (p. 16). In a time of increasing public messages about sexuality and the growth of a culturally diverse society, it was believed that the schools could administer the sexuality of children better than could the parent.

State and city health educators also felt that schools could provide more scientific and rational instruction about sex matters. The work of these social hygiene educators included lectures to school students and courses for women and engaged couples, often through the YMCA. Urania Rauter of the city health department conducted a "March of Health" broadcast every Saturday in 1943 and 1944. In a broadcast on March 15, 1944, Ms. Rauter stated that parents, although well-meaning, often used the "weapons of force and fear instead of the tools of knowledge and education and confident and understanding guidance in their relationship [with their children]."[13]

At the April 4, 1944 school board meeting, a letter was read from the Milwaukee County League of Women Voters. The members requested that

> a well considered program of character education and social and mental hygiene for children be developed appropriate to the needs of varying personalities and levels of maturity, and that means be provided for the supplementing of the training of teachers and the supplying of trained supervisory leadership for carrying out such a program. (Milwaukee Public Schools, 1944, p. 369)

The movement toward more comprehensive social hygiene education in the schools was carefully crafted, however. As had been recommended in 1913 by the American Federation for Sex Hygiene committee on the matters and methods of sex instruction, sex education in the schools was to be implemented conservatively and quietly. It was hardly presented as an usurpation of parental authority. Arguably, it was the deference to scientific authority that contributed to the increasingly strong support for education in social hygiene. Most parents simply were believed to be lacking in scientific knowledge. Thus, it was felt that education in social hygiene would complement the moral guidance and religious training provided by the home and church.

Indeed, the social hygiene education of Milwaukee in the 1930s and 1940s was to maintain the moral distinctions created through the construction of bodies, but with a new formation in pedagogical practice that was to secularize such moral distinctions. The body was defined through such values as industriousness and diligence, and school attendance and leisure activities; any attitudes or behaviors that were "socially approved" or that developed "character" were framed as scientifically neutral (based on the latest theories in biology or psychology). New sex hygiene curriculum technologies could rank, sort, and categorize norms and standards for living so that the social relations and historical formation of such discourses were invisible.

Guided Instruction

By mid-century curriculum documents carried efficient and measurable objectives that could account for students' "health" and "fitness." The goals, objectives, and list of topics to be covered in health, as described in Milwaukee Public School Curriculum Guides, produced new and specific ways in which bodies would be observed and evaluated. This would include a closer and more official view of hygienic practices and social deportment, with a continuing push for "race hygiene"—or care taken to find the proper mate, based on race, class, religion, and genetic potential.

A prime emphasis at this time was on social grooming, for preparation to marriage and family. Consider the following heading in the Human Relations unit in the *Junior High Health Instruction Guide Health Course: Suggested Health Topics for Grade Nine* (Milwaukee Public Schools, 1959): "Pupils are justifiably interested in acceptable social deportment and fashions" (p. 7). Another subheading in the same unit stated: "Dating is a unique American custom. We accept and value it as part of the growing up process of our boys and girls" (p. 38).

While historical analysis makes clear a discursive shift toward "dating" as a transcendent and universal construct, its underlying historical, social, and economic geography is veiled. Represented in curriculum documents as normal for all adolescents, the notion of dating is tied to developmentally appropriate human growth and development. Standards thus are set so that each pupil can examine his or her own patterns of dating and appraise those patterns as normal or abnormal. It is possible to understand this categorization as introducing dating as a problem of social administration; however, it is placed in a language that supposes that dating is a "natural" outcome of the human growth and development process.

In an MPS proposed Family Living outline, dated August 2, 1950, the notion that appearance and grooming were synonymous with successful family and social life is evident. The outline included sections on "Individual Development"; "Changes in the American Family"; "Successful Family Life—The Family Council"; "Health, Safety, Recreation, and First Aid Activities"; "Boy–Girl Relationships"; "Marriage"; "Parenthood"; "The Consumer and Home Management"; and "Family in the Community." The unit on health and safety has a subheading entitled "Appearance and Personal Hygiene." The section incorporated information on the proper care of skin, hair, nails, feet, teeth, nose, and throat, as well as on posture and clothing. The information on posture included the item: "relationship of posture to health, economic, and social status" (p. 3). The discussions of proper care of feet and teeth each have the following subpoint: "effect on personal appearance" (pp. 3, 4).

This outline points to the social significance of "hygiene." Contained within the discussions are certain assumptions of what it meant to be a successful male and female in the 1950s. Although the curriculum points to posture, care of hair, teeth, and so on, as universal standards of personal hygiene, in fact, these instructions for proper hygiene represented particular social and moral standards. Underlying these standards is a political economy of the body in which the body is defined in its social utility: The relationship of posture to economic and social status, for example, indicates an underlying concern for social status beyond the threat of ill health.

Throughout the period under study, public health and curriculum documents refer to the need for people to develop a positive attitude toward the program of eugenics. By mid-century, however, such instruction had been framed by scientific, rational curriculum objectives, which easily masked the regulatory elements of such a program.

Illustrations of the way in which curriculum objectives normalized the underlying social construction of eugenic principles can be found in the 1955 and 1959 MPS health instruction guides, for junior high. The 1955 guide (Milwaukee Public Schools, 1955) includes a heading in the Physiology and Diseases unit entitled "Preparation for Parenthood." This section suggests that the student: "1. Knows something of the simpler facts of heredity and eugenics. 2. Knows something of the physiological changes that are taking place in the boy and girl at this period and of their relationship to character and personality" (p. 48). It is clear from the latter statement that moral qualities were believed to be based in human "nature" and to be heritable.

In the 1959 guide, a subunit is entitled "Seventh graders begin to differ from younger boys and girls socially, emotionally, and physically" (Milwaukee Public Schools, 1959, p. 50). In the section on "Internal changes and developments in seventh graders" (p. 52), the following activity is listed: "Raise mice or rabbits, mating pure white and pure black to show transmission of hereditary qualities through genes" (p. 52).

This activity, one among several listed, is to teach seventh graders that people are biologically and genetically different from one another. When the specific language of the activity is examined, however, certain social and cultural values become evident. This particular activity leaves the reader to question the propriety of interracial mating; the discursive practice privileges the breeding among "pure white" or "pure black" mice or rabbits over that of white with black animals.

Instruction in health and sex education, throughout the period under study, emphasized the youth's responsibility to distinguish among people their biological and genetic characteristics. However, hierarchies between individuals and groups are constructed in these discourse practices. The underlying message to youths was that "selective" breeding produced better offspring; the children of interracial, or of mentally "inferior," parents were of less worth and, often, deemed a danger or a burden to society.[14, 15]

The classificatory and hierarchical distinctions constructed in such discourses were made possible through the increasingly scientific and exacting curriculum technologies of schooling. That is, curriculum objectives thoroughly and exactly described, defined, sorted, and measured appropriate social and sexual behavior. In new ways, scientific curriculum allowed for both the construction and maintenance of disciplinary power: It observed and judged the lives, thoughts, actions, and souls of school children.

In summary, a prevalent indication of twentieth-century schooling in the human sciences, including sexuality education, was that students would be increasingly available for both social and self-observation and scrutiny. However, the scientific and technical means by which this practice was made possible obscured the social and historical struggle behind the construction of normal male and female behavior. In a Foucaultian sense, modern "technologies," such as health department statistical data and curriculum standards, were incapable of making moralizing judgments visible and available for critique.

In the following section, I will discuss the ways in which female, male, and adolescent bodies were legitimized as "normal" through the sanctity of the biological sciences.

NORMALIZATION THROUGH THE BIOLOGY OF THE SEXES

The State of Wisconsin had passed a Hygiene Law in 1885 requiring that every school district provide for instruction in physiology and hygiene with emphasis on the effects of stimulants and narcotics on the human system (Patzer, 1924). While this law was directed specifically toward the effects of drugs (what might be described today as "Alcohol and Other Drug Education"), the importance of the notion of "hygiene" cannot be overstated. Hygiene, as is the case with the term "health" today, meant more than the absence of pathogens. It contained socially negotiated directions that went beyond the bounds of a scientific study of pathogenic activity. In the same way, the discourses of "sex hygiene" were embedded with values that, while seemingly neutral, objective, and scientific, clearly interpreted what it meant to live in a sexually "healthy" manner.

Thus, when Milwaukee School Board Director Richardson suggested in his June 1912 Director's Report that sex hygiene instruction might be introduced into the high schools, an important caveat was added: Richardson asserted that dangers of such instruction in the high schools "would be greatly lessened if our young people were instructed by parents in lessons of self-denial in every direction" (p. 500). Richardson argued that young people should have "more exercise in saying 'no' to opportunities for self-indulgence" (Milwaukee Public Schools, 1912, p. 500).

The language of such public calls for sex instruction makes clear the broader meanings behind hygiene. Taken at scientific value, instruction in sex hygiene would incorporate only information on the specific pathways of microbes in the transmission of "venereal" diseases, or the mechanisms by which male sperm fertilize the female egg, or the physiological processes of labor and delivery. However, the discourses of sex hygiene in the early twentieth century contained social foundations beyond a study of the body's microphysiological processes: Sexual experimentation in youths was considered "indulgent." A more deeply embedded assumption was that there existed a psychosexual "drive" or "impulse" in youths, and particularly males, that must be "denied" in order to live sexually hygienic lives.[16]

This scientific rationalization of human sexual behavior was embodied by notions of "normal" male and female sexual impulses and desires. The form of health instruction, and the public discourses about the dangers of sexual experimentation as espoused by Health Department leaders, give insight into the way in which male and female bodies were defined and conceptualized in early-twentieth-century Milwaukee sex education.

As mentioned previously, the health educators for the city were concerned primarily with the lives of particular teens. Those deemed most dangerous were those believed to possess a biological and psychological predisposition to sexual promiscuity.

Although youths who left school early were targeted for failings in their personal character, there was little discussion or focus on the social conditions in which many youths lived. Instead, the health department, through the schools, was positioned to intervene in the social conduct of youths through education regarding transmission of venereal diseases and healthful activities to prevent such afflictions. In examining health department reports and essays, as will be highlighted in more detail next, it is evident that the high rates of the "twin" sexual diseases were viewed as a preponderance of ignorance and a failure of will against the "naturally" occurring and powerful male sex drive.

Venereal Disease: The Cause of Licentiousness

The naturalization of social conditions and circumstances could be found in campaigns conducted by the City Health Department against the dangers of "licentiousness." It was commonly believed that the new vaudeville shows, and later movies, contained stimulating visual scenes that could whet, physiologically and/or psychologically, the "sexual appetite."

Deputy Commissioner of Health Koehler stated in 1918: "Sexual immorality is the cause of venereal disease and the further anyone remains from sexual immorality either in thought or action, the better it will be for his health."[17] Koehler's assertion is that immorality, not microbe activity, is the cause of venereal disease transmission. Likewise, Milwaukee's Health Commissioner George Ruhland argued in 1919 that the function of the new Bureau for Venereal Diseases was to treat as well as to "lessen, if not eliminate, these diseases, by showing their danger, and by giving reliable and safe instruction on what constitutes a normal and healthful sex life" (Milwaukee Health Department, 1919, p. 8).

The notion of "normal" sex life cannot be taken out of the context of "normal" social behavior. First, a social and moral code was embedded in the language of "danger." Second, it was implied that individuals who sought to view sexually explicit materials, movies, shows, and so forth, were displaying abnormal behavior. This pathology was drawn from a scientific discourse that legitimated the notion that viewing of such materials triggered a psychosexual impulse to action. Thus, the stage was set for a disciplinary code of conduct: Human beings, and particularly males, were seen as naturally possessing a difficult-to-control sex drive. However, the prevailing code also reinforced the belief that it was respectable (i.e., normal) to deny such an appetite. The male self is, thus, sharply "divided"—through both the construction of a strong sexual impulse and the construction of a strong code of ethics regarding the equally normal behavior of sexual "repression."[18]

Added to this complex set of disciplinary behaviors is the psychosexualization of "vulgar shows." The most glaring illustration of such practices is an early statement made by Koehler: "It would appear ludicrous to take food away from a man and give him an 'appetizer' instead. It is likewise very inconsistent to attempt to abolish prostitutes and permit agencies to increase the demand for prostitution" (Milwaukee Health Department, 1918, p. 8).

This discourse constructs prostitution as a social institution predicated on an essential female pathology; contained within the discourse is the presupposition that prostitutes are biologically and morally predisposed to such activity. Given the right stimulus—vulgar shows—and the right conditions—the presence of "erotic" women—normal men will find it difficult to go sexually "hungry." The comparison between food and sex is not coincidental. Both are considered "essential" (read "male") drives.

Koehler continued his campaign against licentiousness in later years, claiming that

vulgar shows whether they be in the form of motion pictures, vaudeville, or drama, are responsible for more exposure to venereal disease than any other factor.

The automobile, intoxication, and immodest dress may all encourage exposure to venereal disease, but none as much [as] do some of the modern shows. (Milwaukee Health Department, 1927, p. 6)

Koehler's statement is drawn from a particular scientific discourse that normalizes and universalizes the body. It is a discourse that assumes that there is a scientifically verifiable cause and effect to the viewing of modern shows and the incitement to copulate indiscriminately, thus causing the spread of venereal diseases. In addition, the discourse is productive of clear distinctions between appropriate and healthy dress and dress that is believed to cause sexual excitation. It signifies that some apparel and wearing of apparel is modest and some is immodest. Imbedded in such a discussion is the notion that the wearing of less apparel contains psychosexual significance: In this case, it justifies the belief that the female body is capable of sexual titillation.

Central to this analysis is the construction of the normal. Self-knowledge in sex education discourses was made possible through scientific evidence. There is little question that sexual and social rules for conduct contained their basis for *legitimation* not in social theories, but in biological theories. Males and females came to know themselves as sexually appropriate or pathological according to their desire; although libido was believed to be psychobiological in nature, it was biological science that directed this impulse and biology that would determine how these impulses would be acted on or denied in males and females. Although the biological sciences as they cohered with new discourses in developmental psychology would change the way in which gender would be constructed in sexuality discourse practice by mid-century, it is important to first discuss the ways in which normal sexuality shifted from dangerous or vile in nature, to positive and productive—in females, males, and adolescents.

From Vile Impulse to Productive Force

Valorized in the early-twentieth-century Milwaukee Health Department public documents was the notion of a natural, but difficult-to-control, psychosexual drive of males. At the same time, these discourses were distinctive of and categorical of particular women who were believed to possess such a drive. Prostitutes especially were targeted as women with abnormally high libidos. It was purported that these highly "sexual" women were, as was the case with males, more likely to act on their impulses in the presence of certain "aphrodisiacs": licentious movies, shows, pictures, access to the automobile, and so on.

As with male high school dropouts, "wayward" young women became a target of citywide public health efforts.[19] Health department demographic data per se did not allow any analysis of the economic or social basis for prostitution, and essays seldom took a stand against economically driven prostitution. The fact that recent immigrants and lower-income women disproportionately represented the ranks of prostitution and people afflicted with venereal diseases was mostly left unchallenged in health department discourses as evidence of a social or political etiology.[20] Instead, the scientific tables and records constructed a sexual pathology, distinguished along national, race, gender, age, income, and other lines.

By far the most important and valorized conceptualizations of womanhood, as postulated by the public health discourses, were those that had to do with caretaking: of the home, the family, school children, the race. It was believed that women possessed a natural instinct toward nurturing and procreation. Medical officers in the health department even stated that women, by nature, had a stronger "interest" in sanitation than did men.[21]

The shift in gender constructions in sexuality education discourses occurred most dramatically at the time when there was a confluence of new theories regarding sexual impulses, human growth and development, and family life. By the 1940s, women were constructed as not only having a sexual impulse, but containing such for the purposes of providing a "happy" family life. That is, both men's and women's sexual drives would be reconstructed in such a way as to redefine the sexual and social territory between men and women.

The New Woman

A significant illustration of this shift can be found in one of the reference materials for sex education in Milwaukee Public Schools: Biester, Griffiths, and Pearce's *Units in Personal Health and Human Relations* (1947). These authors cited a 1938 study conducted by Lewis Terman, which described more specifically the new expectations for marital relationships. It listed several factors that contribute to a happy marriage, including "the adequacy of the wife's orgasm" and "equality or near equality in the strength of the sex drive in husband and wife" (p. 198).

While it is questionable whether these studies were mentioned directly in health education classes, new meanings regarding sexuality, and for sex education, were formed, based on certain social and cultural norms. For both men and women, there would be a shift in the way in which they would view, and examine, their bodies. Biological and psychological science had justified what were new social relations between men and women. The discourse on sexual response within marriage not only explicitly defined normal sexuality, but implicitly cast all other forms of sexual behavior as abnormal.

Adolescence: Construction of a Psychosexual Identity

In the 1940s, theoretical work in the psychology of sexuality allowed for the formation of new, institutionalized norms for youthful sexuality—first in adolescents, and then in children. Sexuality came to be defined in terms of stages of development. This new categorization would change the way people thought about sexuality: The sex impulse would be expressed rhetorically as vital, healthy, positive, and productive. It was not dirty, vile, evil, or destructive, argued Frances B. Strain in *New Patterns in Sex Teaching* (1940).

Strain's volumes, *New Patterns* and later *The Normal Sex Interests of Children* (1948), would be two of the most common references for social hygiene education in Milwaukee schooling. In 1949, the State Board of Health recommended Biester, Griffiths, and Pearce's *Units in Personal Health* and Strain's *New Patterns* as the best social hygiene materials available.[22]

In a 1947 report by the Milwaukee Public School health committee (comprising a home economics, physical education, sociology, and commercial teacher), objectives are listed under the family living section for grades 10–12. Among other things, the students are to develop "wholesome" relationships with the opposite sex, to understand that desire for independence from the family is normal, and to know the physiology and psychology of the reproductive and glandular systems.

The new combined science of developmental psychology and physiology contained an epistemology that framed instruction in the "stages of adolescence." Biester and colleagues (1947) described the characteristics of the new adolescent body as follows: Adolescence roughly encompasses ages 12 to 22; emotional changes accompany physical changes at puberty; human reproduction is the same as animal reproduction; the body is not enjoyed for leisure; the human body is advanced—unlike primitive bodies; and reproductive parts are for reproduction. Although the language used in the description of adolescence made these notions of the body seem neutral, it is clear that moral criteria were being applied to humans as if they were a "natural animal."

A 1948 Wisconsin State Board of Health publication entitled *The Parent's Part* described the "modern" attitude toward social hygiene education. It suggested that a hopeful sign in postwar America was the increasing interest in training children for family life. This booklet stated that there were four stages in sex development. The first is at 4 to 5 years of age, when the child is curious and wants to know about the body, differences between the sexes, and the origins of babies. "This is the time for helping him to establish objective attitudes toward the body" (p. 7). The second stage is from 6 to 9 years of age. This stage is a "latent period as far as sex is concerned" (p. 7). According to this source, young children (ages 4 to 5) are curious about sex, but lose that interest between the ages of 6 and 9. The third stage is ages 10 to 11. This is when the "physical and emotional changes of puberty begin" (p. 7). The booklet suggested that this child will need assistance in the emotional adjustment to adulthood.

The final stage in sex development is adolescence—again defined as between the ages of 12 and 22. At this point, "interest in sex is full blown. Dating, love, choosing a mate, marriage, reproduction, and family relationships are of great interest and importance to both boys and girls" (p. 7). In adolescence, the young boy and girl are to understand that "the new sensations and impulses that come to them at this time are indications that their bodies are being prepared for the duties and responsibilities of motherhood and fatherhood" (p. 12). The double standard did not disappear, however. Girls were to "learn once and for all the danger of illegitimacy connected with irregular intercourse" (p. 13), and boys must learn "that the loose girl is a potential source of sex diseases" (p. 14).

These rather extended excerpts and discussions are illustrative of the way in which the new formations in sexuality framed and constructed normal behavior in children and adolescents. Young people could be trained toward social living by inculcating in them the biological and psychological "truths" about their bodies as they changed and "matured." Changing scientific "understandings" of human growth and development made the new social construction of childhood and adolescence appear natural and essential.

Detailed descriptions of the stages of adolescence constructed a normal male and female child whose bodily proclivities could be readily observed and monitored—not only by her/himself, but by others. Developmental discourses conceptualized a curious and naturally "sexual" child. However, it was not typical (i.e., normal) for this same child, between the ages of 6 and 9, to have an interest in sex. By ages 10 to 11, youths are constructed as needing guidance in order to adjust to the inevitable pull of hormones that begin to manifest themselves by age 12 in feelings of independence, attraction to the opposite sex, and, most of all, a yearning for the culminating institution of parenthood. Again, these discourses distinguish between normal male and female behavior: While girls were warned of illegitimacy and boys of sex diseases, there is no indication that boys could be considered "loose"; only females were designated in discourse as such.

Central to this discussion are the changes in the ways in which adolescent sexuality would be institutionalized. Whereas in the 1910s and 1920s it was clear that the sexual drives of youths were more likely to be described along class, race, gender, and age lines (i.e., libidinous youths were male; dangerously libidinous youths were teenage males and females of lower-income classes, recent immigrants, and school dropouts), by midcentury, youths were more likely to be stratified according to universal measures. The notion of dangerous sexuality would be more appropriately tagged to youths in accordance with their failure to fall within the normal range of biological, emotional, and psychological stages of growth and development.

The biology and psychology of the sexes had shifted to the point where all children and youths were viewed as having, a priori, a sexual nature. While on the surface it would appear as if this shift represented a more "democratic" way of thinking about youthful bodies, underlying such an epistemological framework was a new form of discipline and regulation of youths: They could still be viewed as dangerous and pathological if their physical maturation and social and sexual attitudes and behaviors fell out of the bounds of the well-defined developmental measures.

The descriptions of the ways in which male, female, adolescent, and children's bodies were normalized in the mid-century discourse practices of Milwaukee sex education represent both continuities and breaks with the past. While in the early decades, females and teens were defined as sexually normal only within the bounds of their disinterest or diligence in "saying no to sex," by the 1940s and 1950s, a shift in epistemologies had signaled new formations of a natural and normal sexual interest in women, teens, and children. In fact, a shift in discourses made clear the responsibilities that married women were to embody in terms of sexual desire: By mid-century, married women were to examine their own sexual adequacy in relation to how "responsive" they were to their husbands. At the same time, youths were to celebrate their own natural, a priori sexual nature, but only if thoughts and behaviors fell neatly within the bounds of the quantified guidelines for developmental measures.

However, in continuous fashion, the biological and psychological sciences became the overriding authority for what was considered normal behavior in sexuality discourses. That is, whether early in the century or in the late 1950s, the authoritarian nature of the human sciences, including genetics, obscured the continual human, social struggles and debates that provided the backdrop for construction of the "normal" body.

CONCLUSION

In the early decades of the century, discussions regarding sexuality, whether conducted in the home, church, or school, were considered potentially dangerous. That is, the discussion of sexuality itself was considered capable of inciting youths to sexual experimentation. Underlying this belief, however, was a more fundamental thought that, if conducted with extreme care, discussion of human reproductive biology would have a dissuasive, rather than provocative, "effect" on students. Students would see and hear the dangers of sexual experimentation and as a result would embody the belief that sex outside of marriage was dangerous and immoral.[23] Indeed, certain youths who were sexually active did "embody" such an identity: The discourses regarding the dangers of sexual activity and the vile and immoral element of such habits constructed distinct sexual natures that were either normal or pathological.

Fundamentally, the power of the new, mid-century scientific discourses on sex went beyond their intended purpose, which was to counter unwholesome information. In a Foucaultian sense, power was exercised through the ability of the scientific discourses to make the categories and attitudes described a "fact" of nature, so that the "child will feel sex is natural. If he knows about body parts and functions he won't be impressed by unwholesome attitudes" (Biester, Griffiths, & Pearce, 1947, p. 115).

This shift in discourses constructed new ways in which the sexual body would be essentialized. On the surface, it can be viewed as a move from negative to positive: Sexuality by the 1940s no longer was talked about as evil, vile, and negative, but natural, normal, and productive. It became institutionalized in pedagogical practice as a breakthrough, as progress toward the emancipation of our "true," sexual selves. It represented the "liberation" of not only men's bodies, but women's, adolescents', and children's as well.

In a Foucaultian sense, however, it is possible to see the disciplinary and regulatory aspects of such discursive practices and call into question their claims to truth. While speaking of sexuality appeared to free, it was spoken of in a scientific language that was considered largely beyond debate. In this sense, the mid-century changes in the will to tell youths about their sexuality represented a new form of past regulation: Bodies were monitored and distinguished, but by new rules and codes of conduct.

Implications for such analysis rest in the potential for scientific curriculum discourse to obscure social and political relations. Present-day debates over school sexuality education share an ancestry with the social construction of past curricula. In a Foucaultian manner, new conceptualizations of the body, and new instructions for "appropriate" sexual and social behavior found in official curriculum materials on such current health issues as teenage pregnancy and HIV/AIDS, might well be investigated for underlying normalizations of the self—those that distinguish, categorize, and limit human potential.

NOTES

1. See Barbara Defoe Whitehead's article entitled "The Failure of Sex Education" (1994). Also see Kantor, "Attacks on Public School Sexuality Education Programs: 1993–94 School Year" (1994).

2. This research is compiled in Judith Rabak Wagener, *A Social Epistemology of Sex Education in the Milwaukee Public Schools: 1910–1960* (unpublished doctoral dissertation, University of Wisconsin–Madison, 1991).

3. See Popkewitz (1991) for an analysis of the notion of social epistemology.

4. This notion of governing, or power, was first developed in Michel Foucault's *Discipline and Punish* (1979) and is explored in various forms in his later works. His historical studies trace the shift from top-to-bottom sovereign rule in the premodern period to a circulatory form of power as it is located in unstable and multiple institutions in the modern era. See *Power/Knowledge* (1980b, pp. 72, 81, 97–98); *History of Sexuality* (1980a, pp. 92–98); also see Foucault, "Governmentality," in Burchell, Gordon & Miller, *The Foucault Effect* (pp. 87–104, 1991).

5. For an important and more thorough discussion of forms of legitimation in modernity, see Berger and Luckmann (1967) and Berger, Berger, and Kellner (1973).

6. Again, the notion of circulatory power is important here. Foucault described modern power as strategic rather than juridical, tied to the power of the sovereignty. While recent immigrants and other individuals did have a lower standard of living than the "native" Milwaukeans, who were mostly of German descent, the theoretical position taken is that differences among groups were neither biologically determined nor structurally bound. Foucault's postulate is that while social, political, and economic structures provided a broad context for the lived experiences of recent immigrants, power inhered in the rationality with which individuals were ranked, sorted, and segregated according to age, gender, income, race, and so on.

7. For further analyses of the eugenics movement, see Bleier (1984); Chorover (1979); Devlin and Wickey (1984); Gould (1981); Haller (1984); Hostadter (1955); Kevles (1985); Lewontin, Rose, and Kamin (1984); Pickens (1968); Vecoli (1960); Wiebe (1967).

8. Milwaukee County Historical Society (MCHS), crime clippings file, February 5, 1909.

9. *Evening Wisconsin*, vice clippings file, July 27, 1906, no page given, Milwaukee Legislative Reference Bureau (LRB).

10. Lizzie B. Kander papers, University of Wisconsin–Milwaukee, Area Research Center (ARC), May 29, 1907, pp. 14–15.

11. *Milwaukee Journal*, January 21, 1919, n.p., Milwaukee Public Library (MPL).

12. See Foucault, *Discipline and Punish* (1979) for a detailed description and discussion of the ways in which modern bodies have been anatomically divided and coded according to a political economy—a modern strategy that can be traced to penal practices.

13. State Board of Health, Sex Education Series 891, University of Wisconsin–Milwaukee, ARC.

14. In the MPS reference book, *Units in Personal Health and Human Relations,* Biester et al. (1947) stated that "mentally superior parents usually do not have mentally inferior children, and likewise, mentally retarded parents do not have mentally superior children" (p. 61).

15. For a more thorough discussion of the hereditarian notions prevalent throughout the century in Milwaukee sex education discourses, see Rabak Wagener (1991).

16. In the January 1919 *Bulletin of the Milwaukee Health Department* an article by the U.S. Public Health Service stated: "Thousands of personal instances testify to the large part that ignorance has to play in the *downfall* of girls and the *infection*

of men" (p. 14; emphasis added). The language of such discourse makes clear the difference in normality between women and men: Women were considered normally above sexual promiscuity and those who participated were then put in a *lower* position of social evaluation; sexual impulses in men, however, were normal and thus moral.

17. *Bulletin of the Milwaukee Health Department*, October–November 1918, p. 7.

18. Although space limitations do not permit a more thorough discussion of Foucault's critique of the notion of "sexual repression," a valuable discussion of such a political construct can be found in *The History of Sexuality* (1980a).

19. See discussions and debates in *The Milwaukee Journal*, November 19, 1913; December 21, 1919, p. 6; February 18, 1921; April 22, 1921.

20. For example, in the 1916 *Annual Reports of the Commissioner of the Milwaukee Health Department* (Milwaukee County Historical Society, Madison), 50% of the deaths from syphilis occurred in "foreign"-born Milwaukeans, who represented less than half of the total population. This same trend occurred in the 1917 records. See *Annual Reports of the Milwaukee Health Department*: 1914–1920. (University of Wisconsin–Milwaukee, Area Research Center).

21. See *Bulletin of the Milwaukee Health Department*, September 1920.

22. See State Board of Health, Sex Education Series 891, November 17, 1949.

23. This was cited continually as a "benefit" of sexuality education, as postulated by national leaders in the early decades of the century. See Lloyd and Bigelow (1904); Balliet, Bigelow, and Morrow (1912); Galloway (1913); Foster (1914); March (1919); and Gallichan (1921).

REFERENCES

Balliet, T., Bigelow, M., & Morrow, P. (1912). *Report of the special committee on the matter and methods of sex education.* New York: American Federation for Sex Hygiene.

Berger, P., Berger, B., & Kellner, H. (1973). *The homeless mind: Modernization and consciousness.* New York: Vintage.

Berger, P., & Luckmann, T. (1967). *The social construction of reality.* New York: Anchor Books.

Biester, L., Griffiths, W., & Pearce, N. O. (1947). *Units in personal health and human relations.* Minneapolis: University of Minnesota Press.

Bleier, R. (1984). *Science and gender: A critique of biology and its theories on women.* New York: Pergamon.

Burchell, G., Gordon, C., & Miller, P. (1991). *The Foucault effect: Studies in governmentality.* Chicago: University of Chicago Press.

Chorover, S. (1979). *From genesis to genocide.* Cambridge, MA: MIT Press.

Corner, G., & Landis, C. (1941). *Sex education for the adolescent.* Chicago: American Medical Association.

Devlin, D., & Wickey, C. (Winter, 1984). "Better living through heredity": Michael

Guyer and the American eugenics movement. *Michigan Academician*, 6(2), 199–208.

Foster, W. (Ed.). (1914). *The social emergency.* Boston: Houghton Mifflin.

Foucault, M. (1977). *Language, counter-memory, practice: Selected essays and interviews* (D. F. Bouchard, Ed.; D. F. Bouchard & S. Simon, Trans.). Ithaca, NY: Cornell University Press.

Foucault, M. (1979). *Discipline and punish: The birth of the prison* (A. Sheridan, Trans.). New York: Vintage.

Foucault, M. (1980a). *The history of sexuality: Vol. 1. An introduction* (R. Hurley, Trans.). New York: Vintage/Random House.

Foucault, M. (1980b). *Power/Knowledge: Selected interviews and other writings by Michel Foucault, 1972–1977* (C. Gordon, Ed. and Trans.). New York: Pantheon.

Foucault, M. (1986). *The history of sexuality: Vol. 3. The care of the self* (R. Hurley, Trans.). New York: Vintage.

Foucault, M. (1991). Governmentality. In G. Burchell, C. Gordon & P. Miller (Eds.), *The Foucault effect: Studies in governmentality* (pp. 87–104). Chicago: University of Chicago Press.

Gallichan, W. (1921). *A textbook of sex education.* Boston: Small, Maynard.

Galloway, T. W. (1913). *Biology of sex for parents and teachers.* Boston: Heath.

Gould, S. J. (1981). *The mismeasure of man.* New York: Norton.

Haller, M. H. (1984). *Eugenics: Hereditarian attitudes in American thought.* New Brunswick, NJ: Rutgers University Press.

Hostadter, R. (1955). *Social Darwinism in American thought.* Boston: Beacon Press.

Kantor, L. (1994, August–September). Attacks on public school sexuality education programs: 1993–94 school year. *SIECUS Report*, pp. 11–16.

Kevles, D. (1985). *In the name of eugenics.* New York: Knopf.

Kliebard, H. (1975). The rise of scientific curriculum making and its aftermath. *Curriculum Theory*, 5(1), 27–38.

Kliebard, H. (1986). *The struggle for the American curriculum, 1893–1958.* Boston: Routledge & Kegan Paul.

Korman, G. (1967). *Industrialization, immigrants and Americanizers.* Madison: State Historical Society of Wisconsin.

Leavitt, J. W. (1975). *Public health in Milwaukee, 1867–1910.* Unpublished doctoral dissertation, University of Chicago.

Lewontin, R. C., Rose, S., & Kamin, L. (1984). *Not in our genes.* New York: Pantheon.

Lloyd, F. E., & Bigelow, M. A. (1904). *The teaching of biology in the secondary school.* New York: Longmans, Green.

March, N. H. (1919). *Towards racial health.* New York: Dutton.

Milwaukee Health Department. (1918, October–November). *Bulletin.* Milwaukee, WI: Author.

Milwaukee Health Department. (1919, November–December). *Bulletin.* Milwaukee, WI: Author.

Milwaukee Health Department. (1921, April). *Bulletin.* Milwaukee, WI: Author.

Milwaukee Health Department. (1927, October–November). *Bulletin.* Milwaukee, WI: Author.

Milwaukee Health Department. (1936, September). *Bulletin.* Milwaukee, WI: Author.

Milwaukee Public Schools. (1912). *Annual report: Board of School Directors.* Milwaukee, WI: Author.

Milwaukee Public Schools. (1920). *Annual report: Board of School Directors.* Milwaukee, WI: Author.

Milwaukee Public Schools. (1926, February). *Our high school girls.* Milwaukee, WI: Author.

Milwaukee Public Schools. (1912). *School Board Proceedings.* Milwaukee, WI: Author.

Milwaukee Public Schools. (1955). *Junior high health instruction guide health course: Suggested health topics for grade nine.* Milwaukee, WI: Author.

Milwaukee Public Schools. (1959). *Junior high health instruction guide health course: Suggested health topics for grade nine.* Milwaukee, WI: Author.

Olson, F. I. (1960). The socialist party in the union in Milwaukee, 1900–1912. *Wisconsin Magazine of History, 44*(2), 110–116.

Olson, F. I. (1987). City expansion and urban spread: Settlements and governments in Milwaukee County. In R. M. Aderman (Ed.), *Trading post to Metropolis: Milwaukee County's first 150 years* (pp. 1–89). Milwaukee: Milwaukee County Historical Society.

Patzer, C. (1924). *Public education in Wisconsin.* Madison, WI: State Superintendent's Office.

Pickens, D. K. (1968). *Eugenics and the progressives.* Nashville, TN: Vanderbilt University Press.

Popkewitz, T. S. (1991). *A political sociology of educational reform: Power/Knowledge in teaching, teacher education, and research.* New York: Teachers College Press.

Rabak Wagener, J. (1991). *A social epistemology of sex education in the Milwaukee public schools: 1910–1960.* Unpublished doctoral dissertation, University of Wisconsin–Madison.

Reese, W. J. (1981, Spring). Partisans of the proletariat: The socialist working class and the Milwaukee schools, 1890–1920. *Educational Quarterly, 21*(1), 3–50.

Ring, D. (1968). *The Milwaukee socialists' attitudes toward the public schools, 1907–1915.* Unpublished senior thesis, University of Wisconsin–Milwaukee.

Still, B. (1948). *Milwaukee: The history of a city.* Madison: State Historical Society of Wisconsin.

Strain, F. B. (1940). *New patterns in sex teaching.* New York: Appleton-Century.

Strain, F. B. (1948). *The normal sex interests of children.* New York: Appleton-Century.

U.S. Census. (1900). *Twelfth census of the United States: Vol. 1. Population.* Washington, DC: U.S. Government Printing Office.

Vecoli, R. J. (1960, Spring). Sterilization: A progressive measure? *Wisconsin Magazine of History, 43*(3), 190–202.

Whitehead, B. D. (1994, October). The failure of sex education. *The Atlantic Monthly, 274*(4), 55–80.

Wiebe, R. H. (1967). *The search for social order, 1877–1920.* New York: Hill & Wang.

Wisconsin State Board of Health. (1948). *The parent's part.* Madison: Author.

Woehrmann, P. (1987, Autumn). Milwaukee German immigrant values: An essay. *Milwaukee History, 10*(3), 78–94.

PART III

Disciplining and the Deployment of Power

7

Born-Again Teaching?
Governmentality, "Grammar,"
and Public Schooling

BILL GREEN

Literacy debates and associated public campaigns organized around notions of educational "crisis" and the decline of "standards" remain powerfully current, and recurrent, in advanced industrial societies. How such quintessentially social phenomena are to be understood is an important and fascinating matter for scholarly inquiry, with implications not simply for education studies but for social theory more broadly. In what follows, I want to explore specific aspects of this, drawing in particular on the work of Michel Foucault with regard to new problematics of power, governmentality, and the state. Two examples will set the scene.

In a recent editorial in *Phi Delta Kappan*, the focus was on what was depicted as a significant misrepresentation of literacy and public education in the United States. It opened as follows:

> The Department of Education . . . chose the beginning of the new school year to release the results of a study on "Adult Literacy in America." And American newspapers responded with uniformly negative headlines that implicitly indicted school performance. ("Shame on the Press," 1994, p. 355)

What is noteworthy here is the manner in which the argument is conducted. Understandably enough perhaps, it speaks from a certain positioned practice within the discourse of literacy and educational professionals. It marshals a counter-reading both of the report in question and of its press representations on the basis of certain claims to and assertions of "truth" and "science." In doing so, it enters into a now familiar process in such debates, not only opposing science to ideology or rhetoric but also failing to appreciate or even recognize the discursive and symbolic complexities at issue here:

> A report that should have reinforced the public's view of the value of public education was instead allowed—by the nation's press—to demoralize teachers and administrators and to reaffirm the widely held (but erroneous) view that public education is failing to educate. . . . American education deserves better. ("Shame on the Press," 1994, p. 355)

What are we to make of this? There is a note of almost helpless frustration here, a constrained chagrin mingled with dismay and even a measure of hurt: Why are "they" saying such things about "us"?

My second example is taken from a similar situation in Australia. A recent outbreak of the so-called literacy debate has featured an emphasis on grammar. Articles appeared in major newspapers under headlines such as "Grammar crucial to unlocking language," "Verbal abuse," "Writing's on the wall for DIY literacy," and "The literacy war." One article, racily entitled "Verbs with verve spark a new war of words," made the front page. At issue here was a gathering momentum toward the restoration of explicit grammar teaching in Australian schools, as part of a (re)new(ed) public-policy emphasis on literacy. Debate centered on the rival claims of, on the one hand, "traditional grammar" and, on the other, "functional grammar," the latter derived from the systemic-functional linguistics of Michael Halliday. As the front-page article put it, "Battle lines have been drawn over the suggested introduction of a new method of teaching grammar in primary and secondary schools," something that was likely to cause "an upheaval in English teaching." Moreover,

> introducing it [i.e., functional grammar] to Victoria would see a return to a more traditional school grammar after almost twenty years of teaching methods that encourage greater freedom of expression in students' writing, sometimes, say critics, at the expense of construction and sense. (Richards, 1994, p. 1)

Notwithstanding the claims that the new approach differed considerably from "traditional grammar," it is clear that within this context what was important was what they had in common, that is, explicit attention to grammar as such. Importantly, this was presented as a "return," and in effect a rejection of 2 decades or so of what elsewhere is described variously as "unconventional" and "experimental" forms of educational practice. This is, again, familiar territory.

What particularly interests me here, though, is the photograph accompanying it. It features a classroom scene, shot across a group of students at their desks; the teacher is presented at the whiteboard, marker in hand, working off what would seem to be an exercise. The caption reads, in part, "Ms Jennifer Haynes teaches language rules to a Camberwell Girls Grammar School class." She is later identified as the president of the Australian Association for the Teaching of English, and it is clear that she has no particular endorsement for grammar teaching conceived in the terms of either the article or this latest manifestation of the debate more generally. Yet what happens here, in effect, is what I want to call the discursive production of the scene of teaching. That is, there is a powerful symbolic dimension to the staging of this scene that marks it out as, in a quite precise sense, over-determined. The teacher in question has since indicated that she was asked explicitly to participate in this particular staging and that originally, as she understood it, she was not to be included. At the last moment, however, she was drawn in, in accordance with what would seem the "on-the-spot" judgments and requirements of professional ideology and practice on the part of the newspaper personnel and their associated sense of news-value. What is it, then, that makes such a scene newsworthy? What is, over and above its generic role and function in newspaper textuality, its social meaning? In what follows, I will undertake some preliminary inquiries into these matters, with reference specifically to notions of governmentality, grammar, and English teaching.

THE "RE-BIRTH" OF THE TEACHER

To answer these questions, it is necessary to turn to the larger picture of educational politics, with reference particularly to the post-1960s period. This has been described variously in terms of the cultural and educational offensives of the New Right and of "the liberal-conservative restoration" (Shor, 1986); other linked formulations include what Ball (1990, 1993) describes as the contradictory dynamics of "conservative restorationism" and modernization, and also the notion of "postmodern educational reform" (Whitty, 1991), understood through the lens of a new economic order of performativity, commodification, and hyper-rationality (Wexler, 1987).[1] Something of the complexity of the particular educational-political settlements at issue here is captured in Ball's (1990) account of the British experience of the 1980s:

> Thatcherism attempts to stand both for modernisation and progress and for tra-
> dition and stability. The neo-liberal influence emphasises an orientation to the
> future, constant adaptation to new circumstances and an absence of state con-
> trols; the neo-conservative influence stresses an orientation to the past, tradi-
> tional values and collective loyalties. *Education is thus contested in terms of its
> role in both restoring authority and responding to the contemporary logic of capital-
> ist development.* (p. 213; emphasis added)

Similar contradictions and tensions are to be observed elsewhere in the
educational world, and that they continue to resonate in the New Age of
Clinton, Keating, Major, and others is unlikely to be disputed. What is especially marked in these struggles is the role and significance of teaching and
the teacher. As various commentators have noted, teachers have long been
at the center of the storm of New Right educational politics, with fierce
contention over what counts as teaching. Accordingly, Ball (1990) points
to "confused and contradictory views" of what he explicitly calls "the
'new teacher,' ranging from the innovative and competitive petit-professional
to the harassed, reactive teaching technician" (p. 214). What is particularly noteworthy in this regard is the simultaneous de-construction and
re-construction of the teaching body. Attacks on teachers and a concerted
struggle against organized forms of "teacher power" are fundamental to the
educational politics of the post-1960s, perhaps reaching their apotheosis in
the late 1980s and early 1990s. What is involved here is an attempt to challenge, demonize, and dismantle the image of teaching as it has become associated with "Progressivism" and the always mythic 1960s, and at the same
time to reinvent, regenerate, and restore another image in its place, in an
exemplary instance of discursive and symbolic politics.

What is also striking, however, is that this clearly is not something restricted to the erstwhile Right; quite the contrary, in fact, with arguments
from the self-proclaimed Left increasingly vociferous in their denunciation
of the new Demon figure of the Progressive teacher, often specifically identified with English teaching and related pedagogies. How is this to be understood? What explains what on the face of it appears par excellence to be
a case of strange bedfellows and unholy alliances? Or, to put it somewhat
differently: What are the conditions of possibility and intelligibility for something like this to emerge now, in the last decade of the twentieth century, in
all its emergent (post)modern glitter?

We also can ask questions about the manner in which teaching and
teachers are represented in the cultural-symbolic field, and why the media
might be motivated especially at this time to portray teachers, literacy, and
public education as they do, from newspapers to recent cinematic produc-
tions such as *Stand and Deliver* or even *Pump Up the Volume*. How does the

teacher figure in the public imagination, then, and why? My larger concern here is with the social dynamics of crisis and change in public schooling, and with understanding contemporary educational politics as an historical problem par excellence. Hence, the focus in this chapter is, on the one hand, on "literacy" and "grammar" as normative symbolic categories, and, on the other, on English teaching as both representative of public schooling—its constraints and characteristics—and a synecdoche for public schooling. There is a very real sense, that is, in which English teaching as a distinctive curriculum domain is linked specifically and directly to the emergence and consolidation of public, mass compulsory, "popular" education and schooling, organized under the auspices of the state and in accordance with various governmental initiatives and imperatives (Goodson, 1988; Hunter, 1988). In this formulation, a particular relation exists between "governmentality" and "the modern state," a reciprocal relation in terms of which nonetheless "power relations have come more and more under state control" (Foucault, 1983, p. 224), and is realized as various forms of pastoral power and social welfare.

Crucial to this account is what I want to call the figure of the Teacher, as a central term within what is in effect both a social imaginary and a certain complex cultural-symbolic field. This figure is to be seen as significantly associated with the very notion of authority itself; a further critical factor here is the cultural and pedagogical link between language and authority, within the contexts of both school and society. In what might be called the normative classroom, a certain relation holds between speech and silence, and between speaking-positions corresponding to structured inequalities of power/knowledge relations. The normal situation is one in which teachers speak and students listen; alternatively, students read and write, essentially in silence. This is also a relation between activity and passivity, with the teacher's active, directive role in the classroom economy to be contrasted with the student's role, which is characteristically passive and reactive. Further, it is also a relation between a relatively powerful minority and a relatively powerless majority, which arguably has a certain symbolic value not simply as a microcosm of social relations more generally but also as a model for such relations. That is, the classroom conceived in these terms becomes itself a representation of a certain form of social organization, and also (re)productive in this regard. In such a situation, then, there is an important connection to be made between the teacher's "voice" and social power, and between speaking and authority. This admittedly schematic outline of the normative idea of the classroom has the further dimension that the teacher is institutionally charged with the in(tro)duction of students into socially authorized relations of knowledge and power, and differential access to the universe of discourse. Consequently, there is considerable investment in the idea of teaching gener ally, and teachers have a correspondingly high symbolic value. This is, curiously enough, notwithstanding the relatively low status and often negative image of the profession, something that is intimately tied into the contradictory dynamics of mass compulsory schooling (as "popular education"), but also something that is becoming increasingly apparent, as the crisis in education deepens and seemingly reaches toward the critical point.[2]

However, all this cannot be understood adequately without taking into account that teaching is itself a contested category in cultural and curriculum discourse, and perhaps particularly so in the current educational climate. The tendency is to see it in traditional, normative terms, within the framework of the so-called "educational paradigm" (Willis, 1977) and the modern classroom system (Hamilton, 1980, 1989). It is this perspective that I have identified with the symbolic figure of the Teacher. My argument is that the post-1960s period of crisis and change in English teaching, and of educational crisis more generally, can be grasped as a time when this figure has seemed particularly at risk, partly as a consequence of larger forms of cultural and social change and partly as their cause. This helps explain the vehemence of the attacks on teachers that characterize this period, and the growing movement toward "teacher-proof" forms of curriculum and assessment, together with a heightened emphasis on teacher accountability and the surveillance and control of teachers' work (Ball, 1990). Certainly part of the impetus for this is provided by new economic imperatives, and the felt need to secure a closer, more organized relation between education and the economy, thereby seeking to reassert the service role of public schooling in relation to capitalist society in a time of general socioeconomic crisis.

But there is arguably more at issue than this. There would seem to be an excess of anxiety and concern in this regard, which suggests that the cultural-symbolic dimensions of educational crisis need to be taken more directly into account. There has been much debate in recent times about the apparent movement away from traditional forms and practices of education and teaching into what is widely seen as a new laissez-faire style, largely identified with the educational project of Progressivism. Referring more particularly to educational reform in the United States, Tyack and Tobin (1994) point, for instance, to what they describe as "the tumultuous sixties" as "a time of optimistic innovation when reforms in the grammar of schooling burst into public attention and then largely disappeared" (p. 455). This articulates readily with concern over standards and the question of authority, pedagogical and otherwise. Fundamentally at issue is the widely perceived and essentially mythical problem of "politically-motivated teachers" (Ball, 1987, p. 32); that is, teachers subversive of established systems of authority, order, and hierarchy, not just in their own classrooms—now much less educationally recognizable as a result of the move toward oracy, groupwork, and developmental learning, and indeed seen as tending toward the "chaotic"—but in school and society more generally. This is something identified especially with the subject English.

The so-called Progressive revolution was short-lived, however, if indeed it can be said to have occurred at all. This was, in fact, one of the central findings of the Bullock Report (Department of Education and Science [DES], 1975), and it has been confirmed ever since (e.g., Mayher, 1990; Willinsky, 1990). But the myth has persisted of "permissive" teachers refusing both their authority and their responsibility and hence contributing in significant ways to the moral disintegration of society and the prospect of a new "barbarism." The myth constructs the teacher, and more particularly the English teacher, as "folk-devil," therefore, since it is within the political space of the English classroom that the nexus between language and discipline, culture and authority, is most explicit and hence most vulnerable. As Ball (1987) argues, "The symbolic and political functions of the Bullock Report are probably in the long run of greater significance than its specific findings" (p. 31)—indeed, the latter were quickly glossed over, precisely because they ran counter to expectations about falling standards and radical teaching methods. Ball (1987) wrote, "The Bullock Report served as a vehicle for restructuring English":

> Its role was symbolic in giving public censure to significant aspects of "new wave" English and in creating space for the insertion of alternative concepts of the role and purpose, and form and content of English teaching. It gave credibility to those voices which said "things have gone too far." (p. 39)

From the mid-1960s on, there have been quite remarkable and decisive patterns of crisis and change in the nature, character, and fortunes of English teaching, as an integral activity in the social practice of schooling. It has been a time of marked turbulence and excitement. But it has not been entirely without precedence. Medway (1986) has observed that the 1960s were, in fact, "a second period of crisis" (p. 331) for the profession, following a period of over 40 years in which, in the United Kingdom, it "ran along basically the same grooves" as those established in the first 3 decades of the century, especially the years 1906–1921, when the subject English first firmly established itself as a school subject of significant and even pre-eminent status.[3] This is endorsed by Ball (1983, 1985), who notes that, once the state had "established a framework of indirect control over the curriculum through the examination system," there followed an extended period where there was minimal state intervention in schooling, its major representative, the Board of Education, having "virtually abdicated any direct control over curricular provision and the classroom work of teachers" (1983, p. 85).

In the specific case of English teaching, there was an early period of intense struggle in which advocates for the subject-discipline mobilized arguments and support, culminating in the Newbolt Report (1921), by general consensus a major document in the formal establishment of the subject English in the school curriculum (Willinsky, 1991). This period was extremely decisive in setting the agenda for subsequent curriculum development and change in English teaching. Indeed, Ball (1983) stated: "In specific relation to English, much of the contemporary conflict and conceptual precariousness evident involving practitioners can be understood in terms of the first emergence and early development of the discipline and the strangely 'segmented' nature of its professional community" (p. 83). Concerned with the larger picture of English studies, King (1983) goes further, suggesting that the Report is decisive in what he calls "the birth of the teacher" in relation to the "newly constituted field of 'English'" (p. 25). His analysis joins up with the important work of Hunter (1987, 1988) in this respect, seeing English as "the privileged embodiment of a formerly more widely-used pedagogy" (King, 1983, p. 33), itself understood as a central strategy through which governmental initiatives and state intervention in popular education were achieved (Hunter, 1987). The significance of this argument is that it establishes an important continuity between the emergence and consolidation of "popular education," in the more general sense, and that of English teaching. Both involve specific forms of response and reaction to crisis, and both involve the construction of a distinctive cultural figure—the Teacher, conceived in social-disciplinary terms as "an embodiment of certain emulable norms of conduct and expression" (King, 1983, p. 25).

This connection between popular education and English teaching is an important matter. It concerns the way in which English teaching, as a distinctive pedagogical practice, is inscribed in a larger process of governmentality (Foucault, 1991) and hence must be understood as "the outcome of a highly specific governmental technology and rationality," a particular social-administrative discourse, in terms of which it is "a relatively late mutation" (Hunter, 1987, p. 581). For Foucault, there has been a growing movement from the mid-sixteenth century onward, with a particular localization to be observed in the mid-eighteenth century, toward the establishment of a new system of power involving the "sovereignty–discipline–government" complex (Foucault, 1991, p. 102). Within this complex, the concept of government—which Foucault (1991) calls "the problematic of government in general" (p. 88)—involves the following: "How to govern oneself, how to be governed, how to govern others, by whom the people will accept being governed, how to become the best possible governor" (p. 87). This entails, in turn, "three fundamental types of government, each of which relates to a particular science or discipline: the art of self-government, connected with morality; the art of properly governing a family, which pertains to economy; and finally the science of ruling the state, which concerns politics" (p. 91). This is based on a particular rationality, an ordering principle for the "body politic" conceived as the union and indeed the integration of individual, family, and state, complexly interrelated in terms of a series of relays and mirror effects. What is at issue here is the proper exercise of authority, as a productive force in "the right disposition of things" (p. 93). Moreover, this is to be seen most emphatically as a rational, legitimate matter, rather than simply the application of violence or coercion. Foucault cites a metaphor employed by one early commentator on "the art of government": "the king of bees, the bumble bee, who . . . rules the bee-hive *without needing a sting*" (p. 96; emphasis added). Not that there is no "sting" in government and leadership conceived in this way; rather, it is not necessary, and is perhaps even counterproductive, if there are other, more artful means at hand. The qualities associated with this are "patience, wisdom and diligence" (p. 96), qualities fitting a long, gradual, graduated, and even evolutionary process in the administration and management of social complexity.

A crucial consideration in this regard is the link between governmentality and the (modern) state, within an understanding of social power in terms of the interplay of distinct registers of "domination," "exploitation," and "subjection–subjectification" (Foucault, 1983, p. 213). Moreover, as Foucault observes, with reference to the specific relationship between modernity, power, and subjectivity, "basically power is less a confrontation between two adversaries [violence, coercion] or the linking of one to another [consent] than a question of government," in its original, "very broad meaning":

> "Governmentality" does not refer only to political structures or to the management of states; rather it designated the way in which the conduct of individuals or of groups might be directed: the government of children, of souls, of communities, of families, of the sick. It did not only cover the legitimately constituted forms of political or economic subjection, but also modes of action, more or less considered and calculated, which were destined to act upon the possibilities of action of other people. To govern in this sense, is to structure the possible field of action of others. (Foucault, 1983, p. 221)

Importantly, this allows for an understanding of the specificity of power, culture, and the social, dis-engaged from any necessary reference to political economy or the mode of production. It therefore greatly expands the possibilities for and, among other things, enables a more dynamic view of education as a field of power relations.

A key point to make here is the usefulness of the notion of governmentality for understanding the practice of pedagogy; indeed, the pedagogical character of governmentality is captured, for instance, in Foucault's depiction of its most appropriate qualities (patience, wisdom, diligence). It is illuminating, therefore, to move from this to consider the image of the teacher most characteristic of post-Dartmouth English teaching, and specifically the way the relationship between teaching and authority typically has been presented.

Boomer (1988), for instance, a central figure in more recent reformulations of the New English, makes the following assertion:

> Teachers teach most profoundly what they are at the core. The lasting lesson is the demonstration of the self as it handles its authority and those under its authority. At the same time this "self" demonstrates how it in turn responds to those in authority over it. (p. 31)

It is interesting to read this in the context of the previous discussion of governmentality. Personal authority and pedagogical authority are effectively identified. The notion of a "demonstration of the self"—in effect, a staging of the self—is both fundamental to the curriculum discourse of the New English and intensely problematical. It depends on a particular understanding of the relationship between subjectivity and governmentality, not simply assuming, for instance, that a core exists, a foundational sense of self, but also, more actively, constructing an imaginary unity in this regard. A second implication is that more is being communicated in the pedagogical encounter than simply what is said—certainly one way in which the message system of the so-called hidden curriculum works. At the same time, pedagogical communication of this kind involves a movement beyond language per se. Such a formulation clearly is linked discursively with the following, taken from the Martin Report (Education Department of Western Australia, 1980):

> How a teacher teaches is rooted deep in his [sic] personal history. Being concerned with children, and authority, and friendship—and love—his behaviour has powerful links with his own childhood, with his authority figures and his emotional attitudes to this. This is true also of parents—who also are teachers. (p. 23)

Once again we see the intimate association of authority and identity, and further, the assertion of a fundamental connection between teaching and parenting, thus bringing together pedagogical and familial discourses in a manner that indicates very clearly the relationship between governmentality and educational practice. Dixon (1967/75) similarly indicates the ambivalence and complexity of the teaching role when he observes: "The English teacher tries to be a person to whom pupils turn with that sense of trust" (p. 8) necessary for the exploration and expression of personal experience, whether it be in talk, drama, or writing. This links up with the work on the expressive function in language usage and the audience category of "trusted adult" (Britton, Burgess, Martin, McLeod, & Rosen, 1975), which are central features of the conceptual edifice of the growth paradigm associated with the New English and the London School.

What these statements make explicit is something that is powerfully implicit throughout: the concept of demonstration. This is a key notion in process pedagogies generally, and in the area of literacy education specifically, although clearly it has a wider curriculum significance (Willinsky, 1990). A central demonstration is that provided by the teacher him/herself, as not simply an active participant in the culture, including the culture of literacy, but also an emblem of the dominant culture. What needs to be recognized is that, in every case, students are caught up in a particular relationship with a teacher, one that is always intimate, interactive, transactive, and negotiated, and characterized by a certain form of the expression of pedagogical authority.

King's (1983) reference to "the institution of a new teacher–pupil relation" (p. 20), actively constructed and formalized in the textual practice of the Newbolt Report, must be seen in context, as a particular culmination of the emergence of "the ordinary popular school teacher" (Hunter, 1987, p. 575). This figure embodies "a sophisticated apparatus of pastoral surveillance and moral training" (Hunter, 1987, p. 575), who serves as a representative—more strongly, an image—of cultural authority, and a significant presence who combines distance and proximity, the cultural and the personal, and who also both enacts and conveys the lived complexity of social discipline and moral regulation. The teacher, that is, is a representative of the organic integrity of the state and, importantly and increasingly, of the nation (as both alibi for and primary expression of the state), by way of a displaced identification.[4] Pedagogical authority here is ultimately associated with cultural authority, its promise, its achievement, and its supreme value, as well as its fragility. Hunter (1987) describes the emergence of state-sponsored teacher training, following the collapse of monitorialism, as "the historical formation of an apparatus for forming a new category of person, installed within a new social relationship (the teacher–student couple), and supported by a new moral technology" (p. 580). He goes on to observe the birth of the teacher in the following terms:

> At the centre of this new space of regulated freedom [i.e., the modern classroom] appeared a new figure who combined authority and intimacy; a figure who relayed new social norms through a purpose-built personality—part friend, part parent, part exemplar—which children would want to emulate; finally, a figure through whose unobstrusive yet ever-present gaze children could look at themselves and see the kind of person they must become. (p. 580)

The shift is from what, elsewhere, he calls "the regulation of norms" to "the regulation of images" (Hunter, 1984, p. 72), an "unstable transition" that, in actual schooling practice, is likely to mean a combination of normative and imaginary regulation. Within what he describes as "the normalized system of the classroom," which appeared in its modern form toward the end of the eighteenth century, the teacher's role is particularly significant: "The role of the teacher was determined by its positioning, *at once symbolic and actual*, as the point from which this normalizing surveillance emanated" (Hunter, 1984, p. 68; emphasis added).

This is clearly something still underway, although the rise into prominence of the New English since the 1960s probably has involved a further mutation in this process of transition and consolidation.[5] King's (1983) account of what he calls "a techné of self," involving the production of an "individuated subjectivity" and "practices of self-governance" (p. 21), focuses specifically on the Newbolt Report as a central agency in a larger discursive network operating at the time. His argument is that the Report establishes and formalizes a new disciplinary mechanism whereby the population at large, subject to a compulsory schooling regime, is socialized into a congenital subjectivity:

> The Report set up a student–text–teacher relation within a larger system of moral training from which, in many ways, we have not escaped. The Report consolidates a form of moral pedagogy such that, in an emerging national education system, "English" becomes the space where students declare their private experience in a public form. (King, 1983, pp. 26–27)

Under this system, the student actively engages in his or her own self-production, essentially via the practices of reading and writing. Literature, realized in a particular way, becomes a disciplinary "mechanism of self-interrogation" (King, 1983, p. 25), based in a specific pedagogy combining truth and pleasure; English, as the modern realization of popular literary education, becomes precisely a discipline of pleasure, operating in different but related ways across primary, secondary, and tertiary levels of schooling. Not that this total coverage of the schooling system is accomplished in the Newbolt Report; however, it is set in motion, and it is the extraordinary cultural-educational project of the Scrutiny movement that consolidates it, at least in the tertiary and secondary systems (Doyle, 1989). It is only in relatively recent times that the specific disciplinary effects of literary pedagogy, conceived in the general form of the Newbolt paradigm, has been extended to primary schooling, notably as an extension of the New English (Willinsky, 1990). The pattern is established in the Newbolt Report, however.

As King (1983) observes, in a particularly resonant passage in the present context:

> Significantly it is the child/pupil's "self-expression" and "self realization" which becomes the key to its correction. The proposed mode of pedagogy doesn't impose something on the student but rather uses the student's self-expression to generate a system of non-coercive correction. (p. 25)

The distinctive feature of this pedagogy is a focus not just on texts, realized and verified in a particular way and operating therefore as a principle of social management, but also on the ever-present, supervisory figure of the teacher, at once a Model Reader and a supreme exemplum. Significantly, teaching and examining are linked up as disciplinary measures, something that becomes increasingly more visible as a major site of tension, conflict, and contradiction in the further development of English teaching, exacerbated by the paradigm shift of the post-Dartmouth era.[6] For King, the Report "solved" a problem of some magnitude for the national-cultural project underway at the time, aimed at constructing and consolidating a new hegemony through education:

> A form of teaching was needed which could place the teacher–student relation at its centre, in a new kind of way, such that the student would be open to infinite non-coercive correction. The moral stature of the teacher had to be established, as the embodiment of certain norms and as the point at which a disciplinary system corrected students in an embodied fashion. The teacher becomes a point of relay for the construction of an autonomous, self-policing "pupil-life," literally an *ascetic life*. (King, 1983, p. 27)

The teacher, as both the expression and the embodiment of cultural authority—"a point of relay between [literature as a storehouse of human experience] and the pupil" (King, 1983, p. 26)—initiates into the culture the student, who thus is constructed as a self-governing agent who recognizes that authority as legitimate, necessary, self-sufficient, and noncoercive. To become disciplined, and therefore productive as a reader, is to be "socialized" into the culture, such that one is both enabled and also, in a quite specific sense, "made safe." Literary education, as a species of moral instruction and training, hence becomes an important means of the production of consent, whereby subjects come to a willing acceptance of, if not an active complicity in, their own submission, paradoxically in the very assertion of their autonomy. Importantly, however, it is not just inculcation into literary culture that is at issue here; rather, entering into the symbolic order in this way becomes of particular importance in the maintenance and renewal of social order more generally.

It is for these reasons, in large measure, that the state withdrew from direct involvement in the course of English teaching after Newbolt, a stance that it maintained until the mid- to late 1960s. The means to social regulation had been secured, however uneasily (Donald, 1985), principally through the curriculum consolidation of English as a text-based literary pedagogy, organized by a new instrumentality: the teacher–student couple. This is not to say that all English teaching in the "inter-crisis" period, 1920–1960, proceeded smoothly and without conflict, nor does it mean that there was a totally successful realization of literature-based English teaching across schooling generally. As various commentaries indicate (e.g., Ball, 1985; Mathieson, 1975; Mayher, 1990), there was still a considerable grammarian emphasis in much classroom practice. Also, a consistent, psychology-based Progressivism persisted, in which children's writing, particularly in the literary-creative mode, was of particular importance. Nonetheless, the literary character in this period of English teaching, as a school-based subject-discipline, would seem a matter of general consensus.

The Newbolt Report focuses and culminates, then, an intense process of cultural politics, out of which modern English teaching emerges. Significantly, the "birth of the teacher" and the emergence (birth) of modern English teaching coincide with, and indeed are generated out of, a time of crisis—hence Medway's (1986) assertion of the 1960s as "a second period of crisis" (p. 331) for the profession. Much curriculum change emanates from this period (Green, 1995).

Central to this was a change in the authority relationships and dynamics of the English classroom. This is succinctly expressed in one report in the following manner:

> Perhaps the most marked change in English teaching and learning is the value now given by many teachers to students' own utterances, spoken or written— utterances of their own experiences, their own thoughts and feelings expressed and accepted in their own personal formulations. And this kind of communication presumes the notion of sharing. Students have often complained that their English teachers have only been interested in how they said things, not in what they said. To anyone trying to communicate, it is frustrating in the extreme to find the audience is not interested in the communication itself, but only its form; this may account for some of the widespread hostility to English. (Education Department of Western Australia, 1980, p. 54)

Further, English curriculum change of this kind is seen as

> itself part of a changing conception of learning which gives a different meaning to teaching. It represents a movement away from the ages old transmission

model of learning with the teacher as the font of all knowledge and power, towards a model based on negotiations between teachers and taught. (Education Department of Western Australia, 1980, p. 54)

This reconceptualized view of teaching involves a complex and ambivalent attitude toward pedagogical authority, and important consequences for English classroom practice, as well as for the social relations of the school generally. This is made explicit in Dixon's (1967/75) account of what is involved in the shift from previous "skills" and "cultural heritage" versions of English teaching to one concerned with "language and personal growth" (p. 4). Significantly, the shift can be thought of in terms of a foregrounding of learning rather than teaching in curriculum practice, and hence a decisive change in the nature of pedagogical authority. As Medway (1980) writes:

Under the guise of just another curriculum subject, [English] has come to enact nothing less than a different model of education: knowledge to be made, not given; knowledge comprising more than can be discursively stated; learning as a diverse range of processes, including affective ones; educational processes to be embarked on with outcomes unpredictable; students' perceptions, experiences, imaginings and unsystematically acquired knowledge admitted as legitimate curricular content. (p. 11)

What the post-Dartmouth shifts in emphasis involve, further, is a shift from writing into speech—from the politics and associated social relations of the written language to those of the spoken language.[7] It is important to see this in the context of institutionalized, compulsory schooling, as a social mechanism of constraint and control and the regulation of discourse and meaning, achieved precisely through a certain "ritualization" of language and the symbolic order (Foucault, 1981) of the kind more readily associated with literacy and writing. Viewed in this way, the new emphasis on spoken language and its spill into school writing becomes the mark of a popular-democratic impulse, a groundswell of movement from below (Willinsky, 1990). Ball (1987) picks up on this point to assert the ascendancy of "popular culture" over "literary culture" in the New English, the former to be linked to language and speech ("the knowledge of the masses"), the latter to literature and writing ("elite knowledge"), seeing in these developments a clear instance of at least the possibility for cultural politics and ideological struggle (Green, 1995).

What needs to be appreciated, however, is the sheer difficulty that this shift in emphasis involves, both on the level of mainstream classroom practice and in terms of public intelligibility.[8] The very principle of pedagogical authority itself is changed, as well as its general mechanism. It involves opening up the social space of the classroom to difference and heteroglossia, to the plurality and proliferation of voices and interests, and hence to conflict and contestation. This is in large part because a significant disjunction operates between the version of curriculum expressed in English teaching as a theoretical discourse and that embodied and transmitted in schooling as an institutional practice. The "transmission" classroom, that is, is functional; it represents a highly effective and productive social management strategy—hence its persistence (Hamilton, 1980; Hunter, 1984). In contrast, the "interpretation" classroom—and perhaps even more so, the "negotiation" classroom—is from this perspective dysfunctional or even counter-functional, in that it goes against the grain not only of the dominant educational paradigm, as folklore and common sense, but also of the conventions and commonplaces of cultural authority and social order. According to the dominant social logic, that is, it literally does not "make sense" (it is ungrammatical); pushed further, it constitutes an active affront. English teaching conceived in this manner, then, exhibits both an oppositional and an alternative significance, neither of which makes for comfort; taken together, there cannot help but be contradiction and conflict, along with an attendant anxiety. Description of this kind of English teaching, taken to the limits of its own logic, as ultimately a "deschooling" project, becomes not only more understandable but also illuminating and even compelling.

Given this, it becomes possible to see post-Dartmouth English teaching emphatically within the terms of crisis. It was a crisis both of legitimation and of authority. Whereas previously the English teacher had an assured (that is, established, preconstituted) role and identity, a stable professional center, this changed; the profession was in a quite specific sense "decentered," and nothing had been provided that was able to fill the gap effectively or satisfactorily. To understand this, we need to return to the Newbolt Report.

What was established there, and later consolidated in the cultural-pedagogical work of Leavis, Richards, and their cohorts, was a new pedagogical formation organized around the teacher–text–student triad. First, it rested on a systematic relation between the authority of the text and that of the teacher, and between these and cultural authority. Second, it involved a process whereby the student was caught up in a speculary relationship to both the text and the teacher, separately and in their interaction. The student's engagement with the text, his or her identification with it, conceived as a quite specific socialization effect, was mediated by the teacher; the teacher was, therefore, a significant and necessary intermediary in the transactions between the student and the social-symbolic order, as realized through the culture of literacy. As the student takes on his or her structured identity, the teacher, doubtless in all due and proper humility, falls away, allowing the student an authorized autonomy not only in reading but also in life itself. As King describes it, the teacher–pupil relation is a central feature of this kind of social-disciplinary strategy. However, it rests on the insistence of the significance and priority of the teacher: "The teacher must exist before the pupil" (Newbolt, 1921, p. 25; cited in King, 1983, p. 33). Not only "prior to," King observes, but also in the presence of; in short, an insistence on the teacher's crucial significance as at once role, identity, and function.

In the post-Dartmouth period, however, this kind of authority and its associated legitimation, as well as its "role-identity," were no longer available to the English teacher. There are several reasons for this. One is certainly the shift in emphasis from transmission to interpretation orientations in curriculum (Barnes, 1976), and hence from a teaching focus to a learning focus.[9] This meant a definite ambivalence in terms of pedagogical relations. Given that the introduction into the classroom of students' histories, experience, cultures, and interests means that expertise and authority now rest with the student(s), teachers need to adopt a new stance, fashion a new speaking and enunciative position, one that acknowledges these shifts in what might be called epistemic authority, while maintaining a necessary measure of pedagogical authority. Achieving this becomes a matter of maintaining an often precarious balance—something that has been compounded, often, by the equally precarious balancing act required to negotiate the social relations of the wider school context, to say nothing for the moment of the larger cultural field. What made the teachers' task even more difficult was that, in opening up the classroom to student culture, to difference (Burgess, 1988), teachers found themselves, more often than not, in a situation where their training, history, and skills—largely if not overwhelmingly in the literary-critical mode—were of little real help in understanding, let alone teaching, the texts in question. The teacher, in short, was "de-skilled" and effectively "disempowered," specifically with regard to the normative pedagogical form.

Given, then, that authority no longer resided in literary expertise, conceived as a matter both of canonic knowledge and of technique, alternatives needed to be sought. One such alternative—which was directly related to new investment in writing pedagogy (Gilbert, 1989)—was the increased emphasis on the personal authority of the teacher him/herself; the teacher, that is, as a person. This is neatly captured in the passage from Boomer (1988) quoted previously, concerning "the demonstration of the self": "Teachers teach most profoundly what they are at the core" (p. 31). Pedagogical authority resides in the self, that irreducible core of the human being conceived in all its ultimate plenitude. The teacher, therefore, as exemplum; a "trusted adult" (Britton et al., 1975), one who cares, has patience, diligence, and wisdom, and also reads and writes—a model par excellence. It is an extraordinary demand, and resonant with contradiction and complexity. What it names, in essence, is the exemplary governmental subject: the Teacher.

ON GRAMMAR, GOVERNMENTALITY, AND EDUCATION

What would an account of English teaching, grammar, and governmentality have to teach us, over and beyond providing a case study in the history and politics of public schooling? Relatedly, what might be the general implications or indeed the international reference of an account addressed largely to recent manifestations of educational crisis and change in the United Kingdom? What, specifically, does all this have to contribute to understanding the historical nexus between English teaching and public schooling, as a distinctive form of social-disciplinary power? I want to take up these questions now, in focusing more directly on the significance of the socio-symbolic figures of grammar and the teacher (or teaching). My organizing thesis is that these are profoundly intricated, within a general economy of the educational-political imagination.

What must be recognized at the outset is that the discourse of English teaching is formed out of a number of what can be called reciprocating axes within a single educative strategy. These include what I am particularly concerned with, here and elsewhere: the implicit relationship between literature and grammar. Much recent work has been done on the former category in this regard, including my own efforts (Green, 1990; Hunter, 1988; Morgan, 1990). How does grammar figure, then, as the "other side" of the discourse of English teaching? First, it is useful to understand grammar in this context as a rule-resource system for living and meaning. As such, it involves conditions of possibility and intelligibility for social statements of various kinds, including but not limited to those pertaining to language and the body. In this sense, grammar is not to be conceived as a matter of science or truth, but rather of rhetoric and ideology, or more precisely, of socio-symbolic power. Hence it must be considered not so much from the perspective of linguistics as from that of politics and philosophy, or political philosophy. For my present purposes, this requires, then, what might be described as a Foucaultian account of grammar.[10] Second, what is now to be conceived as a specific or strictly delimited genealogy of grammar involves accounting for its forms of emergence in the present, as one manifestation of the historicity of schooling. Put simply: Why grammar now? What is it about grammar that merits social and discursive analysis, as part of a larger politics of education?

Something of this can be gauged from recent work by Frances Christie (1990, 1993). This is particularly relevant because she features significantly in the "literacy wars" scenario introduced at the outset of this chapter. Working from within a systemic-linguistic framework, which has been identified elsewhere as the Sydney School (Lee, 1995), she has been prominent in arguing for the importance of "overt teaching and learning about language" (Christie, 1993, p. 102) in English teaching and language education more generally. To this end, she has advocated the introduction of what is known as functional grammar, in sharp contrast to so-called traditional grammar. It needs to be said, too, that her arguments are framed by a clear concern for social equity, operating within the rubric of critical social literacy. Hence the position represented here is to be identified more with the Left, conventionally conceived, than with the Right. Notwithstanding this, it can be seen as participating in, and actively contributing to, what has been described here as a general program of liberal-conservative reorganization. For that reason, it is pertinent to draw attention to its larger socio-symbolic contextualization.

For Christie, what is at issue is what she calls "the decline of rhetoric and the corruption of grammar." She documents the manner in which language education moved from being integrally linked to meaning and purpose, and hence to social participation and practice, to being divorced and dissociated from life and linked instead to schooling. From the eighteenth century, through the nineteenth century, to the twentieth century, she traces a narrative of "decline," "corruption," and "deviation"; as language education is progressively subsumed within popular, public schooling, it enters into what might be called—paradoxically—the social condition of the Fall. This is narrated within a conceit of the so-called "received tradition," which effectively corresponds to and persists through the history of schooling itself. This is evident in the fact that, for her, a major referent of "the decline of rhetoric and the corruption of grammar" is precisely the historical nexus between English teaching and public education. This in turn enables her to read in that history a Progressive deviation from the norm—that is, the preferred, normative conditions and practices of rhetoric, grammar, and education as they were prior to roughly the mid-eighteenth century and presumably will be after what she presents as the "error" of the New English. For Christie, the post-Dartmouth discourse of English teaching represents not so much a refusal of the received tradition of grammar instruction as its apotheosis and its culmination. Thus, all of schooling's history converges on this moment of realization when monstrosity erupts on the scene of pedagogy in the form of the anti-teacher, the Progressive (English) teacher who effectively refuses his or her responsibility and who abdicates authority in deference to the "other" (the learner, the student).

Of particular concern here is the teacher-as-facilitator, that is, one who simply attends to the learner learning, or guides him or her toward cultural and personal understandings. Hence Christie (1993) advocates "a directly

interventionist role on the part of the teacher to bring about improved opportunity for students to use [language]. Such a role is not 'facilitative' of growth;
rather, it involves overt teaching and guidance of students as they learn language" (p. 78). Hence:

> In this view, unlike the romantically conceived individual who is involved in
> some sort of journey of "personal discovery," the individual is seen much more
> as an apprentice: one who is initiated into ways of operating and dealing with
> experience through guidance, advice, and experimentation with the models of
> others. (Christie, 1993, p. 100)

That is, there is a direct association in arguments such as this between grammar and teaching, between the teaching of grammar and the grammar of
teaching.[11] I intend this latter phrase partly in the Wittgensteinian sense, to
indicate that teaching needs to be grasped both as a social concept and as a
social practice. As such, it is organized in accordance with and within the
terms of a distinctive social grammar, "regulat[ing] the possibilities of how a
particular practice might be recognized or interpreted" (Rizvi, 1993, p. 136).
With respect to teaching as a normative concept, with a quite definite and
delimited social intelligibility, this is something subject to training, something
learned in and through discipline and also—significantly—"discipleship."
Further, "the goal of any training is to draw individuals into an established
grammar, a shared practice; to initiate them into a community of persons
bound together by their allegiance to the rules of a particular discourse"
(Rizvi, 1993, p. 136). What is important here is that there is a crucial tension
between the professional discourse of teaching and the larger social logic that
constrains and contextualizes it—to employ a more Foucaultian formulation, the logic of "the social."

From this angle, there is no significant difference between grammar as
a category of contemporary linguistic science, within the Hallidayan tradition, and as a feature of traditional schooling, and hence between functional
grammar and traditional grammar.[12] This is clearly indicated in recent manifestations of the literacy debate in Australia, for instance, in headlines such
as "Grammar comes back into fashion" (1993, p. 8), which specifically addresses the introduction of functional grammar into "school literacy education," noting that "the lack of emphasis on teaching grammar in the nation's
schools since the late 1960s has been identified by employers, academics and
commentators as a major cause of declining literacy standards in the community." The research evidence against claims such as this has been noted time
and time again (e.g., Hartwell, 1985), and yet "the continuing pressure to
teach more grammar is one of the most enduring aspects of the common

sense of language education" (Mayher, 1990, p. 32). More is at issue, that is, than truth per se.

At this point, then, it is appropriate to look more specifically at other historical work on grammar and English teaching. Walker (1986, 1990) has investigated the history and politics of grammar instruction in Canadian education, with reference specifically to Nova Scotia and Newfoundland. As he notes: "The factors that influenced nineteenth-century educators in their decisions about grammar teaching were linguistic and social as well as educational" (Walker, 1986, p. 23). Indeed, it would appear functional for grammar to be incorporated into English lessons and the practice of schooling, notwithstanding the difficulty teachers experienced or the "torment" such lessons represented for students. Grammar, linked to written language and to standardization and regulation, served as an exemplary instrument of social discipline. Among several explanations, including its links to a doctrine of "mental discipline" and the discourse of "faculty psychology," Walker draws attention to the significance of what he calls, variously, "linguistic fundamentalism" and "authoritarian fundamentalism," observing what he describes as "an interesting parallel between the predominant nineteenth-century conception of language and a twentieth-century religious ideology that clarifies the power of the prevailing ideology of language in the final decades of the last century" (Walker, 1990, p. 164). Hence:

> In the 1890s, linguistic propriety was a singular doctrine, and, in accordance with the wider academic curriculum of the time, it was external to the individual child. Grammar was a body of knowledge that had to be mastered as a prerequisite to proper speaking and writing upon which, together with polite manners and an approved religion, depended full participation in respectable society. (Walker, 1990, p. 165)

A further study of English curriculum history and politics, in part focused on the 1980s in the United Kingdom, indicated very clearly what can be described as a new "grammarian turn" in public debates over national curriculum, schooling, literacy, and English teaching (Ball, Kenny, & Gardiner, 1990). The official and preferred view of language and language pedagogy, which is first elaborated in the policy document *English from 5 to 16* (DES, 1984), sets the scene for the later work of the Kingman (DES, 1988) and Cox (DES, 1988/89) Reports. The following is indicative:

> Many pupils are taught nothing at all about how language works as a system, and consequently do not understand their mistakes or how to put them right. We suggest that if some attention is given to the examination and discussion of the structure of the language pupils speak, write, read, or listen to for real purposes, their awareness of its possibilities and pitfalls can be sharpened. In the

course of this, it is reasonable that they should learn such grammatical terminology as is useful to them for the discussion of language. (DES, 1984, p. 14)

There are several points to note here. First, the emphasis on teaching is significant. Knowledge of language "as a system" is directly linked to teaching, as knowledge that teachers have and are to transmit to their students. Accordingly, that "many pupils are taught nothing" about language "as a system" is automatically seen to imply that they know nothing in this regard. It also works on the assumption that the knowledge in question is necessarily articulate and explicit, rather than tacit and implicit. Further, knowledge of this articulated, explicit kind, identified as it is with teachers and teaching rather than learners and learning—that is, something that teachers have and students do not, by definition—links up with the notion of grammar and linguistic terminology, in ways that figure significantly in subsequent reports. Terminology is something that needs to be taught, as in any specialist knowledge domain. The linguistic orientation in such a formulation is very evident; that is, the way linguistic science figures here, however that is understood (Lee, in press). Moreover, the stance taken is highly rationalist; because students do not know about "language as a system," or at least have not been taught about it, they cannot "understand their mistakes or how to put them right"—the use of the word *consequently* is particularly significant in this regard, I suggest.

Part of what is at issue here is certainly the de-emphasis on knowledge about language in New English and other child- and learner-centered pedagogies (Rothery, 1989). This is something that must be understood historically as well as ideologically, however, since it stemmed from an explicit reaction to previously dominant forms of pedagogy in which language exercises figured significantly. Of course, this cannot be disengaged from matters such as the effects of institutional and cultural changes on curriculum and schooling, or from questions of politics and ideology. All the same, it is important not to overlook the historical element, and hence the strategic aspect of the move away from prescriptive teaching of language and grammar. As Stubbs (1989) notes: "Grammar was dropped from many English syllabuses as one part of a child-centred movement in teaching, which also had as an explicit part of its aims to change teacher–pupil relations in schools" (p. 239).

The two need to be seen together, in fact. Grammatical knowledge, as traditionally understood, equates readily with notions of teaching, authority, and expertise. Therefore, to move away from explicit teaching of grammar is to move away from a certain authoritative position, with particular regard to language knowledge and expertise. The move is away from teachers' grammatical expertise, something that they themselves have been taught and that needs to be taught to students, toward a focus on the learner's experience and associated forms of expertise, which includes that tacit knowledge relating specifically to their language experience.

What is most relevant about this exchange and the position taken on language study in the 1984 document, however, is the way the term "grammar" functions both symbolically and politically. This is consistent, in fact, with a history of policy developments and government initiatives, and with official moves in the British national curriculum debate to restore traditional forms of pedagogy, particularly those involving language and grammar. Hence, as Ball, Kenny, and Gardiner (1990) write, "to a great extent the discourse of critique mounted by the Black Paper ideologies of the 1970s" (p. 70)—traces of which were clearly discernible in Bullock—had become government policy by the end of the 1980s. The common ground between government and the media on questions of language, grammar, teaching, and standards, within a general discourse of educational crisis, is particularly notable. Noting that the *English from 5 to 16* document "urge[s] that grammar, spelling and punctuation should be brought to the forefront in English teaching," Ball and his colleagues (1990, p. 70) go on to indicate how matters such as this were interpreted and recontextualized in the media, citing various examples of selective reporting and willful misreading. This is a point Stubbs (1989) also makes, with reference to the later Cox Report, and it has been in fact a particularly noticeable feature of British educational politics since the 1970s. Cameron and Bourne (1988) counterpose a statement from the then Secretary of State for Education, Kenneth Baker, with one reported in the *Observer* newspaper. The latter, published in 1982, was a feature article by an independent school headmaster, John Rae, on the topic "The decline and fall of English grammar." Rae makes it very clear that, for him, grammar is linked decisively to the notion of conduct, and this is achieved rhetorically via the concept of rule. As Cameron and Bourne (1988) gloss his argument, children need to be taught grammar so that they come to realize that "there are rules of conduct: people may not simply do as they please, either in language or in any other kind of social interaction. Rejecting grammar is one mark of a society which rejects rules, and the result is anarchy" (p. 150). They cite the following from Rae's article:

> Grammar was a predictable victim of the self-indulgent sixties. It was associated with authority, tradition and elitism. Grammatical rules, like so many other rules at the time, were regarded as an intolerable infringement of personal freedom. (Cameron & Bourne, 1988, p. 150)

As Rae goes on to propose: "The overthrow of grammar coincided with the acceptance of the equivalent of creative writing in social behaviour" (Cameron & Bourne, 1988, p. 150). This is familiar territory in the educational climate of the New Right, as Shor (1986) and others have indicated. What is widely perceived as the breakdown of traditional institutions and associated patterns of authority and value in the post-1960s period is linked to permissive pedagogical practices and the cultural shifts associated with television, youth culture, and rock music. The concept of grammar is, therefore, particularly significant in this context, as at once symptomatic and symbolic. In Cameron and Bourne's (1988) terms, clearly "grammar is to bear an enormous symbolic weight, being associated with the values of hierarchy, order and rule—*government in general*. That is why it is both passionately advocated and passionately opposed. A return to grammar marks a return to the associated social values" (p. 155; emphasis added).

Research such as this enables the argument that current moves toward the restoration of traditional (normative, conventional) practices in education and schooling, including those associated with grammar, are best seen as similarly motivated. What Christie conceives within the terms of corruption and decline, with "real" grammar contrasted with "school" grammar—in effect, essence with institution—might well be seen otherwise. Could it be that this distinction is itself problematical? Might not this so-called corruption and decline be read, rather, as functional to schooling, and as linked organically to the social invention of the urban schoolteacher (Jones, 1990) and the modern classroom system (Hamilton, 1980), and later the textbook? More to the point, as Christie correctly indicates, grammar became decontextualized and abstracted over the course of the eighteenth and nineteenth centuries. It is also no accident, of course, that this coincided with the emergence and consolidation of state-sponsored, mass compulsory schooling. For Christie (1993):

> A scholarly preoccupation with grammar, a declining value attaching to speech, and a corresponding [ascendent] value attaching to writing, had caused a shift in approaches to the study of the English language by the early years of the nineteenth century. (p. 93)

This needs to be linked directly to "the development of elementary schooling"—as she puts it, "at the same time, and for historically related reasons," bringing with it "various practices for teaching and disciplining children in large numbers" (Christie, 1993, p. 93). Writing and schooling thus come together in the conjoint expression of disciplinary and pastoral power. On the one hand, there is the emergence and consolidation of literary education, built upon a new understanding of authorship, textuality, and commentary, linked to which is "the exemplary text–teacher–authority triplet" (McHoul, 1991, p. 206; Hunter, 1988). On the other, there is the humble grammar lesson, much less a matter of the government of love and the love of government than of "drills-and-skills," in the rhetoric associated with reform movements such as the New English or, much earlier, first-generation Progressivism in the United States. The movement is from a pedagogy of love as the cornerstone of the good teacher to one predicated on various modulations of coercion and violence, not all of which were symbolic in nature and effect. The teaching of grammar in the mass compulsory context of the modern school becomes necessarily a prescriptive exercise in discipline and training, and in the management of complexity; it is far less a labor of love, even on the part of the most dedicated teacher, and even in accordance with "an official emphasis on 'gentle' pedagogy" (Curtis, 1988, p. 238), and "more a torment than a benefit" to teacher and students alike (Walker, 1986).

This registers a key principle here: the "failure" of social programs such as those associated with literary education and modern schooling—the inevitable disjunction between the realms of theory and practice, discourses and effects. The significance of this, here, lies first in what Jones (1990) sees as fundamental to the genealogy of the urban schoolteacher, more specifically toward the end of the nineteenth century: "The failure of the teacher to effect an urban reformation" elided with "a larger concern about national decline and the implications of the extension of the franchise after 1868" (p. 67). As he notes: "The [nineteenth-century] teacher occupied an intensely ambivalent strategic position" (Jones, 1990, p. 66), something that in fact would appear common across national systems, in, for instance, Canada West (Curtis, 1988) and Australia (Smith, 1990), and extends into the present time. Hence, Jones points to the social formation of a distinctive "image repertoire" ("the teacher as an ideal father, a good and rational parent, and eventually, in an interesting reversal of gender, a good and nurturing mother") into which is nonetheless inscribed a necessary "failure":

> This image repertoire congeals in the formation of the good teacher and plays consciously across the classrooms and staffrooms of the contemporary urban school. These images occupy a technology that orders and examines the phenomenon of urban growth. This technology, moreover, has always failed. The genealogy of the urban schoolteacher is the passage of a failure which, paradoxically, induces a more extensive examination of the need for urban schooling. (p. 75)

A crucial aspect of this image repertoire revolves around the symbolic category of grammar, as evoked in the recent manifestations of an always renewable literacy debate with which I opened this chapter. Grammar lessons represent habituated relations of embodied authority,[13] an imaginary field linking nostalgia and desire, including social and cultural anxieties around questions of change and generation, language and authority, structure and freedom, discipline and disorder. Consider, for instance, the typical distribution of knowledge, power, and desire in the grammar lesson, the arrangement of bodies and architecture, the social play of question, answer, and judgment: the structure of participation in the social-symbolic order of the classroom, thus linking school and society. Herein lies the power and significance of the recent re-invention of teaching, in all its visibility and potency, and the moral fervor that attaches to the re-birth of the Teacher and the restoration of pedagogical authority, in all its familiarity and normative pleasure. Ball (1993) is strikingly apposite in his observations on this program of renewal. As he writes, apropos of recent developments in British education in the wake of Thatcherism, a major theme in recent policy and public formulations "is nostalgia, an educational Victorianism which represents education, to parents in particular, in terms of familiar images of 'traditional' pedagogic forms":

> This is a form of cultural popularism organised around notions of discipline, authority and learning. The Victorian classroom and the grammar school are the lost objects of desire, standing for a time when education was simple, when learning meant doing and knowing what you were told by the teacher. Kenneth Clark's classroom has desks in rows, the children silent, the teacher "at the front," chalk in hand, dispensing knowledge. This powerful image of "the teacher" and of "teaching" makes perfect sense to parents in ways that new teaching methods and new teacher–student relationships do not. Many recognise in this fragments, images, laments of their own schooling. (Ball, 1993, p. 209)

That is surely at least one manifestation of crisis and change in public schooling today that haunts us all, poised as we are on the cusp between modernity and postmodernity, and new forms of power, governmentality, and the state. The scene of grammar thus contains within itself important social lessons that remain compelling today, yoking together educational politics and historical imagination in a renewed understanding of curriculum, schooling, and the symbolic order.

CONCLUSION

In the newspaper article cited at the outset of this chapter ("Verbs with verve spark a new war of words"), a commentator is quoted as saying that the current outbreak of the "literacy debate," featuring "Professor Christie and her new wave," evidenced a "desperate attempt to claim territory. The functional grammar people are evangelical about it [i.e., the new 'functional grammar'], as if it is going to save the world" (Richards, 1994, p. 1). We have already seen a similar zeal in conservative back-to-basics proponents, in the spirit of what Ball (1993) describes as "cultural restorationism." The extraordinary public reception of the arguments of Bloom, Hirsch, and others in the United States, although by no means tied (at least directly) to the question of grammar per se, can be similarly understood (Aronowitz & Giroux, 1991). At issue fundamentally is a felt need to return to the traditional social virtues and markers of distinction and authority, of structure and discipline—the right order of things. Central to this is clearly the restoration of the symbolic figure of the Teacher, an impossible fiction, as indicated here, but nonetheless one with real effects in terms of the social dynamics of subjectivity, power, and worldly "salvation" (Foucault, 1983, p. 215).

NOTES

My thanks to Alison Lee and Jo-Anne Reid for their advice and assistance in the preparation of this chapter, and to Marie Brennan for her editorial forbearance.

1. Note that it is best always to understand terms such as "restoration" rhetorically, i.e., as contradictory concepts employed variously to refer to contemporary social dynamics and tensions of crisis and change, invention and renewal.

2. It also needs to be said that any such assessment of teachers and teaching needs to take into account that the profession characteristically has been constructed, materially and symbolically, as "women's work" (Apple, 1986)—a point given further significance when the historical connections between gender and English teaching are recognized (Doyle, 1989). Elsewhere in the same context, Doyle (1989) refers to "the particular character of English as an institutionalized and gendered pedagogic discipline" (pp. 4–5).

3. For a historical assessment of English teaching in the United States, see Applebee and Purves (1992); for an international overview, see Britton, Shafer, and Watson (1990).

4. Elsewhere, Hunter (1988) refers specifically to "the transference of the exemplary attributes of the popular school teacher to the teacher of English" (p. 65).

5. For a critical assessment of the Bullock Report in this regard, specifically within the Hunter–King framework of analysis, see Patterson (1993).

6. As King (1983) observes, "The Newbolt Report [is] forced to argue the necessity for and the impossibility of examinations" (p. 28)—a contradiction that remains at the very heart of New English pedagogy. The Dartmouth Seminar of 1966, involving English educators from North America and the United Kingdom, commonly is viewed as a key moment in the formation of the New English (Dixon, 1967/75; Mayher, 1990).

7. See Gilbert (1989) for a critical assessment of this matter.

8. Apropos of English as "a highly significant case within the school curriculum," Medway (1990) points out that "at least in certain of its contemporary forms, it is manifestly strange" (p. 2), or eccentric, and hence even different. At the same

time, I would stress that the contemporaneity of this difference (as ab-normality) needs to be understood in the context of the historical production of the norm of teaching and schooling more generally.

9. A further development here is the notion of a distinct negotiation orientation (Boomer, Lester, Onore, & Cook, 1992). Whether this is simply a further mutation in interpretation, constructivist pedagogy or a movement, potentially at least, into a new socially critical form remains to be seen.

10. The present work clearly is only an initial or opening moment in such an undertaking. It would require a more intensive and systematic account of the discourse of grammar as well as of discourses on grammar and study of the various surfaces upon which the category "grammar" is and has been inscribed.

11. Note a similar usage of the term "grammar" in Tyack and Tobin (1994). They write: "The basic 'grammar' of schooling, like the shape of classrooms, has remained remarkably stable over the decades. By the 'grammar' of schooling we mean the regular structures and rules that organize the work of instruction." Further: "Much of the grammar of schooling has become so well established that it is typically taken for granted as just the ways things are. It is the departure from customary practice in schooling or speaking that attracts attention" (p. 454).

12. The same point holds for the linguistic-scientific claims of transformational-generative grammar in the Chomskyan tradition, which has been more influential in the North American language education context (Langer & Allington, 1992; Mayher, 1990).

13. As Curtis (1988) writes with regard to "the centrality of 'habituation' in pedagogical practice": "Students habituated to certain kinds of behaviour at school would exhibit that behaviour outside of school. The efficacy of 'respect for authority', for instance, lay not in students' mental appreciation of its moral correctness, but in their practical behaviour towards authority" (p. 377).

REFERENCES

Apple, M. W. (1986). *Teachers and texts.* New York: Routledge & Kegan Paul.

Applebee, A. N., & Purves, A. C. (1992). Literature and the English language arts. In P. W. Jackson (Ed.), *Handbook of research in curriculum* (pp. 726–748). New York: Macmillan.

Aronowitz, S., & Giroux, H. A. (1991). *Postmodern education: Politics, culture and social criticism.* Minneapolis: University of Minnesota Press.

Ball, S. J. (1983). A subject of privilege: English and the school curriculum 1906–1935. In M. Hammersley & A. Hargreaves (Eds.), *Curriculum practice: Some sociological case studies* (pp. 61–88). London: Falmer Press.

Ball, S. J. (1985). English for the English since 1906. In I. Goodson (Ed.), *Social histories of the secondary curriculum: Subjects for study* (pp. 53–88). London: Falmer Press.

Ball, S. J. (1987). Relations, structures and conditions in curriculum change: A political history of English teaching 1970–85. In I. Goodson (Ed.), *International perspectives in curriculum history* (pp. 17–45). London: Croom Helm.

Ball, S. J. (1990). *Politics and policy making in education: Explorations in policy sociology*. London: Routledge.

Ball, S. J. (1993). Education, majorism and "the curriculum of the dead." *Curriculum Studies, 1*(2), 195–214.

Ball, S. J., Kenny, A., & Gardiner, D. (1990). Literacy, politics and the teaching of English. In I. Goodson & P. Medway (Eds.), *Bringing English to order: The history and politics of a school subject* (pp. 47–86). London: Falmer Press.

Barnes, D. (1976). *From communication to curriculum*. Harmondsworth: Penguin.

Boomer, G. (1988). Struggling in English. In B. Green (Ed.), *Metaphors and meanings: Essays on English teaching by Garth Boomer* (pp. 31–41). Adelaide: Australian Association for the Teaching of English.

Boomer, G., Lester, N., Onore, C., & Cook, J. (1992). *Negotiating the curriculum: Educating for the twentieth century*. London: Falmer Press.

Britton, J., Burgess, T., Martin, N., McLeod, A., & Rosen, H. (1975). *The development of writing abilities (11–18)* (Schools Council Research Studies). London: Macmillan.

Britton, J., Shafer, R. E., & Watson, K. (Eds.). (1990). *Teaching and learning English worldwide*. Clevedon: Multilingual Matters.

Burgess, T. (1988). On difference: Cultural and linguistic diversity and English teaching. In M. Lightfoot & N. Martin (Eds.), *The word for teaching is learning: Essays for James Britton* (pp. 155–168). London: Heinemann.

Cameron, D., & Bourne, J. (1988). No common ground: Kingman, grammar and the nation. *Language and Education, 2*(3), 147–160.

Christie, F. (1990). The changing face of literacy. In F. Christie (Ed.), *Literacy for a changing world* (pp. 1–25). Melbourne: Australian Council for Educational Research.

Christie, F. (1993). The "received tradition" of English teaching: The decline of rhetoric and the corruption of grammar. In B. Green (Ed.), *The insistence of the letter: Literacy studies and curriculum theorizing* (pp. 75–106). Pittsburgh: University of Pittsburgh Press.

Curtis, B. (1988). *Building the educational state: Canada West, 1836–1871*. Philadelphia: Falmer Press and London, Ontario: Althouse Press.

Department of Education and Science. (1975). *A language for life* (Report of the Committee of Inquiry [The Bullock Report]). London: Her Majesty's Stationery Office.

Department of Education and Science. (1984). *English from 5 to 16: Curriculum matters 1*. London: Her Majesty's Stationery Office.

Department of Education and Science. (1988). *Report of the Committee of Inquiry into the Teaching of English Language* (The Kingman Report). London: Her Majesty's Stationery Office.

Department of Education and Science. (1988/89). *English for ages 5 to 16* (The Cox Report). London: Department of Education and Science and the Welsh Office.

Dixon, J. (1967/75). *Growth through English: Set in the perspective of the seventies.*

London: National Association for the Teaching of English and Oxford University Press.

Donald, J. (1985). Beacons of the future: Schooling, subjection and subjectification. In V. Beechey & J. Donald (Eds.), *Subjectivity and social relations* (pp. 214–249). Milton Keynes: Open University Press.

Doyle, B. (1989). *English and Englishness.* London: Routledge.

Education Department of Western Australia. (1980). *The Martin report: What goes on in English lessons* (Case Studies from Government High Schools in Western Australia). Perth: Author.

Foucault, M. (1983). The subject and power. In H. L. Dreyfus & P. Rabinow (Eds.), *Michel Foucault: Beyond structuralism and hermeneutics* (2nd ed.) (pp. 208–226). Chicago: University of Chicago Press.

Foucault, M. (1991). Governmentality. In G. Burchell, C. Gordon, & P. Miller (Eds.), *The Foucault effect: Studies in governmentality* (pp. 87–104). Chicago: University of Chicago Press.

Gilbert, P. (1989). *Writing, schooling and deconstruction: From voice to text in the classroom.* London: Routledge.

Goodson, I. (1988). *The making of curriculum.* London: Falmer Press.

Grammar comes back into fashion. (1993, November 27–28). *The Weekend Australian,* p. 8.

Green, B. (1990). A dividing practice: "Literature," English teaching and cultural politics. In I. Goodson & P. Medway (Eds.), *Bringing English to order: The history and politics of a school subject,* (pp. 135–161). London: Falmer Press.

Green, B. (1995). Post-curriculum possibilities: English teaching, cultural politics, and the postmodern turn. *Journal of Curriculum Studies, 27*(4), 391–409.

Hamilton, D. (1980). Adam Smith and the moral economy of the classroom system. *Journal of Curriculum Studies, 12*(4), 281–298.

Hamilton, D. (1989). *Towards a theory of schooling.* London: Falmer Press.

Hartwell, P. (1985). Grammar, grammars, and the teaching of grammar. *College English, 47*(2), 105–127.

Hunter, I. (1984). Laughter and warmth: Sex education in Victorian secondary schools. In P. Botsman & R. Harley (Eds.), *Sex, politics and representation* (pp. 55–81). Sydney: Local Consumption Series 5.

Hunter, I. (1987). Culture, education and English: Building "the principal scene of the real life of children." *Economy and Society, 16*(4), 568–588.

Hunter, I. (1988). *Culture and government: The emergence of literary education.* London: Macmillan.

Jones, D. (1990). The genealogy of the urban schoolteacher. In S. J. Ball (Ed.), *Foucault and education: Discipline and knowledge* (pp. 57–77). London: Routledge.

King, N. (1983). "The teacher must exist before the pupil": The Newbolt report on the teaching of English in England, 1921. *Literature and History, 13*(1), 14–37.

Langer, J. A., & Allington, R. L. (1992). Curriculum research in writing and reading. In P. W. Jackson (Ed.), *Handbook of research in curriculum* (pp. 687–725). New York: Macmillan.

Lee, A. (in press). Questioning the critical: Linguistics, literacy and pedagogy. In

P. Freebody, S. Muspratt, & A. Luke (Eds.), *Constructing critical literacies: Teaching and learning textual practices.* New York: Hampton.

Mathieson, M. (1975). *The preachers of culture: A study of English and its teachers.* London: George Allen & Unwin.

Mayher, J. S. (1990). *Uncommon sense: Theoretical practice in language education.* Portsmouth, NH: Boynton Cook/Heinemann.

McHoul, A. (1991). Readings. In C. D. Baker & A. Luke (Eds.), *Towards a critical sociology of reading pedagogy* (pp. 191–210). Amsterdam/Philadelphia: John Benjamins.

Medway, P. (1980). *Finding a language: Autonomy and learning in school.* London: Writers and Readers Publishing Cooperative/Chameleon Books.

Medway, P. (1986). *What counts as English: Selections from language and reality in a school subject at the twelve year old level.* Unpublished doctoral dissertation, University of Leeds, School of Education.

Medway, P. (1990). Into the sixties: English and English society at a time of change. In I. Goodson & P. Medway (Eds.), *Bringing English to order: The history and politics of a school subject* (pp. 1–46). London: Falmer Press.

Morgan, R. (1990). The "Englishness" of English teaching. In I. Goodson & P. Medway (Eds.), *Bringing English to order: The history and politics of a school subject* (pp. 197–241). London: Falmer Press.

Newbolt Report. (1921). *The teaching of English in England: Being the report of the Department Committee appointed by the President of the Board of Education to inquire into the position of English in the education system of England.* London: Her Majesty's Stationery Office.

Patterson, A. (1993). "Personal response" and English teaching. In D. Meredyth & D. Tyler (Eds.), *Child and citizen: Genealogies of schooling and subjectivity* (pp. 61–86). Brisbane: Institute for Cultural Policy Studies, Griffith University.

Richards, C. (1994, June 24). Verbs with verve spark a new war of words. *The Age,* p. 1.

Rizvi, F. (1993). Children and the grammar of popular racism. In C. McCarthy & W. Crichlow (Eds.), *Race, identity and representation in education* (pp. 126–139). New York: Routledge.

Rothery, J. (1989). Learning about language. In R. Hasan & J. R. Martin (Eds.), *Language development: Learning language, learning culture* (pp. 199–256). Norwood, NJ: Ablex.

Shame on the press [Editorial]. (1994). *Phi Delta Kappan, 75*(5), 355.

Shor, I. (1986). *Culture wars: School and society in the conservative restoration 1969–1984.* Boston: Routledge & Kegan Paul.

Smith, R. (1990). William Wilkins's saddle bags: State education and local control. In M. R. Theobald & R. J. W. Selleck (Eds.), *Family, state and control in Australian history* (pp. 66–90). Sydney: Allen & Unwin.

Stubbs, M. (1989). The state of English in the English state: Reflections on the Cox report. *Language and Education, 3*(4), 235–250.

Tyack, D., & Tobin, W. (1994). The "grammar" of schooling: Why has it been so hard to change? *American Educational Research Journal, 31*(3), 453–479.

Walker, L. (1986). *"More a torment than a benefit": English Grammar in Nova Scotia schools in the nineteenth century* [Mimeo]. University of Lethbridge, Faculty of Education.

Walker, L. (1990). The ideology and politics of English grammar: An 1894 Newfoundland example. In I. Goodson & P. Medway (Eds.), *Bringing English to order: The history and politics of a school subject* (pp. 162–184). London: Falmer Press.

Wexler, P. (1987). *Social analysis of education: After the new sociology.* London: Routledge.

Whitty, G. (1991, October). *Recent education reform: Is it a post-modern phenomenon?* Paper presented at the Conference on Reproduction, Social Inequality and Resistance: New Directions in the Theory of Education. University of Bielefeld, Germany.

Willinsky, J. (1990). *The new literacy: Redefining reading and writing in the school.* New York: Routledge.

Willinsky, J. (1991). *The triumph of literature/The fate of literacy: English in the secondary school curriculum.* New York: Teachers College Press.

Willis, P. (1977). *Learning to labour: How working class kids get working class jobs.* Farnborough: Saxon House.

8

The Deployment of Information Technology in the Field of Education and the Augmentation of the Child

DAVID SHUTKIN

By the late twentieth century, our time, a mythic time, we are all . . . theorized and fabricated hybrids of machine and organism; in short, we are cyborgs.

—Donna Haraway, *Simians, Cyborgs, and Women*

A multiplicity of institutional concerns are steering objectives of schooling to reflect an emphasis on technology as tools to systematically enhance the cognitive skills of children by *augmenting* their rational capacities. References to augmenting human capacities with technology emerge in 1963 in the work of Douglas Englebart. While on staff at Xerox Palo Alto Research Center (PARC), Englebart (1963) described a psychological domain that integrated technology to increase the human capacity for approaching complex problem situations, for gaining appropriate comprehension of these situations, and for deriving solutions for them. In the field of education, as the design, production, and implementation of technologies, including computers, telecommunications, and television, have been reduced to these instrumental concerns, these are not neutral tools simply providing educational opportunities for children. Instead, such practices can be analyzed as a *deployment of information technology* in the field of education.

I borrow the concept of *deployment* from Michel Foucault (1979, 1980b), who used the concept *dispositif* to organize his analyses of discipline and of sexuality.[1] The concept of deployment emerges in the work of Foucault (1972, 1979, 1980a, 1980b) as he shifts his thinking from an analysis of power as repressive to an analysis of a productive power. Foucault (1980a) asks what enables the effectivity of power or why do people accept it? His answer: Power is more than a prohibitive force that says no; power "produces things, it induces pleasure, forms knowledge, produces discourse. It needs to be considered as a productive network which runs through the whole social body" (p. 119). Power acts upon the actions of others (Foucault, 1982). For instance, Foucault (1980b) notes that the family as an institution and the sexuality of the child, as objects of investigation and regulation, were reorganized, restricted, and intensified through relations with other institutions. He refers to these relations as a deployment. Technologies, as interrelated elements of a deployment, are produced through, but are also productive of, power relations in the field of education. As a form of power, the actions of the deployment of information technology modify the actions of "others."

Following Foucault, I describe productive relations of power through which technology currently is deployed in the field of education. My concern is with how the deployment of information technology is organized and productive of a body of knowledge and facts and its organization and production of discourses, institutions, and social practices. To analyze the deployment of information technology in the field of education, I discuss discursive practices across a multiplicity of institutions: the discipline of psychology, private business, higher education, the media, and state government. These institutions have their own stakes; they are competitive, they have their own agendas, and they are governed by their own rules and social relations. However, these institutions are not autonomous; instead, through their multiple interrelating elements they mutually condition each other and the field of education.

While an objective of these multiple interrelating elements may be the automation of school environments with local area networks, the Internet, and laser disc technology, the subjectivity of children is constructed through these practices. Put another way, across the field of education, "the child" is being constructed as a subject of the deployment of information technology. Weedon (1987) describes the social practices of constructing subjectivity in discourse as follows:

> Forms of subjectivity are produced historically and change with shifts in the wide range of discursive fields which constitute them. . . . As we acquire lan-

guage, we learn to give voice—meaning—to our experience and to understand it according to particular ways of thinking, particular discourses, which pre-date our entry into language. These ways of thinking constitute our consciousness, and the positions with which we identify [and] structure our sense of ourselves, our subjectivity. (p. 33)

This analysis of the deployment of information technology and the subjectivity of children focuses on the social and historically specific practices to use technology to augment the rational capacities of "the child." To underscore this concern and to draw attention to its operations, I make repeated references to the child. As the subject of the discursive practices of this deployment, the child is positioned as *Homo rationalis*, as a coherent, rational, and noncontradictory (i.e., unified) individual; a source of conscious action whose mental capacities can be augmented with technology (Marshall, 1992; Walkerdine, 1984).

Through the discursive practices of this deployment emerges the conditions in the field of education that legitimate psychological practices to reorganize the rational functioning of the child with technology. These practices conform to a vision of educational change that relates technology to cognitive development. From the classroom to the laboratory, such practices deploy technology with the goal of augmenting the development of the rational capabilities of the child's mind.

The subjectivity of this child as *Homo rationalis* is guaranteed through the authority vested in historically specific discourses on technology and human progress, such as the Cartesian cogito. However, through my analysis of relations between the subjectivity of the child and technology, I conclude with evidence of an historical break. The concern for the cognitive development of the child simultaneously includes developing the capabilities of the child and a child/machine system. Thus, for some psychologists and educators, through this re-production, the intellectual partnership of the child with technology challenges the historically specific integrity of the child as a unified subject. These psychological practices to augment the mental capacities of the child with technology perhaps fail in their instrumental objective to guarantee the unified subject and might even present a challenge to the foundation of psychological practice in the Cartesian cogito.

THE DEPLOYMENT OF INFORMATION TECHNOLOGY
AND THE INSTANCE OF SAN FRANCISCO *GTV*

The interrelating elements of the deployment of information technology in the field of education can be explored by analyzing the social construction of a particular educational laser disc referred to as *GTV*. I focus my analysis of *GTV* by constructing an intertextual analysis of an article titled "San Francisco *GTV*," written by Mary Ellen McDonnell (1992), an administrator with the San Francisco Unified School District. As an instance of the deployment of information technology in the field of education, this article, published in the teacherly journal *The Computing Teacher*, suggests the interrelationships of a multiplicity of institutions, including state government, media, social science, and philanthropic institutions in steering the curriculum of a local school district. As I analyze this article, I describe the practices of *The Computing Teacher* as an instance of the practices of media institutions and the efforts of the International Society for Technology in Education. I discuss the endeavors of Apple Computer and the George Lucas Educational Foundation, among other private philanthropic institutions. I also discuss the State of California curriculum framework and the 1983 California Assembly Bill 803 as interrelating aspects of the deployment of information technology.

To analyze a deployment is to engage in what Bernauer (1990) describes as strategic thinking. It is the objective to look less for a single linear path of explanation than for a series of tactical approaches to a field of power/knowledge such as the field of education. Foucault (1980b) writes, "In the family, parents and relatives became the chief agents of a deployment of [the child's] sexuality which drew its outside support from doctors, educators, and later psychiatrists" (p. 110). In this context, Bernauer (1990) describes a deployment as "a heterogeneous ensemble of discourses, institutions, architectural arrangements, administrative procedures, and so forth" (p. 145). It is, then, the objective of the analysis of a deployment to first describe historically specific relations of productive power established among these elements.

GTV is a four-sided, two laser disc set about U.S. history recently introduced to the San Francisco middle schools. The laser discs are relevant to the eighth-grade social studies curriculum, McDonnell (1992) explains, as they contain the sounds, pictures, and stories of "the history" of the United States. The laser discs incorporate various forms to present U.S. history, including 3-minute videos, still images, music, maps, and the texts of fictionalized autobiographies.

The laser discs are flexible and can be used with a hand-held remote and a video monitor. With a computer, children can guide their own study of U.S. history. There are search functions, tables of contents, captioned descriptions, and other aids for easy access and navigation through the discs. Teachers might use the discs as simple visual aids, playing segments to introduce units; still photographs are easily used for discussions or for review. The *Create a Show* software allows students or teachers to rearrange the documents to construct a lesson, a presentation, a report, and so on. A word processor also is included to encourage students to write their own texts. The laser disc hardware easily interfaces with video cassette recorders, enabling students to produce their own videos with voice-over narration. McDonnell (1992) notes that children have prepared reports on westward expansion, the Depression, the Civil War, and the Industrial Revolution using the discs.

GTV was developed by Apple Computer, LucasFilm, and National Geographic. Each of these corporations, directly and through their philanthropy, is dedicated to the implementation of technology into the schools. In May 1990, *GTV* was introduced to all San Francisco middle schools by these three corporations. Included in the package were Apple computers, a video monitor, and a laser disc player.

Pacific Telesis, a fourth corporation, provided a generous grant to train a teacher representative from each middle school. Initially there were 4 days of training, during which teachers learned how to set up the hardware and run the *GTV* software. Two more days of training were devoted to learning the various applications of *GTV*. Further training was conducted at the LucasFilm's Sky Walker Ranch. At these training sessions, additional teacher representatives became involved as the sessions focused on integrating *GTV* within the context of the State of California curriculum guidelines.

A form letter I received from the George Lucas Educational Foundation (the Lucas Foundation) describes their concern about education and heightening the "vast imagination and curiosity" of children (George Lucas Educational Foundation, 1992). George Lucas, the letter informs, believes that the emerging interactive multimedia such as *GTV* can help transform education. The Lucas Foundation was established to pursue three goals: create a vision of a technology-enriched educational system; facilitate the exchange of ideas among "experts" on the future of education; and disseminate information about educational change. Through the development of prototype software such as *GTV*, the Lucas Foundation will pursue its goals to transform education with technology.

The Lucas Foundation hosts meetings to facilitate the exchange of ideas among experts on the future of education. These experts from the fields of education and technology are invited to contribute to the production of Lucas Foundation professional development videos. These videos have been distributed among educators, policy makers, and others for professional development and to show "how today's perception of teaching and learning must change if education is to keep pace with our rapidly-changing, highly technological society" (George Lucas Educational Foundation, 1992, p. 2). With these videos, the Lucas Foundation is attempting to act as a catalyst to "help others vision what is possible and to inform them of what is essential" (George Lucas Educational Foundation, 1992, p. 2).

McDonnell (1992) explains that *GTV* correlates with the State of California social studies curriculum framework. As mentioned earlier, part of the *GTV* training was dedicated to how the software can be used in the context of the State of California curriculum framework (McDonnell, 1992). The State of California also has adopted a long-range educational technology plan for California schools (California State Department of Education, 1986):

> The legislature has demonstrated its belief that technology and technology based curriculum materials should be infused into the educational system in support of comprehensive educational reform. In 1983, the legislature enacted Assembly Bill 803 (Chapter 113, Statutes of 1983) which authorized and expanded Educational Technology Local Assistance Program. (p. 5)

As explained in the long-range plan, the bill and the long-range plan are to provide a guide for state and local education administrators, teachers, parents, community groups, business leaders, and others who are interested in the implementation of information technology in the California public schools. The plan refers to the need for restructuring and revitalizing of education in the United States as outlined by reports such as *A Nation at Risk* (National Commission on Excellence in Education, 1983) and *A Nation Prepared* (Carnegie Forum on Education and the Economy, 1986). Several intentions or "philosophical parameters" are outlined by the bill and described in the long-range plan for the use of information technology in education. These include seeking the involvement of the business sector, equitable access to technology by all California students, and preparing students with the necessary skills for employment.

The San Francisco *GTV* project effectively has sought the involvement of the business sector, and the project also is attempting to use the *GTV* curriculum for cognitive skills development. Once students and teachers have developed the necessary technical skills to operate the hardware and software of *GTV*, explains McDonnell (1992), teachers can turn their attention to curriculum development "that strengthens geography skills, fosters creativeness, and involves such thinking skills as interpreting, analyzing, comparing and contrasting, synthesizing and evaluating" (p. 38). In this way, the San Francisco *GTV* project is steered by the state but it also defers to the discursive practices of social science and the authority of cognitive psychologists who define the significant pedagogical relations among technology, cognition, and skills development.

GTV, McDonnell (1992) explains, has been promoted through the work of National Geographic, which distributes a video made by high school students. This video incorporates images downloaded from the *GTV* laser discs with voice-over narration produced by the students. Students also have demonstrated *GTV* for parents, for the media, and at educational technology and social studies conferences. *The Computing Teacher,* the journal that published McDonnell's (1992) article, "San Francisco *GTV,*" also engages in these promotional activities.

The form and content of *The Computing Teacher* suggest that its audience reads for ideas that will translate into practical classroom application. In this way, the article "San Francisco *GTV*" represents the genre of *success story,* as McDonnell (1992) concludes:

> As teachers, it is to our advantage to be prepared to exploit the rapidly changing technologies. . . . Because of the possibility of addressing an even wider range of student learning styles, the use of laser disc technology to improve instruction and learning will increase. GTV has helped us prepare for this change. (p. 38)

But "San Francisco *GTV*" is more than that. Through its form and the story it tells, this article refers to the deployment of information technology as it is an instance of it. *The Computing Teacher* is published by the International Society for Technology in Education (ISTE). ISTE recently has merged with the Association of Educational Communications and Technology (AECT) to form an international organization with thousands of members. ISTE publishes several journals, each directed to a different sector of the educational technology field (teachers, researchers, technology managers); it works with educational technology corporations, academic researchers, and governmental institutions. ISTE sponsors annual conferences, lobbies policy makers, and has published its recommendations for the implementation of technology in schools in a report titled *Vision:* TEST *(Technologically Enriched Schools of Tomorrow)* (Braun, 1990), to which I refer below. As *The Computing Teacher* is sponsored by corporations through advertisements, the articles written for it make constant references to these corporations, as I have demonstrated.

The authority that this deployment constructs does not form an oppressive power that says NO. Rather, it is a modern, productive form of power that says YES (Foucault, 1980b): Develop and implement new technologies; engage in research; enact government policy; offer professional development opportunities; define expertise. Do these things to reform the practices of schooling and to realize progress.

While it may appear to have a unified form as it refers to a reform initiative, there is no singular, linear, or uniform deployment of information technology in the field of education. There are numerous and simultaneous instances of the deployment of information technology. Government policies define curricular objectives and the educated child. Philanthropic institutions define expertise, conform to government policies, and underwrite research and the implementation of curricula. Through their practices, journals define the concerns of a teacherly audience, legitimate research, and effective pedagogies. Professional organizations lobby policy makers, prepare research documents, and encourage the formation of a supportive community through annual meetings and conferences. At these events and through journals, businesses advertise the hardware and the software to achieve the objectives of schooling. While there is no real discontinuity between these instances, at the same time the deployment does not constitute a monolithic strategy. Rather, following Bernauer (1990), this deployment is an heterogeneous ensemble of discourses, institutions, social practices, and technological forms. In his study of the family, Saraceno (1984) makes similar references to the works of Foucault. He states that the relationship between the family and the state is neither linear nor one-sided, as there are many forces, groups, and movements giving rise to the formation of often conflicting and fragmentary social policy and practices.

Established through the productive relations of power of this deployment, is a constant and mutual conditioning of its heterogeneous ensemble of elements (Bernauer, 1990; Foucault, 1980a, 1980b). In his discussion of Foucault and the concept of deployment, Bernauer (1990) describes the effects of this mutual conditioning "in which the strategy's negative and positive consequences, whether desired or not, effect harmonious or contradictory relationships between the various elements that make up the field under examination, and evoke adjustments among the elements" (pp. 145–146). Donzelot (1979) describes this nonlinear deployment of power/knowledge in his analysis of the family as "a whole series of bridges and connections between public assistance, juvenile law, medicine, and psychiatry" (p. 89). In his analysis of educational reform, Popkewitz (1991) explains that an ensemble of mechanisms and procedures emerges regionally and in dispersed sites that taken together produce a regulatory system of power relations. This ensemble includes the shifting role of federal and state governments, which are increasing their involvement in the steering of public education. It is an ensemble of mechanisms and relations between government and other institutions that produces a network of practices that reformulates the social regulation of schooling and of children. As Popkewitz (1991) writes, "There is no clear demarcation between governmental and civil institutions as they mesh in the establishment of social regulation of education" (p. 126).

In the instance of the San Francisco *GTV* project, technology development, state education policy, philanthropy, professional development, academic research, the media, marketing, and so forth, mutually condition each other. Through this mutual conditioning, as things happen during a deployment, intentional or otherwise, and as conflicts and accords emerge to sustain the deployment, these various and dispersed elements become adjusted to one another. It is through this mutual conditioning that the very form of technology developed by Apple Computers is adjusted to state education policy. And it is through this mutual conditioning that the theories of cognition and practices of skills development advanced through research resemble the interests of LucasFilms, the themes published in *The Computing Teacher*, and the education policy established in the State of California. Through this mutual conditioning, the practices of one institution influence the practices of another, and the various elements of the deployment adjust to one another. It is this process of mutual conditioning that shapes and steers the trajectory of the deployment of information technology and the augmentation of the rational capacities of the child in the field of education.

AUGMENTING THE MENTAL CAPACITIES OF THE CHILD FOR AN INFORMATION AGE

It is not only theories and methods that are constructed through the discursive practices of the deployment of information technology; as the deployment constructs and organizes a body of knowledge and facts about human beings, the child is constructed as its subject. As the deployment narrows the purposes of schooling to the instrumental concerns of a postindustrial society, the deployment also narrows the range of subject positions made available to children. Marshall (1992) explains:

> Related to the concept of "subject-to" or "subjected" is the "subject position", which refers to ways one is ascribed a "position" within various discourses. For example, we are each assigned a subject position according to gender, race, ethnicity, family, region, as well as according to a variety of other discourses (as woman, as white, as Irish, as a daughter, as a Midwesterner, as a consumer, etc.). (p. 82)

Among a multiplicity of subject positions, children are positioned within a discourse on technology and education as the "augmented child" whose rational mental capacities are to be increased with information technology, and from this position children are invited to make sense of themselves, information technology, and schooling. In this way, children become a site and subject of discursive struggles for their identity (cf. Weedon, 1987).

Across the field of education, the reduction of schooling to the augmentation of mental capacities or cognitive skills is underscored by Secretary of Labor Robert Reich, who emphasizes education for skills development. He writes, "Instead of emphasizing the transmission of information, the focus is on . . . refining four basic skills: *abstraction, system thinking, experimentation,* and *collaboration*" (Reich, 1991, pp. 229–230). Reich concludes that the most fortunate students in the United States are students who develop these cognitive skills. All students are to have this opportunity, according to former Secretary of Labor Lynn Martin, not only the 15–20% of school children in the United States who attend either elite private schools or the finest suburban and urban schools (Department of Labor, 1992).

As early as 1988, the United States Congress Office of Technology Assessment (OTA) issued a report titled *Power On! New Tools for Teaching and Learning*. This report is read widely and has been quite influential, as it is cited often by educators, researchers, and policy makers. The focus of the report is on performance and productivity gains by students using information technology. Improvements in learning, writes the OTA (1988), do in fact result from the new information technologies for some children. The OTA (1988) reports success stories; the first example is the use of new technologies to do chemistry and physics simulations. With the new technologies, children are capable of doing science. In a second scenario, it is concluded that with computer technology, the child can learn reading, writing, and arithmetic, and with telecommunications, students in remote areas can learn calculus, foreign languages, and physics. The OTA (1988) report suggests that the child's capabilities are augmented by information technology; it is implied that without telecommunications, for example, these children would be unable to learn calculus.

Writing in *The Computing Teacher*, Doris Ray (1991), of the Maine Computer Consortium, explains that there are many ways that information technologies can support a child's development of higher-order cognitive and metacognitive skills. Software publishers, Ray (1991) tells us, have produced numerous products such as simulations and research tools that support the teaching of problem-solving and thinking skills. There is software available for helping students improve their memory. Hypermedia applications can be used by students to help them develop evaluation and communication, synthesis, and analysis skills through designing and producing media projects and presentations.

Looking to the discipline of mathematics in the field of education, there are further instances of this educational discourse on information technology. Dr. Kenneth Hoffman, Professor of Mathematics at the Massachusetts Institute of Technology, is featured in the mathematics section of the 1992 *Electronic Learning* special report on school reform and information technology (Bruder, Buchsbaum, Hill, & Orlando, 1992). In this teacherly journal, he discusses shifts in the conceptualization of mathematics, explaining that with technologies such as the computer, we are shifting how we learn and teach mathematics and what we learn as mathematics. Hoffman stresses that with the low cost of computers, especially calculators, there need be less emphasis on paper and pencil skills (Bruder et al., 1992).

In 1989, the National Council of Teachers of Mathematics (NCTM) issued new skills-based standards. Bruder, a regular contributor to *Electronic Learning*, comments that the NCTM standards cannot be achieved by children without technology (Bruder et al., 1992). These standards are to stress analytic, problem-solving, and creative aspects of mathematics thinking. To attain the NCTM standards of mathematics thinking, an educator featured in the *Electronic Learning* report, Ellen Hook from Granby High School in Norfolk, Virginia, stresses the use of graphing calculators. She comments that children are led to discovery and have learned to ask why and to draw their own conclusions. In the first year the children used these calculators, says Hook, "test scores have been excellent; 80% of this high school's graduating class is going to college, with a graphics calculator in their hands" (Bruder et al., 1992, p. 23).

Dr. Diane K. Erickson (1992), Professor of Education at Oregon State University, also advocates the use of the graphing calculator. Reporting in the pages of *The Computing Teacher*, Dr. Erickson comments that the graphing calculator can be used to develop skills in pattern recognition and functions, as recommended by the NCTM. In one mathematics activity she refers to as *dancing functions*, the purpose is for the child to study the effects of varying a, b, c, and d in the graph $y = af(bx + c) + d$ and its relationship to the graph $y = f(x)$. The graphing calculators, Erickson (1992) explains, provide a new opportunity to explore mathematics. Without the graphing calculators or a personal computer, it would take literally weeks to sketch all the graphs required for this activity. However, with the graphing calculators, the children produce graphs to animate a dance sequence that helps them develop skills in pattern recognition.

The merging of this educational discourse on information technologies with a discourse on the postindustrial society is made explicit in a section about at-risk students, economics, and technology in *Vision*, the final report published in 1990 by the International Society for Technology in Education. Prepared to assist American educational decision makers, the ISTE report explains:

> The waste of potentially productive lives cannot be tolerated in a society that values the life of each of its citizens. Even if, as a nation, we wish to ignore the social dimension of this waste, we cannot ignore its business consequences. As we move into the Information Age, businesses need highly skilled employees in increasing numbers. For the sake of our national economic health, we cannot accept a generation of increasing numbers of under-prepared workers. Both for humanitarian and business reasons, we must consider the immediate future as the *Era of Human Capital Development*. (Braun, 1990, p. 11)

Similarly, Haycock (1991) explains that cognitive skills are becoming a veritable survival kit for the twenty-first century, and Collins (1991) discusses that public schools in the United States face the challenges of reorganizing to prepare students to productively function in a postindustrial society. Students and schools in general are immersed in a society that is in a transition to the uses of information technology, and the instrumental purpose of schooling is to prepare the child for the instability of shifting markets and for his or her future role in this postindustrial society. Schools are to supply a system of state-sponsored corporate institutions with capable workers flexible enough to shift from assignment to assignment as their skills are required by one institution and then by the next (Harvey, 1989; Robins & Webster, 1989; Smart, 1992).[2]

There is nothing new in advocating that the development of skills should determine the curriculum of schooling. This is one of several tactics that are historically part of the social and political struggles over education policy and curriculum in the United States (Kliebard, 1986). However, the present context has its historical specificity; informed by the discourse on the post-industrial society, it is a response to the emergence of computer and telecom-munications technologies. Through the deployment of information technol-ogy in the field of education, the child becomes the subject of these tactics designed to restructure education, while the child also is subjected to and becomes the subject of technology. These are tactics of power through which the rational capacities of children are regulated. What it means to be an educated child is changing through the discursive practices of this deploy-ment. This is an historical process occurring through the everyday practices of people working to change public education.

AN URGENT NEED: POSTINDUSTRIAL SOCIETY, SCHOOLING, AND INFORMATION TOOLS

In the initial stages of a deployment, Foucault (1979, 1980a, 1980b) explains, there is an objective course of action to address an historically specific prob-lem, crisis, or *urgent need*. A deployment often is analyzed as a specific for-mation responding to an urgent need. Thus, a deployment serves a strategic function, as Burchell (1981) pointed out in describing the 1949 Children's Act as an event in the emergence of social work as a profession in a reorga-nized field of social government. In his analysis, Sutton (1983) discusses how in the 1820s, the legal relation of children and their families to the state un-derwent profound changes. And Carrier (1983) establishes that learning disability emerged from obscurity to become an authorized category of edu-cational abnormality in the 1960s. The emergence of a strategic function is evidenced by its influence in the discursive fields that constitute it and by the significance of the need. In the case of the deployment of information technology in the field of education, this strategic function or urgent need is the preparation of children with the requisite mental capacities or skills for a postindustrial society. Functioning to rationalize the deployment of information technology in the field of education, this psychological discourse on children and mental capacities uses signifiers such as *the age of information, the twenty-first century, the information revolution,* and *the postindustrial society* almost interchangeably.[3]

The ensuing analysis of this discourse is informed by Foucault's (1981, 1982, 1991) analyses of governmental rationality, which form an approach to the problem of the increase in the political power of reason and rationality for the management of society. It is not "rationality in general" that I question; rather, I question the specific administrative rationality of the deployment of information technologies in the field of education. This focus is emphasized by Foucault (1981):

> The government of men by men—whether they form small or large groups, whether it is power exerted by men over women, or by adults over children, or by one class over another, or by a bureaucracy over a population—involves a certain type of rationality. . . . The question is: how are such relations of power rationalized? (p. 254)

As it is constructed in the context of education, the discourse on the postindustrial society maintains that schooling in the United States is antiquated and more relevant for an industrial era than for an era in which information is reified and exchanged as a commodity. Schools are to respond to these institutional concerns by reorganizing the curricular and administrative practices of schooling to reflect this new era. It is rationalized that the space of schooling is to be brought into an age of information; current initiatives to reform schooling are to achieve nothing less than a restructuring of the nation's schools for a postindustrial society in an information age. To express the changes needed in this new era, Stonier and Conlin (1985) write this poem in the prologue to their book, *The Three Cs*:

Sometime,
during the second half of the 20th century,
    Western Society evolved from an industrial
        to a post-industrial, or to be precise,
an Information Society.
Education for an industrial society
    centered on teaching the *Three Rs*:
'Reading, 'Riting, and 'Rithmetic'.
Its aim was to produce
    a disciplined work force—
        punctual, conformist, specialized—
           to operate
the brute machinery of the nation-state.

Education for an information society
will centre on the *Three Cs:*
'Children, Computers, and Communication'.
Its aim will be to produce
a creative work force—
adaptable, entrepreneurial, interdisciplinary—
to help solve
the problems of this planet (p. xi)

Through a reductive and totalizing discourse on the postindustrial society, the urgency of the deployment of information technology in the field of education is rationalized. My analysis of this discourse is informed by Poster's (1990) critique of the totalizing discourse on the postindustrial society and by Foucault (1980b), who refers to the work of totalizing discourse in his analysis of the relations between truth and power when he writes: "Each society has its regime of truth, its 'general politics' of truth: that is, the types of discourse which it accepts and makes function as true" (p. 131). The incorporation of this discourse on the postindustrial society within the deployment imposes reductive structural categories of a postindustrial society that function as the truth of social reality.

Across the field of education, the postindustrial society frequently is reduced to a monolithic social structure (Collins, 1991; David, 1991; Perelman, 1987; Reigeluth, 1992; Sheingold, 1991; Stonier & Conlin, 1985). In one instance, the educational technologist Charles Reigeluth (1992) claims that from the agrarian age to the industrial age to the postindustrial or information age, society has experienced massive changes that have altered its structural organizing principles (cf. Poster, 1990).[4] In the agrarian age, he argues, education is organized as the one-room schoolhouse, and in the industrial age, schooling conforms to an industrial assembly-line model. But, Reigeluth (1992) questions, how are "we" to restructure schooling now that society conforms to the structures of the information age? As an instance of this totalizing discourse, Reigeluth's (1992) discussion reduces the intricate social, economic, and political forces of historical change to the discrete structural categories of a monolithic society. Through this discourse on the postindustrial society, problems in the current education system are associated with their "archaic" design for an industrial society. In this way, Reigeluth (1992) legitimates a reified construction of the postindustrial society as it inevitably determines the purpose of initiatives to reform the education system. Resembling reports such as the Carnegie Report of the Task Force on Teaching as a Profession (1986), Reigeluth (1992) concludes that the education system must change to reflect societal changes in an age of information. He writes:

Now that we are entering the information age, we find that paradigm shifts are occurring or will likely soon occur in all our societal systems. . . . It is clear that paradigm shifts in society cause (or require) paradigm shifts in *all* societal systems. . . . It is little wonder that we again find the need for a paradigm shift in education. (Reigeluth, 1992, pp. 9–10)

By distinguishing the postindustrial society from everything that came before it and, ostensibly, from anything that might follow, the discourse of Reigeluth's (1992) totalizing structural analysis posits a regime of truth. Such structural models of the postindustrial age, Poster (1990) argues, attempt to encompass "the entire history of humanity in a schema that distinguishes the new from the old" (p. 23). Thus, the strategic function of this discourse on the postindustrial society is to render invalid elements of industrial society that inform current educational practices as well as to render invalid those educational practices and theories directed at changing schooling that do not conform to the structural categories of postindustrial society.

The interrelations between the institutions of the deployment of information technology, including government and the field of psychology, form coalitions that establish practices such as *GTV*. The practices of these coalitions are rationalized by the urgent rhetoric constructing monolithic historical events such as the postindustrial society or the age of information. Yet the actual practices of social regulation are locally enacted. In this way, reform in education is not constituted by a single hegemonic force, nor does a dualism of centralization and decentralization adequately describe this network of practices steering reform in education. Within the context of a shift to decentralization, community involvement, and other practices, the effect of this network or coalition of practices, which is to narrow the range of local participation and the purposes of schooling, is obscured (Popkewitz, 1991). However, social regulation is not an evil to be abolished. Indeed, this is what schooling does (Popkewitz, 1991). Instead, what must be challenged are specific networks of social regulation, including the deployment of information technology, that narrow the purposes of schooling and the range of subject positions made available to children.

A MODERN VISION OF EDUCATION: PROGRESS, TECHNOLOGY, AND *HOMO RATIONALIS*

The search for an epistemological subject who would be the locus of unbiased certitude is usually traced to the seventeenth century. The *locus classicus* of this position is, of course, Descartes.
—Paul Rabinow, "Masked I Go Forward"

In this section I situate the discursive practices of the deployment within an historical juncture. I argue that information technologies are deployed in the field of education to guarantee the development of the augmented child as a unified and rational subject. I maintain that the deployment of information technology forms an historically specific instance of a merging of an educational discourse on the cognitive development of the child with a modern faith in technology. Through this merging, an educational discourse forms that reduces human progress to the augmentation of the mental capacities of the child with technology. This discourse is a re-production of an eighteenth-century conflation of the goals of technological progress with the Western experience of humanity and a foundationalist emphasis on the Cartesian cogito and its unified, rational subject.

From the seventeenth, to the eighteenth, and into the nineteenth century, a social vision merges ecclesiastical ideals of human progress with a faith in technological progress: Technology is to augment the capabilities of the individual. In the seventeenth century, notions of progress combine advances in the social organization of human beings and a Christian notion of self-perfection with an emerging ethos of technological progress. This is evidenced in the seventeenth-century writings of Jonathan Edwards, who expresses a millennial social vision about progress, technology, and the human condition (Mumford, 1970). Edwards claimed that "Heaven would at last come down to earth and 'mechanick philosophy' would bring this about" (Mumford, 1970, p. 198). In this way, improvements in technology, or what was described as a philosophy of mechanics, were matched by improvements in "divine knowledge," leading to an eventual renewal of both human nature and the physical environment.

Into the eighteenth century, goals of technological progress and the Western experience of humanity were to conflate. "Mechanical progress and human progress came to be regarded as one; and both were theoretically limitless" (Mumford, 1970, p. 197). This doctrine of progress is evidenced in the eighteenth-century writings of Edward Gibbon, whose polemics of a cumulative progress suggest that every new age of humanity increases and builds upon the wealth, happiness, knowledge, and virtue of the preceding age (Mumford, 1970). Every new technology, it was claimed, lent credence to an unqualified association with improvements in the human condition until technology, associated with progress, became the measure of humanity. By the nineteenth century, the doctrine of technological progress was used to support the theory of natural selection: Human progress was guaranteed as long as technological invention and the consumption of its products were conceived as the goal of humanity. The inevitability of human progress, even conceived as occurring by fits and starts, by evolution and retrogression, was guaranteed by the doctrine of technological progress (Mumford, 1970).

This technological progress traces too from mid-seventeenth-century Cartesian rationalism and its quest for foundational knowledge (Toulmin,

1990). Following the murder of King Henri IV and the ensuing chaos of the Thirty Years' War, from 1618 to 1648, this Cartesian rationalism takes on broad intellectual appeal. The practical, local, and timely philosophical skepticism associated with Montaigne and Bacon was replaced by a quest for foundational knowledge (Toulmin, 1990). It was the unified and rational individual that was constructed as the foundation for this Cartesian rationalism, as thought was believed to transcend lived experience. Marshall (1992) writes:

> The accepted "birth of the human subject" as a distinct presence with specific attributes is commonly dated as occurring in the seventeenth century and is associated with Descartes: the act of doubting everything and anything as an act of thought could at least assure the certainty of the subject's own being (*Cogito ergo sum*/I think therefore I am). Thus Descartes set thinkers on the path of reifying this thinking subject who searched for certainty and Reason, which then becomes the source of knowledge and of truth. (p. 85)

From its foundation in the unified and rational subject, the cogito discloses a search for universal scientific truth and the technological means to control nature.[5] This Cartesian emphasis on foundational knowledge combines an emerging vision of technological progress with a Christian notion of self-perfection as echoed by Jonathan Edwards. Descartes writes:

> I perceive it to be possible to arrive at knowledge highly useful in life; . . . to discover a practical method by means of which, knowing the force and action of fire, water, air, the stars, the heavens, and all the other bodies that surround us . . . we might also apply them in the same way to all the uses which they are adapted, and thus render ourselves the lords and possessors of nature. (Mumford, 1970, p. 78)

Thus, in Western culture from the seventeenth century, the unified, rational subject of Cartesian rationalism is constructed in tandem with the construction of technological progress.

If in the seventeenth century, technological progress emerged as a discursive practice founded on the unified and rational subject of Cartesian thought, in the twentieth century, Piagetian psychology applies this foundational knowledge to the individual subject's capacity to progress and develop (Walkerdine, 1984, 1988). Not unlike belief in a constant, technological progress, the child, within a rational science of psychology, is seen as developing or progressing through stages and in time. Situating Piaget's developmental psychology as a discursive practice within the field of education, Walkerdine (1984) writes:

It is because he sees the cogito, *Homo rationalis*, as the desired goal that he asserts the naturalness of the progression from emotion to reason. . . . The above characterization of Piaget's early work . . . is meant to demonstrate the necessity of understanding his work in terms of a set of conditions which made it possible within a particular body of scientific discourses and regulatory practices. . . . Its positioning within an ensemble of discursive practices is precisely what ensures its form and its take-up in a particular manner, in helping legitimate and redirect forms of classification of stages of development as regulatory and normalizing pedagogic practices. (pp. 176–177)

This psychological discourse on child development is based on the unified integrity of the individual child who is to develop through successive stages toward rationality. With such psychological discourse practices, the knowledge of the capacity of the child's mind is naturalized, as it is produced as a biological category of scientific research.[6] This psychological discourse continues to have an impact on the ensemble of discursive practices across the field of education, including the deployment of information technology. By the late twentieth century, discursive practices of psychology apply technological invention to develop the cognition of the child. For instance, in Bruner, Oliver, and Greenfield's (1966) study of the psychology of child development, he reasons that certain culturally specific technologies will "amplify" a child's cognitive development. This reasoning also is evidenced in Englebart's (1963) research into the augmentation of human capabilities with technology. In a paper written while on staff at Xerox PARC, Englebart (1963) described a "conceptual framework for augmenting human intellect with computers":

We refer to a way of life in an integrated domain where hunches, cut-and-try, intangibles, and the human "feel for a situation" usually coexist with powerful concepts, streamlined terminology and notation, sophisticated methods, and high-powered electronic aids. (p. 1)

Two hundred years following the merging of the doctrine of technological progress with the "Western experience of humanity," advances in technology are used to legitimate and authorize current initiatives to reform schooling. However, this doctrine of technological progress has undergone a further shift: Through a merging of developmental psychology with the doctrine of technological progress, technology becomes, in the words of Pea (1985), "an indispensable instrument of mentality" (p. 175). Thus, the augmentation of the mental capacities of the individual child with technology offers a *technological* guarantee for the developmental progress of the individual child as the unified and rational subject of the deployment of information technology in the field of education.

THE AUGMENTED CHILD AND THE INTERDEPENDENT COMPONENT OF TECHNOLOGICAL SYSTEMS—QUESTIONS AND CONCLUSIONS

> Once the tool is understood and used regularly, the user feels wanting if it is not available because it has opened up new possibilities of thought and action without which one comes to feel at a disadvantage. It becomes an indispensable instrument of mentality, and not merely a tool.
> —Roy D. Pea, "Beyond Amplification"

In this concluding section, I analyze educational practices deployed to ensure the development of this unified and rational child. These practices relate technology and cognitive development to the construction of the child as a subject of the deployment of information technology in the field of education. These practices are influenced by what I referred to earlier as a *mutual conditioning*, as they are adjusted to the ensemble of elements of the deployment. However, because of the mutual conditioning of this ensemble of elements, Foucault (1980a, 1980b) explains, there are also *unforeseen effects* of these practices. In this way, I argue that the child, while positioned as the unified individual subject of the deployment, simultaneously is constructed as an interdependent component of a technological system. Thus, I conclude this chapter with a challenge to the ontological foundation of the child as a unified subject of Cartesian thought and technological progress. The unified, rational subject no longer can be positioned as the foundation of psychological discourse any more than technological practices, as applied to the field of education, guarantee the reproduction of this subject. As a result of a shift in discursive practices through initiatives to deploy information tools to reform the practices of schooling and to increase the mental capacities of children, the subject of these practices also shifts. The unified subject of the child is destabilized through the very uses of technology recently deployed to guarantee this subject as the foundation guiding psychological practices in the field of education.

To disclose shifts in the discursive practice, I first discuss a concern for determining the boundaries between the child and technology. This concern is evident across the field of education. As Ray (1991) explains, computers are far better at managing information and performing low-level, mechanical functions than are children. Children should be relieved from the tedium of performing such tasks as addition and subtraction and rote memorization of facts and details, as there are fewer reasons today for schools to teach these low-level cognitive and repetitive skills. Through partnerships, in which the computer carries out low-level mechanical processes such as adding or sorting numbers, the child does not need to concentrate on or in some instances even learn such processes. Salomon, Perkins, and Globerson (1991) write:

> It can be argued that work with specific computer tools might redefine and restructure the learning and performance task. . . . The performance of such a partnership between a human and technology could be far more "intelligent" than the performance of the human alone. (p. 4)

In their discussion of activities such as the *dancing functions*, Salomon and colleagues (1991) refer to an *intellectual partnership* between child and technology. The personal computer or the graphing calculator are not unlike the hoe, the microscope, the camera, and the slide rule, which, according to Salomon and colleagues (1991), represent technologies that require the active participation of a user. Moreover, in the intellectual partnership of the computer and child, the computer assumes part of the intellectual responsibility for completing the task at hand. In a discussion of the mathematics software *AlgebraLand*, Pea (1985) explains, "*AlgebraLand* reorganizes the learning in a way that appears to highlight more fundamental skills to be learned—the functional system of mathematical thinking for the equation-solving task" (p. 173). Such improvement is discussed by John Seeley Brown (1984) of Xerox PARC, who developed *AlgebraLand*. He describes this mathematics software as an "idea amplifier." With *AlgebraLand*, children no longer need be responsible for performing mechanical algebraic calculations. Instead, they can concentrate on executing high-order, problem-solving strategies and developing higher-order cognitive skills. Thus, working with the computer, the capabilities of the child, defined as the efficiency and the speed with which children develop high-order skills, are augmented (Brown, 1984). Considering the outcome of an algebraic equation solved by a child, Pea (1985) explains that a child's *ability to solve problems* was augmented by the use of *AlgebraLand*. However, he does not conclude from this that the child's *problem-solving ability* was augmented (cf. Bruner et al., 1966; Englebart, 1963). Rather, Pea (1985) reasons, there are two distinct practices referred to in this instance. *AlgebraLand* augmented the joint system of the child's problem-solving ability. *AlgebraLand* did not augment a fixed mental capacity called "problem-solving ability." Thus, Pea (1985) concludes, the child together with *AlgebraLand* conjoin to produce a unique child/computer partnership or what he refers to as a functional system for problem solving.

Alternatively, Salomon and colleagues (1991) refer to Olson (1986) to explain that psychologists may always have implicitly conceptualized this subject as a *joint system* or as child/computer partnership. "Almost any form of human cognition requires one to deal . . . with technology. To attempt to characterize intelligence independently of those technologies seems to be a *fundamental* error" (Olson, 1986, cited in Salomon et al., 1991, p. 5; emphasis added). Salomon and colleagues (1991) then attempt to reconcile the individual child and the child/computer partnership by questioning what it means to conceptualize intelligence as "the property" of a joint system. They write, "Once we couple intelligent technologies with a person's ability, the emphasis might shift to *examining the performance* of the *joint system*" (Salomon et al., 1991, p. 5; emphasis added). In this context of the *joint system* of the child/computer partnership, they pose a query: What if the human partner is removed from the system and retains only a naive ability to function? Using the example of expert medical systems, they raise what is for them an ethical question: What if the function of the technological component reduces the system's need for an intellectual contribution from a human partner? To resolve what they refer to as a "dilemma," Salomon and colleagues (1991) define two means, one systemic and the other analytic, for assessing the intelligence of joint systems. To do this, the once unified subject of psychology is simultaneously positioned within mutually exclusive conceptual frameworks:

> The systemic approach examines the performance of the whole system and judges the products of its joint intelligence without distinguishing the contribution of the human partner from that of the technology. In contrast, the analytic approach examines the specific kinds of mental processes that the human partner contributes. . . . From a systemic point of view what counts is the overall level of performance of the system, not of the individual in it. . . . By using the analytic approach, we can continue to conceive of ability manifested by them while working with an intelligent computer tool. (p. 5)

As I discussed previously, through a psychological discourse, the individual child is thought to develop or progress through stages not unlike the constant progress of technology. The practices of psychology are to guarantee the development of this individual child. Thus, the examination and assessment of performance emerged in the discipline of psychology to scientifically measure and account for differences in the development and cognitive ability of the child (Walkerdine, 1984). However, as I discussed, there is a shift in the practices of psychology. Reports, such as *Vision* (Braun, 1990), referred to previously, have documented gains in individual student achievement as student abilities are augmented with technology. There, a clear distinction is maintained between the subject of the child and the machine. Yet, through the psychological practices to augment the child's capabilities with technology, there is a sudden multiplying of the subject of psychology. This is evidenced in the work of Salomon and colleagues (1991) and Pea (1985). While they attempt to maintain the integrity of the individual subject, they also recognize a functional child/computer system; both the systemic and the analytic subject are to develop and be assessed through the techniques of psychology.

While the foundation of psychology is grounded in the unified individual subject, the augmentation practices designed to guarantee the production of this subject for a postindustrial society serve to destabilize the subject. Mental measurement, test results, and so forth, no longer can provide unambiguous evidence that the individual child, apart from any technology, has developed appropriate mental capacities. Nor do they provide evidence of a unified, rational individual child.

As the subject is destabilized, so too are the discursive practices of psychology. The rules that determine whether to conceptualize or evaluate a "systemic" or an "analytic" child are socially constructed through the same practices that historically have produced the multiplication of this subject. While the psychological foundation of these practices and the "analytic" subject that these practices are to guarantee are one and the same, through the practices of this psychological discourse this foundation is being questioned and challenged. A new discursive practice emerges in the field of education; there is a crisis: What is the subject(s) of the deployment of information technology and how is the subject's performance to be measured, disciplined, and corrected?

The deployment of information technology in the field of education is productive of and produced through relations of power. Situated within historically specific discursive practices that relate progress, technology, and cognitive development to the production of the unified and rational individual subject, this deployment narrows the objectives of schooling. Through analysis of the mutually conditioning elements of this deployment, including the emphasis on cognitive development, a shift in the conceptualization of the child in the context of education and technology becomes evident. Can the child be conceptualized independently of his or her relation with technology? Augmenting the rational capacities of the child with technology results in the development of the capabilities of a child/machine system. This is expressed through classroom instances of using technology and through research into the development of the child's mind. Failing in its instrumental objective, this intellectual partnership of the child and technology destabilizes the integrity of the child as a unified individual subject. These practices thus present a challenge to the foundation of psychology in the Cartesian cogito; if the child cannot be constructed as a subject independently of any relation with technology, can the mind be assumed to be a guarantor of its own unified rationality?

NOTES

1. In the English translation of the first volume of Foucault's (1980a) book, *The History of Sexuality*, there is a section titled "The Deployment of Sexuality." Translated back into the French, "deployment" refers to *dispositif.*

2. For example, I think here of Manpower and Quality Temps.

3. While there is no shortage of social theories that attempt to explain the concept of the postindustrial society, I cannot and do not intend to survey this literature here. For an introduction to analyses of the postindustrial society, see Harvey (1989) and Smart (1992).

4. My choice to discuss Reigeluth (1992) was not arbitrary. In 1992, he was recognized as the most influential academic in the field of educational technology (Hattendorf, 1992).

5. While the *Discourse* is in part autobiographical, it is, as its name suggests, a discourse or a narrative document of the emergence of modernity and the search for truth in the sciences (Balz, 1952; Markie, 1992).

6. In this way, the scientific practice of studying the development of the child, including developmental psychology, is associated with Darwin's "A Biographical Sketch of an Infant" (Walkerdine, 1984).

REFERENCES

Balz, A. G. A. (1952). *Descartes and the modern mind.* New Haven: Yale University Press.

Bernauer, J. W. (1990). *Michel Foucault's force of flight: Toward an ethics for thought.* Atlantic Highlands, NJ: Humanities Press International.

Braun, L. (1990). *Vision:* TEST *(technologically enriched schools of tomorrow). Final report: Recommendations for American educational decision makers.* Eugene, OR: International Society for Technology in Education.

Brown, J. S. (1984). *Idea amplifiers: New kinds of electronic learning environments.* Palo Alto, CA: Xerox Palo Alto Research Center, Intelligent Systems Laboratory.

Bruder, I., Buchsbaum, H., Hill, M., & Orlando, L. C. (1992). School reform: Why you need technology to get there. *Electronic Learning, 11*(8), 22–28.

Bruner, J. S., Oliver, R. R., & Greenfield, P. M. (1966). *Studies in cognitive growth: A collaboration at the Center for Cognitive Studies.* New York: Wiley.

Burchell, G. (1981). Putting the child in its place. *Ideology & Consciousness,* no. 8, 73–95.

California State Department of Education. (1986). *Long-range educational technology plan for California schools.* Sacramento: Author.

Carnegie Forum on Education and the Economy. (1986). *A nation prepared: Teachers for the 21st century* (Report of the Task Force on Teaching as a Profession). New York: Carnegie Corporation.

Carrier, J. G. (1983). Masking the social in educational knowledge: The case of learning disability theory. *American Journal of Sociology, 88*(5), 948–974.

Collins, A. (1991). The role of computer technology in restructuring schools. *Phi Delta Kappan, 73*(1), 28–36.

David, J. L. (1991). Restructuring and technology: Partners in change. *Phi Delta Kappan, 73*(1), 37–40, 78–80, 82.

Department of Labor. (1992). *Learning a living: A blueprint for high performance.* Washington, DC: U.S. Government Printing Office.

Donzelot, J. (1979). *The policing of families* (R. Hurley, Trans). New York: Random House.

Englebart, D. C. (1963). A conceptual framework for the augmentation of man's intellect. In P. W. Howerton (Ed.), *Vistas in information handling* (pp. 1–29). Washington, DC: Spartan Books.

Erickson, D. K. (1992). Dancing functions from a graphing calculator. *The Computing Teacher, 19*(8), 24–26.

Foucault, M. (1972). *The archaeology of knowledge and the discourse on language* (A. M. Sheridan Smith, Trans.). New York: Pantheon.

Foucault, M. (1979). *Discipline and punish: The birth of the prison* (A. Sheridan, Trans.). New York: Vintage.

Foucault, M. (1980a). *The history of sexuality: Vol. 1. An Introduction.* (R. Hurley, Trans.). New York: Vintage.

Foucault, M. (1980b). *Power/Knowledge: Selected interviews and other writings by Michel Foucault, 1972–1977* (C. Gordon, Ed. and Trans.). New York: Pantheon.

Foucault, M. (1981). Omnes et singulatim: Towards a criticism of "Political Reason." In S. M. McMurrin (Ed.), *The Tanner lectures on human values* (Vol. 2; pp. 225–254). Salt Lake City: University of Utah Press.

Foucault, M. (1982). The subject and power. *Critical Inquiry, 8*(4), 777–789.

Foucault, M. (1991). Governmentality. In G. Burchell, C. Gordon, & P. Miller (Eds.), *The Foucault effect: Studies in governmentality* (pp. 87–104). Chicago: University of Chicago Press.

George Lucas Educational Foundation. (1992). *Edutopia.* San Rafael, CA: Author.

Haraway, D. (1991). *Simians, cyborgs, and women: The reinvention of nature.* New York: Routledge.

Harvey, D. (1989). *The condition of postmodernity.* Oxford: Basil Blackwell.

Hattendorf, L. C. (1992). *Educational rankings annual.* Detroit: Gale Research.

Haycock, C. (1991). Resource-based learning: A shift in the roles of teacher, learner. *NASSP Bulletin, 75*(535), 15–23.

Kliebard, H. M. (1986). *The struggle for the American curriculum 1893–1958.* New York: Routledge & Kegan Paul.

Markie, P. (1992). The cogito and its importance. In J. Cottingham (Ed.), *The Cambridge companion to Descartes* (pp. 140–173). Cambridge: Cambridge University Press.

Marshall, B. K. (1992). *Teaching the postmodern: Fiction and theory.* New York: Routledge.

McDonnell, M. E. (1992). San Francisco *GTV. The Computing Teacher, 19* (5), 37–38.

Mumford, L. (1970). *The myth of the machine: The pentagon of power.* New York: Harcourt Brace Jovanovich.

National Commission on Excellence in Education. (1983). *A nation at risk: The imperative for educational reform* (A Report to the Nation and the Secretary of Education). Washington, DC: U.S. Government Printing Office.

Olson, D. (1986). Intelligence and literacy: The relationships between intelligence and the technologies of representation and communication. In R. Sternberg & R. Wagner (Eds.), *Practical intelligence: Nature and origins of competence in the everyday world* (pp. 338–360). New York: Cambridge University Press.

Pea, R. D. (1985). Beyond amplification: Using the computer to reorganize mental functioning. *Educational Psychologist, 20*(4), 167–182.

Perelman, L. J. (1987). *Technology and the transformation of schools* (ITTE Technology Leadership Network Special Report). Alexandria, VA: National School Boards Association.

Popkewitz, T. S. (1991). *A political sociology of educational reform: Power/Knowledge in teaching, teacher education, and research.* New York: Teachers College Press.

Poster, M. (1990). *The mode of information: Poststructuralism and social context.* Chicago: University of Chicago Press.

Rabinow, P. (1982). Masked I go forward: Reflections on the modern subject. In J. Ruby (Ed.), *A crack in the mirror: Reflexive perspectives in anthropology* (pp. 173–185). Philadelphia: University of Pennsylvania Press.

Ray, D. (1991). Technology and restructuring: Part I. New educational directions. *The Computing Teacher, 18*(6), 9–20.

Reich, R. B. (1991). *The work of nations preparing ourselves for 21st-century capitalism.* New York: Knopf.

Reigeluth, C. (1992). The imperative for systemic change. *Educational Technology, 32*(11), 9–13.

Robins, K., & Webster, F. (1989). *The technical fix: Education, computers and industry.* New York: St. Martin's Press.

Salomon, G., Perkins, D., & Globerson, T. (1991). Partners in cognition: Extending human intelligence with intelligent technologies. *Educational Researcher, 20*(3), 2–9.

Saraceno, C. (1984). The social construction of childhood: Child care and education policy in Italy and the United States. *Social Problems, 31*(3), 351–363.

Sheingold, K. (1991). Restructuring for learning with technology: The potential for synergy. *Phi Delta Kappan, 73*(1), 17–27.

Smart, B. (1992). *Modern conditions, postmodern controversies.* New York: Routledge.

Stonier, T., & Conlin, C. (1985). *The three Cs: Children, computers, and communication.* Chichester, England: Wiley.

Sutton, J. R. (1983). Social structure, institutions, and the legal status of children in the United States. *American Journal of Sociology, 88*(5), 915–947.

Toulmin, S. (1990). *Cosmopolis: The hidden agenda of modernity.* New York: Free Press.

United States Congress Office of Technology Assessment. (1988). *Power on! New tools for teaching and learning.* Washington, DC: U.S. Government Printing Office.

Walkerdine, V. (1984). Developmental psychology and the child-centered pedagogy: The insertion of Piaget into early education. In J. Henriques, W. Hollway, C. Urwin, C. Venn, & V. Walkerdine (Eds.), *Changing the subject: Psychology, social regulation and subjectivity* (pp. 153–202). New York: Methuen.

Walkerdine, V. (1988). *The mastery of reason.* New York: Routledge.

Weedon, C. (1987). *Feminist practice and poststructural theory.* Oxford: Basil Blackwell.

9

Disciplining Bodies: On the Continuity of Power Relations in Pedagogy

JENNIFER M. GORE

> If we recognise ourselves in Foucault's discourse, this is because what to-
> day, for us, is intolerable is no longer so much that which does not allow
> us to be what we are, as that which causes us to be what we are.
> —Miguel Morey, "On Michel Foucault's Philosophical Style"

The history of educational reform is littered with discarded ideas and practices, with policies that were never enacted—at least not as they were intended—and with libraries of academic theories well past their shelf life.

Despite the diversity of educational ideas and enormous intellectual labor invested in educational change, the experience of schooling, probably for
most readers of this text, bears some remarkable similarities. For instance,
what Philip Corrigan (1991) refers to as the "tightening of bodies" that accompanies schooling is manifest in generations of former and current students who raise their hands to speak, who ask permission to leave rooms,
who tense up in examination situations, who beam with the tiniest expressions of approval. Our similar experiences of schooling are also evident in
the quick recognition of teachers and students in a range of social situations,

and our assumption of (or resistance to) those positions in adult pedagogical situations as diverse as teaching an adolescent to drive a car, sharing a recipe, or learning about parenting. One need only watch young children "play school" to observe the longevity of certain schooling practices.

It is my contention that the apparent continuity in pedagogical practice, across sites and over time, has to do with power relations, in educational institutions and processes, that remain untouched by the majority of curriculum and other reforms. With the exception of Bernstein (1975, 1990), Bourdieu and Passeron (1977), and a handful of others who have drawn on their work, educational researchers have paid little attention to the microlevel functioning of power in pedagogy.

In this chapter, I address two specific questions that contribute to the investigation of power relations in schooling: How do power relations function at the microlevel of pedagogical practices? To what extent is the functioning of power relations continuous across different pedagogical sites? The arguments I construct in response to these questions will be informed by Michel Foucault's analytics of power and my own empirical study of four distinct pedagogical sites.

This work has its origins in my sense that the range of practices and relationships possible in classrooms—whether school or university, informed by technocratic, critical, or feminist philosophies—was limited. In my earlier analysis of critical and feminist pedagogy discourses (Gore, 1993), I concluded that the specific instructional practices advocated were not so different from the practices of mainstream educators. I speculated that the institution of schooling might produce its own "regime of pedagogy," a set of power-knowledge relations, of discourses and practices, which constrains the most radical of educational agendas. Conducting an empirical investigation of pedagogical practice seemed the necessary next step in my attempt to understand and subsequently alter long-standing institutional practices.

FOUCAULT ON POWER RELATIONS

Foucault's analytics of power was helpful in conceptualizing this study, for its focus on the micro-functioning of power relations. Once declaring himself a "happy positivist," Foucault (1981) sought to ground his ideas in empirical events. Methodologically and theoretically, then, I chose to explore pedagogical practices from a Foucaultian perspective on power.

Foucault (1977) argues that "disciplinary power" emerged with the advent of modern institutions and extended throughout society, so that continuities in power relations are evident not only in schools, hospitals, prisons, factories, and other institutions, but also outside of these institutions: "A certain significant generality moved between the least irregularity and the greatest crime: it was no longer the offence, the attack on the common interest, it was the departure from the norm, the anomaly; it was this that haunted the school, the court, the asylum or the prison" (p. 299).

Foucault's concept of disciplinary power explicitly shifts analyses of power from the "macro" realm of structures and ideologies to the "micro" level of bodies. Foucault (1980) argues that unlike the sovereign power of earlier periods, disciplinary power functions at the level of the body:

> In thinking of the mechanisms of power, I am thinking rather of its capillary form of existence, the point where power reaches into the very grain of individuals, touches their bodies and inserts itself into their action and attitudes, their discourses, learning processes and everyday lives. (p. 39)

Foucault (1980) elaborates the invisibility and pervasiveness of power in modern society: "The eighteenth century invented, so to speak, a synaptic regime of power, a regime of its exercise within the social body rather than from above it" (p. 39). Using the exemplar of the Panopticon, with its normalizing surveillance, Foucault describes disciplinary power as circulating rather than being possessed, productive and not necessarily repressive, existing in action, functioning at the level of the body, often operating through "technologies of self."

There is a scholarly debate over whether Foucault's analysis of power was particular to penal institutions or intended to characterize all of modern society. There is general agreement that Foucault provided a careful elaboration of specific techniques of power in penal institutions—techniques of surveillance, normalization, individualization, and so on. What seems to be in question is the extent to which his analysis of penal institutions was intended to apply to other institutions—the extent to which he was illustrating a general theory of society with the penal example, or tentatively proffering a general theory that emerged as a result of his investigation of prisons. Certainly, without doing the same kind of sustained analysis, Foucault (1983) made observations about the functioning of power in educational institutions:

> Take, for example, an educational institution: the disposal of its space, the meticulous regulations which govern its internal life, the different activities which are organized there, the diverse persons who live there or meet one another there, each with his own function, his well-defined character—all these things constitute a block of capacity–communication–power. The activity which ensures apprenticeship and the acquisition of aptitudes or types of behavior is developed there by means of a whole ensemble of regulated communications (lessons, questions and answers, orders, exhortations, coded signs of obedience, differentiation marks of the "value" of each person and of the levels of knowledge) and by

means of a whole series of power processes (enclosure, surveillance, reward and punishment, the pyramidal hierarchy). (pp. 218–219)

I interpret this passage as evidence that while Foucault illustrated his analysis of disciplinary power with reference to other institutions, he left the detailed analytic work to those "specific" intellectuals with a closer attachment to education. The analysis of select passages from Foucault's vast (and sometimes contradictory) work is a common form of scholarly engagement with his ideas. Rather than contribute further to these debates on the basis of claims to have read Foucault better than others, I have taken up the question of power relations in pedagogy on the basis of an empirical study of contemporary pedagogical sites.

POWER RELATIONS IN PEDAGOGY

Four diverse sites were selected in the hope of being able to construct some broad statements about power relations in pedagogy. The sites were high school physical education classes with an explicit focus on bodies; a first-year teacher education cohort, working with three lecturers; a feminist reading group; and a women's discussion group that met for the purpose of intellectual stimulation, usually via reading courses provided by community education organizations.

One part of the study[1] involved putting Foucault's techniques of power in penal institutions to the test of relevance for contemporary pedagogical functioning. Put simply, I was asking the question, "Are the mechanisms of schooling like the mechanisms of prisons, in terms of the micro-practices of power Foucault identified?" It probably will not be surprising that my research yielded a "positive" result—that I found the techniques of power that Foucault elaborated in prisons applicable to contemporary pedagogical practice—especially given Foucault's (1983) view that "the fundamental point of [power] relationships, even if they are embodied and crystallized in an institution, is to be found outside the institution" (p. 222). Finding what one looks for in research has been both a perennial problem and a source of comfort for many researchers. I would emphasize, however, that it would have been possible to not find these techniques of power, especially not in each of the sites, diverse as they were.

Techniques of Power

In the remainder of this chapter, I briefly elaborate each of the eight major techniques of power that I investigated in order to demonstrate, first, that they are readily recognizable—that they exist in pedagogical interaction—and, second, that they were found in all of the sites studied. Next, I present some cross-context comparisons based on quasi-quantitative analysis. Finally, I make some statements about the usefulness and dangers of the approach I have taken.

As Foucault (1983) says, analyzing what happens in the exercise of power relations is "flat and empirical" (p. 217). The following segments of data, taken from field notes or transcripts,[2] are certainly that. While contextualizing and categorizing are joint components needed in qualitative research (Maxwell & Miller, 1993), demonstrating techniques of power in order to show that they exist in pedagogy requires only the systematic process of categorization. Furthermore, especially without the specific context of each session in which these data were collected, each event or episode is open to multiple interpretations and many episodes could appear equally legitimately in more than one category. Indeed, the majority of episodes were coded for multiple practices of power, indicating the co-incidence and rapidity with which power is enacted.

Surveillance. Without turning, the teacher says "Zac, you know I can always tell your voice" (PE).[3] Surveillance was found frequently during our[4] observations—where surveillance was defined as "supervising, closely observing, watching, threatening to watch, or expecting to be watched." Consider the following additional examples:

> The teacher goes to the board where she draws a smallish rectangle in the bottom right corner and writes inside it "B1" to indicate that Bill has one demerit point. (PE)

> Elisabeth conducts a roll call. . . . She then conducts an exercise aimed at putting names to faces: each student, starting from the back row, must give his or her name and tell of one school experience. (TE)

> Because Judith is the only one who seems to be making any defense of the book, Carol continually looks at Judith when she critiques as if it is a personal debate. This goes on for some time until Judith says in protest, "Don't look at me." (FEM)

> "Well, since then I've read about 10 other books. I just pushed the other one to the back."
> "It's not memorable, is what you're saying there, hey?"
> "Well, it was for a time."
> "What page did you get up to, Elaine?"

"Did you get that far, Judith?"
"127. I got to." (noises of surprise)
"Oh, I only got to 75."
"This is one-upwomanship!" (laughter)
"You only did half of what she did!" (in a self-mocking tone)
"I know."
"Well, I didn't read it. That gives me the other end of the continuum."
(FEM)

In these examples, teachers monitor students, and students monitor each other. Surveillance singles out individuals, regulates behavior, and enables comparisons to be made.

It is important to remember the productiveness of power. Foucault (1977) declared: "A relation of surveillance, defined and regulated, is inscribed at the heart of the practice of teaching, not as an additional or adjacent part, but as a mechanism that is inherent to it and which increases its efficiency" (p. 176). More generally, Foucault (1988a) said:

> Power is not an evil. . . . Let us . . . take something that has been the object of criticism, often justified: the pedagogical institution. I don't see where evil is in the practice of someone who, in a given game of truth, knowing more than another, tells him what he must do, teaches him, transmits knowledge to him, communicates skills to him. The problem is rather to know how you are to avoid in these practices—where power cannot not play and where it is not an evil in itself—the effects of domination which will make a child subject to the arbitrary and useless authority of a teacher, or put a student under the power of an abusively authoritarian professor, and so forth. (p. 18)

At least some of the surveillance practices outlined above, such as getting to know the names of one's students and keeping students "on task," can be seen as serving purposes productive for pedagogy.

Normalization. "Okay, so what we want and hope that you will have competence in by the end of your teacher education program, is that you'll be able to articulate and defend a personal theory of education, which is moral and socially just, because you are involved in a moral enterprise. You're making judgments all the time about goodness and worth, judgments about whether this particular learning activity is a worthwhile learning activity, whether a decision that you've made in managing . . . a learning difficulty in the classroom is a fair and just decision. So the whole notion of teaching as social practice is that it's an ethical practice. You'll be able to communicate effectively to your pupils, your peers, the people with whom you work, and the community at large. It's very important that teachers can justify what they do and that they can learn from each other" (TE). Foucault (1977) high-lighted the importance of "normalizing judgment," or normalization, in the functioning of modern disciplinary power. He explained that such normaliz-ing judgment often occurs through comparison, so that individual actions are referred "to a whole that is at once a field of comparison, a space of differentiation and the principle of a rule to be followed" (p. 182). For the purposes of my research, normalization was defined as "invoking, requiring, setting, or conforming to a standard—defining the normal." The following examples, like the one above, should be readily recognizable:

> Ingrid also dislikes Eisenstein. She thinks a better feminist representa-tive could have been chosen. She feels that Eisenstein is "too giggly," not serious enough about the issues. (FEM)

> Kate gives an example of a student at the institution who, because of his religion and upbringing, believed that corporal punishment had a place in schools. Kate finds this "hard to come to grips with." She un-packs the assumptions behind this student's belief. Then she asks if his belief was justifiable: Educationally—No. Corporal punishment does not promote learning. Morally—No. He has no right to do this to an-other person. Socially—No. This behavior does nothing to promote harmonious relationships in the world. Politically—No. It is against the law. She says, "End of argument." (TE)

Whether in relation to participants in these pedagogical settings, or in rela-tion to other people or views, reference to standards appears to be a common feature of pedagogy. Educating is about the teaching of norms—norms of behavior, of attitudes, of knowledge. Here, the productiveness of power would seem to be a fundamental precept of pedagogical endeavor.

Foucault's view of power relations as enacted at the site of the body also is readily demonstrated in the following examples of normalization:

> I hear the class teacher telling her, "Success breeds success." Clearly both teachers are urging her to try to improve her marks. Amy, her back to the class as she is "encouraged" by the two teachers, pulls her windcheater hood over her head (as if to retreat into the security of it). (PE)

> A girl climbs on the stage behind the teacher and looks over his shoul-der: "Oh, you're writing reports." He glances at her with an annoyed expression: "Shh. If I blow this, it has to go right round to everyone again," he tells her (i.e., one mistake will require all those staff respons-

ible for this student's report to rewrite it. No errors or crossing out is permitted on this "official" document). (PE)

A young girl is seen standing looking in from the door. The teacher's back is toward her, but the girls in the class see her and one calls out, "Yes, can I help you?" (taking on the teacher's role). (PE)

The girl who pulled the hood of her jacket over her head while being singled out and challenged by teachers probably was doing so not because she was cold, but in response to an exercise of power. Similarly, it was a student's movement onto the stage and another's standing at the doorway that prompted reactions—or, in Foucault's terms, prompted "actions upon actions"—and so set up relations of power.

Exclusion. There is a great amount of discussion as students fire questions or make observations about body building. One of the girls makes a statement about how "disgusting" female body builders look and that it is "not natural" (PE). The category of exclusion was used in my research to mark the negative side of normalization—the defining of the pathological. Foucault refers to exclusion as a technique for tracing the limits that will define difference, defining boundaries, setting zones. Exclusionary techniques are pervasive in pedagogy, as demonstrated in Tyler's (1993) genealogical research that found that, even in kindergarten, some children, some dispositions and behaviors, are constructed as "better," while others quickly are excluded. One long-term aim of my research is to identify techniques of power that need not be as they are in pedagogy—to identify what Foucault (1988c) called "spaces of freedom." Examples of exclusion from my study follow:

The women criticize the tutor, saying, "There's no comment on our work" and "he even has poor grammar." Julie says, "He just doesn't answer our questions; he's not extending us." (WG)

A boy was sent to sit on the side of the court. He seemed to go without much reticence, and also without the kind of spectacle some students create in these situations. (PE)

She said something I disliked and she's not a feminist, so I wrote rather a longish letter, pointing out that I wanted them to take it into account and also pass it on to her. (FEM)

Mrs. Fernley says, "Come on. You cannot be chatting merrily and writing at the same time." A girl says, "Wanna bet?" Mrs. Fernley:

"You can't write and read." A student says, "We never do, we just write." (PE)

> Now when you look at some of the literature on viewing teaching as problematic, some people say that teachers operate at different levels. I do have some problems where people talk about levels because it implies a hierarchy and I think it's very difficult to rank teachers into some kind of hierarchy. . . . [I prefer] more of a continuum, that as teachers we can view our practice as ranging from this end of the continuum as quite unproblematic right through to this end of the continuum, extremely problematic. (TE)

In these examples, there is the exclusion of individuals—in one case the bodily removal of a student from the activity. Particular identities and practices also are excluded, as are ways of constructing knowledge.

Very often exclusion and normalization occurred together, where the pathological was named in the process of establishing the norm. Canguilhem (1991), one of Foucault's teachers, argues that in the question of which comes first, the normal or the pathological, the normal is logically first, but empirically second. Some of these examples, including the last one from the teacher education site, illustrate Canguilhem's point. A pedagogy that does not set boundaries, that does not normalize and pathologize, is almost inconceivable.

Classification. Ingrid offers the view, taken from a book she has read, that men are warlike and conquering by nature, while women are peaceful and sedentary. Therefore, women are much more likely to be forcibly oppressed (FEM). Differentiating groups or individuals from one another, classifying them, classifying oneself, is another common technique within Foucault's elaboration of disciplinary power and was found within the pedagogical sites investigated. Some additional examples are provided:

> Kate states that the teacher who operates as a critical analyst will take on different roles: coach, mentor, facilitator, listener, questioner, comforter, model, etc. Some of these roles will be active, she said, others will be passive—depending on the situation. Kate continues by discussing the operation of teaching as totally unproblematic or taking a more critical approach. Those who operate under the latter will see teaching as far more complex. (TE)

> But once again Ingrid disagrees, saying that the "libertarians" promoted it. "Libertarians" is said in a derogatory tone. . . . Maxine sug-

gests that the author indulged in this sort of relationship because she was a "creative type" and wanted to experience everything in life. (FEM)

Zac returns to his seat as a conversation develops about the awarding of some Australian beauty crown to a male. The teacher remarks that she sees it as "a step ahead," but Zac is baffled about how a "guy" could win the competition. The teacher explains that he had raised a lot of money for charity and that the competition "has to be non-sexist." Madeleine remarks that the winner "is a Nancy." (PE)

Helen asks if the others have seen a photo of the author—she describes her as a "large, masculine, person." One of the women jumps in with the comment: "Well, someone married her!" (WG)

Mrs. Fernley arrives and says, "Right-o. Your tests. Some of you did very well. Some of you didn't do very well." (PE)

As these examples illustrate, pedagogy proceeds via classificatory mechanisms—the classification of knowledge, the ranking and classification of individuals and groups. A whole tradition of educational research has addressed problems associated with the reproductive sorting functions of schools. Examining specific micro-practices of classification may be one way of intervening in these problems.

Distribution. "What we've organized for the tutorials is . . . some second- and third-year students [who] would like to have a chance to share with you some of their experiences of the practicum. . . . We'll break into smaller groups and we'll actually withdraw, so you'll be able to say those things that you really do want to discuss that you might be feeling a bit tentative about" (TE). Foucault also argues that the distribution of bodies in space—arranging, isolating, separating, ranking—contributes to the functioning of disciplinary power. The exercise of power via techniques of distribution is evident in the following examples:

"The people who are going to be working with you are Kate, Elisabeth, and myself, and our room numbers and our phone numbers are there. And it might be now an opportune time to just mention who will be your tutor for the groups that meet at 12.30. . . . Um, Group 1, . . . you know which groups you're in don't you? You know which groups you've been placed in? (long pause) So Group 1, which has Katie Adams, and Sue Allan, and Michelle Alexander, and a whole lot of other people, you'll be with me and you'll be in room 32. So those I'm with are in 32. Those of you who are in Group 2 will be with Elisabeth in 50, and those of you who are in Group 3 will be with Kate in room 45A. Do you want me to repeat those? Has everybody got it?" (TE)

The teacher moves Robert's desk, apparently in an attempt to prevent him from talking to his mates, and to avoid his distraction from the questionnaire. (PE)

While the teacher is handing out sheets at the back of the room, one of the boys near the front gets up from his seat and hits another boy in the front row. The "victim" calls out, "Miss," but the teacher is busy, her back turned toward them as she distributes the sheets. The "attacker" glances at her briefly to see if his actions have been detected, but seeing the coast is clear, he returns to his seat. (PE)

Another boy runs back from jumping and ever so subtly wheedles his way in, way ahead of the end of the line. (PE)

Madeleine asks other girls if they want to skip with her. A few decline. She then asks me and I decline too. Madeleine turns with some exasperation, it seems. Bill finally accepts her invitation. When Bill is done, Zac is called upon by Madeleine. He says, "Do I have to?" and acts very reluctant, but skips anyway. Madeleine then asks Shaq to skip, saying, "Shaq, come over here." He comes over but says he wants to skip by himself first. He says he wants to get warmed up. Madeleine does not accept this. She skips double time and tells another boy to run in and join her. Several of the students laugh at this. Madeleine says to one boy, "Go play with yourself. I'm skipping." She is encouraged by Annalise to try "double dutch" (I think that's with two ropes turning in opposite directions). Madeleine goes off to the storeroom and emerges with a huge, heavy tug-of-war rope. Both of the teachers seem to have left the hall at this point. . . . The students laugh raucously at Madeleine's new rope. Several others join in, swinging the huge rope, which makes a solid thud each time it hits the floor. (PE)

These examples illustrate a wide range of distributive techniques, from teachers assigning rooms, physically moving bodies, requiring students to form groups, to students moving themselves or imploring others to do so.

Individualization. "But when I was reading, I kept thinking, would I have the moral courage, or the emotional courage, to do what she has just done?" (WG). Giving individual character to oneself or another is a common technique of power in pedagogy, as illustrated below:

> "I grew up in the _____ suburbs. I went to a country Teacher's College. I was sent to _____ area for my first school. I then went to the inner city. I'm now teaching on the _____. So, I've really come quite full circle around NSW, I think. And what it's done in the time that I've been teaching primary school is that I've had to change myself. I've had to rethink what I was doing as a teacher." (TE)

> She encourages a student to run and practice the jump, saying, "Patrick." As he unenthusiastically approaches the mat, walking rather than doing a proper run-up, the teacher calls out, "Go Patrick!" He complies, but without putting any effort into the action. (PE)

> Meanwhile a discussion has begun about Monica Seles suing German tennis for the injury that was inflicted upon her and the financial losses involved. Annalise says, "She's pretty young," I think implying that she has time to recover and become Number 1 again. Curt says, "I think she's pretty," an unusual admission from an adolescent male, I thought, until he continued with, "I like the way she grunts, Miss!" (PE)

> At this point another of the girls enters the class, saying, "Sorry I'm late, Miss." She explains that she has been to see one of the other teachers to see whether she could "drop PD." Madeleine interrupts, claiming, "No she wasn't, Miss. She's been in the toilets." (PE)

> The group is unanimous in its dislike for the text. Somebody asks whose idea it was to read it. I think Carol points the finger at Ingrid, who says that she hasn't read it for a long time but doesn't remember it being that bad. (FEM)

Totalization. "Teaching as a profession requires us to go on engaging in professional development throughout our careers. . . . So I hope we can model for you what we're asking you to do in your own professional lives" (TE). At the same time as individualization is a common technique, totalization, the specification of collectivities, giving collective character, forms a readily recognizable element of pedagogical activity. Sometimes totalization is achieved through simple linguistic structures, such as using the word "we," as in the following examples:

> Elaine states that "we think of dilemmas as a choice between two evils, but that it is now more appropriate to think of them as two alternatives." (TE)

> "But she's really the same as all of us. I mean, if we traveled in an area like that (Afghanistan), we would form our own opinion . . . and we'd then come home and tell it all, writing letters about what we thought." (WG)

At other times, totalization involves addressing whole groups of participants in the pedagogical site or elsewhere:

> We enter the small video viewing room at the far end of the library with the students. I comment that the back row is already taken. One girl says, "We are Year 11 students, after all!" (PE)

> A boy remarks in relation to Mrs. Fernley's forthcoming long service leave, "Teachers are always going away. It's a great life." (PE)

> "One of the main effects of alcohol is that it gives you a high. That's why people drink it. It's not because they love the taste, although some people do, but I would suggest that most people drinking beer for the first time, for example, probably wouldn't like its taste." (PE)

> "I think the Australian male has changed. . . . Lots of women didn't question things much then, because they weren't economically capable." (WG)

As these examples show, while totalizing is clearly a technique used in pedagogy for governing or regulating groups, students and teachers also "totalize" themselves by naming themselves as part of various collectives.

Regulation. "The subject, as you can see, is assessed on a pass/fail basis. And we're intending that to be the case because we hope that the course will be intrinsically interesting" (TE). Regulation was defined in my research as "controlling by rule, subject to restrictions, invoking a rule, including sanction, reward, punishment." While all of the previous techniques of power could be seen to have regulating effects, this category was used specifically to code incidents in which regulation was explicit, as in the following examples:

"Madeleine, that's your fourth infringement." Madeleine makes some excuse, asking the teacher, "Did you see that?" Nevertheless, and without much further persuasion from the teacher, Madeleine collects her things and leaves the room, saying, "And I'm not coming back!" (I don't get the impression that she feels too much animosity over the incident, as she was quick to comply with the teacher's decision. I was aware that one of the class rules involved allowing four infringements in any week, and any further violations required students spending two lessons in the library and the expectation that they would catch up on the work that they had missed. Madeleine's exit precipitated a discussion among the boys about how many "demerits" each of them had.) (PE)

"You've probably been told in all your other classes about the idea of plagiarism and cheating and things and it's very important that you start right from the first day, that you do get a copy of the referencing procedures and that you use them and you do reference your material correctly. And if you have problems with understanding the reference system, then you come to see me and I'll show you how to do it. But it is vital that you do reference your material, that you don't just use great big chunks of other people's work without acknowledging it. It's not appropriate and it won't be accepted." (TE)

"That did change, but it wasn't until 1942 in fact, the early 1940s, that aboriginal people could actually legally, they were legally able to go to Western schools." (TE)

When the discussion turns to the "caring" argument relating to quarantining HIV positive people, Ingrid says that this is done in Sweden under an humanitarian guise. Most of the group seems incredulous over this policy. The group discusses the effect of such a policy. Carol says that people who thought they might be HIV positive would not submit for tests because of a fear that they would be interned in one of the separate HIV communities. Therefore, these people "go underground." Somebody points out that this is the converse of the Australian policy. (FEM)

"But it was because we decided to answer every question, he says here, 'the topics for discussion at the end of each lecture are suggestions only, to be used as much as you require, to stimulate and guide discussion.'" (WG)

As with other categories, regulation sometimes involved reference to knowledge, not only reference to group rules or restrictions.

To the extent that this whole set of examples resonates with readers, conjuring up memories of similar incidents as teachers, students, or members of other groups, I trust I have demonstrated that these categories have been useful and relevant for the analysis of classroom power relations. In what follows, I outline some broader insights that have emerged from the analysis of data thus far conducted.

Continuities Across Pedagogical Sites

Many educational theorists would expect quite different practices of power in the four disparate sites in which my study took place. For instance, some feminist, critical, and other radical pedagogues have argued that their classrooms should or can do away with power. From this perspective, where power is often an evil to be done away with, less power might have been expected in the feminist and teacher education[5] sites than in the others. From the perspective on power informing this study, however, no site was free of power relations and no site "escaped" the use of techniques of power. Rather, as the examples demonstrate, the broad techniques used in the exercise of power relations were found in the radical and mainstream, and the institutionalized and noninstitutionalized sites.[6] Hence, my speculative view that the institutionalization of pedagogy within schools and universities constrains radical agendas might not be supported by the study, as a generalized claim. Instead, it seems that pedagogy, as a modernist enterprise, has some continuous features across quite different locations. This continuity might be accounted for, in part, by the fact that participants in the noninstitutionalized sites were adults—people who had already been subjected to and had learned the governmental processes of pedagogy.

Finding these techniques in contemporary pedagogical practice is not surprising, given Foucault's view of the disciplinary techniques of prisons as having their beginnings in pedagogy:

> Foucault emphasizes in *Discipline and Punish* that the disciplines linked to the panopticon were first used in secondary education, then primary schools, then the hospital, then the military barracks, and only later the prisons. So the panopticon was not dispersed into society from the prison; on the contrary. (Kelly, 1994, p. 370)

While a continuity in pedagogical practices across time is suggested by this passage, and while there is certainly considerable evidence in popular literature on schooling, and in the memories of generations of students and teachers (Southgate, forthcoming), of minimal change over time, my own study was not designed to "test" continuities over time, but continuities across sites.

As the above examples illustrate, I am able to claim continuity in the broad "techniques of power" for each of the four sites investigated. While the specific effects of those practices of power may have varied across sites, I can say with some confidence that power relations in pedagogy were enacted via techniques of surveillance, normalization, exclusion, distribution, and so on. These techniques were often productive for pedagogical (or other) purposes. Perhaps Foucault's (1977) statement about surveillance as inherent to pedagogy and as increasing its efficiency, holds also for the other techniques. Part of my ongoing analysis is oriented toward identifying specific forms of surveillance, normalization, and so on, that were necessary for teaching, and those that may have been peripheral, such as regulating students' dress and eating habits in classrooms, for instance.

The examples also demonstrate that each of the techniques of power, as I defined them, was employed in a number of ways: Sometimes, they functioned in the construction of knowledge; at other times, they functioned in the construction of relations among participants in the various sites; at yet other times, they functioned in the construction and maintenance of particular subjectivities (often defining oneself). Moreover, as already indicated, these techniques of power also occurred frequently in combination, illustrating the rapidly circulating functioning of power relations, and highlighting Foucault's view that power relations are simultaneously local, unstable, and diffuse, not emanating from a central point but at each moment moving from one point to another in a field of forces (Deleuze, 1988). The complexity that this analysis embraces is, in my view, illustrative of the ways in which a Foucaultian analysis of power in schooling can complement and extend past analyses, and aid the empirical study of power.

In order to draw comparisons between and within sites, and between and among the techniques of power, the relative frequency of each technique of power was calculated, where each segment of data had been coded with the multiple techniques of power that could be discerned. When examining these frequencies across all sites, I found that individualization and totalization were the most common techniques. Foucault (1988b) writes of the kind of rationality in which institutions are grounded, a rationality characterized by the integration of individuals in a community or totality that results from a constant correlation between increasing individualization and the reinforcement of the totality. This "rationality" was most obvious in the teacher education site, not surprisingly, given that we observed a first-year cohort of students in their introductory subject, where a certain kind of teacher was being produced.

Across all sites, there was also substantially less use of regulation (explicit reference to or enactment of rules, sanctions, etc.) and surveillance (observational techniques) than of the other techniques. This "finding" is consistent with Foucault's elaboration of the increasing invisibility of governmentality in modern society. The "Panoptic" operation of surveillance (which is invisible but constantly possible) may well have had an impact on specific practices enacted by participants, but was not visibly exercised as frequently as were normalizing and other practices. Observing that which is "invisible" is, of course, a problem. Nevertheless, the subtle techniques that I have called, after Foucault, normalization, classification, exclusion, and so on, were much more frequently observable than direct surveillance and regulation.[7]

As already stated, I am not attempting to argue that the techniques of power were configured identically regardless of pedagogical site. Differences were evident between sites, even in the few decontextualized passages I have presented above. Foucault's view of power as operating in capillary style, from the infinitesimal, does not imply that there are no patterns in the circulation or functioning of power. For instance, the examples provided, however open to multiple readings, suggest that teachers and students exercised power differently. That is, in many cases, students' power was "reactive" rather than "active" (Deleuze, 1988). Power circulated in these sites, but the exercise of power certainly was not equal for all participants.

CONCLUSION

My study responds to those critics who have accused Foucault of a totalizing characterization of modern disciplinary society, and of a representation of power that it is not possible to go beyond or free oneself from. Donnelly (1992), for instance, finds difficulty with Foucault's notion of panopticism "when he generalises the notion and empties it of all specific context," rather than when he, genealogically, "deploys it to make intelligible actual practices" (p. 202). While supporting Foucault's detailed genealogical work, Donnelly is critical of what he terms Foucault's "epochal" arguments about modern society. He argues that Foucault fails to demonstrate adequately the development of modern disciplinary society. I posit that Donnelly (and other critics like him) revile what they read as a pessimistic vision of society on the basis of their own theoretical and political desires for accounts of modern society that privilege human agency, if not continuing hope in revolution.

In my view, such reactions to Foucault's conception of modern disciplinary society emerge, at least in part, because Foucault's notion of power relations is so different from traditional conceptions of power and because of the strength of discourses attached to dominant notions of power. Foucault's modern disciplinary society is gloomy only if the very presence of power (diffuse and pervasive, as Foucault posits it) is troubling. However, Foucault (1983) was not troubled by the simple presence of power: "The exercise of power . . . incites, it induces, it seduces, it makes easier or more difficult" (p. 220). Difficult as it sometimes is in the context of hierarchical institutions, Foucault's analysis of power implores us to remember power's productiveness.

Power's pervasiveness, then, seems to be a problem primarily for those who would wish to remove power, because they continue to understand it as somehow sinister, rather than embracing Foucault's (1983) point that "a society without power relations can only be an abstraction" (p. 222). We are all familiar with the operation of power at the microlevel, as the resonance of my examples with readers probably bears testimony. However, this functioning of power remains largely invisible in our daily practices, unless we are looking for it. The microlevel documentation of power relations provided in this chapter demonstrates why the removal of power relations (conceived in this way) is inconceivable.

However, and this is the crucial point of my study and of this chapter,

> to say that there cannot be a society without power relations is not to say either that those which are established are necessary, or, in any case, that power constitutes a fatality at the heart of societies, such that it cannot be undermined. (Foucault, 1983, p. 223)

Through his genealogical method, Foucault presented himself as documenting the way society is and how we have come to be the way we are, rather than prescribing a new social form through the declaration of normative positions. Nor was he proposing a form of power that leaves no space for activism or change: "All my analyses are against the idea of universal necessities in human existence. They show the arbitrariness of institutions and show which space of freedom we can still enjoy and how many changes can still be made" (Foucault, 1988c, p. 11).

As Francois Ewald (1992), Director of the Foucault Center in Paris, says, "We have a responsibility with regard to the way we exercise power: we must not lose the idea that we could exercise it differently" (p. 334). Documenting the techniques of power outlined in this chapter, identifying which seem essential to pedagogical enterprise and which might be altered, is my own contribution to thinking about how educators might exercise power differently.

In bringing about educational reform, I argue that we must know what we are and what we are doing (in education), in order to begin to address adequately how we might do things differently. I recognize the potential enactment of the very governmental processes of modern society that Foucault studied, and in part criticized, with this attempt to document techniques of power in pedagogy. But pedagogy's governmental influence, both within and beyond schooling institutions, is enormously powerful in the control of populations. Attempting to understand those processes and remove those that are harmful cannot, in my view, be any more dangerous than maintaining what already exists.

The microlevel focus of Foucault's analytics of power, therefore, not only is useful for understanding power's operation in specific sites, as demonstrated here, but also has clear potential in addressing change possibilities. That is, the Foucaultian approach enables us to document what causes us to be what we are in schools, and hence, potentially, to change what we are. Given the continuing widely documented negative effects of schooling for many students and teachers, such change seems a worthy pursuit.

NOTES

I am grateful to the Australian Research Council for the funding that has supported this study, to all who participated in the research, and to James Ladwig, Gavin Hazel, and Marie Brennan for their comments on earlier drafts of this chapter.

1. I want to emphasize that the scope of the overall project is clearly much larger than can be conveyed within this chapter. There are many other theoretical and methodological concerns that I am addressing elsewhere.

2. These episodes have been selected randomly by simply opening, for each category, the file of data segments that were coded with that technique of power. The number of coded segments per category per site ranged from four episodes of regulation in the feminist site to 746 episodes of distribution in the physical education site.

3. Pseudonyms are used throughout and other identifiers have been removed or changed. The data source is coded PE for the physical education site, TE for the teacher education site, WG for the women's discussion group, and FEM for the feminist reading group. Transcripts are distinguished from field notes via quotation marks. The transcripts have been edited slightly, in order to facilitate reading. Given the multiplicity and complexity of pedagogical events, no truth claims are made for these data. As Bourdieu, Chamboredon, and Passeron (1991) say, we need to "renounce the impossible ambition of saying everything about everything, in the right order" (p. 10).

4. My research assistants, Erica Southgate and Rosalie Bunn, and I spent approximately 6 months in each of the sites, during 1993, making detailed observational notes and audio tapes of all group meetings during that period.

5. The teacher education program was driven by strong critical and feminist educational perspectives.

6. For further examples that substantiate this point, see Gore (1994).

7. Average proportions for each category indicate the following as the most to

least common practices across all sites: individualization, 24.7; totalization, 17.8; exclusion, 16.5; classification, 15.8; normalization, 15.7; distribution, 14.0; surveillance, 5.4; regulation, 4.8.

REFERENCES

Bernstein, B. (1975). *Class, codes and control: Towards a theory of educational transmissions.* London: Routledge & Kegan Paul.

Bernstein, B. (1990). *The structuring of pedagogic discourse.* London: Routledge.

Bourdieu, P., Chamboredon, J.-C., & Passeron, J.-C. (1991). *The craft of sociology: Epistemological preliminaries.* Berlin: De Gruyter.

Bourdieu, P., & Passeron, J.-C. (1977). *Reproduction in education, society and culture.* London: Sage.

Canguilhem, G. (1991). *The normal and the pathological.* New York: Zone Books.

Corrigan, P. R. (1991). The making of the boy: Meditations on what grammar school did with, to, and for my body. In H. A. Giroux (Ed.), *Postmodernism, feminism, and cultural politics* (pp. 196–216). Albany: State University of New York Press.

Deleuze, G. (1988). *Foucault.* Minneapolis: University of Minnesota Press.

Donnelly, M. (1992). On Foucault's uses of the notion of "biopower." In T. J. Armstrong (Ed. and Trans.), *Michel Foucault philosopher* (pp. 199–203). New York: Harvester Wheatsheaf.

Ewald, F. (1992). Summary of discussions. In T. J. Armstrong (Ed. and Trans.), *Michel Foucault philosopher* (p. 334). New York: Harvester Wheatsheaf.

Foucault, M. (1977). *Discipline and punish: The birth of the prison.* New York: Pantheon.

Foucault, M. (1980). Prison talk. In C. Gordon (Ed. and Trans.), *Power/knowledge: Selected interviews and other writings by Michel Foucault, 1972–1977* (pp. 109–133). New York: Pantheon.

Foucault, M. (1981). The order of discourse. In R. Young (Ed.), *Untying the text: A post-structuralist reader* (pp. 48–78). Boston: Routledge & Kegan Paul.

Foucault, M. (1983). The subject and power. In H. L. Dreyfus & P. Rabinow (Eds.), *Michel Foucault: Beyond structuralism and hermeneutics* (2nd ed., pp. 208–226). Chicago: University of Chicago Press.

Foucault, M. (1988a). The ethic of care for the self as a practice of freedom. [Interview]. In J. Bernauer & D. Rasmussen (Eds.), *The final Foucault* (pp. 1–20). Cambridge, MA: MIT Press.

Foucault, M. (1988b). The political technology of individuals. In L. H. Martin, H. Gutman, & P. H. Hutton (Eds.), *Technologies of the self: A seminar with Michel Foucault* (pp. 145–162). Amherst: University of Massachusetts Press.

Foucault, M. (1988c). Truth, power, self: An interview with Michel Foucault. In L. H. Martin, H. Gutman, & P. H. Hutton (Eds.), *Technologies of the self: A seminar with Michel Foucault* (pp. 9–15). Amherst: University of Massachusetts Press.

Gore, J. M. (1993). *The struggle for pedagogies: Critical and feminist discourses as regimes of truth.* New York: Routledge.

Gore, J. M. (1994, November). *Power and pedagogy: Within and beyond the schooling institution.* Paper presented at the annual conference of the Australian Association for Research in Education, Newcastle.

Kelly, M. (1994). Foucault, Habermas and the self-referentiality of critique. In M. Kelly (Ed.), *Critique and power: Recasting the Foucault/Habermas debate* (pp. 365–400). Cambridge, MA: MIT Press.

Maxwell, J. A., & Miller, B. A. (1993). *Categorization and contextualization as components of qualitative data analysis.* Unpublished manuscript.

Morey, M. (1992). On Michel Foucault's philosophical style: Towards a critique of the normal. In T. J. Armstrong (Ed. and Trans.), *Michel Foucault philosopher* (pp. 117–128). New York: Harvester Wheatsheaf.

Southgate, E. (forthcoming). Collective memory and discourses of schooling (tentative title). Doctoral manuscript, University of Newcastle.

Tyler, D. (1993). Making better children. In D. Meredyth & D. Tyler (Eds.), *Child and citizen: Genealogies of schooling and subjectivity* (pp. 35–60). Griffith University, Brisbane: Institute of Cultural and Policy Studies.

PART IV

The Opening/Closing of Pedagogical Spaces

10

Performing the Self: Constructing Written and Curricular Fictions

DAVID SCHAAFSMA

We have to create ourselves as a work of art.
—Michel Foucault

In this chapter I examine the function of constructing fictions—the stories, poetry, and plays written by individual students, and the curricula created by teachers and students and enacted in classrooms—in the process of performing the self. The site of my analysis is the writing of one 13-year-old, African American schoolgirl, Rashema Steward,[1] over the course of one semester in the context of Don Chevako's urban English classroom. The curriculum of the class was organized according to an "inquiry-based" approach, where students were invited to explore questions arising out of the conditions of their lived lives, imagine and develop forms to shape answers to their questions, and take action in their lives and communities on the basis of their research.

While my primary goal is to argue, on the basis of one student's writing, for a particular approach to the analysis of student writing, my secondary but closely related goal is to argue for a similar approach to the analysis of writing curricula such as Don's. The theoretical frame for my analysis owes much to a range of theorists working in performance, literacy education, and the sociology of knowledge, but one of my primary concerns in this chapter is to explore how (especially) the later work of Foucault might be useful in analyses of writing and writing curricula. Foucault was a philosopher; his project is not my project. Still, I have found his work relevant for exploring some questions I have about this field of study, so as I analyze both Don's writing curricula and Rashema's writing, I engage with him (and others) in conversation on these issues.

FOUCAULT AND ROOM FOR MANEUVER IN DISCOURSE

In one of Foucault's early writings he says that his purpose in analyzing the discursive practices of disciplines was to "unmask discourses as practices that systematically form the objects of which they speak" (1975, p. 49). As he says:

> Truth is a thing of this world: it is produced only by virtue of multiple form of constraint. And it induces regular effects of power. Each society has its regime of truth, its "general politics" of truth: that is, the type of discourse which it accepts and makes function as true; the mechanisms and instances which enable one to distinguish true and false statements, the means by which each is sanctioned; the techniques and procedures accorded value in the acquisition of truth; the status of those who are charged with saying what counts as true. (1980, p. 131)

Discourses are viewed here as domains within which power and authority are conferred on some and denied to others. Discourse operates in particular sites, within certain rules of inclusion/exclusion, providing boundaries invested with institutional support and correlated with a variety of social, political, and administrative practices. It is seen primarily as a means of constraint, a set of techniques and procedures emanating from a particular regime of truth. Discourse is a "violence" done to people, a practice imposed on them by "a body of anonymous and historical rules" (Foucault, 1972, p. 117), with rupture the only apparent means of escape.

While it will be clear from my analysis that the disciplining discourses of public school education and writing curricula do in part construct persons, it is also important to see that rupture may not be the only possible "strategy" as a response to such discourses. If to "unmask" discourses of domination was Foucault's stated purpose for his early archaeologies, a somewhat different overall purpose for his work is revealed in his later writing: "My objective for more than twenty five years has been to sketch out a history of the different ways in our culture that human beings develop knowledge about themselves" (1990, p. 17).

In another, later essay, Foucault also clarifies that his work is "not about what it is impossible for us to do and to know, but it will separate out, from the contingency that has made us what we are, the possibility of no longer being, doing, or thinking what we are, do, or think" (Rabinow, 1984, p. 46). Foucault acknowledges that the human capacity for resistance to domination and the capacity for self-creation are possible, although there are social and political limits to the exercise of those capacities. In still another later essay (Dreyfus & Rabinow, 1983), he makes a distinction between technologies of power, which determine the conduct of individuals and submit them to certain ends or domination, and technologies of the self, which he defines as permitting "individuals to effect a certain number of operations on their own bodies and souls, thoughts, conduct and way of being, so as to transform themselves in order to attain a certain state of happiness, purity, wisdom" (Foucault, 1990, p. 18). Technologies of power and self should be seen as in relation, in dialogue, in struggle with each other, which reconfigures power as more than simply a tool for domination and/or reproduction. In addition to the cracks, ruptures, and failures in every system, the process of becoming "one's own subject" also involves strategies that are possible within existing power relations.

Thus, we can see in his later work that Foucault seems to discover what Ross Chambers (1990) calls "room for maneuver," where discourse gets considered not just in terms of the effects of subjection and domination. As Foucault says, "There are two meanings of 'subject': Subject to someone else by control and dependence, and tied to his own identity by a conscience or self-knowledge" (Dreyfus & Rabinow, 1983, p. 212). What follows from this is that "discourse can be both an instrument and an effect of power, but also a hindrance, a stumbling block, a point of resistance and a starting point for an opposing strategy" (p. 201). Speech can be said or seized differently, Foucault sees in his later work, and can function as a form of action. Power in discourse is thus not a structural, monolithic entity. It is not only repressive, or dominating. Power positions individuals as subjects, but also provides opportunities for struggle. As Foucault says, the will to truth takes place in the context of an "agonism," a struggle between "power and freedom's refusal to submit" (Dreyfus & Rabinow, 1983, p. 222).

Drawing on the work of Foucault and others whose work in some ways extends or complements his perspective, I argue for an approach to writing and curricula that recognizes the constitutive force of discourse, a construction of the self through technologies of power and the self, recognizing the often oppressive governmentality of technologies of power, while acknowledging that such discourses are always multiple and thus sometimes ambiguous and contradictory, but certainly not totally determining. This is a view of discourse that presupposes individuals' capacities as actors within a given setting, capacities that are always in struggle, in agonism, in dialogue, but capacities that can contribute to what Colin Gordon (1991) calls "the changing shape of the thinkable" (p. 8). Before I proceed to an analysis of Rashema's writing, then, it will be useful to see how Don's curriculum was enacted, as a way of understanding how the discursive practices of Rashema's schooling may have in part socially and culturally constructed her.

CONTEXTS FOR RASHEMA WRITING: "INQUIRY-BASED" CURRICULUM AND THE URBAN SCHOOL

At the time of this writing, Rashema is a 13-year-old, African American schoolgirl living in Milwaukee's northwest "projects" area. This past year, the one in which I first met her, she attended the M. L. King Neighborhood Academy, a public middle school that is housed in the M. L. King Neighborhood Center. An "alternative" school, M. L. King focuses its program on "at-risk" students who have "special needs." Many of the students are a year or more behind in school and are multiply labeled by the school system.

As in most urban school systems, the Milwaukee Public School system's discursive practice of designating M. L. King Neighborhood Academy as "alternative"—like the label "at-risk" that is attached to Rashema—is a pejorative one and is accompanied by material inequities: generally fewer resources for alternative schools than for traditional schools. Usually, the designation "alternative" within an urban school system, like the various labels associated with "lower tracks," is a supposedly neutral label meant to indicate a school's "troubled" adolescents, who usually are also economically disadvantaged minorities.[2]

The school last year housed 80 at-risk (and otherwise variously and multiply labeled) students. During 1993–94, the school's population nearly doubled, with no increase in staff. I—accompanied regularly by one or two students from the Secondary English certification program I directed—was a regular visitor/participant-observer/assistant in Don Chevako's English classroom that year, particularly the first 2 class periods of the day, classes that were specifically associated with the Write for Your Life (WFYL) project, of which, with Patti Stock, I was the co-director and Don was one of the participating teachers.

Teachers in this project, supported by a grant from the Bingham Trust, conduct a range of "inquiry-based" curricula in their classrooms, in various ways inviting students to write stories, poems, plays, videos, essays, or any other form of presentation about issues of health and well-being in their lives and communities. The teachers in the project take seriously what Maxine Greene (1978) suggests: that schools should provide "occasions for individuals to articulate the themes of their own existence" and that "students must be enabled to encounter curriculum as possibility" (p. 18), and embrace her suggestions as goals. One way teachers involved in the project propose to accomplish these goals is through making discursive space for the stories teachers and students share with each other and their communities.

The name of the project calls attention to its focus on student writing—the improvement of which is a central project goal—and on its relevance to students' lives and communities. All the participating teachers in various ways claim to embrace a view of writing as social action, and most of them can give evidence of an approach that reflects those beliefs. A central goal of the project for most teachers has been to encourage students to take action, if possible, "beyond" writing with regard to specific issues they have chosen to explore on their own or their communities' behalf, and students in WFYL classrooms have the opportunity to write grant proposals to the project's co-directors to support student projects that may serve their schools or communities.

ESPERANZA AND DON'S STUDENTS: WRITING THE SELF[3]

The class Rashema attended included 13 girls, three of them white, and the rest African American. All of the students lived in the general vicinity of the school. Don's approach was what we have called inquiry-based, focusing as much as possible on negotiating the curriculum with the students according to their interests and needs. Early on, the impetus for many of the student writings in this class came from personal connections students were making with daily readings in *The House on Mango Street* by Sandra Cisneros (1991). Don chose this initial reading for the course, after the girls had made some of their interests known.

Cisneros's book is dedicated "A las Mujeres (To the Women)" and relates through a series of very short vignettes the story of Esperanza Cordero, a teenager growing up in the Spanish quarter of Chicago. The book jacket describes the novel as "semi-autobiographical," and Don early on encouraged his students to think of themselves as writers of their own worlds, as both Cisneros and her first-person narrator Esperanza identify themselves. The girls read of Esperanza's encounter with run-down tenements, boredom, eccentric neighbors, the death of her grandfather, and an emerging awareness of the sexual world, and they said they liked the book. They told us they felt they could relate to Esperanza's experience of growing up, the story of a girl who enjoys spending time with her friends, but feels oppressed by her urban surroundings and never sees them as "home."

Early in the semester, students in Don's class read short chapters from

The House on Mango Street aloud and shared stories—usually initiated by "invitations" from Don—based on their own "reader responses" to Cisneros's vignettes, stories about owning their first bikes, about special friendships or bitter animosities. These early stories included one girl's story of anger about the prevalence of homelessness in the area, and her commitment to doing something to help those she was encountering. Don, knowing how little many of these students had written in school, encouraged a range of writing, especially early on, with much student choice about the form and content of the writing. The result was primarily what usually might be identified as "personal" writing based on students' lives and concerns, most of it in the form of stories and poems. Some writing, including essays, debates, and plays, was directed toward "social" or community issues such as racism, gang violence, and homelessness.

After many girls had read their writing one morning, one student read aloud a section from *Mango Street,* entitled "Darius and the Clouds," and students wrote in response to this passage. Rashema wrote a story of her miscarriage and shared it with the class. After a few moments of silence, Don said, "You know, I was really impressed with your story, but I was wondering whether you could actually cause a miscarriage just by jumping up and down."

Keisha responded, "You know, I think in order to have a miscarriage the woman has to have some sickness down there, and then . . . I don't know, then the baby just goes away. You have a miscarriage." Another student, Roni, said her mother had had a miscarriage, too, but she thought her mother had not been sick at all when she had the miscarriage. A general discussion ensued about how it is that miscarriages occur, and it was clear that although several girls had intimate experience—their own, their relatives' and their friends'—with sex, childbearing, and loss of life, neither Don, these girls, or I had a satisfactory explanation of how and why miscarriages occur.

Don posed a question: "Is this something worth finding out? Is this something you think is worth exploring?"

Most of the girls seemed to agree that it was.

"Well," Don said, "If you wanted to find out the answer to the question of why miscarriages happen, what would you do, how would you proceed?" Several girls answered: "Call a nurse!" "Talk to a doctor!" "Go to the clinic." "Planned Parenthood." Don asked: "Who will call a doctor or nurse or clinic so they can come and visit us or so we can visit them and get some answers to our questions?" Several volunteered to call different "expert" individuals and agencies.

"Maybe someone could come in and talk to us about pregnancy and having babies and miscarriage," Don said. "Would it be interesting to study that?" The girls seemed to be very interested in that as a possible research project.

Out of one 13-year-old schoolgirl's (Rashema's) story about her own miscarriage, a curriculum began to emerge, my story of which gives a brief picture of Don's version of an inquiry-based classroom.

POWER IN THE PERFORMANCE OF PROGRESSIVE PEDAGOGIES

In thinking of curriculum as others as have done, as both multiply performative and politically situated (Dyson, 1992; hooks, 1994; Phelan, 1993), I occupy a contrasting perspective to the approach of most district and state curriculum guides and textbooks, which represent classroom learning as a linear, monologic process of transmission and cognitive "acquisition." Such a view of teaching and learning is about the performance of social expectations and norms, the teacher and her students as "performers" of district curricular initiatives. As we begin our brief analysis of the curriculum in Don's classroom as one that performs in somewhat different ways than district mandates, it is important to keep in mind Foucault's notion of the technology of power in schools that in part shapes students. We also must acknowledge with various researchers (Gilbert, 1991; Lensmire, 1994; Luke, 1990, 1991; Schaafsma, 1996; Walkerdine, 1990, 1994) the disciplinary power . operating in particular "whole language" and similarly Progressive classrooms. Curriculum always entails a selection from culture, a privileging of certain values over others, and all literacy practices are implicated in certain ideological considerations (Gere, Fairbanks, Howes, Roop, & Schaafsma, 1992; Luke, 1990). As Luke (1991) points out, "No approach to literacy is neutral. All are utterly implicated in distributing to and perhaps depriving children and adults of power, knowledge, and competence to particular economic and political ends" (p. 135).

Luke (1990) further describes pedagogy as a "form of inscription, of body writing and mapping" (p. 2). Acknowledging with Luke and Foucault that all curricula involve strategies of social and moral regulation, we must begin by asking what regimes of truth, what kinds of body writing, are present in WFYL classrooms such as Don's. Don's curriculum, as one part of the WFYL project, follows an inquiry-based or whole language approach. This approach encourages (and, as in most classrooms where teachers are in power, expects and prods) students to write about often troubling aspects of their lives based on a belief that personal and social change are both possible and worth pursuing. Particular assumptions about individuals' possibilities for acting on community and self, and assumptions about the improvement of self and society (which might be seen as consistent with Enlightenment notions) through writing and self-reflection must be acknowledged and interrogated in this project.

Students are, in a sense, invited to "make their bodies present" in Don's curriculum in ways that they are not in other curricula. Still, is a kind of self-monitoring or perhaps confessional process also encouraged within this "emancipatory" approach, where students are encouraged daily to share stories of their personal lives? Gilmore (1994) points out that autobiographical and confessional writing (especially, we might add, within the context of the classroom) "always unfolds within a power relationship" (p. 112), and this relationship is present in this classroom, as in many others. To what extent do WFYL teachers such as Don privilege—even authorize through assessment procedures—the intensely, even traumatically, personal in this project? If the body is possibly too absent in most mainstream classrooms, is it possible that it might be too (and, in perhaps subtle ways, coercively) present in classrooms such as Don's?

While the material inscription of children through literacy training happens in all classrooms, the notion of praxis, reflecting on the world and acting on the basis of those reflections to change the world, and learning to cope with it on a daily basis (Fiore & Elsasser, 1988; Freire & Macedo, 1987) are central assumptions and grounding principles in WFYL project classrooms, inscribing children in particular ways that other classrooms do not. In the WFYL project as it has been constructed in Don's classroom, reading and writing are seen as critical acts of interpreting the world through language. In Don's classroom, student texts are honored as literature; student text-making is seen as an important self-constructing activity, a way of making sense of the world. There is a confidence in language use as self- and world-constructing activity. Students are encouraged to research shared and "personal" and community concerns together through their writing as they feel necessary, and they are both supported and challenged to become more articulate in the process of their research.

Like any other pedagogy, progressive pedagogies such as the one we have described in Don's classroom can ignore teacher–student power relations. When Lensmire (1994) speaks of the "underside of children's relations that workshop advocates have not confronted" (p. 388), when Gilbert (1991) calls attention to the stories of racism and sexism that are present in whole language, story-centered classrooms, and when Orner (1992) helps us see the need to "interrupt the calls for student voice in 'liberatory education'" (p. 74), sometimes (because of its individualistic and personalistic focus) it is important to also investigate such gaps and fissures in Don's classroom. Although Don's curriculum generally does focus on student and community needs, and at times does specifically invite (for instance) investigations of racism and sexism within both the classroom and the community, his approach would still appear to privilege a notion of the individual as autonomous agent of her own destiny. "Personal" and what is usually recognized as "creative" writing takes a more central place in Don's classroom than does community action, and certain kinds of personal writing (i.e., confessional) seem to be privileged over others and are seen as in some respects "natural."

Writing is not a natural response to the world, though; as Luke (1991) points out, it could be seen as among other things taking up a position in a discourse, and of bringing certain subject positions into existence. The role of teachers can be, as the WFYL project intends, to help students "learn to skillfully negotiate—and indeed to contribute to the transformation of—the complex world we share" (Dyson, 1994, p. 26), but the question is how to support and strengthen alternative subject positions in discourse, how to provide students tools for unmasking dominant discourses in the classroom in the context of performing themselves. We have to adopt social, political, and cultural frames of reference for teaching and analysis of texts, and some of Don's teaching only begins to do that.

Still, in spite of concerns we might have about the "moralizing" effects of Don's (and other) WFYL curriculum, its emphasis on literacy as invitations relevant to life seems to me to offer more possibilities for students than the (perhaps) rather different normalizing effects of the traditional public school approach, with its top-down emphasis on the district-mandated, regulatory examination process and the fixed, textbook-based curriculum. Most of the students in Don's classroom have been shaped by the disciplining discourses of public school education; they have been tracked, suspended, expelled from the system. In a sense, his curriculum is intended to help students resist the techniques that have objectified his students, techniques that usually are outlined in detail in each elaborate file that accompanies a student to M.L. King. Literacy may, as Luke points out, not entail power for individual readers and writers, but in Don's classroom the approach to literacy learning seems to be one step to where students can begin acting on their own and their community's behalf.

DIALOGUE AND THE "INDIVIDUAL" WRITER

Don's curriculum is much like the one Patti Stock (1995) describes, where students investigated their lives together through "growing up stories" that they read and wrote and revised for publication. Stock reveals, in her close attention to students' writing and talking with each other and teachers, one way in which the classroom can be performative rather than merely representational for students: through dialogue. As she points out, curriculum plans are always to some extent just that: plans, at least partly dependent on student engagement in the process of performance. Students always enact curricula with teachers. Curriculum is never in any instance entirely imposed because students are never completely passive.

According to Stock, there are two kinds of dialogue that take place in the classroom: dialogues between self and other and dialogues between self and (an)other self. The dialogues between self and other are those in which teachers and students engage with one another; the dialogues between self and (an)other self are those in which students engage with the selves—the personae—they created for themselves in the stories they told and the literature they wrote (Stock, 1995).

The concept of self-as-dialogue helps us explore the ways discourses in part shape or perform student writers, while also helping us find the ways students might become to some extent performers of their selves and become more than victims of those discourses, more than objectified by and subjected to their exclusionary aims. The particular view of writing and writing curriculum as performing the technologies of power and self that I argue for here depends on a view of reality—self, culture—as in part socially constructed through discourse, and of discourse as constitutive of reality. Yet identity categories in such a conception of discourse-as-dialogue are open and resignifiable, precisely because they are constructed continuously from so many available sources. As Bakhtin (1981) says, "Verbal discourse is a social phenomenon—social throughout its entire range and in each and every one of its factors, from the sound image to the furthest reaches of abstract meaning" (p. 259). In my view, when students such as Rashema write, they do not "discover" themselves or get in touch with or "express" their "true" selves, as is still the most common way of speaking about such issues in writing studies.

Just as it is opposed to a singular notion of identity categories, the perspective on student writing that I argue for here opposes notions of "author," "voice," and "imagination" as "expressing" or speaking for/from a singular and essential identity, and endorses a view of self as multiple—voices/subjectivities—discursively and interactively and contradictorily constituted, open to shifts and changes as discourse shifts. Author, voice, and imagination are not just waiting to be expressed, but like identity categories, must be seen as historical events (Foucault, 1984a) that are continuously performed.[4] Like identity categories, such discursive functions are resignifiable, because they are constructed from so many available sources.

FOUCAULT AND THE STUDY OF THE INDIVIDUAL WRITER

Still, as we know, writers in fact do construct texts, and it is fundamental to my argument that text-making to some extent reconstitutes discourse in the very act of its making. As Foucault says: "Each discourse undergoes constant change as new utterances are added to it" (Dreyfus & Rabinow, 1983, p. 54),[5] making it clear that he might have something to contribute to our analysis of the writing of "individual" utterances—socially constructed though they may be—within writing curricula.

One of the best ways we can understand some aspects of Foucault's (1986) perspective on writing is to examine his only book-length study of a single writer. Very often in this book about the French surrealist writer Roussel, Foucault makes statements that are consistent with his early perspective on discourse: "The historical world in which we live cannot be dissociated from all the elements of discourse which have inhabited this world" (p. 177). The language we use, he says, is "already said, already present" and in "one way or another determines what can and cannot be said afterward" (p. 177). In an interview following his study of Roussel, however, he reveals a perspective with which students of autobiography and memoir might be familiar. Of a writer's relationship to his work, Foucault says: "I believe that it is better to try to understand that someone who is a writer is not simply doing his work in his books . . . but that his major work is, in the end, himself in the process of writing his books. . . . The work is more than the work: the subject who is writing is part of the work" (p. 184). He also says that it is the desire of the writer when writing "to become someone other than who he is. Finally there is an attempt at modifying one's way of being through the act of writing" (p. 182). It is this transformation of his way of being that Foucault felt he observed in Roussel, and that we may begin to see in other writers such as Foucault or in student writers.

Yet, how does that transformation take place in writing, if not always through a strict representation of events? It is, I would argue, through a kind of language performance. Foucault (1986) talks of the "core of language" in his book on Roussel as the "field of imagination," not as a mirror of reality or a one-to-one correspondence. In analyzing this field, Foucault helps us appreciate the productive power of Roussel's writing "in which as the subject approaches the meaning deepens in secrecy" (p. 4). Roussel's language, Foucault says, speaks to us "from a threshold where access is inseparable from that which constitutes its barrier" (p. 4). Language in Roussel is a "space of infinite uncertainty. . . . Each word at the same time energized and drained, filled and emptied by the possibility of there being yet another meaning, this one or that one, or neither one nor the other, but a third, or none" (p. 11). Through his elusive prose, Roussel seems to perform the nature of language as "undecidable," open to interpretation.

Writing, as Foucault discusses it especially in his later work, is an interplay of signs arranged less according to the signified context than according to the very nature of the signifier. Writing unfolds; it invariably goes beyond its own rules and transgresses limits. If all writing is indeed in some respects "autobiographical," it also is not always clear where the correspondence is between life and art. Writing, as Foucault (1984a) sees it at this point, is "creating a space into which the writing subject constantly disappears" (p. 102).

Using "all the contrivances that he sets up between himself and what he writes," the writing subject in Foucault's conception of writing "cancels out the signs of his particular individuality" (p. 102). This view of the effects of power of rhetorical strategies applies as much to apparently or explicitly "author-saturated" texts such as autobiographies and memoirs as to explicitly "author-absent" texts such as technical reports. The writer is reduced to "nothing more than the singularity of his absences" (p. 102) through his stylistic approaches, and we are asked to imagine writing as an absence—as an "excess" of the author (p. 105). Consistent with our earlier discussion, the notion of author that emerges here in Foucault's later work is a variable and complex function or effect of discourse, not an essential quality. As Shari Benstock puts it: "Writing the self is a process of sealing and splitting that can only trace fissures of discontinuity, not reveal or confess the self as coherent or 'organic'" (Felman, 1993, p. 23).

If we are to more fully appreciate what Foucault's contribution to an understanding of writing might be, it is also important to see him as a writer, a creator of particular kinds of texts and worlds. Writing a range of texts, he clearly occupies different subject positions and rhetorical strategies in discourses; he is not monolithic, occupying the same position at all times. He shifts and changes his perspectives on issues over time. He also, in one late interview, admits that his works may be seen as "fragments of autobiography," to be understood in terms of the events and perspectives on events that he took on his life. He repeatedly admits his debt in the shaping of his thought and writing to teachers such as Georges Canguilhem and philosophers such as Nietzsche and Heidegger. In this respect, we can see Foucault's recognition of thought and language as social and cultural constructions.

It is with this sort of background in mind that we are encouraged, when analyzing student texts, to examine a range of texts, attempt to understand the various positionings within the texts in terms of social and cultural events in a writer's life, and to explore what the purposes of such text-making might be. Thus we can begin to see an approach to writing as self-construction that is not merely representational, but performative, and not merely performative of social expectations, but performing in certain places a disruption of those expectations. Although Foucault (1986) insists on the inadequacy of language to represent reality with any degree of finality, the naming of one's world is nevertheless a crucial process to undertake: "Without names to identify them, things would remain in darkness" (p. 165). For him, "language alone forms the system of existence" (p. 161), even a language that cannot quite express our understanding, one that continuously must perform the self and world.

To have considered Foucault as writer and as student of an individual writer is useful as we begin to examine some of the dimensions of Rashema's writing. We might begin to see one aspect of student writing as a technology of the self, a fictional strategy that both is a struggle against the privileges of knowledge and opposition against mystifying representations imposed on people, and also still constructed to some extent in and through the technologies of power. To begin our analysis of Rashema's writing, it is important to keep in mind that her texts reveal a dialogue with and a struggle between existing and ever-changing power relations, both "open" to possibilities and tied to what in part constructs her. We have to consider who she is, her position of power, and the various institutional contexts in which she happens to be situated, and at the same time see the multiplicity of possibilities in her language use.

RASHEMA WRITING

Rashema, as one student in Don's classroom, helped to shape the curricular beginning of her class' inquiry into pregnancy and miscarriage through her writing, in response to the reading of *Mango Street*, about the conditions of her own life circumstances. In the process, she begins to engage through that writing, I would contend, in the second kind of dialogue to which Stock (1995) refers, a dialogue with multiple selves or personae. Rashema, like many others in her class, wrote in response to classroom reading and both "personal" and shared social concerns, and invited response to her own writing from students in her class and from students in other WFYL classrooms in the form of drawings, poetry, stories, and essay responses. During a 4- to 6-week period, she wrote several poems, including, within 2 or 3 days following the discussion on miscarriage, this poem:

The Petal of the Rose Is Drowning

Death should come upon me

Let the earth raise
And the people cry

The clouds are floating
The birds are singing

The petal
of the rose
is drowning

If one were only to read this poem by Rashema, one might be tempted
to make a quick judgment about the "nature" of her "voice." Considering
it in the light of the "revelations" in the story of her miscarriage, one might
too narrowly read only "suicidal" or "grief-stricken" constructions of selves
in the text.[6]

While these interpretations may, in fact, be relevant to consider, she also
wrote another poem during this time period:

Pink Flowers

Pink Flowers are special
You can express your self
Many people dress in pink
Every where you go you will see
Pink/pink baby lotion, pink roses;
pink pants pink shoes.
Just think of the word

pink

Seen together, these writings work against simplistic notions of what
constitutes "identity" for Rashema. With the possibly frightening cry, "Death
should come upon me," from "The Petal of the Rose Is Drowning," juxtaposed with the playful, "Pink Flowers are special/You can express your self/
Many people dress in pink," from "Pink Flowers," we may begin to imagine
very different subjectivities being explored in dialogue. Any particular line or
poem might persuade readers to mistakenly assume that the (single) "self"
of Rashema is a "victim," or "courageous," or other reductive descriptions,
when it is clear from her writing that she is in fact far more complicated.

While issues of identity/multiple subjectivities are relevant when we consider these poems, we also can read them as a disciplining of self through the
inscription of a particular notion of sexuality. In "Pink Flowers" Rashema
constructs a self in a color stereotypically associated in U.S. culture with girls,
sweetness, and happiness. The references to "baby lotion" in this poem may
or may not be connected in some way to her miscarriage, but they certainly
are associated with particular kinds of gender roles. Lines about "expressing
your self" through color also can be associated with a cultural emphasis on
fashion for girls. In other respects, "Pink Flowers" itself may be viewed as

an effect of disciplining technologies of power. Color poems, for instance, are common "creative writing" exercises in English classrooms, forms widely available to students such as Rashema. She is, in these poems, in many ways well within the frame of acceptable English classroom discourses.

The texts of Rashema that we have touched on thus far can be viewed as revealing multiple subjectivities, subjectivities that are not fixed, that are constructed in the texts, and disciplining technologies of power and the self. Rashema is using language to construct her self, or selves, and is constructing—for those of us willing to interpret her words—contradictory motions within her texts that in part reflect her struggle to exist within ever-changing power relations.

Perhaps the clearest example from Rashema's writing exhibiting these "contradictions" or multiple subjectivities is a poem/letter "To My Baby," which was written a few weeks later, after Rashema discovered that she was once again pregnant:

To My Baby

Hi, baby.
I can't give you a name right now
because I don't know what you are,
but I really hope you are a boy
so I can name you Tiquan Demond Johnson.
I want you to have pretty green hazel eyes
and pretty silky hair.
I want you to be long and skinny.
I want you to be a basketball player.
I want you to go to college.
I want you to get a high school degree.
I just want you to be successful.
I want you to be good.
I don't want you to be like me,
a nothing having a bad life,
wanting things I can't get,
had a job but got fired because of laziness,
never wanting to go to school,
had all kinds of boyfriends I didn't really like,
I was in a gang,
I was the queen of Gangster Disciples,
my best friend Spencer died
and I wanted to get out of the gang
and I couldn't because I was the queen of GD,

and if I really wanted to get out
I was going to have to die,
so I didn't really want to get out of that too bad
or I would have died.
I lived in a junky house.
My mother was a hard worker
but she really didn't have any money to buy me what I want,
she bought me stuff like AF shoes
(that's like Payless shoes)
and everybody would talk about me,
they'd call me names and they would be rude and hit on me,
pull my hair and sometime they would cut my hair.
But I got hip, I started wearing fresh clothes,
I started having boyfriends
And getting pregnant and having miscarriages,
I had three miscarriages.
I was a bigtime dope dealer.
Everybody looked up to me.
I was Shema Mac.
Love, Mommie

The narrator of this (possibly) "autobiographical" narrative poem reveals what seem to be contradictory strategies, from the hopes for her unborn
child: "I want you to have pretty green hazel eyes/and pretty silky hair./I
want you to be long and skinny./I want you to be a basketball player./I want
you to go to college./I want you to get a high school degree./I just want
you to be successful./I want you to be good" to an (apparently) anguished
assessment of her own life: "I don't want you to be like me,/a nothing having
a bad life,/wanting things I can't get,/had a job but got fired because of laziness,/never wanting to go to school,/had all kinds of boyfriends I didn't really
like," to her (again, apparently) proud strut: "But I got hip, I started wearing
fresh clothes,/I started having boyfriends" to another abrupt admission in
the next clause: "And getting pregnant and having miscarriages,/I had three
miscarriages." The way she concludes the poem is a construction of contradictory impulses, too, a vision of a life in transition: "I was a bigtime dope
dealer./Everybody looked up to me./I was Shema Mac./Love, Mommie," each
line suggesting another possible self and world, her ambivalence about dealing drugs, her nickname Shema Mac depicting one self, her potential as a
"Mommie" depicting yet another.

As in the other poems, technologies of power and self work in dialogue:
When the narrator speaks of not wanting her baby "to be like me,/a nothing
having a bad life," she may be seen as internalizing the regulatory gaze/objec-

tifying techniques of the institutions that repeatedly have identified her as "bad." She reflects the regulatory gaze of the management where she was fired when she refers in a confessional manner to her "laziness" as the cause of her being released, and to the objectifying discourse of the gang of which she is a member when she speaks of being "the queen of Gangster Disciples," and being "a bigtime dope dealer" where "everybody looked up to me."

Rashema also constructs an attitude of regret over her best friend Spencer's death and recalls this event's leading her to want "to get out of the gang," yet realizes too that her power position of "queen" of the Gangster Disciples prevents her from ever getting out of the gang: "I was going to have to die,/so I didn't really want to get out of that too bad/or I would have died." Her struggle with voices seems apparent in this poem as she creates a seemingly different persona at every turn.

One more poem seems to indicate what writing means for Rashema:

The Magic Box and the Pencil

I imagine a box
Of joy and peace and air.
No people are around,
No animals, no radio or television
No nothing but this one magic box
And a pencil.

I can't ever leave that box.
I can draw anything I want.

One way to read this poem is to see it as an acknowledgment of discursive boundaries, on the one hand, and yet a recognition of discursive possibilities within those limits, on the other.

In keeping with Foucault's (1986) analysis of Roussel, we can see the ways in which discourse in part constructs Rashema, the ways technologies of the self are in dialogue and struggle with technologies of power. As with Roussel, the language that she uses to construct her identity seems to "hover in a space of infinite uncertainty" (p. 11). Writing, as Foucault says of Roussel, creates for Rashema "a space into which the writing subject constantly disappears" (p. 102). Who is Rashema? We read and think we know, and then read on and she appears to be someone rather different, confounding our pursuit of a fixed notion of identity. But therein lie the possibilities in her writing, in the very indeterminancy of the act of speaking her self.

Through the act of writing, Rashema "writes to become someone other than [s]he is" (Foucault, 1986, p. 182). She "creates herself as a work of art," as Foucault suggests we must do, out of the possible languages that are available to us. As Bakhtin (1981) says, "Each word tastes of the context and contexts in which it has lived its socially charged life. . . . As a living, socio-ideological concrete thing, as heteroglot opinion, language, for the individual consciousness, lies on the borderline between oneself and the other. The word in language is half someone else's. It becomes 'one's own' only when the speaker populates it with his one intention, his own accent, when he appropriates the word, adapting it to his own semantic and expressive intention" (p. 293). The collection of Rashema's writing that we have examined here might be seen as in some respects making the language that in part shapes her "her own," as one possible means to effect change in her community and life.

PERFORMING THE POLITICS OF FICTION

One way to think of the nature of Rashema's performance—not unlike Foucault's or Roussel's with respect to its constitutive properties—is to think of it as a fiction, a construction of reality in language. Michel De Certeau (1986) speaks of the slippery, decidedly nonlinear uses of fiction for the purpose of contributing to our understanding of the nature of understanding:

> Fiction plays on the stratification of meaning: it narrates one thing in order to tell something else; it delineates itself in a language from which it continuously draws effects of meaning that cannot be circumscribed or checked. . . . It is "metaphoric"; it moves elusively in the domain of the other. Knowledge is insecure when dealing with the problem of fiction; consequently, its efforts in an analysis (of a sort) that reduces or translates the elusive language of fiction into stable and easily combined elements. (p. 202)

Foucault (1979) said of his own work:

> I am fully aware that I have never written anything other than fictions. For all that, I would not want to say that they were outside the truth. It seems plausible to me to make fictions work within truth, to introduce truth-effects within a fictional discourse, and in some way to make discourse arouse, "fabricate," something which does not yet exist, thus to fiction something. (p. 75)

To think of Foucault as a writer of fiction here is not necessarily to equate his work with that of the novelist (although one could begin to argue this). It is to see him, like other writers, like Rashema, as a constructor of a fictional, performed world.

To see Foucault and Rashema as different kinds of writers of "fiction" is also to see the possibilities for understanding the relationship between writing such fictions and existing power relations. A key question for Foucault in his later writing was, "How can the growth of capabilities be disconnected from the intensification of power relations?" (Rabinow & Dreyfus, 1983, p. 211). His answer to his own question was, in part, the act of writing "fictions," works that could challenge dominant discursive practices. In a sense, Rashema's writing can be seen as yet another kind of challenge to those practices that in part form her.

Writing can be seen as one strategy of opposition, as one form of resistance to counter some of the effects of power. Foucault (1981) stated what he hoped to accomplish as a writer through his own writing:

> To give some assistance in wearing away certain self-evidentnesses and commonplaces about madness, normality, illness, crime and punishment; to bring it about, together with many others, that certain phrases can no longer be spoken so lightly, certain acts no longer, or at least no longer unhesitatingly, performed, to contribute to changing certain things in people's ways of perceiving and doing things, to participate in this difficult displacement of forms of sensibility and thresholds of tolerance,—I hardly feel capable of attempting much more than that. (p. 37)

For Foucault, writing was a political act. In examining the different social movements of the 1970s and 1980s, he observed: "All of the present struggles evolve around the question: who are we? They are a refusal of these abstractions, of economic and ideological state violence which ignores who we are individually, and also a refusal of scientific or administrative inquisition which determines who one is" (Rabinow & Dreyfus, 1983, p. 212).

In looking at what the political uses of writing might begin to be for Rashema, we can consider Carolyn Forche's (1993) view of the poet as witness, and the potential for the act of writing to become a kind of witnessing and testimony: "In an age of atrocity witnessing becomes an imperative and a problem: how does one bear witness to suffering and before what court of law?" (p. 36). Reality is represented, for writers and witnesses such as Rashema, "through the unexplained (and ultimately irreducible) vehicle of metaphor" (p. 33). What one cannot quite say—the unspeakable, what is beyond complete understanding—becomes represented in metaphorical and performative ways, as something somehow "beyond" language.

In spite of the normalizing functions we might see in them, some of Rashema's fictions of self also might be described as "critical fictions" (Mariani, 1991), written as a part of oppositional culture. As bell hooks sees it, "critical fictions emerge when the imagination is free to wander, explore, transgress" (Mariani, 1991, p. 55). Imagination, a process often associated with the "personal" and the individualistic, sometimes may function in the process of transforming reality. Within communities of resistance, hooks, echoing Forche, points out, narratives of struggle are testimony, the purposes of which include telling what happened, strengthening faith, and developing community.

As Felman and Laub (1992) suggest, "To testify is not merely to narrate but to commit oneself, and to commit the narrative, to others: to take responsibility" (p. 204). For Rashema to begin to testify in her writing in this way, is to employ what Rina Benmayer calls "testimony as a research tool" (Gluck & Patai, 1991, p. 164). To bear witness to the conditions of her own life as students like Rashema have done, is, as Felman and Laub (1992) point out, "to take responsibility for truth" (p. 204). Rashema, the witness of her own life, gives testimony to her lived experience through her writing, and in the process constructs experience for herself.

In particular, the poems and stories of Rashema operate within a long tradition of writing by and about women of color (Cisneros, 1991; Morrison, 1987). Toni Morrison says of the purpose of the writing of women of color: "Each text, each little narrative, is a local, subversive struggle" (Marshall, 1992, p. 176). What is exposed in Rashema's texts is the inscription and description of herself as nonunitary female subject of color living in a world in which she can begin to play a useful part. Speaking of Toni Morrison's *Beloved* (1987), Brenda Marshall (1992), echoing Foucault, says: "It is a will to power: a strategy to allow a people to be the subject of its own history, not as marginalized others, as addenda" (p. 184). The same might be said of Rashema's writing about her life.

Rashema's collection of stories and poems, as performance of her self and culture, and a testimony to her struggle to grow and be, is an example of writing she does for her life. She engages in a process of creation that demonstrates one way she learns. In the work, she appears to imagine and "practice" identities. By enacting a will to power through writing, she "takes responsibility for truth" about her life within the discursive constraints of schooling and cultures.

"We have to create ourselves as a work of art," as Foucault says (Dreyfus & Rabinow, 1983, p. 237). When we view writing curricula and writing as acts of self-construction, we also might begin to view these processes as performing works of art, rather than merely enacting the "given." Maxine Greene (1994) says that "works of art are occasions for exploration, not completion" (p. 218). I would argue that a conception of both student writing and writing curriculum as works of art has to acknowledge the extent to which such works of art are open for exploration and in part shaped by the social and cultural contexts of creation. Such a conception allows for both writing and writing instruction to be seen as performative investigations of the possible.

NOTES

I would like to thank Chelsea Bailey, Kris Kellor, Liz Ellsworth, Tom Popkewitz, Debbie Kinder, Pat Enciso, Brian Ellerbeck, and Susan McMahon for their helpful comments on various drafts of this chapter.

The opening epigraph is from an interview with Foucault by Hubert L. Dreyfus and Paul Rabinow (1983, p. 237).

1. All student names are pseudonyms.

2. See, for example, Jeannie Oakes (1985). The both arbitrary and sometimes pernicious nature of the discursive practice of labeling—an important dimension of the politics of representation—also is addressed in Foucault's (1965) study of the locally and historically specific understandings of what constitutes "madness" in any given age. "Labeling" is, of course, what Foucault might call a technology of power that seeks to classify and reduce certain segments of the population for the purpose of efficient management.

3. The stories about Don's classroom are based on my journal/field notes from the Fall 1993 semester.

4. Several theorists, for example, Phelan (1993), Butler (1990), and Walkerdine (1990, 1994) write about the performance of two particular identity categories, gender and sexuality. As Judith Butler puts it in *Gender Trouble*, "Genders can be neither true nor false, but are only produced as the truth effects of a discourse of primary and stable identity" (p. 136). Butler goes on to add: "Gender is a performance, an identity tenuously constituted in time, instituted in an exterior space through a stylized repetition of acts" (p. 140).

5. Michael Polanyi (1962) agrees: "Every time we use a word in speaking and writing we both comply with usage and at the same time somewhat modify the existing usage" (p. 208). Bronwyn Davies (1993) says it even more pointedly: "Who we are, our subjectivity, is spoken into existence in every utterance, not just in the sense that others speak us into existence and impose unwanted structures on us, as much early feminist writing presumed, but, in each moment of speaking and being, we each reinvent ourselves" (p. 73).

6. Some of Rashema's writing was shared with the school counselor, who subsequently met with her. In a conversation with Rashema about the apparent "death wish" of this poem after she read it aloud in class, she revealed to Don that on the day she wrote the poem, she was writing about times when she had felt "down," including the time of her miscarriage.

REFERENCES

Bakhtin, M. (1981). *The dialogic imagination: Four essays* (M. Holquist, Ed.). (C. Emerson & M. Holquist, Trans.) Austin: University of Texas Press.

Butler, J. (1990). *Gender trouble: Feminism and the subversion of identity.* New York: Routledge.

Chambers, R. (1990). *Room for maneuver.* Chicago: University of Chicago Press.

Cisneros, S. (1991). *The house on Mango Street.* New York: Vintage.

De Certeau, M. (1986). *Heterologies: Discourse on the other.* Minneapolis: University of Minnesota Press.

Davies, B. (1993). *Shards of glass: Children reading and writing beyond gendered identities.* Cresskill, NJ: Hampton Press.

Dreyfus, H. L., & Rabinow, P. (Eds.) (1983). *Michel Foucault: Beyond structuralism and hermeneutics* (2nd ed.). Chicago: University of Chicago Press.

Dyson, A. H. (1992). The case of the singing scientist: A performance perspective on the "stages" of school literacy. *Written Communication, 9,* 3–45.

Dyson, A. H. (1994). Confronting the split between "the child" and children: Toward new curricular visions of the child writer. *English Education, 26,* 12–28.

Felman, S. (1993). *What does a woman want? Reading and sexual difference.* Baltimore: Johns Hopkins University Press.

Felman, S., & Laub, D. (1992). *Testimony: Crises of witnessing in literature, psychoanalysis and history.* New York: Routledge.

Fiore, C., & Elsasser, N. (1988). "Strangers no more": A liberatory literacy curriculum. In E. Kintgen, B. Kroll, & M. Rose (Eds.), *Perspectives on literacy* (pp. 27–42). Carbondale: Southern Illinois University Press.

Forche, C. (Ed.). (1993). *Against forgetting: Twentieth century poetry of witness.* New York: Norton.

Foucault, M. (1965). *Madness and civilization: A history of insanity in the age of reason* (R. Howard, Trans.). New York: Random House.

Foucault, M. (1979). Interview with Lucette Finas. In M. Morris & P. Patton (Eds.), *Michel Foucault: Power, truth, strategy* (pp. 67–73). Sydney: Feral.

Foucault, M. (1980). *Power/Knowledge: Selected interviews and other writings by Michel Foucault, 1972–1977* (C. Gordon, Ed. and Trans.). New York: Pantheon.

Foucault, M. (1981). Questions of method. *Ideology and Consciousness, 8* (11), 37–42.

Foucault, M. (1984a). What is an author? In P. Rabinow (Ed.), *The Foucault reader* (pp. 101–120). New York: Pantheon.

Foucault, M. (1984b). What is enlightenment? In P. Rabinow (Ed.), *The Foucault reader* (pp. 32–50). New York: Pantheon.

Foucault, M. (1986). *Death and the labyrinth: The world of Raymond Roussel* (C. Ruas, Trans.). New York: Doubleday.

Foucault, M. (1990). *The history of sexuality: Vol. 1. An introduction* (2nd ed.) (R. Hurley, Trans.). New York: Vintage.

Freire, P., & Macedo, D. (1987). *Literacy: Reading the world and the word.* South Hadley, MA: Bergin & Garvey.

Gere, A. R., Fairbanks, C., Howes, A., Roop, L., & Schaafsma, D. (1992). *Language and reflection: An integrated approach to teaching literacy.* New York: Macmillan.

Gilbert, P. (1991, June). *The story so far: Gender, literacy and social regulation.* Paper presented at the Gender in Education Conference, Amherst.

Gilmore, L. (1994). *Autobiographics: A feminist theory of women's self-representation.* Ithaca, NY: Cornell University Press.

Gluck, S., & Patai, D. (Eds.). (1991). *Women's words: The feminist practice of oral history.* New York: Routledge.

Gordon, C. (1991). Governmental rationality: An introduction. In G. Burchell,

C. Gordon, & P. Miller (Eds.), *The Foucault effect: Studies in governmentality* (pp. 1–51). Chicago: University of Chicago Press.

Greene, M. (1978). *Landscapes of learning.* New York: Teachers College Press.

Greene, M. (1994). Postmodernism and the crisis of representation. *English Education, 26*(4), 206–219.

hooks, b. (1994). *Teaching to transgress: Education as the practice of freedom.* New York: Routledge.

Lensmire, T. J. (1994). Writing workshop as carnival: Reflections on an alternative learning environment. *Harvard Educational Review, 64*(4), 371–391.

Luke, A. (1990, July). *The body literate: Discursive inscription in early literacy training.* Paper presented at AERA conference, San Francisco.

Luke, A. (1991). Literacies as social practices. *English Education, 23*(3), 131–147.

Mariani, P. (Ed.). (1991). *Critical fictions: The politics of imaginative writing.* Seattle: Bay Press.

Marshall, B. K. (1992). *Teaching the postmodern: Fiction and theory.* New York: Routledge.

Morrison, T. (1987). *Beloved.* New York: Knopf.

Oakes, J. (1985). *Keeping track: How schools structure inequality.* New Haven: Yale University Press.

Orner, M. (1992). Interrupting the calls for student voice in "liberatory" education: A feminist poststructuralist perspective. In C. Luke & J. Gore (Eds.), *Feminisms and critical pedagogy* (pp. 74–89). New York: Routledge.

Phelan, P. (1993). *Unmarked: The politics of performance.* New York: Routledge.

Polanyi, M. (1962). *Personal knowledge: Towards a post-critical philosophy.* Chicago: University of Chicago Press.

Rabinow, P. (Ed.). (1984). *The Foucault reader.* New York: Pantheon.

Rabinow, P., & Dreyfus, H. L. (1983). *Beyond structuralism and hermeneutics* (2nd ed.). Chicago: University of Chicago Press.

Schaafsma, D. (1996). Things we can't say: "Writing for your life" and stories in English education. *Theory into practice, 35*(2), 110–116.

Stock, P. (1995). *The dialogic curriculum.* Portsmouth, NH: Heinemann.

Walkerdine, V. (1990). *Schoolgirl fictions.* London: Verso.

Walkerdine, V. (1994). Gender as performance. In L. Stone (Ed.), *The education feminism reader* (pp. 286–302). New York: Routledge.

11

School Marks: Education, Domination, and Female Subjectivity

MIMI ORNER

As a feminist working in the field of education, I have been struggling to develop nonconfessional modes of talking about the body—our bodies—in ways that address the everyday, lived effects of power on our bodies and that address the specificity and the intertwining of gender, sexuality, cultural background, race, class, size, geographical region, age, and education. Although much has been written "on the body" in recent years, very little of it focuses on our living, breathing, desiring bodies:

> The descriptions and analyses of bodies that [have been] provided lack reflexivity—they fail to account for the bodily practices of the theorists, and they also perpetuate fear of speaking/dealing with the body, a tradition that Spelman calls "somatophobia in feminist theory." (Spelman, quoted in Szekely, 1988, p. 179)

In current educational theorizing, the place of emotions, the irrational, and the body is marginalized. Desire, fantasy, sensuality, and the play of the unconscious are either absent from educational discourse or rendered politically unimportant. "Understanding" often is equated with cognition, with a more or less rational, intellectual, logocentric encounter with the texts and contexts of others. What is undertheorized in education is the emotional, the irrational, the fear, and the guilt that always accompany any attempt to understand. Teaching and learning, at least in part, require the uncovering and recovering of our own and students' implications, interests, and investments in the knowledge being forged. Shoshana Felman (1982) writes:

> Teaching . . . has to deal not so much with lack of knowledge as with resistances to knowledge. Ignorance . . . is a "passion" inasmuch as traditional pedagogy postulated a desire for knowledge—an analytically informed pedagogy has to reckon with "the passion for ignorance." Ignorance, in other words, is nothing other than a desire to ignore. . . . It is not a simple lack of information but the incapacity—or the refusal—to acknowledge one's own implication in the information. (p. 30)

In this chapter, I explore the irrational aspects of teaching and learning in order to locate our "own implication in the information," and to bring the body—our bodies—back into discussions of education. Some of the most important contributions of recent feminist and poststructuralist theorizing have been the deconstruction of the mind/body dualism and the linearity and logic that characterize Western modes of thought. I join with other educators working to reframe the dichotomies that structure education—mind/body, head/emotions, teacher/learner—and the dichotomies surrounding gender, sexuality, race, ethnicity, class, and nation. My approach here centers around investigations of the "body talk" produced by students and myself in an undergraduate Women's Studies/Educational Policy Studies course I taught for 5 years at the University of Wisconsin–Madison. I use writing and commentary by students (in this case, all women students) and myself to examine how our bodies are educated and to look closely at the kinds of knowledges learned through bodily discipline and regulation. I explore with students how these knowledges and practices figure in our constructions of ourselves, in our interpretive frameworks and strategies, and in the meanings we make of educational theories and pedagogical practices.

In this chapter, I argue that stories about schooling often are told in ways that embody the complex disciplinary technologies deployed in schools. Stories told about schooling can be read as living testimonies through which the tellers continue to make sense of their own construction within educational contexts, discourses, norms, and practices. This study focuses on stories told about schooling in order to investigate how it is that "girls," "boys," "women," and "men" are formed in part through schooling, and how it is that we become our own gender overseer—observing, judging, and disciplining every aspect of ourselves.

TECHNOLOGIES OF THE SELF

"Perhaps," said Foucault, "I've insisted too much on the technology of domination and power. I am more and more interested in the interaction between oneself and others and in the technologies of individual domination, the history of how an individual acts upon him/herself, in the technology of the self" (in Martin, Gutman, & Hutton, 1988, p. 19).

The "technologizing of the self" happens in part through the stories we tell others and ourselves about who we are. I am curious to explore how we act upon ourselves in the very narrative formulation of a self, of selves, for public consumption. In what follows, I explore how the self is narrativized in school stories and what this might mean for understanding disciplinary technologies that inform how we make sense of our own subjectivities. I work with school narratives produced by students and myself in order to understand the multifaceted ways in which disciplinary discourses and practices operate in schools to construct gendered subjects. I mean to designate the way in which gender is not a property of bodies or something originally existent in human beings, but "the set of effects produced in bodies, behaviors, and social relations," in Foucault's words, by the deployment of "a complex political technology" (Foucault, 1980, p. 127).

Like many feminists, I extrapolate from Foucault's work to the site where my research questions exist. I employ Foucaultian concepts, frameworks, and strategies over the bounds established in Foucault's writing in order to articulate some of the ways in which femaleness and maleness are constituted in schools. Teresa de Lauretis (1987) argues that

> to think of gender as the product and the process of a number of social technologies, of techno-social or bio-medical apparati, is to have already gone beyond Foucault, for his critical understanding of the technology of sex did not take into account its differential solicitation of male and female subjects, and by ignoring the conflicting investments of men and women in the discourses and practices of sexuality, Foucault's theory, in fact, excludes, though it does not preclude, the consideration of gender. (p. 3)

Foucault's exclusion of gender analysis in his discussion of sexuality has been discussed at length in well-known studies of Foucault's use value for feminism (see, e.g., de Lauretis, 1987; Martin et al., 1988; Probyn, 1993; Ramazanoglu, 1993; Sawicki, 1991). In her characterization of this growing body of literature, Jana Sawicki (1991) divides feminist appropriations of Foucault into two camps—

> namely, those who use his analysis of disciplining power to isolate disciplinary technologies of women's bodies that are dominating and hence difficult to resist,

and those who acknowledge domination and center on cultures of resistance to hegemonic power/knowledge formations and how individuals who are targets of this power can play a role in its constitution and its demise. (p. 14)

Elspeth Probyn (1993) refuses this either/or position and instead suggests that there are other approaches to Foucault's work that feminists may find more helpful at this time:

Indeed, there are other ways of considering discipline and resistance; I want to suggest that we can think of them, along with other Foucauldean notions, as lines of an analysis that can be bent in directions other than those Foucault himself laid out. (p. 115)

In this chapter, I use school narratives as a way to explore the excessive deployment of gender technologies in schools. Along with other feminists, I "bend" Foucault's work to fit my own questions regarding the gendering of girls and boys in schools. I do not remain "loyal" to Foucault's project here (a loyalty he most likely would have denounced as a humanist fallacy anyhow). Instead, I use Foucaultian concepts and insights as I "poach" (de Certeau, 1984) other feminist and poststructuralist work that offers more direct insight into the question of gender demarcation and enforcement in schools.

SCHOOL(ED) STORIES

In Frigga Haug's book, *Female Sexualization* (1987), a group of German feminists document a memory project in which they engage in extended analyses of the education of various parts of their bodies. The central role of schooling in the construction of femininity is demonstrated in this excerpt from the project:

She comes into the classroom one morning to find a group of girls giggling and whispering secretively to each other. The joke seems to be contained in the bag they're passing around. It opens to reveal a bra. One of the girls in the class has bought it the day before. The newcomer stands aside, wishing she could make herself party to the knowledge that centres around the contents of the bag. She can recall her reaction to a remark made by the most popular girl in the class: "You don't need that sort of thing, you're underdeveloped anyway . . ." But she remembers only too well the eyes turned in her direction in the changing room when she stood clad only in leotard or swimming costume. The eyes of the others focused on a part of the body which seemed to be linked with the state of being "developed" or "underdeveloped". She could almost feel the glances cast time and time again in her direction: underdeveloped, underdeveloped. (p. 116)

What I want to focus on are the meanings school stories hold for the teller and the audience. School storytelling involves much more than recalling and recounting anecdotes about locker rooms and the glares of other class members. My emphasis with regard to school stories is not on their formal characteristics, structure, plot development, or denouement. Nor am I interested in the aesthetic choices of the teller. I want to examine why certain stories are marked as significant. Why do certain stories work their way into our own canon to be told and retold? I actively argue against seeing school stories as the mere representation of reality or truth, an entertaining or expressive tradition, or even a rhetorical appeal for consensus on shared meanings and beliefs (Langellier & Peterson, in Mumby, 1993).

Rather, school storytelling, like other forms such as family storytelling, describes a complex, strategic process constrained by social and historical conditions, oriented by a variety of narrative means and structures, framed by the interactional dynamics of telling and audiencing, and punctuated by particular choices and actions (Langellier & Peterson, in Mumby, 1993, p. 59).

I am curious to understand what kinds of stories we tell, what stories are possible in given social and historical contexts. I also want to explore what stories remain unspeakable for women in the context of a Women's Studies classroom, in the context of the university, in our families, with our friends, and in the culture at large. I am drawn to this passage from Valerie Walkerdine's book, *Schoolgirl Fictions* (1990):

> We are not simply positioned, like a butterfly being pinned to a display board. We struggle from one position to another and, indeed, to break free—but to what? . . . what it is that we want to say, what words will take us from the position of schoolgirls to that of powerful women? Is there an authentic female voice? For me the answer lies not, as some feminists have suggested, in some kind of essential feminine voice that has been silenced, but in that which exists in the interstices of our subjugation.
>
> We can tell other stories. These stories can be very frightening because they appear to blow apart the fictions through which we have come to understand ourselves. Underneath stories of quiet little girls are murderous fantasies. These are not there because they are essential to the female body or psyche but because the stories of our subjugation do not tell the whole truth: our socialization does not work. (pp. xiii–xiv)

Is there space for "murderous fantasies" in classrooms, or just stories of "quiet little girls"? After researching the stories produced by class members and myself, I am increasingly convinced that stories of "quiet little girls" are often "murderous fantasies" in disguise, and that the perceived difference has more to do with narrative emphasis and the vicissitudes of reception. For instance, the student story that follows maps the horrific extremes to which women will go to achieve the status of "good girl":

> In Frigga Haug's *Female Sexualization*, she writes about "linkages, feel-ings, attitudes towards other people and towards the world, which have some connection with the body." The majority of my linkages come from having a mother who attended an exclusive, finishing type two year college and a grandmother who won't leave the house until she is totally made up. For me these linkages began very early. The main message was always look your best. When I look at my baby book it is loaded with pictures of a baby dressed to the hilt with little bows scotch taped on her head. I wore the latest children's fashions and if I ever complained I would always be told "beauty before comfort." The phrase still rings in my head often.

Denaturalizing gender in the Women's Studies classroom is a complex undertaking. Readings and discussions help to uncover some of the myriad ways in which we have been taught to behave as women and as men—how we learn to put "beauty before comfort"—to sit, walk, speak, act, and gesture in ways that conform (or refuse to conform) to gender expectations. Female students have recounted memories of learning to sit "like a lady" with legs "unnaturally" forced together, of learning to "throw like a girl," and of "play-ing dumb" around boys. A student writes:

> In third grade my class decided to set up our own baseball team. Al-though I was probably a more skilled baseball player than most of the boys, and though it was one of my favorite games to play, I took my ex-pected position as a cheerleader without protest. I hate that I did that. I can vividly remember my feelings at that time. I knew that I wanted to play, but I didn't have the courage to tell anyone. I even pretended to be excited about cheerleading, getting my mom to help us make ban-ners and t-shirts. But all the while I was sad and dissappointed [*sic*] with myself.

Another student writes:

> The article [*sic*] by Frigga Haug and Others brings to light so many is-sues from my life. I am especially sensitive to the young girl who feels she is deceiving those around her. Many times in my life I have felt that I was really someone other than the person I would have others be-lieve me to be. This article gives me a better understanding of my vul-nerability and my desire to please others at all costs for fear of being

"found out." Remembering the ritual of my First Communion and the preparation for it, learning how to sit, stand, walk "correctly," hair styles, diets—all of these were just a regular part of my life that I didn't consider questioning. I know that somewhere between sixth grade and high school I "forgot" how to throw a baseball/softball side-arm. Girls just didn't throw that way once you reached a certain age where you weren't supposed to be better than boys in sports.

Male students I have taught remember getting hurt on the playground or in a fight, and the pain of holding back their tears. And as Bird has pointed out:

> For boys, any signs of interest beyond the usual male domain of activity can be construed as crossing that barbed wire fence between the genders; of straying from one's real gender to endanger one's proper heterosexual orientation. To take an interest in girls' things is to risk positioning oneself as a girl—to be, in Butler's terminology, boy-as-girl, which in Western culture is synonymous with being a gay male, frequently a reviled social position. How do we react if a boy shows an interest in the touch or feel of a square of satin fabric? Or curiousity about colourful pots of eyeshadow? Or about how a cake is iced? Hush it up! Give the boy a football and pray that he is normal. (Bird, quoted in Davies, 1993, p. 107)

Each of us has memories and semiconscious traces of various gender, sexuality, race, ethnic, and class-based knowledges we have been forced to learn and other "inappropriate" or unwelcome understandings we have been encouraged to forget. The school stories that I tell, that students tell, are sometimes murderous, sometimes funny, sometimes excruciatingly hard to hear. However attached to these stories we may be, it is important that we resist seeing our own canon of stories as the "truth" about ourselves, as un-mediated reflections of reality—past or present. School stories are fictions through which we currently understand ourselves and our experiences of education. Our stories are not the end point—they warrant further investigation into their blind spots and absences. Our own "personal" master narratives must be deconstructed if we are to rethink ourselves and forge new strategies for educational and social change.

By seeing our narratives as temporary, contingent, and context-specific fictions, I aim to disrupt the truth value that often is attached to our storytelling, particularly when we are allegedly revealing "personal information" or "relating our experiences." I want to work against a notion of "feminist expertise," where the "truth" and coherence of women's experience supplants the scientific method and data-collection truths of empirical social science. As Elaine Marks (1984) states:

> Feminist ideologies that have developed in the United States are dependent on the notion that there is a separate, analyzable female experience . . . that women tell their experiences, that is to say tell the truth of their lives, and that this truth obliterates all others. Experience is used to denote a sacred event existing outside language and through which has been revealed an ultimate truth, an indisputable reality: woman's, women's or female identity, nature, essence, self, culture, history. Experience has become the Divine Providence of a secular religion, the sole guarantee of authenticity in writing and in speech. . . . This concept of experience is at the center of a discourse that both believes in truth and limits its origins to autobiographical confessions. . . . It ignores the cliches that are always at work in language and it confuses meaning with reference. This discourse believes in the transparency of language and implicitly claims to know what men and women are. More stubbornly, it refuses to leave any room for the play of the signifier . . . concepts of absence and the unconscious become irrelevant, processes of representation are not acknowledged. The act of negating through which we refuse the established order and propose another is not properly recognized. (p. 99)

The exaltation of experience makes it possible to retain a simplistic notion of identity based on the fiction of a coherent self. Marks continues by stating that this fiction has served the women's movement in some ways but that ultimately we must problematize the notion of experience and question the idea of a fixed and unified self. In working with school narratives produced by women in my Women's Studies course, I find myself frequently resisting the tendency on the part of my students to read their own and each other's stories as the unmediated truth of their experience or as the articulation of their authentic voice.

Instead, I work with students to explore the pleasure and the horror—perhaps even the necessity—of the stories we tell ourselves and others, the stories that have been told about us by our families, friends, and acquaintances. I ask class members to think about why we are invested in telling the particular stories we tell. I encourage students to consider whose vision of them a given story reinforces or challenges. Is it a story that others (family, friends, teachers, acquaintances) have told about us? What are the silences, the unsaid in this particular narrative of the self? How can we move from seeing these stories as the "truth" about ourselves to seeing them instead as data in a prolonged personal, political, and theoretical examination of our complex experiences of education?

OUTSIDE THE CONFESSIONAL

While presenting a draft of this chapter at a conference, I was asked whether there were other "student confessions in my data set." I was stunned as I tried to figure a way out of the two frameworks the speaker established around my research. "Data set" conjures up images for me of positivist experimental design, statistical approaches to "validity," myths and fetishes of "objective," "unbiased" research, and other totalizing, normalizing discourses of Western science. Even worse, however, was the claim that what I was doing involved confession—a practice, a technology I have been firmly set against ever since encountering, in my second year of graduate school, Foucault's explication of the meanings and uses of the confessional.

I explained to the audience member as best I could why I do not consider my work with student narratives to be driven by or underwritten by confession. I tried to explain why I believe the analysis of school narratives and the insight they provide into the marking of gender in schools is not a confessional project. Not all personal narratives are confessional. The school stories that I work with here testify to the disciplinary practices of schooling. They do not seek absolution. I am frustrated that at precisely the moment when women and men of color, white women, lesbians, gays and bisexuals, people living with AIDS, and other marginalized groups begin to tell stories in educational contexts, these speakings are undermined as exaggerated, confessional, self-indulgent, or atheoretical.

The fear of sounding confessional, of getting read as confessional, has become a disciplinary technology in its own right. The public condemnation of "personal writing" has ushered in a retreat to projects that remain detached and intellectualized. The narratives I work with are never far away from the messy feelings, images, sensations, and fears associated with schooling. As a result, readers may find the writing to be excessive, overly dramatic, or otherwise "undisciplined." Those are some of the characteristics that I find most useful. I seek to make use of the excess instead of trying to discipline it back into "reality/truth." To see school stories as testimonials rather than as confessions opens up possibilities for critical and creative interventions into their construction, their circulation, and the production of new selves. As Bordowitz put it:

> There are differences, very significant to me, between the confession and the testimony. Through testimony one bears witness to one's own experiences to one's self. Through confession one relinquishes responsibility for bearing witness to and for one's self with the hope that some force greater than one's self will bear away the responsibilities for one's actions. The testimony is the story of a survivor. The confession is the story of a sinner. Both are motivated by guilt. If

the survivor does not bear witness to his experience, he may blame himself for the pain he feels despite the fact that the pain was caused by another person's actions. If the sinner does not reveal the nature of his sins, he will suffer the consequences of his actions through punishment inflicted by god. The testimony is secular. The confession is religious. Each can involve the other. The testimony is offered to an other, who listens. The confession is posed to an other, who has the power to punish or forgive. They are two distinctly different acts because the precondition for the testimony is a historical cause and the precondition for the confession is a subjective cause. Psychoanalysis engenders both confession and testimony by making subjectivity historical and history subjective. Confession presupposes guilt. Testimony presupposes innocence. Coming out is a form of testimony. Recovery is a form of testimony. Disclosing one's HIV status is a form of testimony. All of these can take the form of confession. Testimony is a means of gaining sovereignty of the self. Confession subjugates the self to a sovereign force. A testimony that leads to confession recapitulates repression. A testimony, performed successfully, can lead toward liberation. (An idealization.) A testimony once started cannot cease. The telling must continue. A confession implies an end, but it is an endless repetition. I want to assume the largest measure of responsibility for myself possible. This can be earned only through a greater understanding of my limits: the limits of my thinking, my actions, my expressions. This is a testimony. (Bordowitz, quoted in Sappington & Stallings, 1994, p. 25)

MURDEROUS FANTASIES AND/AS SCHOOL STORIES

Like the school story from Haug's memory project, women in my class also express fear and humiliation in stories concerning the development (or lack thereof) of breasts and the crises that growing breasts incite in both the story-tellers and those around them. These stories are salient precisely because the tellers are still living through the trauma. Anxiety about breast size and shape does not end upon graduation from high school. The continuing incitement to discourse of female breasts is evidenced across the covers of fashion magazines, on talk shows, and in products and exercises designed to expand, contract, or firm up breast tissue. Furthermore, the plastic surgery and cosmetics industries, which have generated billions from breast augmentation surgery, have come under fire as the health dangers of silicone breast implants have been publicized. Recent disagreement over the efficacy of mammography, confusion over breast self-exams, and demonstrations protesting the lack of funding for breast cancer research contribute to an atmosphere of mistrust and fear, which is inculcated in childhood. An older returning student in my course tells a story of her own schooling in ways that point out the movement from the external observation and discipline of her female body to the investment of her own maturing body with shame, humiliation, and fear:

I went to a one-room country school with grades 1–8. One afternoon our school was having a spelling bee competition with another country school. We all lined up on opposite sides of the room. Everyone's attention was usually focused on the person spelling the word and I interpreted the smiles as approval and encouragement that as a 5th grader I was still standing and spelling against older students. Though at times I sensed that the smiles were slightly different than for others, I felt proud and confident in spite of my usual shyness in these types of situations. Later that evening at home, my sister suggested that I probably should wear a bra with that sweater because every time I was given a word to spell I would take a deep breath and pull my sweater down and you could "sort of" see my breasts. I looked in the mirror and pulled my sweater down at the waist, and sure enough, as the sweater stretched over my chest, I could see not only the shape of my breasts but also two brown spots—my nipples! I felt so embarassed [*sic*]. I put on a bra right away to cover them up. For a while after that I wore a bra all of the time, even to bed. I didn't want to see those two brown spots because when I did I felt this wave of humiliation come over my body.

Through the construction of dualistic modes of thought and the valuation of that which is associated with masculinity, women learn to suppress the body, to identify with the privileged term in binaristic logic leading us to value culture over nature, reason over emotion. For the student storyteller above, there are a series of tensions and incompatibilities surrounding the possession of nipples (visible or not) and the ontological status of spelling bee champion. The question of what is (or should be) visible and what is not, has been noted by others to be a central aspect of female subjectivity (see Irigaray, 1985). The same binary mechanisms between what is (or should be) visible and what should remain hidden, are expressed in Bakhtin's notion of the classical body and the grotesque body. Wolff (1990) expands on this notion:

> The classical body has no orifices and engages in no base bodily functions. It is like a classical statue. It is opposed to the "grotesque body", which has orifices, genitals, protuberances. Francis Barker's . . . study of seventeenth-century Europe documents . . . how the body was increasingly redefined and privatized, its sexual and other needs and appetites denied. . . . Barker analyses these transformations of discourse in relation to changes in class structure, labour demands, and the reconstitution of subjectivity. The "positive body", founded on the exclusion of desires and appetites, which now constitute the "absent body", is the ideal and necessary subject and object of rational science and bourgeois society. (p. 124)

Based on the denial of the self through resistance to temptation, the ascetic imperative plays a particularly prominent role in the construction of femininity. Geoffrey Harpham's analysis of asceticism highlights the ways in which an "ascetic imperative" has covertly structured Western ideas of the body, writing, ethics, and aesthetics. Harpham (1987) writes:

> All cultures are ethical cultures; for the idea of ethics is inescapably ascetical. No matter how hedonistic, materialistic, self-indulgent, wicked, or atomistic they may be, all cultures impose on their members the essential ascetic discipline of "self-denial," formulated by the Christian ascetics as the resistance to what Augustine calls "nature and nature's appetites." (p. xi)

How is it that women historically have borne the brunt of the ascetic imperative? Feminists have been exploring the ways in which women are subjected to discourses that encourage us to suppress or ignore our appetites. Susan Bordo's (1988) work on anorexia nervosa foregrounds these concerns:

> The view that human existence is bifurcated into two realms or substances—the bodily or material on the one hand, and the mental or spiritual on the other . . . appears as the offspring, the by-product, of the identification of the self with control, an identification that . . . [lies] at the center of Christianity's ethic of antisexuality. The attempt to subdue the spontaneities of the body in the interests of control only succeeds in constituting them as more alien, and more powerful, and thus more needful of control. (p. 93)

Approximately one-fourth to one-third of the young women I work with and advise are actively engaged in practices such as restrictive dieting, bulimia, and anorexia. As a feminist, educational researcher, and former restrictive dieter, I want to understand how these disciplinary technologies are deployed in schools from kindergarten through graduate school. I want to change what young girls are learning about themselves, about their bodies, about their appetites (intellectual, sexual, and dietary) inside educational institutions. By fourth grade, 80% of girls in U.S. schools are on diets. By tenth grade, 75% hate the way they look. I continue to hear stories college women tell about ritual weigh-ins in front of potential fraternity brothers (who vote on their desirability via thumbs up or thumbs down) as part of their sorority rush activities. It is no wonder that anorexia and bulimia are rampant on college campuses. Once space is opened in class to analyze issues surrounding body image, excessive dieting, and the denial of female appetites, the floodgates open. I receive journal entries and visits to my office from women who are anxious to discuss these issues.

College women I teach and advise speak frequently about the paucity of sites in their lives where they can talk about the social construction of body image and the relentless pursuit of thinness, understand these issues historically, and link them to other social and political struggles. One student framed it as feminism's dirty little secret—that so many of us have serious issues around body image at the same time that the only available forms of discourse are those that require us to speak as if we are "above" these issues, as if only others are affected by the relentless pursuit of thinness in our culture. As we challenge what counts as legitimate knowledge, we challenge a variety of knowledge forms as well. Since there is no objective or unbiased position from which to understand the world, we need to find alternatives to forms of expression that continue to position us as detached—as removed from the very issues under investigation.

At least half the women in my classes have some close connection (usually themselves or their sister, mother, best friend, or roommate) to bulimia or anorexia. Many are still "practicing," and often it is not possible to tell who by appearance. I have brainstormed with students ways that we might teach about bulimia and anorexia in schools and universities. One woman said she began throwing up after learning about bulimia in a high school health class and watching a film on the topic. Clearly, issues of "body image" and "self-control" are important for women, and schools and universities are key sites in the circulation of meanings around these terms. There is clearly a need for more discussion, for courses that deal specifically with women, food, and body image. One student's narrative points to the centrality of these issues in women's lives:

> I read a book by Maya Angelou where her body begins developing and she becomes afraid she is growing a penis. She starts worrying that this means she is a lesbian. In the book she is forced by her step mother to look up the word "vulva" in the dictionary. Even so, her fears are not quieted until she becomes pregnant. A baby born, she has finally "proved" her femininity.
>
> Maya Angelou's struggle with her own femininity is a story I know well. Last year my male lover was attempting to compliment me by telling me I was androgynous. To his surprise, instead of becoming modest or boasting, or whatever he expected, I was furious! My lover was baffled: isn't that what every feminist wanted to hear? Hadn't I always proudly stated that I was "butch"? What I couldn't seem to explain was that as a male, the privilege he assumed by trying to define my gender joined the chorus of all males, dictating femininity to me. After defining it for me they could somehow conclude that I didn't measure up. This was an issue I had struggled with since puberty, and probably long before.
>
> In kindergarten, although our mom didn't allow us to watch TV, I

had caught enough to develop a "Cindy Brady Complex." I wanted to be just like her. I wanted to have golden curly pigtails and two teeth missing in the front. I wanted to lisp. This television character represented the unobtrusive "cute" girl to me. She was not only small and delicate, she was also completely unoffensive. We divided the female world into two categories: the tom-boy and the Cindy-girl. And although we scorned the latter for her uselessness, we also knew that was the model we were supposed to follow. Even as I strived to be like this early picture of femininity, I knew somewhere that I could never achieve it. I'm sure I did not understand what the implications of such a model would mean in the larger picture. Nor did I understand where to direct the frustration that accompanied this socialization.

Cindy Brady was still inexplicitly looming over me through the sixth grade when the boy who sat near me (ignorantly I may add) called me a "hair lip," drawing me, for the first time, to something concrete to use as a scapegoat for my failure to be just like my favorite Brady: my dark body hair. This also marked the beginning of a long sequence of objectifying and dissecting which accompanied adolescence.

Puberty may have created my breasts, which I treasured, proudly buying my first bra and telling all my friends, but it brought mostly "unfeminine" surprises such as black underarm and pubic hair, and with it, blatant sexuality. I remember cutting and shaving all my pubic hair off once, thinking that it might not grow back. I wonder if Cindy Brady ever had to deal with the itchiness of stubble on the pubic area? She certainly didn't tell Marsha. . . .

As we can see by Maya Angelou's example, the things that inherently distinguish woman from man, such as the vulva, are either nonexistent in society's picture of "feminine" or despised. It never ceases to surprise me when I encounter men who actually believe that "real" women don't have a hair anywhere but on their head. Or the idea that menstruation should be hidden and that breast feeding in public is antisocial.

Womanhood not only becomes vacant of all the things that naturally make us this, but it also turns against itself, to become defined in how well a woman can repress herself. Her clitoris disappears and the "equivalent," although an unfeeling hole, becoming increasingly more valuable the *smaller* it gets, is the vagina.

Feminism at that time did not mean to me to possess "male qualities," but to be a strong woman. But in my head, the idea of "woman" and "feminine" had not been challenged. A true feminist, in my eyes, had to be subtle, yet assertive. She had to outwardly condemn all the societal constructions of beauty and smallness, yet somehow "naturally" maintaining all these qualities. Cindy Brady had been replaced by an even harder to obtain role model: an assertive, self-actualizing person, who could be sexual, and, tough as it may seem, unceasingly a Cindy Brady.

In my senior year of high school I went to my first Michigan Women's Music Festival and saw a fat naked black woman playing volleyball, unself-conscious of her body as a measurement, except in it's [sic] ability to produce enjoyment. At the time, I had been struggling with bulimia, a futile attempt to become "hipless." Although I did not stop compulsive eating until a year later, I believe the picture of that woman playing volleyball was the primary incentive in becoming healthy. My ideas of womanhood and femininity were being openly challenged for the first time. . . .

Although I still bleach the hair on my lip, still wish my hairy legs weren't so hairy, continue to complain about the size of my butt, still take as a slander on my femininity when a customer calls me "waiter," I am in the process of defining my own womanness. To be a woman comes from "in-knowing" oneself. Hopefully, i [sic] won't have to have a baby like Maya Angelou to prove my femininity, nor will I let Cindy Brady define it for me. I am proud of my period, my sexualness, even somewhat proud of my ability to offend people. My body may take up space, but as long as I *take* that space, i [sic] am defining myself. And all of that space is feminine.

My students' struggles to understand their own construction opens up space to think about how we each might intervene in the current technologies of gender operating in schools today. I take Felman's (1982) move to "acknowledge one's own implication in the information" (p. 30) in the confines of a university classroom to imply a kind of responsibility on the part of teachers and students for generating tentative, partial, and context-specific understandings of issues and events. In the context of teaching, this includes uncovering the connections between the personal, the political, the educational, and the theoretical.

THE SCHOOL-AS-LIVED AND THE PROMISE OF THE BODY

Most people who have experienced schooling carry stories. Stories about schooling are significant. The school-as-lived is organized and maintained daily and over time through a multitude of discursive and material practices. Narratives about schools inform how schools are established, maintained, and transformed. Some school stories legitimate meanings and power relations that privilege boys over girls, whites over people of color, rich over poor, heterosexual over lesbian, gay, or bisexual, national over international. The school stories represented here resist these power relations, while pointing to areas in the education of girls and women in continued need of intervention.

The challenge of locating the overseer in our consciousness as multiply positioned, historically located, conscious and unconscious "women" continues. I struggle with students to identify problems and come up with alternatives for what Cherrie Moraga has called "theory in the flesh—where the physical realities of our lives—our skin color, the land or concrete we grew up on, our sexual longings—all fuse to create a politic born out of necessity" (Moraga & Anzaldua, 1981, p. 23).

As both teacher and student, I have lived the contradictions of regimes of the body, particularly as they inform the circulation of power in the university classroom. Where disciplinary technologies of (self) surveillance construct "schooled subjects," I am drawn to exploration. Thinking through the judgments that have been made about us and that we have made about ourselves as students, as females, as members of other marginalized groups, helps to delineate strategies for changing education. If there is any common ground we share as women, it is the relentless surveillance and judgment (by others and ourselves) of our appearance, our femininity, and our abilities.

REFERENCES

Bordo, S. (1988). Anorexia nervosa & the crystallization of culture. In I. Diamond & L. Quinby (Eds.), *Feminism and Foucault: Reflections on resistance* (pp. 87–117). Boston: Northeastern University Press.

Davies, B. (1993). *Shards of glass: Children reading & writing beyond gendered identities.* New Jersey: Hampton Press.

de Certeau, M. (1984). *The practice of everyday life.* Berkeley: University of California Press.

de Lauretis, T. (1987). *Technologies of gender.* Bloomington: Indiana University Press.

Felman, S. (1982). Psychoanalysis and education: Teaching terminable and interminable. *Yale French Studies, 63,* 21–44.

Foucault, M. (1980). *The history of sexuality: Vol. 1. An introduction* (R. Hurley, Trans.). New York: Vintage.

Harpham, G. (1987). *The ascetic imperative in culture and criticism.* Chicago: University of Chicago Press.

Haug, F. (Ed.). (1987). *Female sexualization* (E. Carter, Trans.). London: Verso.

Irigaray, L. (1985). *This sex which is not one.* Ithaca, NY: Cornell University Press.

Marks, E. (1984). Voice IV . . . feminism's wake [Review of *Women and language in literature and society*]. *Boundary 2, 12*(2):99–111.

Marshall, B. K. (1992) *Teaching the postmodern: Fiction and theory.* New York: Routledge.

Martin, B. (1988). Feminism, criticism, and Foucault. In I. Diamond & L. Quinby

(Eds.), *Feminism and Foucault: Reflections on resistance* (pp. 3–19). Boston: Northeastern University Press.

Martin, L. H., Gutman, H., & Hutton, P. H. (Eds.). (1988). *Technologies of the self: A seminar with Michel Foucault.* Amherst: University of Massachusetts Press.

Moraga, C., & Anzaldua, G. (Eds.). (1981). *This bridge called my back: Writings by radical women of color.* New York: Kitchen Table Press.

Mumby, D. (Ed.). (1993). *Narrative and social control: Critical perspectives.* Newbury Park, CA: Sage.

Probyn, E. (1993). *Sexing the self: Gendered positions in cultural studies.* New York: Routledge.

Ramazanoglu, C. (Ed.). (1993). *Up against Foucault: Explorations of some tensions between Foucault and feminism.* New York: Routledge.

Sappington, R., & Stallings, T. (Eds.). (1994). *Uncontrollable bodies: Testimonies of identity and culture.* Seattle: Bay Press.

Sawicki, J. (1991). *Disciplining Foucault: Feminism, power and the body.* New York: Routledge.

Spelman, E. (1988). *Inessential woman: Problems of exclusion in feminist thought.* Boston: Beacon Press.

Szekely, E. (1988). *Never too thin.* Toronto: Women's Press.

Walkerdine, V. (1990). *Schoolgirl fictions.* London: Verso.

Wolff, J. (1990). *Feminine sentences.* Berkeley: University of California Press.

PART V

Intellectual Work as Political

12

Genealogy and Progressive Politics: Reflections on the Notion of Usefulness

INGÓLFUR ÁSGEIR JÓHANNESSON

This chapter focuses on two interrelated problems. First, radical scholars and educational reformers do not see that they are—in the name of historical progress and intrinsic quality of reform proposals—caught in the web of discourses of emancipation and domination. They have not come to grips with how a unitary rational individual in the reform movements toward societal and school change performs this contradiction. Second, many radical scholars have not listened to the ideas of the French historian of systems of thought, Michel Foucault, or properly observed the work of the French sociologist, Pierre Bourdieu, to understand how their conceptualizations contribute to progressive politics.

The chapter begins with a discussion of the notion of usefulness prevalent in radical educational discourse and introduces Foucault's theses on progressive politics and genealogy as an approach to the study of present historical issues. I discuss how his theses relate to the Bourdieuean notion of symbolic capital and the Marxist notion of the chief contradiction, that is, a societal contradiction from which all other contradictions supposedly are derived. Finally, there is a discussion of the compatability of Foucault's notion of the technologies of the self and Bourdieu's notions of social strategies and epistemic reflexivity. In these discussions I often refer to radical educators, radical scholars, educational reformers, or researchers as commonsense labels, not as defined or definable groups, because "groups" can be defined only in relation to the discursive poles that are relevant in a given social field.

Following Bourdieu, I conclude that we, as educational reformers and researchers, collectively must take a reflective stance toward our principles that legitimate the radical educational discourse. I also contend that the usefulness of Foucaultian and Bourdieuean conceptions entails a reflectivity for educational reformers about the discourses of emancipation and domination, as well as about the social, historical, and epistemological relations of taken-for-granted educational ideas and practices.

PRACTICAL THEORIES/REFLECTIVE PRACTICES AND THE NOTION OF USEFULNESS

In the 1993–94 academic year I taught two college classes in Reykjavík. The first was a last-year class for sociology majors at the University of Iceland and the topic was "Theories: Foucault, Bourdieu, Habermas, Giddens"; the second was a class in a certification program in the University College of Education for uncertified teachers in secondary schools and the topic was the relationship among schools, society, and the vocations. In brief, the sociology majors did not challenge that it was appropriate to teach them theory. One of my goals in teaching the sociology class, however, was to show the relevance of Bourdieu's work for the lives of the sociology students, and, of course, they appreciated the fact that his theory was not as far away from daily life as were many other theories. In contrast, the teachers who were doing part-time studies for certification in addition to full-time teaching had the expectation that ideas (theories) be directly relevant (i.e., useful) for their job. That experience is consistent with my previous experience as a teacher educator in the United States and Iceland: Student teachers are interested in having a practical focus in their education, and often they request direct recommendations stripped of conceptual speculations or a skepticism concerning what and how to teach (on student teachers' persistent demand for specific advice, also see Britzman, 1991).

In fact, the interests of these two groups of students are not two separate problems. Sociology students ought to question the relevance of every theoretical position in the manner that Bourdieu has encouraged sociologists to become more reflective of the social relationships of theoretical practice (e.g., Bourdieu & Wacquant, 1992), and teachers ought to think conceptually about the social relationships of what they teach and how they teach it. Intellectual practice of all kinds and physical work must be treated similarly in their conceptual and social relationships. Theory is practice, practice is theory, and these activities can be kept less divided from each other if we rethink their relationships.

As progressive politics aims at changing society, it has been oriented toward practice, and it views history as development toward a more just society (for an analysis of the history of progress, see, e.g., Popkewitz, 1991). Similarly, educational reformers aim at better schools for the children of their country, and they tell the history of educational reforms as the history toward better education. Further, radical intellectuals call for themselves to guide the struggles and help empower the masses. Similarly, educational reformers expect of teachers that they will liberate their students, and of teacher educators that they will enlighten prospective teachers.

Poststructural and Foucaultian critiques of eternal goals and the individual as unitary and rational in various approaches in radical politics and educational reform have made Foucault's conceptions suspect in the eyes of many radical educators. For instance, Apple (1993) worries about how much "grand theorizing" is taking place in radical education. He believes that a

> large part of what is called "critical educational studies" has tended to be all too trendy. It moves from theory to theory as each new wave of elegant meta-theory (preferably French) finds its way here [i.e., the United States]. (p. 6)

Further, Apple argues:

> At times the perspectives of, say, postmodernism and poststructuralism have been appropriated in ways that make them into simply the cultural capital of a new elite within the academy; so concerned about academic mobility and prestige that some individuals have lost any sense of "real" political issues over culture and power in schools. (p. 6)

Although I share Apple's concern about the importance of not losing sense of the politics of educational research, I think he overlooks that the distinction between useful ideas and meta-theory is not a natural distinction but constructed in debates throughout decades of theoretical as well as practical discursive struggles. Ideas need to be conceptualized before they become useful in the present context, and the distinction between useful ideas and meta-theory is capable of blindfolding educators and radicals from a serious consideration of using poststructural/Foucaultian ideas to question taken-for-granted practices and theories. Foucault's ideas, however, are not irrelevant if they are properly conceptualized for a certain use; indeed, Apple (1993) acknowledges that feminists have been able to use Foucault's work to bring issues of gender, race, the body, and sexuality nearer to the center of attention.

Demands for the usefulness of theory are an important theme in radical educational discourse. In their pursuit to bring forward progressive social change, radical educators insist that theorizing is socially useful, suited to guide such change. For instance, Anyon (1994) asks:

> What makes a theory useful? By "useful," I intend that such a theory would make usable recommendations to those who work for a more humanitarian, more equitable society, and, consequently, this theory will have a progressive effect on society itself. (p. 117)

Although Anyon's notion that the usefulness of theory should be judged on how it leads to recommendations is somewhat too narrow, she acknowledges "the assumption of many Marxists, feminists and postmodern/poststructuralists that philosophy cannot be torn from its political context" (p. 117).

In fact, the demand for usefulness is related to positivistic notions of science where theory and method are separated from each other, particularly in statistical research (e.g., Popkewitz, 1991). The positivistic notion suggests that individuals rationally apply "practical" theories. Such an approach is a technical approach that presupposes a very simplistic notion of both intellectual and physical labor. Among radicals and teachers, this approach appears in the preference for theories that are derived directly from experience, and it distinguishes between good and bad theories on preconceived notions of "what works in practice." Popkewitz (1991, p. 233) has observed in radical educational literature a persistent demand for "the last chapter on organic linkages," in which directions for practice should be given. Further, as Anyon (1994) indicates, there is a tendency to judge the credibility of research and other kinds of writing on whether they give specific advice.

The practices of radical educators in defining what is useful have serious consequences: They keep theoretical practice in an ivory tower, and they maintain an elitist gap between those who produce recommendations and those who receive recommendations, whether student teachers or others. The phrase "usable recommendations" is suited to maintain a dualism between theorists as producers of knowledge and those who wait to discover that they need to be empowered by that knowledge. Further, the demand for practical directions places a burden of urgency on the researcher-theorist. For example, politicians are anxious for easy-to-install proposals to use (or at least to let the public think are to be used) or simple rhetorical statements to use in electoral debates. Such demands are suited to dismiss ideas that do not appear easily translatable into "practice" or are not derived directly from the "experience" of "practitioners" (e.g., teachers). This is what I believe has taken place among many radical educators regarding the conceptions of Foucault and Bourdieu; these conceptions do not look easy to install.

The notions of usefulness, experience, and what is practical are constructed notions. Experience, for instance, is not a direct, authentic source; it is always filtered through interpretation (Scott, 1992). But rather than rejecting the demand that ideas should be useful, I wish to broaden the notion of usefulness to include intellectual practices that problematize and conceptualize our own strategies, stances, constructed notions, taken-for-granted ideas, experience, and so forth.

This broader notion of usefulness is designed to avoid dogmatism and preconceived notions of how it might be possible to struggle for our goals (also see Sawicki, 1991). Therefore, it is useful to problematize the eternal goals embedded in history as progress and blur the arbitrary line between useful and not useful recommendations. It is useful to be able to reflect on the historical and social relationships of the positions we adopt. And it is useful to question the idea of the unitary rational leader/teacher capable of enlightening masses of followers/students with his or her superior knowledge. The conceptual "tools" of Foucault and Bourdieu and of poststructural work must provide strategies for teachers and researchers to make sense of their experience and to help find strategies for change.

FOUCAULT'S THESES ON PROGRESSIVE POLITICS

Foucault did not say much about how his ideas were to be "used." His studies were mostly historical studies, genealogies, where he traced the "genes" of current ideas and practices in order to find out how they came to be what they are.[1] In articles and interviews, however, Foucault frequently discussed practical political problems, and in 1968 he remarked on the compatibility between his ideas and historical materialism in the journal *Esprit*. Historical materialism, the approach adopted by Marx and generations of Marxists, presupposes that history is the history of progressive development toward a classless society and that reformers and historians should advocate that goal. The following question, asked by the journal, is apparently in the spirit of historical materialism:

> Doesn't a thought which introduces discontinuity and the constraint of a system into history of the mind remove all basis for a progressive political intervention? Does it not lead to the following dilemma:
>   —either the acceptance of the system,
>   —or the appeal to an uncontrolled event, to the irruption of exterior vio-

lence which alone is capable of upsetting the system? (Foucault, 1978, p. 5; ital-
ics omitted)

Foucault chose to answer the latter question, as it speaks to his concerns
more directly than discussing acceptance of a system would do.[2] At the end
of the article he submitted several hypotheses on what he believed characterizes progressive politics as they ought to be and explained the difference between progressive politics and other politics. These hypotheses follow, along
with brief notes that preface the discussion.

First, a progressive politics "recognizes the historic conditions and the
specified rules of a practice, whereas other politics recognize only ideal necessities, univocal determinations, or the free play of individual initiatives" (Foucault, 1978, p. 24). Traditional Marxist analysis, upon which many radical
accounts in education are drawn, sees economic development as a motor
giving power to what can take place in all other spheres in society and requires that the proletarian revolution be the most important goal, often overriding other objectives, which are considered unimportant. History in this
vein traces history as a journey toward that goal, which means that reform
should be conducted and history written to promote revolution of some sort
(Poster, 1984). Foucault (1978) criticized such history as too bound to a "profound teleology of an original destination" (p. 19). Most radical scholars as
well as historians of education subscribe to some notion of eternal progress
in history, although not all of them should be labeled as Marxists.

Second, a progressive politics "defines in a practice the possibilities of
transformation and the play of dependencies between these transformations,
whereas other politics rely on the uniform abstraction of change or the thau-
maturgical presence of genius" (Foucault, 1978, p. 24). This thesis broadens
the notion of what can be considered change; that is, change does not have
to be a revolution to be important. As, for example, Sawicki (1991) and Apple
(1993) point out, that is very important for feminist struggles, which often
have been marginalized under the wing of working-class struggles. By looking closely into the actual processes of change, we may be able to validate the
"unactualized possibilities" (Sawicki, 1991, p. 57) available to radicals and
educational reformers.

Third, a progressive politics "defines the different levels and functions
which subjects can occupy in a domain that has its own rules of formation"
(Foucault, 1978, p. 24). Those who depend on other kinds of politics believe
that consciousness of the individual is "the universal operator of all transformations" (Foucault, 1978, p. 24). They believe that the individual is an autonomous subject capable of moving things, similar to how the subject in grammar governs the sentence. Consequently, individuals are brought to focus
when successes and problems are evaluated and either praised or blamed.

This perspective has been fairly common in the radical educational discourse, and, as I have argued elsewhere (Ingólfur Ásgeir Jóhannesson, 1992), it appears in the idea of the transformative intellectual who consciously teaches toward progressive social goals (e.g., Giroux, 1985).

Fourth, a progressive politics forms a "practice which is articulated upon the other practices" (Foucault, 1978, p. 24). In other politics, practices are seen as "the result of mute processes or the expression of a silent consciousness" (p. 24) that waits to be awakened by someone, for instance, the transformative intellectual.

If practices are no longer considered the consequence of the pure thought of a unitary rational individual, it is useful to adopt Bourdieu's (e.g., 1988, 1989) metaphor of social field to understand how practices are articulated upon other practices in struggles for acquiring symbolic capital. Symbolic capital in education can be reform proposals or established pedagogical practices that "are perceived and recognized as legitimate" (Bourdieu, 1985, p. 724; also see 1986a). When the metaphor of a field is used, discourse is likened to a space in which groups of people align themselves with certain practices and ideas that have value (symbolic capital) in that field. In a social field there are multiple discursive possibilities for struggles over which ideas and practices count as capital, and reformers respond to the discursive practices, consciously and unconsciously, by employing ideas and practices that have value as symbolic capital to increase their status in the field.

Politics informed by this approach aims at mapping what has the potential of counting as capital in the field in question. For instance, developmental psychology appears to have achieved value as symbolic capital in educational discourse, and ideas that can be linked to psychological arguments are, then, more likely to gain momentum than ideas that run contrary to the psychological standpoints.

Fifth and finally, a progressive politics understands "the manner in which diverse scientific discourses, in their positivity . . . are part of a system of correlations with other practices" (Foucault, 1978, p. 25). Those who depend on other politics may find themselves in a position of trying to give a neutral criticism on some standardized, ahistorical scale (Foucault, 1978). Such a position is often harmful, as its elitism tends to condemn ideas and practices that are not geared to the ideal practice. A genealogical identification of the principles that legitimate scientific discourse, for instance, helps to denaturalize what is considered ideal practice.

I will discuss issues that emerge in Foucault's theses from three foci. First, from the focus of "method," I discuss how the genealogical approach can contribute to a more reflective understanding of schooling by radical educators and researchers. Second, from the focus of purpose or "usefulness," I discuss how genealogical analysis is capable of opening multiple possibilities of rupturing discursive connections, compared with the central status of a chief contradiction of Hegelian Marxism that tends to lock the possibilities for transformation into dogmatic positions. Finally, from the focus of "individuals," I discuss how Bourdieu's notions of social strategies and epistemic reflexivity are compatible with the Foucaultian understanding of technologies of the self.

GENEALOGY, POWER, DISCOURSE

Genealogy, the type of history that Foucault used, traces how discursive themes break up and form a new theme. Discursive themes are, for example, educational ideas and practices, such as centralized examinations and the division of what is taught in schools into subject matter. The genealogical researcher studies conjunctures of discourses, searches for ruptures and breaks in social practices, and identifies the formation of new historical conjunctures.[3]

In my research of educational reform in Iceland, based on the genealogical approach, I focused on how discursive struggles are structured around spectra of legitimating principles (e.g., Ingólfur Ásgeir Jóhannesson, 1991a, 1991b, 1993b, 1993c). The concept of legitimating principles refers to historically and socially constructed patterns of discursive themes that are the available means for individuals to make sense of what takes place in the social field (e.g., Ingólfur Ásgeir Jóhannesson, 1991a). This means that the themes—ideas, talk, silences, behavior—have acquired in previous struggles symbolic capital capable of structuring the discourse into a social field. The spectrum metaphor suggests that connections of discursive themes construct clusters of ideas, talk, silences, behavior, and so on, that can be described as poles. Then individuals (such as reformers or researchers) are attracted to these poles as if they were needles sticking to a magnet.

Once legitimating principles, such as the reform and prereform pedagogies in Iceland in the late 1960s through, at least, the 1980s, have become polarized in struggles over the value of ideas and practices, they tend to become stable and resistant to change. But it is not primarily because of institutionalization or rational arguments (Edelstein, 1987) that have been put forward, that legitimating principles are resistant to change; rather, these principles are produced in the process wherein reformers and others internalize ideas and practices as natural.

To understand the legitimating practices, I have adopted a notion of power as described by Foucault. This notion is different from the prevalent notion in radical discourse, which sees power as repressive and "owned," primarily by the bourgeois class and state institutions. From Foucault's point of view, power is produced and exercised in discursive practices, and it can be described as if it were a net of relationships. Radical educators and Marxists have been reluctant to accept the view of power as exercised and productive, as not coming from one source, because it rejects the view of the individual (or social groups) as a fully autonomous subject. Consequently, they are not likely to examine their own involvement in producing the web of discursive themes—legitimating principles—in which they nevertheless are caught.

The concept of discourse is central to the genealogical approach. According to Sawicki (1991), Foucault defines discourse as "a form of power that circulates in the social field and can attach to strategies of domination as well as to those of resistance" (p. 43). Further,

> discourse is constituted by the difference between what one could say correctly at one period . . . and what is actually said. The discursive field is, at a specific moment, the law of this difference. (Foucault, 1978, p. 18)

From this perspective, discursive practices are not limited to words; rather, discourse refers to the way in which discursive practices are social practices with material effects. This means that discursive practices include the silences in the discourse as much as they refer to spoken and written words (Britzman, 1991; Foucault, 1980b). Patterns of behavior and the organization of schooling are parts of discourse. For instance, the features, even the attitudes, of a teacher in a classroom are a part of the discourse. Similarly, the organization of subject matter is an element of discourse, and what is not in the curriculum "can be as telling as that which is said" (Britzman, 1991, p. 189). Thus, discourse is an inclusive concept; it is a conceptual approach to understanding the relationship between events and thoughts.

This explanation of what is discourse differs from the observations of Zipin (Chapter 13, this volume), who has identified "prediscursive" or "extradiscursive" moments in poststructuralist scholarship. While I believe his observations are correct, my contention is that the Foucaultian concept of discourse refers to the materiality of practices as much as it refers to the spoken and written word. Further, in contrast to Zipin's stance, I see discourse as referring to the history (trajectory) of the discursive themes that currently have capital. Consequently, "historical grounds" of discourse, as Zipin argues, do not exist outside of discourse but are part of it. Finally, the theorizing of "reflexive and integrative agentic capacities" that Zipin calls for, assumes and stresses the importance of "humanness" before discourse. In fact, what is prior to discourse hardly matters because everything that might be there achieves its value (e.g., humanness) in discursive struggles over what counts as capital.

The main strength of the genealogical approach is that it enables us to see how the historical and social significance of discursive themes emerged in a particular place and time. Because there is no intrinsic nature of an idea or fundamental source to which it can be traced, I suggest that an important analytic strategy is to trace the trajectory of a discursive formation by looking at the play of rules and clusters of relations between discursive themes, individuals, and institutions (see, e.g., Foucault, 1978). By trajectory, I mean that the history of a discursive formation is unique, yet has a logic. This logic consists of historically and socially constructed legitimating principles in each social field.

IS GENEALOGY USEFUL? THE DECENTERING
OF THE CHIEF CONTRADICTION

The question of how useful genealogy is for progressive politics may be best answered by pointing out that the genealogist Foucault was himself an engaged social critic who was not pleased with how modern society took for granted the disciplinary power that had made productive power relations largely invisible. Sawicki (1991) tells the story of when she met Foucault in a seminar at the University of Vermont shortly after she submitted her doctoral dissertation on his work. He responded with some embarrassment and suggested to her that she should not spend energy talking about him but do the same as he did, namely, write genealogies. Indeed, Foucault did not use his time to produce a grand theory of change; he examined the trajectories of modern understandings of, for example, madness (1973), medicine (1975), and sexuality (1980a). Others who have employed his method and view on power as productive, such as Popkewitz (1991) and Sawicki (1991), also are interested in affecting current relations of power.

But the genealogist is not likely to compose specific recommendations on the ground of the story that is told, and certainly she or he does not transcend power relations, as Sawicki (1991) points out. In contrast, genealogy is meant to problematize what is considered useful; it redefines where change is possible because it helps to blur a priori divisions between what is important and what is not useful. Genealogy also suggests that we constantly should be prepared to shift strategies and question our previous positions (also see Sawicki, 1991).

One of the ideas in radical education and progressive politics that needs to be interrogated seriously is the idea of the chief contradiction, a central notion in Marxist politics. According to this notion, it is necessary to find the chief contradiction in a society and reverse that contradiction before other work (e.g., reform in education) is likely to give desired results. The chief contradiction in modern Western societies is, of course, between the bourgeois and proletarian classes. This contradiction is supposed to have a status that could, and should, guide other progressive work. For example, Giroux in his early work (e.g., 1983a, 1983b) emphasized the importance of teachers building up counter-hegemonic and emancipatory work in schools, as opposed to doing hegemonic and oppressive work (for a critique of such work, see Ingólfur Ásgeir Jóhannesson, 1992; also see Ladwig, 1992, for an account of work in the social field of radical education).

From a Foucaultian perspective, no discourse is inherently liberating or oppressive (also see Sawicki, 1991). Thus, it is not possible to invent an anti-position, freed from the authority from which we sought freedom—as Giroux's position seems to entail. Positions that are directed against each other exist because of the other position, not because of their intrinsic, ahistorical value. For example, the dominant organization of school subject matter around traditional academic disciplines has legitimacy in part because there is a counter-position called subject integration or thematic studies wherein the traditional subjects are dismissed as an organizing principle (see Ingólfur Ásgeir Jóhannesson, 1991a). If the counter-position did not exist, educators might not realize that the former position is not beyond criticism. But once the less dominant position of integration of subject matter around the themes, such as the environment, becomes dominant, it can seem oppressive to teachers who are used to teaching the traditional subject matter. These teachers have not been liberated from the practices based on the formerly unquestioned notion, but are oppressed by not being able to do what they previously have internalized and know how to do (i.e., teach the traditional subject matter).

The very same ideas and practices can be liberating and potentially dangerous, and they can do this at the same time because they begin to circulate through the social body of the opposition as an unquestioned truth. To point out the potential danger of the counter-position is not to reject, for example, subject integration but to emphasize that it is dangerous to naively believe in its good.

Focusing on power as a possession has led to the location of power in a centralized source. The Marxist location of power in a class has obscured other loci of resistance and hidden networks of power relations that invest not only class but gender, kinship, knowledge, technology, and so on (Sawicki, 1991). Therefore, we must decenter the chief contradiction in Marxism, that is, between the bourgeois and proletarian classes, and not replace it with another contradiction, such as gender, race, or sexuality. The Marxist chief contradiction should be decentered because power does not come from one source and there are multiple loci for resistance that must be carried out in local struggles at the everyday level of social relations (also see Sawicki, 1991).

I do not suggest a wholesale rejection of analyses based on Marxism but demand that we not judge usefulness on such a criterion as a strict focus on the creation of counter-hegemonic positions in education (e.g., Giroux, 1983a, 1983b). When people realize that it is difficult to reverse the chief contradiction, they often give up and find themselves in a situation where they blame themselves for the failure of, for example, a reform proposal. As Urwin (1984) suggests, we should make a distinction between the possibility and the inevitability of change. The genealogical approach does not require that utopias be rejected, only that they be put into an historical and social context with the skepticism that, for example, Foucault and Bourdieu have presented. Socially engaged researchers and critics, whether Marxists, genealogical researchers, or others, are not those who are most likely to give up, because they nurture their visions and utopias rather than valorizing the critiques, as Foucault, rightly or wrongly, has been criticized for at times (Sawicki, 1991).

A genealogical study of epistemological and political connections identifies the multiple possibilities for discursive connections and reminds us that a prudent attitude ought not to prevent us from work that has the potential of disconnecting and reconnecting discursive themes and therefore rupturing business-as-usual. As the genealogist does not have preconceived ideas of where to look and what might "work in practice," the genealogical perspective is especially well suited to search for ruptures that could be exploited in order to bring about change.

SOCIAL STRATEGIES AND EPISTEMIC REFLEXIVITY

If we connect Foucault's notions of genealogy and power with Bourdieuean conceptions, we can extend the notion of usefulness as it relates to critiques and productive social strategies. While Foucault studied the trajectories of discursive practices, Bourdieu allows us to relate discourses to heterogeneous fields and examine the role of individuals in such fields. In particular, Bourdieu's notion of social strategies (e.g., Bourdieu, 1984, 1986b, 1988, 1990; also see Ingólfur Ásgeir Jóhannesson, 1993c, 1994a) is capable of substantiating progressive politics and educational reform by shifting the understanding of what is useful from applicability to a focus on the present legitimating principles operating in a social field.

The notion of social strategies questions the idea that the individual is unitary and rational, capable of applying reason any time when her or his consciousness is awake. In contrast, Bourdieu (1986b) sees social strategies as "the product of a practical sense, of a particular social game . . . , an improvisation that is absolutely necessary in order for one to adapt to situations that are infinitely varied" (pp. 112–113). Social strategies depend on "the pre-verbal taking for granted of the world that flows from practical sense" (1990, p. 68). The strategies are indeed obscure in the eyes of their producers (who are produced by them as well): "It is because agents never know completely what they are doing that what they do has more sense than they know" (1990, p. 69). Often it is said that we are, at the same time, employers and employees of social strategies.

Bourdieu's understanding of the individual, appearing in the notion of social strategies, is similar to that used by Foucault. Based on the network-like notion of power that produces pleasures, knowledge, and discourse, Foucault studied what he called the political technologies of the self (e.g., 1986, 1988a, 1988b). These technologies, which emerged in the past 2 centuries, allow individuals to internalize conceptions and practices such as developmental psychology and curriculum reform as natural phenomena or, to use the Bourdieuean vocabulary, employ them as social strategies. Bourdieu (1990) describes how this happens: "Countless acts of recognition" generate "collective misrecognition" and "constitute investments in the collective enterprise of creating symbolic capital" (p. 68). The acts of recognition are practical calculations that people make because of their belief (they believe in what they are doing), based on a sense of which kinds of strategies will be successful in current discursive struggles. Although institutionalized imposition is a part of the struggles in the social field of educational reform, it is the engagement of individuals in reform practices that is most productive of the beliefs that reformers have. This practical engagement is a process similar to what Foucault (e.g., 1979) has described as surveillance; that is, reformers watch themselves and other reformers so that no one becomes particularly interested in being critical of the collective project.

It is ironic indeed that reformers who believe in modern rational ideas use their supposedly unitary rational selves to put forward ideas (reform proposals) without reflecting on their investment in the practice of working with these ideas. For example, the Icelandic reform beginning in the late 1960s was put forward as an integral way to improve education and increase democracy (e.g., Edelstein, 1987; Ólafur J. Proppé, 1983). It was directed against the allegedly nondemocratic and prescientific prereform pedagogical tradition in Iceland. In the process, the reformers masked the similarities with the prereform pedagogy, not only from the critics and the public, but also from themselves (Ingólfur Ásgeir Jóhannesson, 1993c). This is the process that Bourdieu (1990) calls officialization: "The group (or those who dominate it) teaches itself and masks from itself its own truth, binds itself by a public profession which sanctions and imposes what it utters, tacitly defining the limits of the thinkable and the unthinkable" (p. 108). In a Foucaultian analysis, a similar process is called normalization.

Educational reformers and researchers can become more critical of their ideas and practices by adopting what Bourdieu calls epistemic reflexivity on the relationship between their conceptions and their physical work (theory and practice). What is meant by epistemic reflexivity is "a self-analysis of the sociologist [in this case, the educational reformer or radical educator] as cultural producer and a reflection on the sociohistorical conditions of possibility of a science of society," as Wacquant phrases it (Bourdieu & Wacquant, 1992, p. 36; also see Wacquant, 1990). Wacquant defines "Bourdieu's brand of reflexivity . . . as the inclusion of a theory of intellectual practice as an integral component and necessary condition of a critical theory of society" (Bourdieu & Wacquant, 1992, p. 36). Epistemic reflexivity is not merely a technical method with the criteria that the researcher be critical of the data or formally unbiased. According to Wacquant, there are three criteria in which Bourdieu's reflexivity differs from other approaches:

> First, its primary target is not the individual analyst but the *social and intellectual unconscious* embedded in analytic tools and operations; second, it must be a *collective enterprise* rather than the burden of the lone academic; and, third, it seeks not to assault but to *buttress the epistemological security of sociology.* (Bourdieu & Wacquant, 1992, p. 36; emphasis in original)

Wacquant continues: "It is not the individual unconscious of the researcher but the epistemological unconscious of his discipline that must be unearthed" (Bourdieu & Wacquant, 1992, p. 41). Individuals are seen as epistemic individuals, rather than biographical individuals; they are constructed by objectifying the relationship between the researcher and the discursive themes that are available to capitalize on in the given social field. As an example, Bourdieu (1988) has identified two legitimating principles in the university field in France: the social hierarchy, which corresponds to inherited capital, political power, and prestigious positions, and the cultural hierarchy, which corresponds to scientific competence and intellectual renown. These are the two sets of discursive themes that French academics are, in various proportions, most likely to employ as social strategies, although other themes are not impossible as candidates for capital.

To understand the employment of discursive themes as derived from practical sense, should not be seen as a demand for simply sitting in a chair and thinking (reflecting). Analysis of the available discursive themes in the field assists educational reformers in the conversion of those themes (proposed ideas) into symbolic capital. Reformers need to acquire capital for the proposed ideas within the discursive space of possibilities in which there are no essential physical or epistemological boundaries of the social field. If there were such a priori boundaries of what could count in the field, of course, the reformer's strategies would be useless in the pursuit for change.

This understanding is particularly important for educators; because public education in schools is only a little more than a century old in Western countries, the space for the discourse on education and, especially, reform in education is still a space where the rules of the discourse (i.e., the legitimating principles) are not as stable as in many other fields in society (e.g., the university field in France). It is useful to know that the field of educational reform is a place where change might indeed be possible, and if we were to align ourselves only to existing principles of legitimation we would not be able to affect any change. Investment in such a space is, of course, risky and relatively unpredictable, but the possibilities for change are greater than in many other fields (Ingólfur Ásgeir Jóhannesson, 1993c).

TOWARD A CONCLUSION

The purpose of this chapter was to explore how the ideas of Foucault and Bourdieu were useful in progressive educational politics.[4] During the process of writing, I found that their ideas could not be judged on their own merit unless the prevalent notion of usefulness in radical educational discourse was altered and made broader.

Above I suggested that it was useful to problematize and conceptualize what appears as natural or personal. One of these "natural-looking" themes is the will to reach an eternal goal. My exploration of the trajectory of current discursive themes in educational discourse in Iceland has shown how discursive connections—for instance, the web of cultural assumptions about knowledge and intelligence, congregational pedagogy, nationalistic perspectives, and scientist ideas and practices—are "in charge" of the unitary rational individual as the discursive themes circulate through social networks. Thus, we are continually caught in productive power relations of discursive themes whose taken-for-granted assumptions need to be problematized.

It seems to me that epistemic reflexivity à la Bourdieu, as I use this term, is useful, because it leads sophisticated intellectual practice to consider the competition for capital in the field of educational reform. The genealogical approach to what legitimizes practice also helps radicals and reformers to come to grips with the contradiction of perceiving themselves as rational beings who are caught in productive power relations and struggles over what counts as capital.

The realization that "everything is discourse" has been criticized for having a paralyzing effect on, for instance, educators. I think this is wrong: The notions of epistemic reflexivity and genealogy present a path on which researchers and reformers do not need to become discouraged from being active in reform or politics. If energy is spent on reflecting on present collective beliefs in order to gain a conceptual understanding of the multiple possibilities for discursive connections, then energy does not have to be spent on personal blaming of the biographical individual who perceived him/herself failing. Goals and visions should not be rejected only because they are based on a belief in historical progress, and I believe that epistemic reflexivity allows socially engaged researchers to assume a greater responsibility, moral as well as practical, for their historically situated utopias.

NOTES

1. At first, Foucault called his diggings into history "archaeology" (e.g., 1972). Later he began to describe his work as genealogy (e.g., Foucault, 1978). The work that I draw upon is primarily his later work. Also see Dreyfus and Rabinow (1983) for a discussion on genealogy and archaeology.

2. Foucault's response to the question is article-length and has appeared in an English translation in *Ideology and Consciousness* (Foucault, 1978).

3. The concept of conjuncture is used here in a narrower sense than the French *Annales* school of history and historian Fernand Braudel do. In my usage, *conjuncture* seems to be equivalent to a "complex event," or somewhere between event and conjuncture, as Braudel (1980) uses these terms.

4. The research project has, in many senses, been useful for me, an enthusiastic advocate of radical goals in education. The genealogical approach combined with Bourdieuean notions of social strategies and epistemic reflexivity gives me conceptual "tools" to analyze my position concerning the spectra of legitimating principles in Icelandic education in the mid-1990s. I also have adopted the same perspectives to observe other social fields, such as the discourse on environmental advocacy, in a way that has affected my employment of strategies in that discourse (Ingólfur Ásgeir Jóhannesson, 1993a, 1994c). I now can better avoid blaming myself and other individuals, having come to understand that problems do not arise because the unitary rational individual is not rational enough. Instead of analyzing myself and my opinions and other individuals as biographical individuals, I stress the necessity that epistemic reflexivity be a collective enterprise—in contrast with "the burden of the lone academic" (Bourdieu & Wacquant, 1992, p. 36).

REFERENCES

Anyon, J. (1994). The retreat of Marxism and socialist feminism: Postmodern and poststructural theories in education. *Curriculum Inquiry, 24*, 115–133.

Apple, M. (1993). *Official knowledge: Democratic education in a conservative age.* New York: Routledge.

Bourdieu, P. (1984). *Distinction: A social critique of the judgement of taste* (R. Nice, Trans.). Cambridge, MA: Harvard University Press.

Bourdieu, P. (1985). Social space and the genesis of groups (R. Nice, Trans.). *Theory and Society, 14*, 723–744.

Bourdieu, P. (1986a). The forms of capital (R. Nice, Trans.). In J. G. Richardson (Ed.), *Handbook of theory and research for the sociology of education* (pp. 241–258). New York: Greenwood Press.

Bourdieu, P. (1986b). From rules to strategies (R. Hurley, Trans.). [Interview with Pierre Lamaison]. *Cultural Anthropology, 1*(1), 110–120.

Bourdieu, P. (1988). *Homo academicus* (P. Collier, Trans.). Stanford: Stanford University Press.

Bourdieu, P. (1989). Social space and symbolic power (L. Wacquant, Trans.). *Sociological Theory, 7*(1), 14–25.

Bourdieu, P. (1990). *The logic of practice* (R. Nice, Trans.). Stanford: Stanford University Press.

Bourdieu, P., & Wacquant, L. J. D. (1992). *An invitation to reflexive sociology.* Chicago: University of Chicago Press.

Braudel, F. (1980). *On history* (S. Matthews, Trans.). Chicago: University of Chicago Press.

Britzman, D. (1991). *Practice makes practice: A critical study of learning to teach.* Albany: State University of New York Press.

Dreyfus, H. L., & Rabinow, P. (1983). *Michel Foucault: Beyond structuralism and hermeneutics* (2nd ed.). Chicago: University of Chicago Press.

Edelstein, W. (1987). The rise and fall of the social science curriculum project in Iceland, 1974–1984: Reflections on reason and power in educational progress. *Journal of Curriculum Studies, 19*(1), 1–23. [Often referred to as Edelstein, 1986, because of a typo on page 1 in the journal]

Foucault, M. (1972). *The archaeology of knowledge and the discourse on language* (A. M. Sheridan Smith, Trans.). New York: Pantheon.

Foucault, M. (1973). *Madness and civilization: A history of insanity in the age of reason* (R. Howard, Trans.). New York: Vintage.

Foucault, M. (1975). *The birth of the clinic: An archaeology of medical perception* (A. M. Sheridan Smith, Trans.). New York: Vintage.

Foucault, M. (1978). Politics and the study of discourse (A. M. Nazarro, Trans.; C. Gordon, Rev. trans.). *Ideology and Consciousness, 3*, 7–26.

Foucault, M. (1979). Governmentality (P. Pasquino, Trans.). *Ideology and Consciousness, 6*, 5–21.

Foucault, M. (1980a). *The history of sexuality: Vol. 1. An introduction* (R. Hurley, Trans.). New York: Vintage/Random House.

Foucault, M. (1980b). *Power/Knowledge: Selected interviews and other writings by Michel Foucault, 1972–1977* (C. Gordon, Ed. & Trans.). New York: Pantheon.

Foucault, M. (1986). *The history of sexuality: Vol. 3. The care of the self* (R. Hurley, Trans.). New York: Random House.

Foucault, M. (1988a). The political technology of individuals. In L. H. Martin, H. Gutman, & P. H. Hutton (Eds.), *Technologies of the self: A seminar with Michel Foucault* (pp. 145–162). Amherst: University of Massachusetts Press.

Foucault, M. (1988b). Technologies of the self. In L. H. Martin, H. Gutman, & P. H. Hutton (Eds.), *Technologies of the self: A seminar with Michel Foucault* (pp. 16–49). Amherst: University of Massachusetts Press.

Giroux, H. (1983a). Theories of reproduction and resistance in the new sociology of education: A critical analysis. *Harvard Educational Review, 53,* 257–293.

Giroux, H. (1983b). *Theory and resistance in education: A pedagogy for opposition.* South Hadley, MA: Bergin & Garvey.

Giroux, H. (1985). Teachers as transformative intellectuals. *Social Education, 49,* 376–379.

Ingólfur Ásgeir Jóhannesson. (1991a). *The formation of educational reform as a social field in Iceland and the social strategies of educationists, 1966–1991.* Unpublished doctoral dissertation, University of Wisconsin–Madison.

Ingólfur Ásgeir Jóhannesson. (1991b). ¿Por qué estudiar las reformas y los reformadores? La formación en la reforma educativa como campo social en Islandia, 1966–1991 [Why study reform and reformers? The formation of educational reform as a social field in Iceland, 1966–1991]. *Revista de Educación, 296,* 99–135.

Ingólfur Ásgeir Jóhannesson. (1992). Capable of resisting and entitled to lead: On the historical conditions of the neo-Marxist educational discourse. *Educational Policy, 6,* 298–318.

Ingólfur Ásgeir Jóhannesson. (1993a, September). Innra edli náttúrunnar—hvad er nú thad? Gagrýni á rómantískar hugmyndir um náttúru og útivist [The essence of nature—what is it? A critique on romantic notions of nature and outdoor life]. Presentation at a conference on environmental ethics, Reykjavík.

Ingólfur Ásgeir Jóhannesson. (1993b). Principles of legitimation in educational discourses in Iceland and the production of progress. *Journal of Education Policy, 8,* 339–351.

Ingólfur Ásgeir Jóhannesson. (1993c). Professionalization of progress and expertise among teacher educators in Iceland: A Bourdieuean interpretation. *Teaching and Teacher Education, 9,* 269–281.

Ingólfur Ásgeir Jóhannesson. (1994a, August). Symbolic capital in teacher education in Iceland. Presentation at the twenty-second meeting of Nordic historians, Oslo.

Ingólfur Ásgeir Jóhannesson. (1994b, September). Íslenska uppeldisfraedin: Thétt-ridid net úr ólíkum efnum [The Icelandic pedagogy: A firmly woven web made of different fabrics]. Presentation at a conference entitled Sjónarhorn á sjálfstaedi. Lýdveldid Ísland í 50 ár [Focus on Independence. Fifty Years of an Icelandic Republic], Reykjavík.

Ingólfur Ásgeir Jóhannesson. (1994c). Útivist sem táknraenn höfudstóll: Ordraedan um útivist og náttúruvernd í ljósi kenninga franska félags- og mannfraedingsins Pierre Bourdieu [Outdoor life as symbolic capital: The discourse on outdoor life and nature conservation in light of Pierre Bourdieu's theories]. In Thorvardur Árnason & Róbert H. Haraldsson (Eds.), *Náttúrusýn: Safn greina um sidfraedi og náttúru* [How people see nature: Article on ethics and nature] (pp. 169–181). Reykjavík: Sidfraedistofnun Háskóla Íslands.

Ladwig, J. (1992). *A theory of methodology for the sociology of school knowledge.* Unpublished doctoral dissertation, University of Wisconsin–Madison.

Popkewitz, T. S. (1991). *A political sociology of educational reform: Power/knowledge in teaching, teacher education, and research.* New York: Teachers College Press.

Poster, M. (1984). *Foucault, Marxism and history: Mode of production versus mode of information.* Cambridge: Polity Press.

Ólafur J. Proppé. (1983). *A dialectical perspective on evaluation as evolution: A critical view of assessment in Icelandic schools.* Unpublished doctoral dissertation, University of Illinois at Urbana-Champaign.

Sawicki, J. (1991). *Disciplining Foucault: Feminism, power, and the body.* New York: Routledge.

Scott, J. (1992). Experience. In J. Butler & J. W. Scott (Eds.), *Feminists theorize the political* (pp. 22–40). New York: Routledge.

Urwin, C. (1984). Power relations and the emergence of language. In J. Henriques, W. Hollway, C. Urwin, C. Venn, & V. Walkerdine (Eds.), *Changing the subject: Psychology, social regulation and subjectivity* (pp. 264–322). New York: Methuen.

Wacquant, L. (1990). Sociology as socio-analysis: Tales of "Homo Academicus." *Sociological Forum, 5,* 677–689.

13

Looking for Sentient Life in Discursive Practices: The Question of Human Agency in Critical Theories and School Research

LEW ZIPIN

This is the real power of institutions, that they actively teach particular ways of feeling.

—Raymond Williams, *The Long Revolution*

The term "discursive practices" is increasingly popular in critical school research. The modifier *discursive* puts conceptual stress on the ways in which all practices are bound up in systems of knowledge. Institutional sites are studied in terms of the rule-bound sign systems (discourses) that infuse everyday activities, and that differentiate people in relation to cultural norms that constitute self-regulatory ways of knowing. More or less unconsciously, each person actively embodies subjective dispositions for sensing (1) "self" as distinct from "others" within a complex identity nexus; (2) one's centrality or marginality in relation to rules of ethics and perception that define a "normal" self—norms that are partial historical constructions of "truth," passed off as timeless universal verities; and (3) styles of behavior that it is one's distinctive "nature," as a raced, sexed, classed, or otherwise identified subject, to perform in relation to dominant norms.

Discourse analysis figures prominently in recent school studies that accent diverse critical theories, especially "feminist" adaptations of "poststructuralist," "psychoanalytic," and other critical frameworks. While researchers tend to favor particular theories, they also tend to combine elements from diverse traditions in pragmatic blends, especially in studies that fit theory to the unruliness of lived sites. For example, a Foucaultian insistence that all subjective processes are by-products of power/knowledge may appeal when interpreting behaviors that seem to obey institutional codes, while a "neo-marxist" emphasis on a creative human agency at the center of subjective processes might beckon when explaining what seem like resistive actions. Authors may slip across contradictory theoretical assumptions, often without clear acknowledgment.

At what some call a "high theory" level of debate—the evaluation of competing research programs through philosophical analysis of central assumptions—hybrids of historically and conceptually divergent traditions are more problematic. Many see "deconstructive" and "poststructural" shifts toward a stress on the discursivity of power and practice as strong breaks from neo-marxist or feminist standpoint emphases on (1) the "historical materiality" of salient macro-structural axes of power (class, gender, race, etc.), theorized as grounding the distinct practices, meanings, and identities of people who stand in different positions of social relation; and (2) the basic agency of people to change structural formations. For example, Barry Smart (1986) insists that the Foucaultian poststructuralism he favors—which avoids notions of a "human" agency to make history within situated structural limits—is incommensurable with neo-marxist research. Seyla Benhabib (1991) agrees that this strong "death of the subject" thesis is an incommensurable break, but argues it negates the possibility of emancipatory reasoning about ethics, which she upholds as vital for feminist projects.

This chapter joins debates over some key moves in defining a "strong break" from earlier critical traditions: (1) a *refusal of humanist foundations* for agency—that is, a refusal to assume any "human" capacities as if inborn ontological essences that ground people's agency to originate and transform their social practices and relations; and (2) a stress on the "discursivity" of practice and power *as a way to avoid foundational premises*. To amplify the reasons for an anti-foundational emphasis on discourse—the problems this move addresses in critical theory, research, and politics—I draw on Foucault's writings and, more prominently, on Judith Butler's "deconstructive" extensions of a Foucaultian "genealogic." To highlight problems that, I argue, such moves produce, I explore how anti-humanist discourse theories are both deployed and interrupted in school studies by Valerie Walkerdine and

Bronwyn Davies. Finally, I examine Butler's elegant efforts to theorize a "subject" whose "agency"—as constituted by discourse—requires no "human" foundations. I argue that she tacitly relies on foundational assumptions, and that without some invocation of prediscursively human capacities, a fruitful concept of agency cannot be sustained. While I greet discourse analysis as a valuable development in critical research, I conclude that strong moves to define "discursive practices" so as to preclude questions of how forms of knowledge and power originate in the *humanness* of social practices, fail in their own terms and weaken critical research and politics.

GENEALOGICAL REFUSAL OF THE SEARCH FOR ORIGINS: THE CONSTITUTED SUBJECT OF POWER/KNOWLEDGE

Like other critical scholars, Michel Foucault is centrally concerned with researching *power*. But unlike many, say Best and Kellner (1991), "Foucault methodologically brackets the question of who controls and uses power for which interests to focus on the means by which it operates" (p. 70). This characterization does not hold absolutely; for example, in *Discipline and Punish* (1979) Foucault depicts the eighteenth-century shift, in France, from public torture to sequestered incarceration as an enactment of class power by emergent "bourgeois" professionals interested in stemming riots by "poorer masses" who reacted to punitive spectacles. But more generally, Foucault does not stress massive forms of historical relation—"capitalism," "patriarchy," and so on—as underlying structural grounds of power.

Is this a simple matter of methodological focus on techniques more than social bases of power? In an interview, Foucault (1980) says he stresses "fine meshes of the web of power" in relatively autonomous institutional domains of criminal punishment, psychiatric treatment, and so forth, that "are undoubtedly essential to the wheels of power" but that, when "kept subordinate to the economic instance and the system of interests which this served," are obscured in a "tendency to regard these problems as of small importance" (p. 116). In this statement, Foucault's "methodological brackets" might seem to seek finer focus on micro-contextual nuance, but without negating research that links micro-power to interests that aggregate in broad social-structural positions.

But Foucault's maxims about what power is/is not, in Volume 1 of *The History of Sexuality* (1990), seem a more definitive negation of macro-bases for micro-mechanisms of power. Foucault defines "power" as an always shifting confluence of manifold capillary streams, too dispersed and fluid to locate in individual or collective hands: "Power is not something that is acquired, seized, or shared, something that one holds on to or allows to slip away; power is exercised from innumerable points, in the interplay of nonegalitarian and mobile relations" (p. 94). As such, power has no social-structurally determinate last instances: "Power comes from below; that is, there is no binary and all-encompassing opposition between rulers and ruled at the root of power relations, and serving as a general matrix" (p. 94).

In his genealogy of historical shifts in modes of punishment, Foucault may be seen as countering the Marxist teleologic of a progressive consolidation of socioeconomic class power. He begins with "sovereign" modes of public torture, rooted in aristocratic regimes, which are displaced by "juridical" forms of bourgeois authority, but then by "disciplinary" formations of a "'physics' of power [in which] the hold over the body, operate[s] according to the laws of optics and mechanics, according to a whole play of spaces, lines, screens, beams, degrees. . . . It is a power that seems all the less 'corporal' in that it is more subtly 'physical'" (1979, p. 177). Industrial workplaces are but one institutional domain—along with schools, hospitals, armies, and so on—in which "disciplinary" technologies emerge and converge in subtle regimes of bodily regulation. In this historiography, an increasingly Kafka-esque micro-machinery of power seems less bound to broad social class positions as it becomes more complexly "organized as a multiple, automatic and anonymous power. . . . Discipline makes possible the operation of a relational power that sustains itself by its own mechanism" (pp. 176–177).

Many feminists join Elizabeth Weed (1989) in her concern that "much of post-structural theory . . . in its desire to get beyond the opposition male/female, underestimates the full political weight of the categories" (pp. xvii–xviii). Used wisely, Foucault's conceptual tools enable the study of complex variations in the modes by which women are subjugated in different contexts and eras. But does his conceptual stress on anonymous, unstable dispersions of innumerable points of power permit adequate research or political movement aimed at powers that seem so extensively and durably amassed along nameable and numerable social-historical axes such as "gender"? Stuart Hall (1985) discerns a theoretical tendency to overemphasize how things fall apart, such that no center can hold:

> If you look at discourse theory for example—at post-structuralism or at Foucault—you will see there, not only the shift from practice to discourse, but also how the emphasis on difference—on the plurality of discourses, on the perpetual slippage of meaning, on the endless sliding of the signifier—is now pushed *beyond* the point where it is capable of theorizing the necessary unevenness of a complex unity, or even the "unity in difference" of a complex structure. I think that is why, whenever Foucault seems to be in danger of bringing things together (such as the many epistemic shifts he charts, which all fortuitously coincide with the shift from *ancien régime* to modern in France), he has to hasten to assure us

that nothing ever fits with anything else. The emphasis always falls on the continual slippage away from any conceivable conjuncture. (p. 92, emphasis in original)

Can we lump Foucault with "deconstructionists" who, argue "materialist" critics, metaphorize the materiality of social practices into an "idealist" textual medium of signs that slip in meaning across multiple discourses? After all, Foucault stresses a micro*physics* of practices that emerge historically in *social-material* contexts, which his genealogies enumerate. His assertion of "innumerability" may exaggerate to make an anti-reductive point; and if he seems to mime the teleological error of Marxism, but in the opposite direction (from consolidation to dispersion of power), it may express the excess of his anti-teleological intention: to refuse the idealized metafictions hidden in "historical materialisms." As Foucault (1977) states his Nietzchean genealogic: "Genealogy rejects the meta-historical deployment of ideal significations and indefinite teleologies. It opposes itself to the search for 'origins'" (p. 140).

This assertive *rejection* of "origins" suggests how Foucault's stress on dispersed "points" of power, rather than central "matrices," seeks a definitive break from critical traditions that invoke foundational historical forces by which structural matrices hold together. It clearly applies to meta-"laws" of history, for example, a Marxist teleology by which structures of social relation evolve in a dialectical sequence of distinct forms of economic class struggle, each the basis of sweeping change in institutions and consciousness. Moreover, such "laws" ultimately imply essential forces at the core of "human being"—for example, a productive "drive" to master nature's limitations through techno-economic progress. A foundational "human subject," with an originary "agency" to change historical formations in directions that express its telos, is suggested by Marx (1991a) when he says: "Men make their own history, but they do not make it . . . under circumstances chosen by themselves, but under circumstances directly encountered, given and transmitted from the past" (p. 5).

In an anti-foundational genealogic, to assume an originary agency reifies a metafiction about a "real" human essence. More important, such fictive "universal essences" subtly encode power differentials that critics should oppose. For example, many feminists deconstruct the Marxist telos as a tacitly masculinized "human drive" by which a tacitly feminized "nature" is properly dominated. (I amplify the deconstructive critique of foundations in the next section.) In what Benhabib (1991) calls "strong versions" of this negation of "human agency," no history-making "subject" can be assumed. In the above-cited interview, Foucault (1980) is asked whether "a certain kind of phenomenology" (later termed "Marxist phenomenology") is inimical to genealogical research. He answers:

I don't believe the problem can be solved by historicising the subject as posited by the phenomenologists, fabricating a subject that evolves through the course of history. One has to dispense with the constituent subject, to get rid of the subject itself, that's to say, to arrive at an analysis which can account for the constitution of the subject within a historical framework. And this is what I would call genealogy, that is, a form of history which can account for the constitution of knowledges, discourses, domains of objects etc., without having to make reference to a subject which is either transcendental in relation to the field of events or runs in its empty sameness throughout the course of history. (p. 117)

Genealogy refuses the rational, free-willing agency assumed, in liberal traditions, to reside at the seat of all human subjects: a timeless originator of changing historical knowledges, domains, and so forth. Genealogy also rejects neo-marxist assumptions of a phenomenological capacity by which human subjects, from within limiting conditions of social-structural relations (class, gender, race, etc.), remake themselves and their realities through social communication, intersubjectively recreating the knowledges and practices that accumulate historically and so act upon subjects with constitutive effects, but that originate from a transcendent human agency that impels this social evolution of subjective forms and contents. Rather than reify metafictions of a preconstituted and constituent agency, genealogy historicizes how such fabrications become underlying foundational principles in scientific and "commonsense" thought processes.

Genealogy sees subjectivity not as an originary force, but as a constituted effect of knowledge regimes ("discourses")—bound up in all practices, no matter how silently physical—that inscribe bodies and thus subjugate people through processes that produce subjectivity. Genealogy tends to stress *knowledge* as the stuff of *power*, since knowledge is the stuff of subjective experience. Without a corresponding emphasis on how knowledge forms originate in the activities of people, Foucault often seems unclear as to whether he theorizes "knowledge" as *a* dimension of the social materiality of power that abides in relations among people, or as *the* materiality of power relations. For example, Foucault (1979) says:

We should admit . . . that power and knowledge directly imply one another; that there is no power relation without the correlative constitution of a field of knowledge, nor any knowledge that does not presuppose and constitute at the same time power relations. These "power–knowledge relations" are to be analysed, therefore, not on the basis of a subject of knowledge who is or is not free in relation to the power system, but, on the contrary, the subject who knows, the objects to be known and the modalities of knowledge must be regarded as so many effects of these fundamental implications of power–knowledge and their historical transformations. (pp. 27–28)

Some critics argue that this slippery move from (1) a statement of linkage between "power relations" and "fields of knowledge," to (2) the conflation of "power" and "knowledge" in a single term, confounds the necessary distinction between power relations embodied in knowledge forms, and power relations among living social actors. Only in the latter, argue such critics, can we theorize an agency to produce and change historical forms of knowledge, and to infuse knowledge with power (I amplify this debate later in the chapter). Says Pierre Bourdieu (1993):

> Michel Foucault transfers into the "paradise of ideas" . . . the oppositions and antagonisms which are rooted in the relations between the producers and consumers of cultural works. . . . It is not possible to treat cultural order, the *episteme*, as an autonomous and transcendent system, if only because one is forbidden to account for changes which can unexpectedly take place in this separated universe, unless one attributes to it an immanent capacity suddenly to transform itself through a mysterious form of Hegel's *Selbstbewegung*. Like so many others, Foucault succumbs to that form of essentialism or, if one prefers, fetishism. (p. 179)

Bourdieu suggests that Foucault, in seeking to avoid "ideal" foundational premises such as "human agency," ironically lapses into a textualist sort of "idealism." I do not argue that Foucault (1983) does this consistently or finally; there are passages, especially in later writings, where he indeed seems to define a phenomenological agency of subjects to produce the knowledges and powers that inform subjectivity. But these are rare, undertheorized passages. I argue that a pressure toward idealist "power/knowledge" conflations associates with a strong refusal of foundations. In the next two sections, I examine how Judith Butler pushes this refusal even more insistently than does Foucault.

DECONSTRUCTING THE NORMS OF POWER HIDDEN WITHIN FOUNDATIONS

When power/knowledge transcribes from practical events to subjective dispositions, says Foucault (1977), "the body is the inscribed surface of events" (p. 148). Fraser (1989) elaborates: "For Foucault, the subject is merely a derivative product of a certain contingent, historically specific set of linguistically infused social practices that inscribe power relations upon bodies" (p. 56). Using the term "discourses" to indicate the symbolic systems (or "signs") that "linguistically" infuse practices with power/knowledge, Judith Butler (1990) says, in a Foucaultian vein, that "the subject is a consequence of certain rule-governed discourses that govern the intelligible invocation of identity" (p. 145).

Butler presses further; if genealogy refuses prediscursive essences, she argues, this should include Foucault's "body":

> By maintaining a body prior to its cultural inscription, Foucault appears to assume a materiality prior to signification and form. Because this distinction operates as essential to the task of genealogy as he defines it, the distinction itself is precluded as an object of genealogical investigation. Occasionally in his analysis . . . Foucault subscribes to a prediscursive multiplicity of bodily forces that break through the surface of the body to disrupt the regulating practices of cultural coherence. (p. 130)

That is, notions of a prediscursive body (1) as "surface" for discursive inscription, or (2) as repository of agentic "forces" that lie beneath and resist inscription, also must be seen as discursive fictions, since "the body posited as prior to the sign, is always *posited* or *signified* as *prior*" (Butler, 1993, p. 30, emphasis in original). Nor do we need to essentialize an "agency" outside the discourses that constitute "the subject," asserts Butler (1990):

> The question of locating "agency" is usually associated with the viability of the "subject," where the "subject" is understood to have some stable existence prior to the cultural field that it negotiates. Or, if the subject is culturally constructed it is nevertheless vested with an agency, usually figured as the capacity for reflexive meditation, that remains intact regardless of its cultural embeddedness. On such a model, "culture" and "discourse" *mire* the subject, but do not constitute that subject. . . . This kind of reasoning falsely presumes . . . that to be *constituted* by discourse is to be *determined* by discourse, where determination forecloses the possibility of agency. (pp. 142–143, emphasis in original)

In a later section, I examine how Butler theorizes the agency of a subject constituted yet not determined by discourse.

Along with universally "human" body/mind capacities such as "reflexive meditation," Butler rejects binarized "gender" propensities that some feminists essentialize as foundational grounds for women's agency to transform male institutions (e.g., women's capacity for "caring"). Says Butler (1990):

> There is no ontology of gender on which we might construct a politics, for gender ontologies always operate . . . as normative injunctions . . . setting the prescriptive requirements whereby sexed or gendered bodies come into cultural intelligibility. Ontology is, thus, not a foundation, but a normative injunction that operates insidiously by installing itself into political discourse as its necessary ground. (p. 148)

Supposed prediscursive essences of being (ontologies)—always posited *in* discourse—operate *insidiously* not simply as reifications of fictive traits, argues Butler, but because these presumably generic traits tacitly signify selective norms of identity, enjoining rather than challenging inequalities. The linguistic signs and syntaxes of theoretical premises are never neutral; they encode ethical and epistemological biases—noninclusive values and visions that impose criteria by which certain people are assigned "deviant" (and therefore subdominant) positions in relation to "normal." Foundations insidiously conceal normative biases within assertions of universal truth about nature or history. Butler thus calls for feminist research and politics that do not found themselves on ontologies, but vigorously *deconstruct* the norms latent in such metafictions.

In the next section, I join debates about whether humanist foundations are necessarily "insidious." There is certainly reason for deconstructive vigilance regarding how normative biases may lurk in discursively premised "human" traits. In much "progressive education," universally "human" agentic capacities are invoked to avoid harmful essentializations of gender- or race-based differences. Valerie Walkerdine, in *Schoolgirl Fictions* (1990), compellingly analyzes how the "agency" assumed in certain "progressive" policies and practices encodes norms that tacitly differentiate people. Walkerdine performs Butlerian deconstructions within a Foucaultian genealogy of power/knowledge systems that converge in post-1960s "progressive pedagogy" in Britain. She interrogates notions of agentic energies assumed as inborn in all children: an active curiosity, driven by a primal libido, that prompts learning by experience, developing into self-autonomous rationality if caring teachers nurture the innate urge to choose freely. Says Walkerdine (1990):

> These taken-for-granted assumptions have a complex history involving the production of a range of systems of categories which on the one hand are claimed to be universal, yet at the same time produce differences and effects on class and gender lines. Central to claims of universality are certain truths located in the body. (p. 33)

Walkerdine traces the categorical assumptions of "child-centered" pedagogy to diverse historical domains where relevant power/knowledge systems emerge, circulate, and intersect, accumulating many meanings and connections, often contradictory. For example, nineteenth-century Darwinians saw men as selectively fit for active, abstract reason that creates the culture of the species, and women for passive, concrete nurture that reproduces the species. This appears as a discursive motif within progressive pedagogical rhetoric; but so does the motif of a gender-neutral child-as-active-learner, held among

twentieth-century Piagetian psychologists. We can add Freudian psychoanalysis, Rousseauian romanticism, medical biology, cultural anthropology, welfare and legal systems, and so forth, as contributory nodes feeding the complex discursive confluence of "progressive pedagogy."

Educational policy is thus a rhetorical tapestry woven of many sub-
textual strands, which Walkerdine deconstructs to show the implicit norms
of differential power—threaded through more explicitly "universalist" statements—that discursively permeate spaces where teachers and students are
subjectively constituted. While a prominent strand of discourse defines a
gender-neutral "child" who develops autonomous reasoning by practicing
active choice in classrooms, a concomitant strand defines a "teacher" ("normally" female) who facilitates active choice by sustaining a nurturing
(passive/motherly) role. Parenthetically implicit in these interlacing discursive strands, a male/female power difference infuses the supposedly gender-
neutral categories of "teacher" and "child," with complex effects on those
who embody these engendering codes. Says Walkerdine (1990):

> But if passive, nurturant femininity [is] necessary to produce active learners, . . .
> the education of girls as "children" represents something of a problem. . . . By
> definition, active childhood and passive femininity exist at the intersection of
> competing discourses. For girls, therefore, their position as children must remain
> shaky and partial, continually played across by their position as feminine. Con-
> versely, for boys masculinity and childhood work to prohibit passivity. And in
> both cases passion and irrationality are constantly displaced. . . . If the normal
> child is self-regulating, any overt conflict, a failure of reason, will be displaced
> on to pathology. Yet the pathologies are different for different discourses; for
> example those regulating the normal child (male) and normal femininity. (pp.
> 34–35)

In this analysis, no subject is *ontologically* rational, gendered, and so on.
Walkerdine meets Foucault's (1980) genealogical mandate "to dispense with
the constituent subject" through "an analysis which can account for the constitution of the subject within a historical framework" (p. 117). She treats
biopsychic propensities not as foundations but as consequences, in Butler's
(1990) terms, "of certain rule-governed discourses that govern the intelligible
invocation of identity" (p. 145). The (male) child-as-active and (female)
teacher-as-nurturing are, as Butler says, not ontologies but normative injunctions, embedded in power/knowledge systems that valorize the "universally
rational subject"—an episteme that, according to Foucault, pervades the
"self"-disciplinary regularities of "humanist" institutions. But in subtexts
that help define the "rational subject" of progressive pedagogy, Walkerdine
(1990) finds that female, working-class, and non-white "subjects" are signified as (ab)normally lacking in rational self-control.

Walkerdine (1990) stresses a constituted rather than constituent subject not only in *genealogical analyses of policy rhetoric,* but in *ethnographic analyses of observed classroom events.* In one case, a female nursery school teacher contends with two 4-year-old boys. One boy ruins a girl's Lego construction, calling her "a stupid cunt." When the teacher intervenes, the boys curse her in turns, building on each other's insults: "Get out of it, Miss Baxter paxter," climbs to, "Get out of it, Miss Baxter the knickers paxter knickers, bum," to "Miss Baxter, show your knickers your bum off," to "Take all your clothes off, your bra off," and so on. Ms. Baxter responds mildly: "I think you're being very silly" and, "Sean, go and find something else to do, please" (p. 4).

Noting that readers of this transcript are shocked at how such small boys exert "so much power over the teacher," who tolerates their crudities, Walkerdine asks: "What is this power, and how is it produced?" (p. 5). She answers that the power dynamics between teacher and boys are partly bound up in "progressive pedagogical" injunctions whereby (male) children shall enact their libidinally driven choicefulness, and (female) teachers shall facilitate this agency. Thus the boys "can take the positions of men through language, and in so doing gain power which has material effects" (p. 5). The conceptual grammar of this sentence suggests that language bestows whatever "agency" determines power of position; male assertiveness is a material effect of discursive assignment, not an original cause of the male dominance coded in language.

And yet, classroom struggles are in practice always somewhat indeterminate, says Walkerdine—not because each subject possesses self-originating "agency," but because each is overdetermined by *multiple, contradictory discourses.* Thus, "although the teacher has an institutional position, she is not uniquely a teacher" (p. 5). Classroom encounters evoke "different discursive practices [which] have different and often contradictory histories," in some of which "women are relatively powerful," for example, "practices in which they signify as mothers (for instance in custody cases)" (p. 10). Diverse occasions of interplay among teacher and boys "serve to constitute them as a multiplicity of contradictory positions" (p. 10) in which, says Walkerdine:

> The "material" of the individual provides the potential to be the subject and object of a variety of discourses which produce that individual as sometimes powerful and sometimes powerless. There is in this model no unitary rational subject of progressivism . . . ; neither is the individual a "real" and essential kernel of phenomenological Marxism, whose outer skins are just a series of roles which can be cast off to reveal the true and revolutionary self. (p. 9)

I will later explore how Bronwyn Davies and Butler each try to theorize a nonfoundational ground for "revolutionary agency" precisely in the contradictory play across multiple discourses that constitute "the subject." I will compare these theorizations with "phenomenological Marxist" conceptions of agency.

I want to note that Walkerdine (1990) hesitates to theorize gender identity as entirely determined by discourse. She says:

> There remain certain problems of determination which do not seem to be totally resolved by this [discourse] analysis. Although this essay does raise problems for arguments which advocate direct and linear cause, the economic and the material are clearly crucial. . . . The confining of women to the quasi-domestic, while discursively powerful, remains a site of economic dependence. . . . Similarly, the girls and women do not take up *any* position in *any* discourse. . . . Positions available to them exist *only* within certain limits. These limits are material—not in the sense that they are directly *caused* by the materiality of the female body, but certainly by the limits within which that body can signify in current discursive practices. (p. 14, emphasis in original)

These statements are confoundingly circular in distinguishing "material" from "discursive" and in defining their interaction. I read Walkerdine to say that women and men (and women of different races, and so on) are positioned in structures of relational power that, while not rooted in material body differences, are at least partly grounded in *social-historically materialized* conditions (economic/domestic) that hold the nonlinear plays of multiple discourses within bounds. That is, "material" roughly means "*pre*discursive": There are historical grounds for relative powers of social position that exist independently of how they are signified in discourse, and that limit both (1) how discourses signify positional powers, and (2) how particular people access discursive senses of position. For if schoolgirls are not structurally situated at a prediscursive level, how do they or their teachers know which codes mark *their* subject positions, vis-à-vis boys, within the complexities of "active child" discourse?

By this logic, when oppositional structurings such as "gender" seem to have central weight in so much discourse, we dare assume they point beyond discourse, to historical-material grounds for these power relations. We need *not* assume that gender troubles are grounded in distinct male and female essences; but I will argue later that we *must* then assume an essential (prediscursive) agency of *human* (not gendered, raced, and so on) actors *socially* to materialize and transform historical forms of relational power and knowledge. In the next section, I explore how Nancy Fraser, despite a reluctance to posit "human" ontologies, raises problems with Butler's anti-foundationalism that, I argue, suggest the theoretical necessity of humanist foundational premises.

FEMINIST DEBATE OVER THE GROUNDS OF POWER, IDENTITY, AND AGENCY

In her essay "Contingent Foundations" (1991), Butler allows that "within feminism, it seems as if there is some political necessity to speak as and for *women*" (p. 159, emphasis in original). Yet such *strategic* invocations of wide support for political agendas always imply problematically generalized grounds for unity, argues Butler, whether biological (e.g., "There are those who claim that there is an ontological specificity to women as childbearers.") or social-historical ("There are others who understand maternity to be a social relation that is, under current social circumstances, the specific and cross-cultural situation of women."). Mothering hardly structures all women's lives, notes Butler; such premises function *normatively,* pathologizing many women, provoking "factionalization within the very constituency that is supposed to be *unified* by the articulation of its common element" (p. 160, emphasis in original). The problem extends to invocations of "black women's" identity, or other categories for positional intersections supposedly populated *en masse.* We face a paradox: The terms "feminism," "antiracism," and so on, in signifying common grounds for struggle against systemic inequities, simultaneously codify inequalities within fictive foundations for unity. Says Butler (1991):

> It seems that theory posits foundations incessantly, and forms implicit metaphysical commitments as a matter of course, even when it seeks to guard against it. . . . And yet are these "foundations," i.e. those premises that function as authorizing grounds, are they themselves not constituted through exclusions which, taken into account, expose the foundational premise as a contingent and contestable presumption? (p. 153)

Butler's *feminist* poststructuralist solution does not abandon politics in the name of "women," but stresses the eternal deferral of definitive grounds for named identity—the shifting interplay of multiple discourses that signify "grounds" for "women's" experience—as the endless source of strategically contingent grounds (contingent foundations) for "agency":

> If feminism presupposes that "women" designates an undesignatable field of differences, one that cannot be totalized or summarized by a descriptive identity category, then the very term becomes a site of permanent openness and resignifiability. I would argue that the rifts . . . among women over the content of the term . . . ought to be affirmed as the ungrounded ground of feminist theory. To deconstruct the object of feminism is not, then, to censure its usage, but . . . to release the term into a future of multiple significations, to emancipate it from the maternal or racialist ontologies to which it has been restricted, and to give

> it play as a site where unanticipated meanings might come to bear. . . . Paradoxi-
> cally, it may be only through releasing the category . . . from a fixed referent that
> something like "agency" becomes possible. (p. 160)

That is, constant deconstruction of the norms coded in "grounds" is the only
way continually to resist exclusionary power. Butler stresses a mobile unfixity
in the ways that *terms* reference grounding conditions for social-positional
power, without counter-stressing a "historical-material" massiveness and so-
lidity of power relations. By this resignificatory "agency," Foucault's (1990)
maxim—"power is exercised from innumerable points, in the interplay of
non-egalitarian and mobile relations" (p. 94)—is happily revised: Discursive
"points" of power/knowledge inter-rift to a groundless egalitarianism of
meanings too numerous and mutable to sustain any normative power.

Responding to "Contingent Foundations," Nancy Fraser (1991) faults
Butler for "uncritical, celebratory talk about women's 'differences'" (p. 175).
Butler's extreme anti-normative approach pushes an ethical and epistemological relativism in feminist research and politics—"a mystification," says Fraser (1991), of

> the underlying political problem . . . [of] whether there are real conflicts of inter-
> est among women of different classes, ethnicities, nationalities, and sexual orien-
> tations, conflicts so intractable as not to be harmonizable, or even finessable,
> within feminist movements. . . . The hard question feminist movements need to
> face is one Butler's proposal elides: Can "we" envision new social arrangements
> that would harmonize present conflicts? And if so, can "we" articulate "our"
> vision in terms that are sufficiently compelling to persuade other women—and
> men—to reinterpret their interests? (p. 175)

Fraser's questions are rhetorical. Regarding the reality of massive divisions among women, she says: "Certainly there *are* conflicts when interests
are defined relative to present forms of social organization; an example is the
clash in interests between professional white middle class First World women
and the Third World women of color they employ as domestic workers"
(1991, p. 175). Fraser clearly takes certain "forms of social organization,"
and their weight in defining interest and identity, as substantial in ways that
a stress on constant resignifications elides. Similar regard for the salient
weight of certain historical structurings provokes Walkerdine to invoke a prediscursive "materiality" of economic and gendered conditions that limit discursive senses of "subject position." If some forms of organization are too
weighty, historically, to be reduced to equivalence with numerous others, then
we must *pro*-normatively weigh our reformational meanings and values, says
Fraser: "Feminists *do* need to make normative judgments and to offer emancipatory alternatives. We are not for 'anything goes.' . . . Feminists need both

deconstruction *and* reconstruction, destabilization of meaning *and* projection of utopian hope" (p. 175, emphasis in original).

Fraser borrows a concept of "utopian hope" from an essay by Seyla Benhabib (1991), who theorizes a reconstructive process by which people in diverse, yet commonly subaltern, conditions of experience reflect on their histories and—moved by an "ethical impulse of utopia"—"articulate the normative principles of democratic action and organization in the present" (p. 147). But such reflexive, reorganizing agency, argues Benhabib (1991), must be premised in "situated" rather than "constituted" subjects:

> The situated and gendered subject is heteronomously determined but still strives toward autonomy. I want to ask how in fact the very project of female emancipation would even be thinkable without such a regulative principle of agency, autonomy and selfhood? (p. 140)

In contrast, says Benhabib, Butler's "Nietzschean . . . vision of the self as a masquerading performer" of discourses, with "no self behind the mask," is "a complete debunking of any concepts of selfhood, agency and autonomy"—that is, of reflexive capacities for ethical deliberation by history-making agents who, "vis a vis our own stories," are "author and character at once" (p. 140).

Joining the debate, Fraser (1991) argues that such capacities are indeed theoretically necessary, but need not presume an "ontologically intact reflexivity" (p. 172). Alluding to Butler's concept of a resignifying "agency," Fraser says: "It is clear from her paper that Butler also believes that people have what I shall call 'critical capacities'; we are not pre-programmed pawns but are able to engage in novel actions and to modify social conditions." And we can dissolve "the question, Where do critical capacities come from?" (if not ontological), says Fraser, since "it is perfectly possible to give an account of the cultural construction of critical capacities. Thus, nothing in principle precludes that subjects are *both* culturally constructed *and* capable of critique" (p. 172, emphasis in original). But Fraser offers no such account. When I later examine Butler's account of how constituted subjects enact "agency," I will argue that Butler fails to theorize constructed yet reconstructive critical capacities, and that such capacities do necessarily imply a *pre*constructed "humanness."

Fraser does challenge Butler's rejection of a foundational "subject" simply because it is normative. In characterizing the ontologically intact subject as insidious, argues Fraser (1991), Butler herself "makes normative claims about the relative merits of different *theories* of subjectivity" (p. 173, emphasis in original); that is, the "constituted subject," as signified in theoretical *discourse*, is also normative. Butler (1991) might reply that a "constituted subject" is the only epistemology compatible with a deconstructive methodo-logic by which, if theory "forms implicit metaphysical commitments as a matter of course," it simultaneously knows itself to do so and thus "exposes the foundational premise as a contingent and contestable presumption" (p. 153). I will argue later that such a notion of "contingently founded" theory finesses responsibility for tacit foundations that function noncontingently in Butler's theory of "agency," without which her argumentation falls apart.

Since norms are inevitable, argues Fraser, we must evaluate theoretical epistemologies as "better" or "worse." While agreeing that "foundationalist theories of subjectivity have often functioned as instruments of cultural im-perialism," Fraser (1991) asks: "But is this due to conceptual necessity or historical contingency?" As "emancipatory" instances, she offers "the French Revolution and the appropriation of its foundationalist view of subjectivity by the Haitian . . . Toussaint de l'Ouverture" (p. 173). (Butler might reply that the foundationalized subject of these "revolutions" functioned as a nor-mative ground for false, exclusionary "democracies," which deconstruction ungrounds.) If Fraser sees no conceptual need for a foundational subject, she sees no necessity against it. If foundational invocations sometimes yield "better" effects, Fraser (1991) sees this as a pragmatic use of "bits of cultural discourse whose meanings are subject to 'resignification" (p. 173). Like But-ler, she does not take foundational premises to reference *real* human ontol-ogies.

In arguing that neither humanist nor nonhumanist discourse is free of norms, Fraser questions the purpose of Butler's "deeply anti-humanist" lan-guage. Noting that "what I have been referring to as 'people's capacities' [Butler] describes as 'power's own possibility' and as an impersonal 'signi-fying process,'" Fraser asks: "Why should we use such as self-distancing id-iom? What are its theoretical advantages (and disadvantages)?" (p. 172). I will return to Fraser's questions when I argue that the "critical capacities" Fraser wants to describe as "people's" must in some way assume *human* ontologies, which Butler wants to avoid. In the next section, I probe how Bronwyn Davies's efforts to research "agency" in a Foucaultian/Butlerian mode—as a constituted by-product of classroom "discursive practices"—are interrupted by the very humanist assumptions that, I will argue, neither she nor Butler can avoid.

"AGENCY" AS A CONTINGENT PHENOMENON OF "DISCURSIVE" PRACTICES

At the outset of her theoretical-cum-ethnographic study, "Agency as a Form of Discursive Practice: A Classroom Scene Observed" (1990), Bronwyn Davies announces that she rejects the "definition . . . which assumes that to be a person is to have agency . . . in favour of a definition that shows the way in which agency may be discursively constructed as a positioning available to some but not to others" (p. 341). Davies hails Walkerdine and Lucey's (1989) deconstruction of how middle-class mothers teach children that, in making ethical choices, they enact an inborn freedom of desire. The authors, says Davies (1990), "argue that the ideal of individual freedom or agency is a . . . liberal humanist sham" (p. 341) by which children are constituted with self-regulating norms. Davies agrees that the idea of ontological choicefulness is a normative discursive trope. But if it is "not a necessary element of human action," she argues, agentic choice can be "a *contingent* element, depending upon the particular discursive practices in use, and the positioning of the person in those practices" (p. 344, emphasis in original). A person thus may "have the opportunity (discursively produced but nonetheless real in its effects) to make choices" (pp. 345–346).

Davies (1990) illustrates this "agency" through ethnographic analysis of observed classroom dialogue. For example, Mr. Good, a primary school teacher, asks John and Deb, a brother and sister, about their plane flight during vacation. Mr. Good hails John with a call of adventure: "Was that a thrill! Was that the first time you had been on an aircraft?" He merely asks Deb, "How did you like it on the aircraft?" (p. 351) By these differential addresses, Mr. Good assigns gendered dispositions, says Davies; and again by asking: "Hostesses look after you well? Were they good lookin'? Pretty? (. . . He looks back in John's direction.) Pretty hostess makes a flight very nice doesn't it?" (p. 352). In hailing John as (male) erotic adventurer, argues Davies, Mr. Good tacitly assigns hostess dispositions to Deb. Thus, "Deb is not constituted as one who has agency, one who can be thrilled by the daringness of the adventure of flying in a plane without familiar adults. Her fragility, and her future capacity to attract and care for men have been the only subject positions made available to her in the discourse through which her story is told" (p. 352).

It seems compelling to argue that boys are signified here as subjects who possess an eros-driven "agency" to initiate action, in dominant relation to passive, care-taking girls. Is this not Walkerdine and Lucey's "sham" agency? Do the codes in Mr. Good's speech position boys with greater choice of *how* to be active, or gendered? Davies wants to theorize "agency" as *really autonomous choosings*, emergent in and of "discursive practices." But how can effective choice emerge in classroom practice—yet not from ontological energies inherent in students or teachers, but as a discursive contingency—when the very discourse of "choice" encodes norms that construct "the chooser"?

Davies's ultimate answer recalls Walkerdine's (1990) argument that, in and across practical events, the discourses that constitute "subjects" are multiple and contradictory. Choice arises in the indeterminate tension between discrepant discursive determinants of a "self." In the subject position of "teacher," Mr. Good is *over*-determined with diverse ways of perceiving "students," which he transmits in classroom practice. In shifting moments of dialogue, Davies sees Mr. Good continually to switch codes. By turns that are more or less subconscious, he hails students as social change agents, and as members of status quo society; as having autonomy to make curricular choices, and as subjects of institutional authority; as equal agents in planning classroom agendas, and as if, by gender, they are not equal. The discourses operating in Mr. Good's speech, gestures, and so on, thus constitute students with "alternative ways of seeing and making sense of the world" (Davies, 1990, p. 358) and of themselves as worldly agents.

Mr. Good's sexist norms contradict his humanist ethic that students possess universal creative autonomy, by virtue of which he often does hail girls and boys equivalently. Consequently, says Davies, "the positioning of Deb as fragile does not preclude other positionings as agentic and powerful"; but "her access to . . . [such] positionings . . . will be fraught with tension" (p. 352). In this tension, Deb's "positioning in this classroom as gendered . . . is not a foregone conclusion, simply because Mr. Good hails her as such. . . . She may even, for the moment, align herself in both ways" (pp. 352–353). Despite Davies's initial claim that people may or may not be agentically positioned, depending on discursive contingencies, she seems to theorize an *inevitable* condition of agentic "choice" in the epistemic tensions that constitute any subjectivity (with perhaps greater indeterminacy in girls' subject positions). Says Davies (1990): "The discursive production of self as the unified coherent, humanist whole is always incomplete and fragmented because of the multiple and contradictory discourses to which each person is subject" (p. 346).

Is the "choice" contingent in multiple "self"-positionings a mere calculus of intersecting vectors, predictably resolved in the direction of the most forceful discourse? Or does an agentic "chooser," born from epistemic tensions, take egoic wings as an autonomous capacity to *reflect* how "I" have epistemological room to maneuver, and to *reconstruct* new self-dispositions? "The theoretical problem," says Davies (1990),

> is to understand how any desire can run against the grain of discursive practices through which that which is desirable is located/named/defined. From whence comes the struggle to redefine and resist? Does one simply rebel against one discursive practice one has learned with another that one has also learned is correct? (p. 345)

To answer "from whence comes" struggle, Davies simply asserts a potential, presumably "within" the constituted "self,"

> to recognize the personal and social implications of each discursive practice in which we are caught up—either as speakers or hearers. This allows the possibility of refusal of any particular discourse or one's positioning within it, the possibility of choices between discourses, or the bringing to bear of one set of discursive practices on another to modify them and the positions being made available within them. (p. 346)

But *how* do capacities to reflect upon, refuse, and recombine positions emerge *in and of discourses* that constitute "one's" practical embodiment of "self"-contradictions? Can a spontaneous generation of self-reorganizing intelligence arise with no basis in a human organism prediscursively equipped to take in and remake coherent sense? Anti-foundational stress on a *discursively* constructed "self" brackets biocognitive ontologies; yet Davies never elaborates how self-*re*constructive capacities arise purely in and of discourse. While she probably wants to avoid an organic human basis for critical capacities, I argue that such ontologies are implicit in passages where Davies stresses how *people* take in and remake discourse in living *social* communication. To begin with, Davies (1990), like Walkerdine, sees the need to theorize *historical-social* limits by which "all available discursive practices are not something any individual can automatically take up" (p. 342). Rather,

> each person brings to any episode of collaborative constitution of the world . . . their accumulated personal history—their sense of themselves not only as they are positioned in the present moment but also of themselves as persons who can or cannot be positioned in that way, i.e. as one who is located in certain ways within the social and moral order. (p. 342)

I read two linked motifs in this statement that, I argue, imply "Marxist phenomenological subjects" more than Foucaultian "constituted subjects": (1) In the distinct practical conditions to which one is born and through which one moves in life, one is *always already positioned* in a materialized historical order of social/moral power relations that structure one's access and receptivity to discursive senses of "self"-position; and (2) present social interactions, while prefigured by meanings and relations from the past, are *always also moments of living praxis* in which people collaboratively recreate meanings, practices, and relations. Regarding the first motif, Davies (1990) elaborates:

> The person is a person by virtue of the fact that they use the discursive practices of the collectives of which they are a member. Such collectives might include

children, boys, students, a particular classroom, one's family, etc. Each person can only speak from the positions made available within those collectives through the recognized discursive practices used by each collective. (p. 343)

"Collectives" that position one's use of discourses range from intimate local sites (e.g., classrooms) to broad "memberships" (e.g., boys). While Davies, like Butler, often does treat social "memberships" as matters of discursive definition, in her references to discursive practices "*of* the collectives," "used *by* each collective," and so on, she, like Fraser, also seems to assume underlying historical forms of organization that structure one's practical tendencies to take up certain personal identities from among many that are discursively available.

Whether "collectives" are theorized as discursive and/or prediscursive grounds for self-positionings, Davies does not want to theorize "subjects" who are so positionally determined that they lack self-recreative agency. She asks: "What is it of one's own, then, that can stand outside of and beyond the collective? Choice within the terms provided by others would seem to preclude something of one's own" (1990, p. 342). I have shown how Davies answers that an indeterminate *opportunity* for choice subsists in the over-determined multiplicity of discourses that constitute "the subject." But this does not say how a *capacity* to integrate newly intelligible self-meanings arises in and of the deconstructive clash of discursive terms (Butler's constant "riftings"). Perhaps the press of this "origin question"—From whence comes *reconstructive* agency?—induces Davies to shift (without noting an inconsistency) between (1) arguments in a Foucaultian/Butlerian mode, refusing an originary agency of "subjects" constructed in discursive practices; and (2) arguments in a Bakhtinian/marxian mode, conceiving *"discourse" as constructive communication that originates in an agency of people* who practice. Says Davies (1990):

But, as Bakhtin points out, language is spoken not only *as if it were* one's own— but in speaking is taken on *as* one's own. One's words carry the accretion of others' past usages but are not recitations—rather they are the available fabric with which each person does being a member of the various collectives in which they participate in their own particular way. (p. 342, emphasis in original)

Davies quotes Bakhtin, who says that "language . . . is populated—over-populated—with the intentions of others," but that live speech is a "moment of appropriation," a "seizure and transformation" that forces language "to submit to one's own intentions and accents" through a tensely negotiated social process in which "consciousness lies on the borderline between oneself and the other" (pp. 342–343)—that is, "others" from the historical past who have populated discursive terms with certain senses of meaning, and "others" in the social present who, from diverse positions, put competing spins on popularly used terms.

Davies here joins a theory in which discourse transforms *not* in and of its own significatory stuff, but through "intentional" actors who, at subtle levels of consciousness, sense how they are subjectively constituted by signs populated with many coded intents. New discourse emerges from a human impetus to make sense of self-in-situation and to struggle toward complex meaning in social communication with others who are positioned to see things variously. In invoking Bakhtinian dialogism, Davies assumes a transformative agency that inheres in *people* more foundationally than in discourses that people produce, although the available fabric of new discursive production is a polysemic weave of past communications, carrying the constraints of historical patterns.

In her conclusion, Davies lists "resources" necessary for "agency" to emerge in practice. It is telling that she lists "discursive" *and* "social" resources. The latter type, says Davies, entails an "ability to mobilize the relevant discourses," and "shifts the focus from the discursive practices to the interactive others" (p. 360). That is, it shifts focus from the "discursivity" to the "sociality" of practices. But this social-interactionist phenomenology assumes a humanly founded agency that violates Foucaultian brackets, vexing Davies's anti-foundational mandate to define "agency" not as an inborn capacity of people, but as a contingent by-product of discourse.

Do these humanist vexations result from theoretical carelessness or conceptual necessity? Can Butler vindicate Fraser's claim that a self- and world-transforming "agency"—comprising reflexive and reconstructive "critical capacities"—is accountable within a theory of a constituted subject? In the next section, I argue that Butler's account of a constituted "agency" fails to elaborate such capacities as emergent in and of discourse. Rather, she subtly relies on what I will call "human/social" ontologies, despite her efforts to avoid them.

A HUMAN/SOCIAL ONTOLOGY VERSUS AN
ONTOLOGY OF MEANING

It is worth comparing how Marx and Butler seek to transcend a philosophical dualism—materialism/idealism, objectivism/subjectivism—by stressing *active materialization*. In *The Theses on Feuerbach*, Marx (1991b) says:

> The chief defect of all hitherto existing materialism . . . is that the thing, reality, sensuousness, is conceived only in the form of the *object or of contemplation*, but

not as *sensuous human activity, practice*, not subjectively. Hence, in contradistinc-
tion to materialism, the *active* side was developed abstractly by idealism—which,
of course, does not know real, sensuous activity as such. (p. 121, emphasis in
original)

In *Bodies That Matter* (1993), Butler notes approvingly that, in Marx's thesis,
"activity is understood as constitutive of materiality itself. . . . The materiality of objects . . . is in no sense static, spatial, or given, but is constituted
in and as transformative activity" (p. 250). Indeed, when Butler insists that
"to return to matter requires that we return to matter as a *sign* which in its re-
doublings and contradictions enacts an inchoate drama of sexual difference"
(p. 49), she defends against charges of "linguistic idealism" by offering a "notion of matter, not as site or surface, but as *a process of materialization that
stabilizes over time to produce the effect of boundary, fixity, and surface we call
matter*" (p. 9, emphasis in original).

As Fraser notes, Butler speaks of a *significatory* process, whereas Marx
stresses *sensuous human* activity. Fraser questions the point of Butler's
"deeply anti-humanist" idiom. I answer that Butler thus seeks to elide human
origins for the sensuousness that abides in social practices and stabilizes in
institutional systems of practical sense (power/knowledge, discourse). I argue
that a costly "linguisticism" results, despite Butler's denials. Butler insists
that critics misread her to say "the materiality of bodies is simply and only a
linguistic effect that is reducible to a set of signifiers." Rather, she seeks

to understand materiality as that which is bound up with signification from the
start. . . . To posit by way of language a materiality outside of language is still
to posit that materiality, and the materiality so posited will retain that positing
as its constitutive condition. (1993, p. 30)

Again, there are overlaps with Marx's concept of materiality as *sensuous* activity. Signification is a process of making *sense* in *actively making* "things."
Like Marx, Butler says that no "thing" materializes—whether objects or
meanings—without active linguistic sensation that sediments into and con-
figures "it." In sensuous practice, all phenomena are known, and thus constituted, in the active subjectivity of language (or signs).

Like Butler, Marx was wary of what Foucault (1977) calls "the metahis-
torical deployment of ideal significations" (p. 140). Indicting Feuerbach for
not breaking far enough from German idealism, Marx (1991b) says that
"Feuerbach resolves the religious essence into the *human* essence. But the
human essence is no abstraction inherent in each single individual. In its
reality it is the ensemble of the social relations" (p. 122, emphasis in original).
Marx here means relational matrices (for *neo*-marxists, class, gender, race,

etc.) that exist as historically sedimented grounds for positional forms of subjectivity. Yet we have seen how Marx signifies an inherent "human" condition for the *sensuous* agency of *active* relations among people (which stabilize over time in historical-material matrices). Perhaps Marx means that only in social interactions does a basic human sensuousness come alive. But the invocation of "humanness" as an anthropological first principle (foundation) of socially emergent sense is apparent when Marx and Engels (1991) say:

> Language is as old as consciousness, language *is* practical consciousness that exists also for other men, and for that reason alone it really exists for me personally as well; language, like consciousness, only arises from the need, the necessity, of intercourse with other men. (p. 51)

I read this to say more than that people necessarily communicate in encountering each other. Social communication activates a *need and capacity to make collaborative sense*: to make discourse in social intercourse. That this self-actualizing need/capacity to produce coherent social sense is in and of human "species being" (perhaps we could call it an evolutionary biocognitive capacity, and thus "historical"), is further indicated when Marx (1978) says:

> When I am engaged in activity which I can perform in direct communication with others—then I am social because I am active as a [hu]man. Not only is the material of my activity given to me as a social product (as is even the language in which the thinker is active); my own existence is social activity. . . . My general consciousness is only the theoretical shape of that of which the living shape is the real community, the social fabric. (p. 86)

In social communication, language is an active process, accessing and rematerializing linguistic products, weaving the epistemic fabric of future communication and practical consciousness. But if the circumstantial condition for active language is social engagement, the ontological condition is a basic species being: a human sensuous capacity because of which "I" am socially active.

Butler (1993), in her anti-normative critique of foundations, refuses to prefix a human condition outside of any originating linguistic action. Doing so constitutes "humanness" *in* language, argues Butler, "such that the human is . . . produced over and against the inhuman . . . through a set of . . . radical erasures" (p. 8). Nor will she conceive power relations such as "gender," in language or society, as effects of "human act or expression"; on the contrary, "the [discursive] matrix of gender relations is prior to the emergence of the 'human'" (p. 7), as its constitutive condition. Butler grants that "there is an 'outside' to what is constructed by discourse, . . . for the point has never been that 'everything is discursively constituted'" (p. 8). But she warns that "insofar as the extra-discursive is delimited, it is formed by the very discourse from which it seeks to free itself"—a formation "that includes and excludes, that decides . . . the stuff of the object to which we can refer," always with "some violence, . . . enforcing a certain criterion" (p. 11).

Whatever may exist "outside" discourse, Butler seems to conceive *power* only as the power by which discursively delimited "outsides" enforce normative exclusions. To grant an extra-discursive but undelimitable "outside" thus contributes nothing to research of power, which Butler might as well theorize as only an effect of language. She cannot address how power also might lie outside language, whether in a sensuous power (agency) of people to materialize meaning and practice, or in historically stabilized powers of social-institutional position—including powers by which epistemes linked to certain positions hold centrality over others in "commonsense" uses of terms such as "woman." Rather, Butler confounds power that abides in *social relations among people* with power in and of language. Consider the following passage, in which Butler (1993) seems moved by a need to conceptualize a "social-political" locus of power outside discourse, in order to account for what constrains the agency to "resignify" weighty and persistent forms of power relation:

> If performativity is construed as that power of discourse to produce effects through reiteration, how are we to understand the limits of such production, the constraints under which such production occurs? Are these social and political limits on the resignifiability of gender and race, or are these limits that are, strictly speaking, outside the social? Are we to understand this "outside" as that which permanently resists discursive elaboration, or is it a variable boundary set and reset by specific political investments? (p. 20)

Butler may seem to invoke a social-political domain outside discourse, exerting limits on the ways "gender" and "race" can signify. But she conflates "social-political" and "discursive" by (1) asking if these limits, at first suggested as effects of a social-political "outside," are "outside the social" (i.e., in some foundational essence), and then (2) asking if that "outside" is not, after all, a "discursive" elaboration that is also a "political" investment. In slippery rhetorical moves, Butler blurs analytic distinctions between "social-political" and "discursive." Dorothy Smith (1993) calls such circularity a "discursive solipsism . . . , confining discourse to the phenomenal world of discourse. Where is the social if not in discourse?" (p. 36). Pointing always recursively back to discursive powers to signify "gender" and "race," Butler seems lost when venturing outside her usual brackets around the question: From whence comes power to hold discursive assignments within bounds?

"Confining the subject to discourse," says Smith (1993), "precludes exploring the beyond discourse that substructs and organizes it" (p. 36).

Smith implies a theoretical need for an ontological human/social agency, as in marxian/Bakhtinian phenomenology, by which subjects are capable, in communicative interactions, of endowing practice and knowledge with cohesive organization. She sees no logic by which a capacity to produce complex, yet coherent, systems of language and practice emerges in and of language. Such organizing capacities are grounded not in an actorless "ontology of meaning," says Smith (1993), but in the "social ontology," which is

> an interplay or dialectic in which people coordinate and concert their activities with each other directly or indirectly. The local concerting of people's activities is always . . . contributing to the extended social relations of society and economy. . . . Forms of knowledge . . . are themselves socially organized and enter into the organization of social relations. (pp. 42–43)

Earlier, I endorsed Fraser's critique of Butler's anti-normative stress on endless significations of positional power, which says nothing about how power coheres in fairly extensive, stable forms of social organization (which Butler herself gropes to explain in asking what limits the resignifiability of "gender" and "race"). Like Smith, Fraser sees a need to theorize "subjects" capable of communicative concertings, feeding extended social power relations that do hold form (for better or worse). Yet like Butler, Fraser upholds a postfoundational break from philosophies of consciousness that assume "ontologically intact reflexivity." If she prefers a more "humanized" idiom, and refutes Butler's claim that foundational humanist premises always function insidiously, she still sees "human essences" as "bits of cultural discourse" that can carry helpful or harmful normative valences, depending on context. Unlike Smith, she believes that we can theorize purely constituted subjects who are nonetheless capable of coordinative social action (agency).

In what follows, I argue that the "critical capacities" that Fraser, Davies, Smith, and even Butler seem to require cannot be theorized purely in and of "constituted" subjectivities. I build my argument as I interrogate Butler's elaborated theory of the "agency" of a "constituted subject." Earlier, I cited Butler's (1990) claim that it is fallacious to presume (as Smith does) "that to be *constituted* by discourse is to be *determined* by discourse, where determination forecloses the possibility of agency" (p. 143, emphasis in original). Here is how she refutes this presumption:

> The subject is not *determined* by the rules through which it is generated because signification is *not a founding act, but rather a regulated process of repetition* that both conceals itself and enforces its rules precisely through the production of substantializing effects. In a sense, all signification takes place within the orbit

of the compulsion to repeat; "agency," then, is to be located within the possibility of a variation on that repetition. If the rules governing signification not only restrict, but enable the assertion of alternative domains of cultural intelligibility, i.e. new possibilities for gender that contest the rigid codes of hierarchical binarisms, then it is only *within* the practices of repetitive signifying that a subversion of identity becomes possible. The injunction *to be* a given gender produces necessary failures, a variety of incoherent configurations that in their multiplicity exceed and defy the injunction by which they are generated. Further, the very injunction to be a given gender takes place through discursive routes: to be a good mother, to be a heterosexually desirable object, to be a fit worker, in sum, to signify a multiplicity of guarantees in response to a variety of demands all at once. The coexistence or convergence of such discursive injunctions produces the possibility of a complex reconfiguration and redeployment; it is not a transcendental subject who enables action in the midst of such a convergence. There is no self that is prior to the convergence or who maintains "integrity" prior to its entrance into this conflicted cultural field. There is only a taking up of the tools where they lie, where the very "taking up" is enabled by the tool lying there. (1990, p. 145, emphasis in original)

Like Davies, Butler defines "agency" as an *in*determinacy that inheres in the convergent multiplicity of discursive positionings that *over*-determine "the subject." Butler refines this model with a repetition compulsion: Identities are redundantly enjoined and performed in the instituted practices of schools, and so on. Butler avoids Bakhtinian notions that the original impulse of instituted compulsions comes from people. In *Bodies That Matter* (1993), she says: "There is no power, construed as a subject, that acts, but only . . . a reiterated acting that *is* power in its persistence and instability. This is less an 'act,' singular and deliberate, than a nexus of power and discourse that repeats or mimes the discursive gestures of power." In courtrooms, for example, it is "neither in the subject of the judge nor in his will, but in the citational legacy" that "a contemporary 'act' emerges," and "the speech act . . . derives its binding power" (p. 225, emphasis in original).

Butler avoids a phenomenology of *inter*active reconstruction, as in Davies's "episodes of collaborative constitution of the world." In Bakhtin's *socially* incited "speech acts," people in courts or classrooms repeat citational legacies from personal and institutional pasts, but also "appropriate the word, adapting it to [their] own semantic and expressive intention" (Bakhtin quoted in Davies, 1990, p. 343). They renegotiate meaning, each from their own positional nexus, at a level of sensuous human awareness that Marx calls "practical consciousness": a more or less unconscious level of strategic "intention" that generates intelligible new forms of sense. In Butler's "acts," new sense generates from a "human"-less power/knowledge nexus of citational legacies, transforming in and of their own linguistic "materiality."

Do such transformations entail reflexive or integrative capacities? But-ler's "agency" seems rather a *mechanical slippage*: If "power" is a repetitive performance of citational legacies, "agency" is an *unintended* misper-formance—a "necessary failure" of exact repetition, spinning off "a variety of incoherent configurations." There is the most minimal theoretical need for bodily people here: In channeling discursive injunctions, Mr. Good and his students animate dances of identity; "they" invest performances with life, but nothing more. They bring no prior capacity to "maintain 'integrity,'" by which they collaboratively grasp competing senses in the "conflicted cultural field," and improvise new sense in struggles for consensus. Butler's "agency" to produce change inheres in discursively impelled dances that reiterate choreographic codes, but with *accidental* missteps that "exceed and defy the injunction by which they are generated."

Perhaps to avoid a prediscursive, universal, biosensory component in the "human/social" development of reflexive and integrative capacities (entail-ing memory-storing "bodies"), Butler elides such capacities in her model of agency. But her slippage mechanism says nothing about what substructs and organizes relations, practices, knowledges, and subjectivities; rather, it pre-dicts the steady entropy of "self" and social cohesions. Butler suggests that institutionally binding power systems emerge as "substantializing effects" (1990, p. 145) of a signifying "process of materialization that stabilizes over time" (1993, p. 9). But in the constant resignification of incoherent variety, what stabilizes the process over time? What gravities sustain "rigid binar-isms" in the excessive play of signs? What synergies enable "a complex recon-figuration and redeployment"? What agency selects and integrates the many performative failures into "alternative domains of cultural intelligibility"? As quoted earlier, Butler raises such questions herself. But she begs answering; she only elaborates an "agency" of endless transformative slippages toward a universe of stardust, without massive and cohesive stars.

I recall Hall's (1985) assertion that "the emphasis on . . . the plurality of discourses, on the perpetual slippage of meaning, on the endless sliding of the signifier" goes "*beyond* the point where it is capable of theorizing . . . the 'unity in difference' of a complex structure" (p. 92). I recall Bourdieu's (1993) argument that Foucault, when failing to stress "oppositions . . . rooted in the relations between the producers and the consumers of cultural works," succumbs to a "fetishism" in which epistemes appear to embody the power (agency) of their own production, such that "one is forbidden to account for changes . . . in this separated universe," except by "an immanent capacity suddenly to transform itself" (p. 179). Butler accounts for how power/knowl-edge systems erode in the immanent slippage of significatory tensions, but not how the slippages implode in complex unities that bind tensions.

It is not enough simply to say that "the very 'taking up'" (intelligible reconfiguration) of "the tool" (plural discursive legacies) is "enabled by the tool lying there." Butler must account for *how* incoherent shards of sense meaningfully reconfigure. Her clever stress on *active process* goes only so far. To endow received discursive "legacies"—however compulsively re-enactive—with "rules" that mysteriously enable slippages to reconverge in newly intelligible normative regimes is, in Marxist terms, to fetishize commodified circulations of knowledge with capacities for evaluative sensibility that inhere in the *organic, transformative sensuousness of co-laboring people.* We cannot evade a basic origin premise: Without an originary materializing agency, there are no "legacies" of sense "to begin with."

I argue that when Butler invokes "the possibility of a complex reconfiguration," she summons ontologies that Davies noisily contends with, but that are artfully absent–present in Butler's anti-humanist idiom. A strong discourse emphasis, says Smith (1993), is quietly haunted by a "not-altogether-discourse" that

> appears in oddly undeconstructed forms such as "dominance," "imperialism," "knowledge/power," that operate in the text like the struts of a tent that hold the fabric up. Often these . . . conceptions trail phantoms of discursive pasts, critical theory or Marxist in particular, that are repudiated or rewritten as discursive expressions. . . . Postmodern feminism relies on its unmentionables, relies on what it "knows" but denies that we can know. (p. 36)

Butler relies on phantoms of neo-marxist phenomenology, I argue, for which she must take responsibility as not-quite-contingent foundations. She does not simply theorize "agency" as a play of *in*coherent effects, contingent in discursive enactments. She also alludes to effective coherencies that she lacks conceptual tools to explain. I suggest that critical theorists do better to explicate "bracketed" ontologies than to finesse them.

CONCLUSION: HYPOTHESIZING A NONCONTINGENT "HUMANNESS"

> Praxeology is a universal anthropology which takes into account the historicity . . . of cognitive structures, while recording the fact that agents *universally* put to work such historical structures . . . which they may even radically transform under definite structural conditions.
> —Pierre Bourdieu, "The Purpose of Reflexive Sociology"

Foucault (1980) wants research that "can account for the constitution of the subject"—and of "knowledges, discourses, domains of objects" that constitute the subject—"within a historical framework," but without requiring a "subject as posited by the phenomenologists . . . that evolves through the course of history" (p. 117). That is, we must not invoke universal *human* capacities, "transcendental in relation to the field of events," by which agents *inter*subjectively (phenomenologically) *put to work* the legacy of constitutive knowledges, communicatively reweaving the discursive fabric—and so driving their own cognitive evolution—in the (inter)course of *social*-historical activity.

In their school studies, Walkerdine and Davies adopt this call to account for "human agencies" as constituted, not original. Yet they also heed feminist calls to account for how people's relational positionings seem to polarize within *complex but cohesive* power "structurings" (or "matrices") such as we name "gender," at levels of discourse, practice, institution, and identity. These studies were thus opportune for exploring theoretical/political tensions in the Foucaultian-cum-feminist commitments that frame them: tensions that seem less finessable in ethnographic accounts—which must "speak to" the on-site presence of socially active *people*—than in Butler's elegant philosophical discussion of "signifying" activities. In trying to account for how the numerous and contradictory injunctions that people perform still manage to hold form, I argued, Walkerdine and Davies verge toward theories of a phenomenological agency within structural limits. And in striving to avoid such departures from Foucaultian brackets, I argued, Butler accounts only for slippages away from cohesion—which is not finally acceptable even to Butler (1990), who still alludes to "the possibility of a complex reconfiguration and redeployment" (p. 145), but does not account for *how* this is possible.

There is a clear need to theorize reflexive and integrative agentic capacities; and I see no way to do so without implying a preconstituted "human" component. To stress the "historicity" by which "discursive" practices shift cohesively begs the question: What agency *sub*structs cohesions? In coping with this gap, much "*post*structuralist" research secondarily stresses the "sociality" of discursive practices—with fuzzy acknowledgment, if any, that this entails constructive communication among people. But this still avoids saying what choreographs social/discursive slippages into newly intelligible performances of "self" and "community." If organized, concerted change is not an immanent, mystical "power" (or "agency") of decaying legacies, it must stem from a *human*/social/discursive *sensuosity* by which people, in practice, organically "seize" the indeterminacy of terms, making them sensible (appropriate) in new events.

If using the term "human" enacts selective norms, this is not solved by mysterious hints of an unnamable ground for "possible reconfigurations" of "discursive" practice. Such "bracketing" of foundational terms hardly opens meaningful debate over what the missing ontological term might signify; nor do *interm*inable (and thus meaningless!) resignifications that avoid rather than void Fraser's hard questions about weighty power divisions. Bracketing all inquiry into ontological components of "self"-development makes it impossible to research *how* "gender troubles" (and other nameable power relations) gain "rigid binary" stability in discourses, personal identities, practical contexts (schools), or institutional apparatuses (school systems). Benhabib (1992) argues that mere "decoding of metaphors and tropes about the self" cannot address "*how* the human infant becomes a social self, regardless of the cultural and normative content which defines selfhood." We cannot ask "how a human infant can become the speaker of an infinitely meaningful number of sentences," or "how every human infant can become the initiator of a unique life-story, of a meaningful tale." These questions point to human capacities at the origin of linguistic practices, not vice versa, suggests Benhabib. To address them requires "serious interchange between philosophy and social science" (pp. 217–218, emphasis in original).

Benhabib's questions suggest that development of seemingly universal *meaning-making* capacities has something to do with how a *precontingent* infant humanness enters contingencies of given socializing conditions, including languages that signify "humanness." I suggest we take the sign "human" not as Butler's "insidious" positing that must be neutralized by endless contingency, nor as Fraser's sometimes contingently positive "bit of cultural discourse," but as a site of meaningful *hypotheses* about what *is* noncontingently, ontologically "agentic." Like "gravity" in physics, such an ideal sign addresses hard-to-explain cohesions that cannot be ignored. Its use in social science discourse is, of course, variable, contingent, never capturing "humanness as such." But seriously daring to imagine what "human biosensory" ontologies might help explain social-institutional and cognitive *systems* of power (which Butler herself dares not ignore) does not preclude concern for how norms accumulate, *social*-historically, in the signs in which imagination is active. The *word* "human" is not sacred: If overly baggaged by negative historical valences, other terms can usefully hypothesize *ontologies for which signs cannot be the only "constitutive condition" that "matters,"* since coherency across signs is not explained by signs "in themselves."

My "conclusionary" arguments leave questions hanging: What precise human/social-ontological hypotheses might best help in theorizing reflexive and integrative capacities of subjects who are deeply but not utterly determined by situations? By what human/social-historical processes do gender, race, class, and so forth, become "structuring" determinants of "self" perception and performance? By what "social science" methodologic can we appreciate that the language of research always refracts what it purports to represent, yet still seek to "objectify" social power relations? I here offer two elliptical clues to my answers: (1) I draw on what I call *social-epistemological standpoint theories,* especially those of Bourdieu (1992) and Haraway (1988); and (2) I retain Butler's "agency" of performative slippages within discursively over-determined "subjectivities," *but* I revise this model by premising certain re-integrative biosensory capacities, which I take from Bourdieu's (1977) model for a subject/agent: "the *habitus.*"

REFERENCES

Benhabib, S. (1991). Feminism and postmodernism: An uneasy alliance. *Praxis International, 11*(2), 137–149.

Benhabib, S. (1992). *Situating the self: Gender, community and postmodernism in contemporary ethics.* New York: Routledge.

Best, S., & Kellner, D. (1991). *Postmodern theory: Critical interrogations.* New York: Guilford Press.

Bourdieu, P. (1977). *Outline of a theory of practice.* Cambridge: Cambridge University Press.

Bourdieu, P. (1992). The purpose of reflexive sociology (The Chicago Workshop). In P. Bourdieu & L. J. D. Wacquant, *An invitation to reflexive sociology* (pp. 62–215). Chicago: University of Chicago Press.

Bourdieu, P. (1993). *The field of cultural production: Essays on art and literature.* New York: Columbia University Press.

Butler, J. (1990). *Gender trouble: Feminism and the subversion of identity.* New York: Routledge.

Butler, J. (1991). Contingent foundations: Feminism and the question of "Postmodernism." *Praxis International, 11*(2), 150–165.

Butler, J. (1993). *Bodies that matter: On the discourse limits of "sex."* New York: Routledge.

Davies, B. (1990). Agency as a form of discursive practice: A classroom scene observed. *British Journal of Sociology of Education, 11*(3), 341–361.

Foucault, M. (1977). Nietzsche, genealogy, history. In *Language, counter-memory, practice: Selected essays and interviews* (D. F. Bouchard, Ed.; D. F. Bouchard & S. Simon, Trans.) (pp. 139–164). Ithaca, NY: Cornell University Press.

Foucault, M. (1979). *Discipline and punish: The birth of the prison* (A. Sheridan, Trans.). New York: Vintage.

Foucault, M. (1980). Truth and power. In C. Gordon (Ed. and Trans.), *Power/Knowledge: Selected interviews and other writings by Michel Foucault 1972–1977* (pp. 109–133). New York: Pantheon.

Foucault, M. (1983). The subject and power. In H. L. Dreyfus & P. Rabinow, *Michel Foucault: Beyond structuralism and hermeneutics* (2nd ed.) (pp. 208–226). Chicago: University of Chicago Press.

Foucault, M. (1990). *The history of sexuality: Vol. 1. An introduction* (2nd ed.) (R. Hurley, Trans.). New York: Vintage.

Fraser, N. (1989). *Unruly practices: Power, discourse and gender in contemporary social theory.* Minneapolis: University of Minnesota Press.

Fraser, N. (1991). False antitheses: A response to Seyla Benhabib and Judith Butler. *Praxis International, 11*(2), 166–177.

Hall, S. (1985). Signification, representation, ideology: Althusser and the post-structuralist debates. *Critical Studies in Mass Communication, 2*(2), 91–144.

Haraway, D. (1988). Situated knowledges: The science question in feminism and the privilege of partial perspective. *Feminist Studies, 14*(3), 575–599.

Marx, K. (1978). *Economic and philosophical manuscripts of 1844.* In R. C. Tucker (Ed.), *The Marx–Engels Reader* (2nd ed.). New York: Norton.

Marx, K. (1991a). *The 18th Brumaire of Louis Bonaparte.* New York: International Publishers.

Marx, K. (1991b). The theses on Feuerbach. In K. Marx & F. Engels, *The German ideology: Part One* (C. J. Arthur, Ed.) (pp. 121–123). New York: International Publishers.

Marx, K., & Engels, F. (1991). *The German ideology: Part One* (C. J. Arthur, Ed.). New York: International Publishers.

Smart, B. (1986). The politics of truth and the problem of hegemony. In D. C. Hoy (Ed.), *Foucault: A critical reader* (pp. 157–173). Oxford: Basil Blackwell.

Smith, D. (1993). *The out-of-body experience: Contradictions for feminism.* Paper distributed by the author at a seminar at the University of Wisconsin–Madison. (Available from the Ontario Institute for Studies in Education)

Walkerdine, V. (1990). *Schoolgirl fictions.* London: Verso.

Walkerdine, V., & Lucey, H. (1989). *Democracy in the kitchen: The regulation of mothers and the socialization of daughters.* London: Virago.

Weed, E. (1989). Introduction: Terms of reference. In E. Weed (Ed.), *Coming to terms: Feminism, theory, politics.* New York: Routledge.

Williams, R. (1961). *The long revolution: An analysis of the democratic, industrial, and cultural changes transforming our society.* New York: Columbia University Press.

14

Intellectuals at Work and in Power: Toward a Foucaultian Research Ethic

DAVID BLACKER

THE PROBLEM WITH FOUCAULT

It is by now almost axiomatic that to read Foucault is to struggle with his apparent unwillingness or inability to contribute any *positive* suggestions toward the liberatory praxis that, in his more candid moments, he claims to champion. His analysis of institutions like the prison, for example, uncovers sordid origins, points out alarming trends, and reveals relations of power and domination as ubiquitous. Moreover, he shows how the neo-Orwellian disciplinary techniques perfected in the prison have spread cancer-like throughout our entire social body—into our factories, offices, and schools. Yet despite this dismal and perhaps even dystopian prognosis, Foucault consistently seems to refuse to identify or even outline a cure. It is as if Marx had exposed the evils of the vampire Capital, only then to give a slightly embarrassed shrug when asked, "Well, what can we do about it all?"

I think, however, that this view is misguided. There is, in fact, much in Foucault about what "we" should do and how we should do it. Furthermore, and this seems largely to have been missed in the literature, what he has to say is of particular relevance and importance to—and is even tailor-made for—intellectuals engaged in research within an institutional setting such as the contemporary university.

My effort to demonstrate this has two aspects, negative and positive. Negatively, I will argue that Foucault's enterprise is not, *pace* some of his most influential recent critics, an exercise mired in ambiguity and ultimately self-refutation (Fraser, 1989; Habermas, 1986, 1990; Taylor, 1985). On the contrary, even his most provocative genealogical "arguments" commit no logical faux pas; while perhaps questionable in other ways, there is nothing formally wrong with them. A dose of interpretive charity finds them in fact to be surprisingly clear and crisp—even teachable. My point is not that Foucault adheres to the canons of logic, formal or informal, but that his texts do indeed contain points of entry for readers who neither are nor wish to be fluent in the jargon of most postmodern theory.

After a round of important criticisms several years ago, the view that Foucault undermines himself has now emerged as a general consensus and in some circles is even considered common knowledge. It is claimed that from the standpoint of praxis, Foucault's central "arguments" are self-refuting because they are predicated upon the very humanist ideals that he elsewhere claims to reject. With one hand, he wants to heap scorn upon the liberal humanist project of making the world more "human," that is, more *humane.* But with the other hand, it is claimed, Foucault seems to rely on precisely this sense of the humane in order to generate the shock, the fright, and the outrage we feel when confronted with the techniques of domination he so vividly illustrates. Does he therefore contradict himself? I think not, and the first part of this chapter gestures toward a way of reading Foucault's genealogies that circumvents this accusation, thereby rendering his project more accessible than often is thought.

Once his cards are on the table, though, it remains to be demonstrated that Foucault does not come up short in another sense. Analogous to the charges leveled against "reproduction" theorists in education, those who argue that despite our best pedagogical efforts schooling is doomed merely to reproduce social structures of power and privilege, it is charged that Foucault's theories instantiate what Frederic Jameson (1984) has called a "winner loses logic": Insofar as the oppositional theorist constructs an airtight totalizing account of how domination works, her reader is to that extent made to feel powerless; such a theorist wins by building an "increasingly closed and terrifying machine" (p. 176) but at the same time she loses because the critical potential of her work is deadened, as all strategies for social change seem trivial and hopeless, and are therefore robbed of a motivation that would sustain them.[1] While such fatalism is known to attract an eccentric here and there, most of us would wonder: If we are *truly* doomed, why bother fighting?

In my interpretation, however, Foucault ultimately beats this logic by stepping beyond both reproduction and motivation. To understand just how he does this, one first must develop a sense of his audience, of just who this peculiar author's readers could possibly be. Given Foucault's emphasis on power's microphysics as well as his avoidance of the "indignity of speaking for others," it is clear that he must be somewhat guarded in his prescriptions. But in this case "guarded" does not mean silent. Rather, it means a very deliberate circumscribing of the group to whom he addresses himself. Accordingly, Foucault's more concrete remarks on ethics turn out to concern the subject position from which they are for the most part uttered, namely, that of the institution-bound intellectual. The paradigm case here is not unlike that of Foucault himself, Professor of the History of Systems of Thought at the Sorbonne, that is, a purveyor of university supported and legitimated research.

A METHOD TO THE MADNESS

Nancy Fraser's (1989) trenchant essay, "Michel Foucault: A 'Young Conservative'?" exemplifies the "Foucault has nothing positive to offer" line of criticism. Foucault, she argues, cannot account for the "sorts of normative political judgments he makes all the time—for example, 'discipline is a bad thing'" (p. 42). It seems relatively noncontroversial that the carceral structures illustrated in *Discipline and Punish* (1979) are somehow "bad things." But *why* and *how* is it that we are made to feel this way? What, as another commentator (Jay, 1986) has asked, are the "roots of Foucault's [and our] outrage?" (p. 195). Most of Foucault's writings, after all, seem to evidence, however obliquely, a strong sense of ethical commitment. But what exactly, Fraser asks, is he *against* and what is he *for*? And what are his criteria for deciding either?

Fraser organizes her inquiry into these questions around familiar humanist values like freedom, reason, autonomy, reciprocity, and the like. And she argues that the most plausible way to read Foucault vis-à-vis humanism is that he offers a radical rejectionism based on "substantive normative grounds."

The problem then may be stated as follows: If Foucault offers an uncompromising critique of humanist ideals, then just where does he stand when he critiques them? How can he say anything at all without offering something positive of his own? It has been suggested that the author of *Discipline and Punish,* in fact, stands nowhere; or, more precisely, he has denied himself any critical vantage point. This is because, it is argued, our responses to the panoptical prison—our dread, anger, helplessness—are rooted in the very ideals being challenged: We abhor incarceration because it negates autonomy, cellular isolation, and surveillance because they prevent reciprocity, the recidivism of delinquency because it is irrational, and so on. For these reasons, Foucault's position seems to undermine itself.

It should be recognized that the above criticism takes Foucault's genealogical studies to provide (sustained) arguments. The core problem for Fraser, then, is that Foucault contradicts himself; he must both deny humanism (as he elsewhere claims to do (e.g., Foucault, 1970, 1977) and accept it (in order to make us feel bad). It is as if one could argue against formal logic by using *modus ponens.*

This problem, however, seems to me to be in the end a pseudo-problem. In fact, I see little to support the idea that the genealogies like *Discipline and Punish* or Volume 1 of the *History of Sexuality* (1980a) must be read as self-contradictory. While Foucaultian genealogy indeed presents a host of contradictions, it is by no means *self*-contradictory. Why not read it, assuming one must read genealogy, as an "argument" in the usual sense, as akin to a *reductio ad absurdum* of humanism? Why can it not be an immanent critique that renders humanist discourse problematic by its own standards? That humanism contradicts itself is not the same as saying that the argument demonstrating this fact is itself self-contradictory. Such a move is tantamount to killing the bearer of bad news.

For Foucault, the ideals associated with humanism are not inherently contradictory, but genealogy reveals that their consequential deeds always seem to belie their words. Humanist discourse in the service of "reform" or "progress" all too often has been uttered in order to justify profoundly inhumane actions; it is in this sense, that of the "preponderance of the evidence," as they say in law, that its practical consequences demonstrate its falsity more eloquently than any amount of argumentation could. Thus, genealogy has a strategic import, as it may be said to succeed or fail according to how powerfully its narrative examples, its *histoires* (in the literal French sense of "story" as well as "history"), serve to unsettle established consensus. Foucaultian genealogy may be thought of as high-stakes storytelling, the aim of which, at least regarding the present question of humanism, generates something like the following induction: "They promise us 'Good,' but things turn out bad. This happens again and again and again. Maybe we shouldn't believe their promises anymore." An important part of Foucault's genius is his ability to pull this off, to astonish us and unsettle us by interrogating, "deconstructing," to borrow a word, our "good intentions," our dreams of liberation, our utopias. Even if Foucault is not an historian in the strict, disciplinary sense, after reading him one will never look at, say, Jeremy Bentham's prison-reforming and "humanizing" panopticon in the same way again; no longer does it appear normal or lay claim to common sense. To drive this point home, I will describe briefly three of these narrative *reductios.* I emphasize again that none of these instances, taken by itself, is sufficient to prove the

thesis that the grand ideals of humanism are accompanied by unhuman realities. It is the ensemble that compels, for the long-established pattern seems
unbreakable.

The first example, drawn from the prisons book, is of obvious interest
to educators: the movement toward "hierarchical observation" and "normalizing judgment" that culminates in and is symbolized by the "examination." Here, the promise of formal equality among individuals is the heralded
ideal. We are told, then, that we are all "equal." But even a cursory examination makes it obvious that human beings, varying as they do in physiognomy,
talents, intelligence, and so forth, seem anything *but* equal. Still, the humanist's (perhaps one might substitute Progressive reformer's) cry persists:
"Equal! Equal!" By a complex process of inculcation, we come to accept this
ideal—whatever it means—and are lead to search for this elusive "equal";
the chase is on to identify some underlying sameness, something held in common by everyone onto which one can pin this "equal" (to the donkey of
meritocracy, for example). Seeking desperately for what makes us the "same,"
and unable to find anything concrete, we readily accept a content given by
hegemonic power. "Power abhors a vacuum," as they say. We are made into
"individuals" and "cases"—we are made to conform to an externally manufactured ideal.

When conformity becomes the reigning norm (perhaps at first a hardly
noticeable shift from the equality ideal), a process is initiated that leads to
an ever more finely tuned streamlining and ranking in accord with that norm.
Those who deviate must be brought into line; they must be disciplined, pun-
ished, IQ-tested. The categories of the "deviant" as well as the "normal"
individual in this way are constructed: "The individual is no doubt the ficti-
tious atom of an 'ideological' representation of society; but he is also a reality
fabricated by this specific technology of power that I have called 'discipline'"
(Foucault, 1979, p. 194). The apotheosis of this process is the "examination,"
this newly formed individual's "ceremony of objectification." Here, one is
identified, differentiated, classified, and marked *ad infinitum* in accord with
the norm—a norm that was so inauspiciously borne of equality.

Second is the figure of the delinquent—the failure (or success?) of the
prison system. The slogan this time is "reform" of the convict. "Reform": to
put back together that which has deviated, to heal, to make once again normal. In opposition to a retributive notion of penal justice, the liberal humanist prison is supposed to "correct," educate, and reform the criminal. In this
way, criminal and society are reconciled, the former being restored to his or
her "rightful" place in the latter. Of course, for a large number of convicts
this ideal result is never achieved. In fact, the situation seems, suspiciously,
to be all too often the reverse: The petty criminal is made into an expert, the
amateur into a professional, and the juvenile delinquent into a veteran. Pris-

ons, it may even be said, are designed to fail. Not only are delinquents "failures," Foucault argues, but they also come to serve a useful function; they are integral to the carceral network's spread beyond the prison gate. "Criminals come in handy" (Foucault, 1980b, p. 40).

They become pimps, prostitutes, racketeers, scabs, and—most important—informants. The latter are transformed into a "closed milieu of delinquency, thoroughly structured by the police" (Foucault, 1980b, p. 42). Thus, a self-perpetuating band of "halfway house" figures circulate among the population at large, ever surveying, recording, and reporting back to their keepers. Far from reforming or educating the delinquent, the carceral system vitally depends on it:

> From the late 1830s, it became clear that in fact the aim was not to retrain delinquents, to make them virtuous, but to regroup them within a clearly demarcated, card-indexed milieu which could serve as a tool for economic and political ends. The problem thereafter was not to teach the prisoners something, but rather to teach them nothing, so as to make sure that they could do nothing when they came out of prison. (Foucault, 1980b, p. 42)

From the perspective of the carceral network, delinquency and recidivism are triumphant successes; the former not only perpetuates but extends its influence. "So successful has the prison been that, after a century and a half of 'failures,' the prison still exists, producing the same results, and there is the greatest reluctance to dispense with it" (Foucault, 1979, p. 277).

Our third narrative *reductio* catches in the act the notion of sexual liberty (pursuant to sexual "freedom"). Foucault challenges the popularly held idea that he calls the "repressive hypothesis": the idea that power is essentially "puritanical," and therefore has repressed and inhibited sexual practices and discourse. We are fortunate to live in a sexually "liberated age," having finally made it through a couple centuries of sexual "dark ages"; whereas the more distant past is characterized by a certain "knowing innocence," the seventeenth through nineteenth centuries gave rise to the "repressed Victorian." So the story goes. Upon genealogical examination, however, it comes to light that the Victorian era signaled a large-scale profusion of sexual discourse—one encounters veritable chatterboxes of sexuality who were anything but inhibited. Certainly, sexuality has been shaped by power, but it has not exactly been repressed; in fact, the situation is quite nearly the opposite: Sexual discourse, "far from undergoing a process of restriction, on the contrary has been subjected to a mechanism of increasing excitement" (Foucault, 1980d, p. 12). Power thus has carefully cultivated the field of sexuality.

It reaps its harvest in a number of practices: For example, the proliferation of "confessional" rituals (symptomatic of the priority placed on dis-

covering the truth about one's "deep and hidden" sexuality) effectively incul-
cates the obligation to confess. Usually this confessional obligation is made
manifest through the elicitation of streams of sexual discourse before properly designated authorities like the priest, school counselor, or psychoanalyst.
As Alasdair MacIntyre (1984) has argued in another context, "the therapist"
has become one of the defining character-types of modernity, embodying a
concern "with technique, with effectiveness in transforming neurotic symp-
toms into directed energy, maladjusted individuals into well-adjusted ones"
(p. 30). To uncover buried impulses and fantasies is advertised as "healthy"
and even liberatory, and one dutifully complies in order to be "free." Yet all
the while, the ear of the confessor is listening and recording the confessions;
"sex was taken charge of, tracked down as it were, by a discourse that aimed
to allow it no obscurity, no respite" (Foucault, 1980d, p. 20). Thus, the supposed liberatory process of eliciting sexual discourse helps to refine techniques of domination and generally yields more grist for the disciplinary mill.
More about us is seen; we are opened up, laid bare, and exposed to ever
greater degrees of institutional intervention and penetration. Furthermore,
similar to how prison techniques "colonize" other areas of society, the imperative to confess has come to characterize other social practices. Contemporary society marshals its resources toward this end: "Sex became a matter
that required the social body as a whole, and virtually all of its individuals,
to place themselves under surveillance" (Foucault, 1980d, p. 116).

One interesting illustration of how deeply ingrained the confessional
ethos has become in Western culture is documented by Tobin, Wu, and Davidson (1989) in their book *Preschool in Three Cultures*. Tobin and colleagues
show how in a typical American preschool, children constantly are encouraged to verbalize, to exteriorize, their feelings. Here, for example, is how a
preschool teacher, Cheryl, chooses to break up a fight in the block corner
between 5- and 6-year-olds:

> "Mike, can you tell Stu with words what you want instead of grabbing? . . . Stu,
> when Mike took the block from you, how did you feel? Did you tell him that
> made you angry? Did it make you angry?" Cheryl explained her strategy to us
> when we watched the tape together: "What I'm trying to do there is get them to
> use words instead of their hands to express their feelings. With kids this age, as
> soon as they get angry or frustrated their first reaction is to hit someone. I try
> and get them to realize what they are feeling and to express it verbally." (p. 152)

By contrast, when this interaction is shown to a group of Japanese preschool
teachers, that is, to a group outside of this particular disciplinary matrix
(though of course enmeshed in one of their own, a different one), Cheryl's
mini-confessional ritual looks altogether odd:

Yagi: Wow, that's amazing! Talking so directly with such young children about their feelings.
Taniguchi: The teacher really gets right in there and deals with the problem.
Tanaka: Talking with children about disagreements like that . . . it seems a bit heavy doesn't it? It reminds me of marriage counseling. (p. 152)

American respondents praised Cheryl's approach, though. As Tobin and colleagues note further, "We frequently heard teachers at American preschools encouraging children to express their mood in words: 'Are you having fun?' 'How did you feel during the play when the witch came out? Excited? Scared? How about at the end when the witch was chased away?'" (p. 152) American children, they conclude, are "much less free than children in China or Japan to remain silent and hide their feelings." (p. 153) All of this is not to say that there is necessarily anything sinister going on here, but to illuminate and make problematic, as the genealogies do, what before may have been regarded unproblematically, if it was regarded at all, as simply good common sense—uncomplicatedly "normal."

Regarding the genealogies, then, we have three processes that start with high-flying ideals but that result in base, inhuman realities: "equality-conformity-examination," "reform-delinquent-informer," and "liberation-confession-control." Needless to say, the final products of these triads negate (and then some) the ideals that provided the original impulse. But our discomfort—indeed our outrage—at these results, I argue, need not be based on these ideals. The liberal humanist and Foucault agree that the denial of equality, freedom, and the rest are "bad things." However, the two soon part company. Whereas the humanist continues to champion the ideal in question, claiming perhaps that the problem will be solved when the ideal is fully and properly realized, Foucault sees no reason for such optimism, for the genealogist is enough of a pragmatist to take as counting against their truth the fact that all too many humanist watchwords always (or at least often enough) seem to deliver their opposite. I stress again that, upon my reading, Foucault has not "refuted" humanism nor has he tried to. Instead, he demands of those who use its jargon that they answer for their predecessors' legacy of deceit. Given the genealogical evidence, a comforting—let alone convincing—response seems unlikely.

I have thus far accomplished only the negative task of this essay, viz, that Foucaultian genealogy is not self-undermining. It should be clear that, since he is offering a type of *reductio* against humanist rhetoric, he is not obligated in the course of his argument to offer any positive alternative. So far, so good. But it certainly would be leaving his readers in the lurch to abandon them at this point. Why "problematize" if one has no hint of a solution? So humanism is a lie—then what? It is indeed fair to demand, along with Fraser (1989), that Foucault say, "in terms independent of the vocabulary of humanism, exactly what is wrong with this [carceral] society and why it ought to be resisted" (p. 50). Fraser proceeds to charge Foucault with the responsibility of offering "some alternative, posthumanist ethical paradigm" in order to satisfy her question. And in her view, it turns out that he cannot: An ambiguous silence is all that emanates from the Foucaultian side. It seems we are left with a rather unfortunate choice: "between a known ethical paradigm [i.e., a variant of liberal humanism] and an unknown X" (pp. 50–51). So it falls upon the rest of this chapter to find a response to Fraser's challenge and to fill in the "unknown X."

LOCAL PROBLEMS, LOCAL SOLUTIONS

In order to draw out Foucault's positive ethical project, I must first make some mention of his picture of what needs to be overcome and how to overcome it. To combat effectively the carceral society's "infinitely minute web of panoptic techniques" one needs to acknowledge that contemporary (post-) industrial society is characterized by radically diffuse and localized power relations and that the source and mechanisms of power are not to be found at any single or central site.

The vagaries of Foucault's theory of power relations has been much written about and discussed. All I wish to do here is point out that his supposition that power operates at every level of the social body has deeper implications than often is realized for anyone interested in charting a viable course for social change. For example, Foucault challenges the efficacy (and desirability) of the Leninist model of revolution: a vanguard group, in the name of the oppressed class, seizing the state apparatus and then "changing" the power structure. Such an event may signal a changing of the guards, but is unlikely to alter the basic nature of the firmly entrenched and inertia-bound "power/knowledge regime." As Sheldon Wolin (1988) suggests, Foucault's theory "requests a sharp break with state-centered conceptions of power and, by extension, with revolutionary or radical politics which defined itself by opposition to, or overthrow of the state" (pp. 184–185).

A far more promising theoretical response is to concentrate on power's "microphysics." Since power is not homogeneous and can be approached only at its specific sites of application, one should not expect to gain a useful theoretical purchase at the macrolevel (sometimes Foucault even seems to indicate that there is no such thing as "power" as such). Instead, the proper level of analysis is a worm's-eye view; power must be considered from the "bottom up." In this way, at power's local extremities, its obfuscatory "veil of administrative decency" to a great extent may be stripped away: "What is needed is a study of power in its external visage, at the point where it is in direct or immediate relationship with that which we can provisionally call its object, its target, its field of application" (Foucault, 1980c, p. 97). This is an important aspect of what the genealogies attempt to do.

This is not the place for me to debate the relative merits of Foucault's "phenomenology" and "ontology" of power (if one can even speak in such terms). I only wish to underscore two relevant points. The first I will let Foucault's compatriot and sometime collaborator, the philosopher and psychoanalyst Gilles Deleuze (1988), make for me:

> The theoretical privilege given to the State as an apparatus of power to a certain extent leads to the practice of a leading and centralizing party which eventually wins State power; but on the other hand it is this very organizational conception of the party that is justified by this theory of power. The stakes of Foucault's book lie in a different set of strategies. (p. 30)

One's idea of what one is struggling against has a direct impact on what one *becomes* as one struggles. This, from a strategic point of view, is why it is so important to get away from state-bound power theories; political "revolution" alone is not enough to effect deep and lasting change.

Second, one who aspires to articulate emancipation must acquire a certain theoretical modesty. Given power's (lack of a) nature, one should not expect to be able to utter much about it that holds universally. If the goal is an "autonomous, noncentralized kind of theoretical production, one that is to say whose validity is not dependent on the approval of the established regimes of thought," one should not try to utter liberatory discourse from an authoritative subject position (Foucault, 1980c, p. 81). For instance, some of Foucault's most vitriolic remarks are aimed at theorists (e.g., certain structuralist Marxists, phenomenologists, social "scientists" of various stripes) who try to legitimate their ideas as "scientific"—thereby cashing in on science's aura of authority. One can, of course, still theorize, provided one is ever-mindful of the "tyranny of globalising discourses with their hierarchy and all their privileges of a theoretical *avant-garde*" (Foucault, 1980c, p. 83). The point is that the theoretician, while still important, no longer represents a privileged site for articulating emancipatory discourse.

RESPONSIBLE STRATEGIES IN THE POLITICS OF TRUTH

Instead of espousing "truth," the primary role of the oppositional intellectual should be to combat the way it is arbitrarily mass manufactured and disseminated. This process is a precondition of, and is therefore indispensable to, the functioning of hegemonic power. The intellectual, *qua* participant (or collaborator), is well-positioned to engage in such a task.[2] The battle lines are to be drawn around society's "politics of truth":

> The essential problem for the intellectual is not to criticize the ideological contents supposedly linked to science, or to ensure that his own scientific practice is accompanied by correct ideology, but that of ascertaining the possibility of constituting a new politics of truth. The problem is not changing people's consciousnesses—or what's in their heads—but the political, economic, institutional regime of the production of truth. (Foucault, 1980a, p. 133)

This is not a struggle to emancipate some pristine truth from the distortions wreaked upon it by power or ideology, nor is it a battle on behalf of truth. Such an endeavor would cut against the grain of Foucault's entire project; one does not decenter by recentering some new set of universalizing (contentless) slogans. Rather, as Barry Smart (1986) expresses it, what is required is a "critical examination of the various ways in which we have come to govern our selves and others through the articulation of a distinction between truth and falsity" (p. 171).

In accord with his emphasis on "dispersed and discontinuous offensives" and what he claims to be the "amazing efficacy of discontinuous, particular, and local criticism," Foucault advocates the cultivation of a new personage, the "specific intellectual" (Foucault, 1980c, p. 80). This is to be juxtaposed against the "universal intellectual," a historical phenomenon of the past two centuries, who claims to speak for the collective conscience. The "universal" figure claims to stand outside power, counterpoising to "power, despotism and the abuses and arrogance of wealth the universality of justice and the equity of an ideal law" (Foucault, 1980a, p. 128). One thinks of Locke, Rousseau, Jefferson, Marx. In contrast, the "specific" intellectual derives from a quite different figure: not the "jurist or notable, but the savant or expert" (Foucault, 1980a, p. 128). Foucault identifies the atomic scientist of the 1940s and 1950s as a harbinger of this new type of personage whose expertise is restricted to a particular field. This is not, however, to say her influence is limited. On the contrary, changes in the power/knowledge configuration have made increasingly possible the paradoxical situation that experts in specific fields, especially the natural and applied sciences, enjoy (and bear the burden of) quite general consequences emanating from their activity, often of a magnitude of which their scribal forebears scarcely could have dreamed. Thus, while more enmeshed in power than ever, the specific intellectual has taken on a new strategic significance.

Why does Foucault rejoice at this development? Why is the specific intellectual to be preferred? To answer, the interpreter must move a bit beyond what is explicit in the texts. Taking as much as possible into account, there seem to be two operative principles, which I provisionally label "efficacy" and "honesty." Perhaps not altogether surprisingly, as I will try to show, these two ultimately will devolve into two moments of something very much akin to an updated and specified Nietzschean "will to power."

As Foucault (1983) has stated in an interview: "People know what they do; they frequently know why they do what they do; but what they don't know is what what they do does" (p. 187).[3] This uncharacteristically folksy observation neatly summarizes the basis of what I am claiming is his strategic recommendation for the oppositional intellectual.

"Efficacy," as hinted above, works on a principle of "transversality," to borrow a word from Deleuze (1988, p. 91).[4] The idea is that by restricting one's scope of activity, one often widens and deepens the (potential) consequences of that activity. Perhaps the most dramatic, and in many ways paradigmatic, example of this is the above-mentioned atomic scientist. By focusing on the tiniest sphere human beings can access (viz, the subatomic), one can become, as the U.S. physicist J. Robert Oppenheimer gasped at the test site where the first atomic bomb was detonated, a "Destroyer of Worlds." Another example, perhaps more readily accessible, is the physician. Transversality may be put to an intuitive test here. Consider the following scenario: Awaiting surgery, you are asked to choose between two surgeons to perform your operation. Your options are two licensed physicians, and you are given only one bit of information about each. First is "Dr. Renaissance": cultured, well-read, well-traveled, well-dressed, well-liked, and a soothing bedside manner. Of the second, you know of only one quality: her tried and tested competence at performing the procedure required. At that point, I would argue, you choose the latter, with little equivocation. When efficacy is paramount, all considerations pale before "specific" competence.

I trust that it is not difficult to see how transversality may be extended to a great number of instances—and not all of them "intellectual" in the usual sense. I emphasize that this claim does not entail a belief that one cannot learn or otherwise benefit from spheres outside one's own. But it does indicate the necessity of organizing one's endeavors around a specific locus; to "specialize" in this sense is not necessarily to be compartmentalized. From the point of view of efficacy, then, to lament over contemporary society's increasing specialization is to indulge in a self-defeating nostalgia. The day of the aristocratic "Renaissance Man" ideal has passed.

"Honesty" has two essential components: what I will call "attentiveness" and "effort." Attentiveness means paying attention to the consequences of one's theoretical practice; more specifically, this entails an awareness of how the results of one's efforts are used. Effort is simply the persistent good faith vigilance required to sustain such an awareness. It must be stressed that honesty does not mean a drive toward self-knowledge; it does not entail a hermeneutics of the self, or any other search for the truth about oneself. Rather, it concerns the implications of one's search for truth—not self-absorption, but attentiveness to how one's actions get absorbed by the power/knowledge regime.

This is why Oppenheimer is described by Foucault (1980a) as a "point of transition between the universal and specific intellectual" (pp. 127–128). Despite his left-leaning politics, and although he was "effective," he was not "honest," in the above sense. In fact, and with very few exceptions (e.g., perhaps, Leo Szilard, the Hungarian émigré who seemed sensitive to the dangers of the bomb project early on), Manhattan Project scientists who developed the bomb were stunningly naive about the social and political ramifications their discoveries might have. Edward Teller's statement that it "is *not* the scientist's job to determine whether a hydrogen bomb should be constructed, whether it should be used, or how it should be used" (Boyer, 1985, p. 342), represents perhaps the paragon of dishonesty.[5] Even if one could forgive these scientists their initial political naivete, there are many other striking examples of dishonesty. The blindness to manipulation and exploitation exhibited by certain "progressive" anti-Communists (e.g., the U.S. anarchist Emma Goldmann and the U.S. Marxist-cum-cold-warrior philosopher Sydney Hook later in their lives, the French "New Philosophers" of the 1970s) is vis-à-vis honesty nothing short of scandalous. Although perhaps a bit anarchronistic by now, the basic *motivation* behind Jean-Paul Sartre's remark that "an anti-communist is always a rat," applies full force in the West—today as much as ever.

An important corollary (or perhaps a necessitating factor) of honesty is Anthony Giddens's (1979) observation about one of the primary "modes in which domination is concealed as domination": the "representation of sectional interests as universal ones" (p. 193). In order to sustain its legitimacy, hegemonic power perpetrates (and perpetuates) the fiction that it stands for "common" interests. Major government initiatives from budgets to war and holocaust, for example, are almost always justified by some supposedly shared interest or threat, whether it be the "Red Menace," the "People's This or That," the "Common School," or the "New World Order." Intellectuals should draw a lesson from this principle: They should always ask, "For whom am I claiming to speak?" And they should realize that, as a rule, the wider the claim, the narrower the subject position that it serves. The honest Foucaultian genealogist-philosopher, for example, who claims to overturn basic assumptions, must be especially vigilant with regard to this type of dishonesty:

> There is always something ludicrous in philosophical discourse when it tries, from the outside, to dictate to others, to tell them where their truth is and how

to find it, or when it works up a case against them in the language of naive positivity. But it is entitled to explore what might be changed, in its own thought, through a practice of a knowledge that is foreign to it. (Foucault, 1986, p. 9)

Again, there is nothing here that precludes learning from others or revealing something to them. Foucault only pleads for a certain cautious and self-conscious theoretical modesty.

Honesty and efficacy, then, are two guiding principles for the specific intellectual. I argue that they are best viewed as two moments of an underlying *telos* whose maxim might be expressed as something like, "One should strive to become master of the consequences of one's actions." This represents a new type of self-relation for self-consciously postmodern intellectuals, a necessarily politicized "will to power."

SELF-CREATION AND THE SPECIFIC INTELLECTUAL

I would like to apply the fourfold analysis of ethical self-relations found in Foucault's later writings to the situation at hand, with an eye toward how one might go about transforming a "decadent" universal intellectual into a "healthy" specific one. First, is the determination of the "ethical substance." This is the material that gets "worked on" by ethics; that dimension of the self that provides the target of concern or what, for the individual, constitutes "this or that part of himself as the prime material of his moral conduct" (Foucault, 1990, p. 26). In other words, it is that "part of ourselves, or of our behavior, which is relevant for ethical judgment" (Foucault, 1983, p. 238). In Christianity, for example, the ethical substance consists of one's desires, one's intentions, and one's faith. These are the objects of priestly concern during confession; one transforms them in order to become a better Christian. For the specific intellectual, the ethical substance has to be something like "consciousness," "self-understanding," or, perhaps more broadly inclusive of less cognitive forms of being-in-the-world, the scope of one's awareness of what goes on in one's environment and how one is implicated in it.[6] In the case of the intellectual, this probably means the institutional site of knowledge or "truth" production (e.g., the university, laboratory, newsroom) and its interface with the larger society.

Second is the "mode of subjection": "the way in which the individual establishes his relation to the rule and recognizes himself as obliged to put it into practice" (Foucault, 1990, p. 27). This is the source or basis from which one produces the self-relation. Examples would be the Greek aristocrat who regulates his diet in a fashion that answers to certain aesthetic criteria, or the nonsexist academic who tries to eliminate gender bias from her prose. In short, the mode of subjection for the specific intellectual is "harmonization";

that is, bringing one's words and acts into harmony with one's "sphere of influence," on the principle of avoiding the "indignity of speaking for others" (Deleuze & Foucault, 1977, p. 209). This entails a self-examination into one's very concern for truth, a consciousness of how one partakes in truth's manufacture. Foucault (Deleuze & Foucault, 1977) presents the rationale for harmonization as follows:

> All those on whom power is exercised to their detriment, all who find it intolerable, can begin the struggle on their own terrain and on the basis of their proper activity (or passivity). In engaging in a struggle that concerns their own interests, whose objectives they clearly understand and whose methods only they can determine, they enter into the revolutionary process. (p. 216)

For many intellectuals, harmonization means a narrowing in order to find "their own terrain." (It is, of course, possible, however, that depending on the subject position one is starting from, one might need to widen in order to harmonize; e.g., the bureaucrat whose inculcated narrow vision leads to an excessively laissez-faire attitude toward the action–consequence nexus.) Within the institutional setting, intellectuals should no longer aim to "help" the downtrodden (on balance, Foucault implies, they never did—at least politically). Rather, they should direct their focus toward the power/knowledge arrangements existing under their very noses—arrangements that thwart and pervert their "good intentions."

The third mode of self-relation is "self-practice" or "ethical work": what one does to oneself in order to behave ethically; the means of self-transformation—"asceticism" in a broad sense. The Jew keeps kosher, the Roman uses sexual desire only to have children, the Christian seeks to identify and battle his Satan-induced lust, and so on. On a general level, the ethical work of the specific intellectual is the rigorous practice of honesty and the various forms, depending on the field in question, this may take. This entails a mastery of one's own sphere of inquiry, an attentiveness to "results," and a wariness regarding how those results are used and who uses them. The university-based researcher, for example, must possess a deep and varied knowledge of the object of study (how can one be effective without competence?), ensure that the work has some strategic import (or why bother?), and attend to the ensuing debate (if any) surrounding the work. There is no room for dilettantism, "knowledge for its own sake," or obliviousness to one's audience or to the human antecedents and consequences of one's own research.

Finally is the *telos*: the ultimate goal one is trying to achieve. Christians seek purification or salvation; humanists, freedom or self-realization; and the Greeks, self-mastery. As mentioned above, the *telos* for Foucault's will to power is a new self-mastery—a mastery over one's actions and their results. To put it differently, this means a controlled and self-regulated dissemination of the subject into the world, a positive dissolution. In other words, although transcending power relations is chimerical, one can become a channel or "privileged junction" through which power can be directed. For her part, the intellectual can gain, for example, a more thoroughgoing understanding of the sources and "purposes" of her funding (e.g., grants, contracts, salaries) and use that understanding to more effectively attend to her purposes (some are already quite good at this). Of course, what one is (or is not) will change as one gains control and confidence at doing this by "flexing one's (institutional) muscles," so to speak. This is not self-absorption, but being absorbed into the world: a "losing–finding" of the self. One might even describe it as a new ethic of self-creation that avoids the pitfalls of both narcissistic aestheticism on the one hand, and the alienation of political obsession on the other. The well-defined and border-patrolled "individual" of the humanists, it is claimed, hinders this process:

> Contrary to a fully established discourse, there is no need to uphold man in order to resist. What resistance extracts from this revered old man, as Nietzsche put it, is the forces of a life that is larger, more active, more affirmative and richer in possibilities. The superman has never meant anything but that: it is in man himself that we must liberate life, since man himself is a form of imprisonment for man. (Deleuze, 1988, p. 92)

"Man," as defined by the carceral regime, has nothing to lose but his chains— a process that means, in a word, self-overcoming. It may well be, as Foucault (in) famously puts it in concluding *The Order of Things* (1970), that Man will "be erased, like a face drawn in sand at the edge of the sea" (p. 387). Yet the tide that brings erasure creates new imprints even as it washes away the old. The dissolution of Man is therefore not so much an obliteration as it is a return, yet another new start on an ancient and ongoing journey.

Thus, we can schematize a Foucaultian political ethic for intellectuals engaged in "truth production" (and possibly outline a more general praxeological ethic) as follows:

Ethical substance: Consciousness/self-understanding/awareness
Mode of subjection: Harmonization
Ethical work: Competence/honesty/attentiveness
Telos: Self-overcoming

EXTENSIONS AND IMPLICATIONS

A few considerations are relevant to this schema's extension to other spheres. First is what one might call a "rule of no guarantees." This means that one should not expect any particular individual to be "all-progressive," "all-reactionary," or all-anything, which in turn indicates that it may be time to rethink these categories altogether. This follows from the idea that the subject position is not coextensive with the "individual" and that a pair of discourses may be incommensurable; the expectation of consistency is based primarily on the fiction of a (necessarily) tightly integrated subject. The operation of separating a priori the moral sheep from the goats has become anachronistic; one may well miss crucial opportunities if one dismisses wholesale whoever the theoretical "villain" of one's choice may be—whether Nazi, Marxist, or liberal democrat. In this significant sense, there does seem to be an air of the ethical relativist around the Foucaultian intellectual, at least in that he or she must remain as open as possible to whatever theoretical tools might be "hidden" within any tradition of thought, even historically odious ones. The appropriateness of the tool will be judged by virtue of its relation to the above-described *telos*. It is just not true that one necessarily knows the tree by its fruit. Even though the Foucaultian intellectual is politically engaged, he or she, it seems to me, would abandon the vestigial theological need to either "save" or "damn."[7] Suspicion, always, but never condemnation, the latter being merely the mirror image of utopianism.

Second, as hinted above, in extending the will to power to other spheres of life, the "starting point" and particularities of the subject position in question will have a direct impact on the entire schema. For example, starting from a relatively dis-empowered subject position entails different methods of harmonization and attentiveness (pursuant to the *telos*). While the old-style universal intellectual for the most part "narrows," less empowered subject positions might need to "widen"; thus, the required level of association with others and the type of discourse uttered will vary in accord with situational needs. For example, a school teacher might require a union for efficacy, or an illiterate peasant may need to utter universalizing rhetoric in order to empower his subject position, as someone like Paulo Freire would allow. Crucially, however, there is no central or privileged site for deciding the specific strategies.

Third, given Foucault's emphasis on power's microphysics and the decentralized nature of power relations, it seems clear that an increase in power *qua* "dominating" (i.e., coercion-based authority) does not necessarily lead to a correspondingly efficacious self-overcoming. In fact, dominating, in the ordinary underwritten-by-coercion sense, in most cases would seem to preclude self-overcoming. For example, the nominal "leader" of a large state apparatus must depend on an almost infinitely complex web of power relays, to the extent that one really cannot speak of such a leader as having much real control—at least in the sense required by the above *telos*. Almost by definition such a leader is so rarely "his own man," so to speak.[8] This is not to say, however, that policies never get implemented or that the president or prime minister of a G7 nation does not in some important sense "have" power. It is only to say that how a given choice is made and carried out often has very little to do with "choice" as we usually think of it. Again, it is a question of knowing and controlling what "what they do *does*." Although there are often intersections, self-overcoming in the sense I am attributing to Foucault may well at times proceed along lines different from political and economic power. It may, for example, in the tradition of Gramsci and certain aspects of the contemporary "cultural studies" movement, need to consider horizons more broadly cultural, and hence more sensitive to power's microphysics. Most important, though, self-overcoming must never fear to look where it is so often hardest to: right under its very nose, at the forces and relations of its own production and renewal.

NOTES

1. One might question a certain psychological assumption implied by this criticism, viz, that determinism leads to inaction. One only need recall that the paradigmatic deterministic world view, Calvinism, never lacked for "motivated" adherents.

2. The contemporary "intellectual" might be understood primarily as a "power/ knowledge" category, as opposed to a straightforwardly economic or social one. As classes in Marxist theory are defined by virtue of their relation to the means of production, so might Foucaultian "classes" be defined by their position in the "truth-manufacturing" process. Accordingly, the term "intellectual" may denote persons in spheres other than the academic, such as some doctors, newspersons, lawyers, or even school administrators, and perhaps even teachers in some cases.

3. They claim this quotation is from "personal communication" with Foucault.

4. Although there are similarities, I do not use the term in the same way as Deleuze.

5. Certainly, Manhattan Project scientists knew that the bomb might be dropped on Japan or Germany. Their naivete consisted in not understanding how little say they would have once their discoveries were snatched up by the government. It is also interesting to note that later in his life, Oppenheimer became "honest," and was outspoken in his denunciation of the government's use of the bomb. But with his honesty came intense political persecution. One might draw the lesson that honesty among intellectuals (especially "effective" ones) is very threatening to hegemonic power.

6. There may be affinities between this idea and the Freirean notion of *conscientizacao*. In *Pedagogy of the Oppressed*, Freire (1970) writes, "*Conscientizacao* does not stop at the level of mere subjective perception of a situation, but through action prepares men for the struggle against the obstacles to their humanization" (p. 112).

7. One current example would be the controversial "Heidegger affair." One of the central questions is whether one can salvage aspects of, say, Heidegger's metaphys-

ics or his critique of technology, while also renouncing whatever led him to embrace Nazism. The position being advanced here would counsel a fairly basic form of cautious open-mindedness.

8. I trust the reader will appreciate the gender irony intended.

REFERENCES

Boyer, P. (1985). *By the bomb's early light: American thought and culture at the dawn of the atomic age*. New York: Pantheon.

Deleuze, G. (1988). *Foucault*. Minneapolis: University of Minnesota Press.

Deleuze, G., & Foucault, M. (1977). Intellectuals and power: A conversation between Michel Foucault and Gilles Deleuze. In M. Foucault, *Language, counter-memory, practice: Selected essays and interviews* (D. F. Bouchard, Ed.; D. F. Bouchard & S. Simon, Trans.) (pp. 205–217). Ithaca, NY: Cornell University Press.

Foucault, M. (1970). *The order of things*. New York: Vintage.

Foucault, M. (1977). Revolutionary action: Until now. In *Language, counter-memory, practice: Selected essays and interviews* (D. F. Bouchard, Ed.; D. F. Bouchard & S. Simon, Trans.) (pp. 218–233). Ithaca, NY: Cornell University Press.

Foucault, M. (1979). *Discipline and punish: The birth of the prison* (A. Sheridan, Trans.). New York: Vintage.

Foucault, M. (1980a). *The history of sexuality: Vol. 1. An introduction*. New York: Vintage.

Foucault, M. (1980b). Prison talk. In C. Gordon (Ed. and Trans.), *Power/Knowledge: Selected interviews and other writings by Michel Foucault, 1972–1977* (pp. 37–54). New York: Pantheon.

Foucault, M. (1980c). Truth and power. In C. Gordon (Ed. and Trans.), *Power/Knowledge: Selected interviews and other writings by Michel Foucault, 1972–1977* (pp. 109–133). New York: Pantheon.

Foucault, M. (1980d). Two lectures. In C. Gordon (Ed. and Trans.), *Power/Knowledge: Selected interviews and other writings by Michel Foucault, 1972–1977* (pp. 78–108). New York: Pantheon.

Foucault, M. (1983). On the genealogy of ethics: An overview of work in progress. In H. L. Dreyfus & P. Rabinow, *Michel Foucault: Beyond structuralism and hermeneutics* (2nd ed.) (pp. 229–252). Chicago: University of Chicago Press.

Foucault, M. (1990). *The history of sexuality. Vol. 2. The use of pleasure* (R. Hurley, Trans.). New York: Vintage.

Fraser, N. (1989). *Unruly practices: Power, discourse and gender in contemporary social theory*. Minneapolis: University of Minnesota Press.

Freire, P. (1970). *Pedagogy of the oppressed*. New York: Continuum.

Giddens, A. (1979). *Central problems in social theory: Action, structure, and contradiction in social analysis*. Berkeley: University of California Press.

Habermas, J. (1986). Taking aim at the heart of the present. In D. C. Hoy (Ed.), *Foucault: A critical reader* (pp. 103–108). Oxford: Basil Blackwell.

Habermas, J. (1990). *The philosophical discourse of modernity.* Cambridge, MA: MIT Press.

Jameson, F. (1984). Postmodernism, or the cultural logic of late capitalism. *New Left Review, 146*, 53–92.

Jay, M. (1986). In the empire of the gaze: Foucault and the denigration of vision in twentieth-century French thought. In D. C. Hoy (Ed.), *Foucault: A critical reader* (pp. 175–204). Oxford: Basil Blackwell.

MacIntyre, A. (1984). *After virtue.* Notre Dame, IN: University of Notre Dame Press.

Smart, B. (1986). The politics of truth and the problem of hegemony. In D. C. Hoy (Ed.), *Foucault: A critical reader* (pp. 157–174). Oxford: Basil Blackwell.

Taylor, C. (1985). *Philosophy and the human sciences.* Cambridge: Cambridge University Press.

Tobin, J. J., Wu, D. Y. H., & Davidson, D. (1989). *Preschool in three cultures: Japan, China, and the United States.* New Haven, CT: Yale University Press.

Wolin, S. S. (1988). The politics of Michel Foucault. In J. Arac (Ed.), *After Foucault: Humanistic knowledge, postmodern challenges* (pp. 179–201). New Brunswick, NJ: Rutgers University Press.

About the Editors and the Contributors

Bernadette Baker is a postdoctoral research fellow at the University of Queensland, Australia. Her research interests include the use of history, multicultural education, feminist, and poststructural theories in teacher education.

David Blacker is in the Department of Educational Administration and Foundations at Illinois State University. He is currently at work on a book that explores often neglected aspects of education's moral nature.

Marie Brennan is at Central Queensland University in Australia. Her main interests are in state educational policy and reform projects, gender and education, and research methodology.

Lynn Fendler is in the Department of Curriculum and Instruction and is a teacher of English as a Second Language at the University of Wisconsin–Madison. Her research interests include philosophy of education, feminist theory, and research paradigms.

Jennifer M. Gore is at the University of Newcastle, New South Wales, Australia. She is author of *The Struggle for Pedagogies* and co-editor of *Feminisms and Critical Pedagogy*. Her major current teaching and research interests are in sociology of education, curriculum theory, gender and education, and poststructural theory.

Bill Green is at Deakin University in Australia. His interests are in the cultural politics of literacy and curriculum.

Sakari Heikkinen is at the University of Helsinki. He has studied industrialization and standards of living in Finland in the nineteenth and early twentieth centuries. He currently is engaged in a research project on the history of Finnish economics during the same period.

Kenneth Hultqvist is at the Stockholm Institute of Education. His research interest is in history of modernity. He has been developing a history of the present through studies of Swedish discourses of the preschool child, youths, and the science of psychology.

Ingólfur Ásgeir Jóhannesson has taught at the Icelandic College of Education and the University of Iceland, and is now Professor of Education at the University of Akureyri.

Mimi Orner is in the Women's Studies Program at the University of Wisconsin–Madison. She is currently co-authoring a book with Elizabeth Ellsworth on representational practices in education. She also authored *Teaching Otherwise: Feminism, Pedagogy and the Politics of Difference* (1995), which explores new directions in feminist research, theorizing, and pedagogical practice.

Thomas S. Popkewitz is a Professor of Education in the Department of Curriculum and Instruction at the University of Wisconsin–Madison. His writing has centered on a political sociology of educational reform in teaching, teacher education, and research; he has published several books and articles on these topics.

David Schaafsma is an Assistant Professor of English Education at Teachers College, Columbia University. His research interests include narrative inquiry, literacy education, and poststructural theory.

David Shutkin is at Ohio State University, College of Education, Department of Cultural Studies. His interests include technology studies, curriculum theory, and poststructural thought. Currently, he is researching a book on technology, social regulation, and radical pedagogy.

Jussi Silvonen is at the University of Industrial Arts, Helsinki. He has been concerned with the history of psychology, qualitative methods in social studies, and higher education policy. He currently is engaged in a project developing computer-assisted methods and programs. He also works on problematics of social construction of historical identity of academic psychology.

Hannu Simola is a researcher in the Department of Teacher Education, University of Helsinki. After teaching in varied settings from primary schools to higher education and publishing a few papers, he was chosen Junior Fellow of the Academy of Finland. Currently, he is preparing his doctoral thesis on the constitution of the teacher in Finnish educational discourse during this century.

Judith Rabak Wagener is an Assistant Professor of Health Education at Northern Illinois University in Dekalb, Illinois. Her interests are sociopolitical formation and re-formation of health education curricula.

Lew Zipin is in the Department of Educational Policy Studies at the University of Wisconsin–Madison. His scholarly interests focus on critical theories of power, institutions, and the constitution of identity, and on critical methods for researching the operations of power that shape identity in school contexts.

Index